MONETARY AND FISCAL POLICY

Also by Douglas Fisher

MONEY AND BANKING
MONETARY POLICY
MONETARY THEORY AND THE DEMAND FOR MONEY
MONEY, BANKING, AND MONETARY POLICY
MACROECONOMIC THEORY: A Survey

Monetary and Fiscal Policy

Douglas Fisher

NEW YORK UNIVERSITY PRESS
Washington Square, New York

Library of Congress Cataloging-in-Publication Data
Fisher, Douglas, 1934–
Monetary and fiscal policy.
Continues: Macroeconomic theory, a survey. 1983
Bibliography: p.
Includes index.
1. Macroeconomics.   2. Fiscal policy.
3. Monetary policy.   I. Fisher, Douglas, 1934–
Macroeconomic theory, a survey.   II. Title.
HB172.5.F54   1988   339.5′2   87–5478
ISBN 0–8147–2587–2

4/10/89   Emery Pratt   45.00

To my wife

Contents

Preface

This is a study of the theoretical literature on monetary and fiscal policy as this literature has evolved over the last twenty-five or so years. The format adopted here is the survey, but in view of the considerable volume of material available, the survey has been very selective, with the emphasis on seminal studies or on studies that seem to lay out the issues in a particularly clear way, rather than on the inclusion of everything that seems of merit. The reader of these pages should bear in mind that this is the policy part of a two-volume survey (the first, which appeared in 1983, is *Macroeconomic Theory: A Survey*). As a consequence most of the work on the basic structural equations of macroeconomics – on consumption functions, investment functions, and the like – has been put aside as we concentrate in this study on the policy issues, accepting whatever structural hypothesis seems appropriate for the problem in hand. This has created a few problems, since the material of the two surveys often overlaps, but book-publishing and time constraints have left us no other course of action. In any case it is the judgement here that the material in this survey – with its strong anti-structural/rational-expectations flavour – stands nicely by itself.

The details of the book are laid out in the first part of Chapter 1 and will not be repeated here. Suffice it to say that by the time Chapter 7 rolls by, practically all of the main topics in the recent macroeconomic policy literature will have appeared, complete with empirical discussions (for the definition of theory here is a broad one) to help to highlight the issues. If there is any drift to the study it is away from simplistic policy designs – let us say of the 'reaction function' variety – and toward designs which make use of what we might call a 'rational – Keynesian – Monetarist synthesis'. This is, of course, an uncompleted synthesis and there is always the danger that things will come unglued – and a fresh wave of controversies break out – but that is no reason to avoid trying to put things together and so we will plough on here, even though there may well be vultures perched in the branches above.

There are several things missing from this survey – broad as it is – and these must be charged against my account. For one thing, while there is a very detailed discussion of 'money-growth' models in Chapter 5, these models do not employ rational expectations. To be sure, there is a little of this material in Chapter 4, where recent extensions to 'rational expectations policy' are considered, but for the most part this part of the growth literature is neglected. It was my judgement that the complexity of this genre would have caused it to eat up much more space in the study than its small audience would have justified; so it was left out. For a second thing, I have not, generally, considered the 'open' economy policy literature except in those cases in which some of the originators of the material thought this would have a major (usually empirical) effect. On the whole I am not convinced that 'opening up' everything would do much more than complicate the theoretical issues, but in any case my main reasons are practical: considerations of time and space simply dominated this decision. The one issue that was not excused from attendance in the two surveys is the topic of 'currency substitution', but this was actually covered in the first volume, in the chapter on the demand for money, and so is not repeated here.

My biggest debt is to Jeffrey I. Bernstein of Carleton University, who contributed the solutions which make up the bulk of Chapter 5 on money-growth models. It is to be understood, I trust, that any errors found therein are mine. Lilyan Fulginiti provided me with some especially valuable bibliographical work, and the following offered useful comments on one or more chapters of the study: John Steven Clark, Walter Coleman, Paul R. Johnson, David McDonald, Khalid Mustafa and John Seater. My wife read the entire manuscript and contributed enormously to the readability of the final product, and the whole manuscript was capably typed through many drafts by Rehsif Guod.

DOUGLAS FISHER

1 An Overview: Basic Policy Models without Rational Expectations

> One of the functions of theoretical economics is to provide fully articulated systems that can serve as laboratories in which policies that would be prohibitively expensive to experiment with in actual economies can be tested out at much lower cost.
>
> R. E. Lucas, 1980, p. 696

1.1 INTRODUCTION

This chapter is designed to serve three purposes. In the first place we need to introduce the subject material of this study – to provide an overview – as a kind of prediction of what is coming. In this part of the discussion certain perceptions and prejudices can be laid on the table, too. We will do this in the remainder of this section, after we finish the preliminaries. Our second purpose in this chapter is to introduce some of the technology of the macropolicy literature. That is, while most of this technology will be laid out as we go along, a certain amount of basic statistical and mathematical material should be emphasised at the beginning in order to get things going. Finally, for our third purpose, we wish to lay out a series of basic macroeconomic policy models that have become standards in the literature.

Broadly speaking, the models we will be considering are typically set-up as follows. The authorities are assumed to have at their disposal certain instruments (e.g. a tax rate or the money supply) which they can vary in order to influence certain objective variables (e.g. the rate of change of prices or the variance of real income). To aid them in their task the authorities construct formal models and consult informed opinion, both as to what to do in particular circumstances and as to what values of the objective variables they should try to achieve. They also rely on the projections of the objective variables that are obtained from the forecasts of dynamic macroeconometric models (under various policy – that is, instrument – settings).

Chapter 1 takes this essentially conventional – and certainly old-fashioned – point of view of the policy process both because it is a particularly straightforward story and because, it will be argued, it still describes the way many economists (and practitioners) actually think about policy. The discussion will not be left in this antiquated state, though, and the remainder of the book basically qualifies and extends the results of Chapter 1. In Chapter 2 we will look at the literature on the Phillips curve as it has evolved from a simple prescription in the activist policy design, through the expectations (natural-rate) hypothesis, to the Lucas supply function (in which policy effects exist, at the most, in the short run). In Chapter 3, using rational-expectations theory, we will rework much of Chapters 1 and 2 and add a considerable amount of recent material on the real business cycle. The debate here concerns (a) the effectiveness and efficiency of policy when economic agents can correctly perceive the policy, (b) just how rational are expectations, (c) how we then explain the apparent effectiveness of macropolicies, and (d) what the potential and actual causes of fluctuations in economic activity are (and what role active macropolicies play in these fluctuations). Chapter 3, though, does not tell the entire story about rational expectations and macropolicy, and the discussion continues into Chapter 4. The purpose of Chapter 4 is to consider recent extensions of the literature and to dig into much of the empirical work on the subject. Thus, Chapter 3 presents the basic models and some particularly mainstream recent theoretical work while Chapter 4 dissolves into a series of extensions, quibbles, etc., which often have significant policy implications that unfortunately present distractions to the clean lines of the basic theory.

Those who believe that rational expectations has totally reshaped the macropolicy literature will find Chapters 3 and 4 the central part of this study. Be that as it may, other formal results still have to be considered, especially with respect to a growing economy. Chapter 5, then, basically completes the theoretical survey by extending Chapters 1 and 2 into the dynamic (growth) area; the work of Sidrauski, Sargent and Wallace, and Turnovsky are typical of this essentially theoretical discussion of recent money-growth policy models. In this case there are no empirical results to look at although the policy issues, involving, for example, the role of the deficit, are still numerous.

After Chapter 5 the organisation of the material is a little less compact, and the nature changes considerably toward 'institutional' results. Up to this point in the study only passing reference has been made to the long running dispute between the Keynesians and the monetarists – or their predecessors and successors. This is fine, as far as it goes, but there are still substantial disagreements over some of the matters appearing in Chapters 1 to 4 and, more importantly, it is possible to gain some leverage – perspective, really – by reviving these issues. Therefore, both monetarism and Keynesianism appear in Chapter 6. Chapter 6 also presents a further discussion of the problem of the deficit (if there is a problem). There will be, of course, some technical material discussed along the way, but these discussions will be considerably less dominant as the discussion drifts toward the 'practical' end of the spectrum. For example, Chapter 6 looks at the 'reverse causation' debate (involving the question of whether income 'causes' money rather than the converse), and both Chapters 6 and 7 consider certain technical matters about fiscal policy that were not really appropriate in the earlier more general discussions. Among the topics is a discussion of just how to measure the strength of the fiscal influence. Chapter 7, finally, presents a detailed discussion of the appropriate objectives of macroeconomic policy, a discussion of an important distinction between targets and indicators, and a consideration of what is involved in the selection of monetary and fiscal instruments. The discussion here is illustrated with contemporary examples although, to be sure, we will drop in certain rational-expectations results, in so far as they provide additional leverage on some of the older debates. Chapter 7, though, should not be thought of as an afterthought, but as a collection of important policy-related topics with both fiscal and monetary dimensions that have been put at the end to avoid cluttering the earlier discussion.

As a matter of principle, before we go on, we should note some important general points about our treatment of the subject. Most importantly, especially because it will give us the most difficulty, we should note the necessity of fully integrating fiscal and monetary policies throughout the study; this reflects the simple fact that the two policies are entwined both in effect and in objective and, furthermore, work through some of the same channels as they develop. More specifically, it is now believed that there is no fiscal instrument (e.g. tax policy) and no fiscal objective (e.g. growth) that can be handled independently of a monetary instrument (e.g. open-market operations) or a monetary objective (e.g. price-level stability). For example – just to present the issues – a tight-money policy to reduce inflation may raise interest rates and reduce employment in the short run, thus imposing a burden on the fiscal authorities in the form of higher interest rates (on the debt) and higher transfer costs (for unemployment compensation). This burden must be borne in some way – in short, it must be financed; as a consequence, the ability to chart an independent fiscal course – once a monetary policy has been established (and vice versa) – is sharply restricted. There are many other complications of this sort, as we shall see.

A second point of principle, and it follows immediately, is to note that any policy discussion will clearly depend on the state of the art in economic modelling and estimation. This qualification refers both to the capacity of the models that we use and to the richness of the empirical material that we can attach to these models. With regard to modelling, the basic choices concern what paradigm to adopt (Keynesian, monetarist, or 'new' classical – comparative/static or dynamic, etc.), the division between what is taken to be endogenous and what is exogenous, and what functional form is to be used to represent the hypotheses that we derive from the basic theory. Here, of course, we are limited both by what is presently in economists' tool kits as well as by what is technically feasible in the given circumstances. With regard to the empirical work, there is another set of tools (as provided by statisticians) to look over, as well as a number of strategic considerations involving

(a) the accuracy and appropriateness of the data,
(b) the level of disaggregation that might produce stable and sensible results (if any), and
(c) which sectors we might want to emphasise.

Thus, the results we ultimately squeeze out of any set of data will be conditioned by these considerations and, we can assume, will change as technical progress in both economics and econometrics establishes new and better tools with which to work the data.

1.2 SOME BASIC STATISTICAL CONSIDERATIONS: IDENTIFICATION AND OMITTED VARIABLES

We have suggested that a major part of the modelling effort requires a marriage between statistical and, let us say, economic-theoretic considerations. We will be emphasising the economics in much of this book, but it is actually efficient – particularly in view of our interest in empirical results – to lay out some broad statistical issues that apply pretty much across the spectrum of the theoretical models that we will be looking at. We begin with the concepts of the *reduced form* and the *structural form* of a basic econometric model. We do this both because it provides a general framework and because the distinction itself has been much discussed in the policy literature.

When we refer to something as *structural*, we generally mean a relation that is based directly on the behaviour of economic agents. An aggregate consumption function in which consumption depends on income and the interest rate is thus a structural relation in this sense. More generally, we can conceive of the structure of an entire economy as a series of equations, such as those in Equations 1.1, in which the relations between variables (x, y) are arbitrarily written out as completely interactive linear equations.

$$
\begin{aligned}
\alpha_{11} y_{1i} + \cdots + \alpha_{1p} y_{pi} + \beta_{11} x_{1i} + \cdots + \beta_{1q} x_{qi} &= e_{1i} \\
\vdots \qquad \vdots \qquad \vdots \qquad\qquad \vdots \qquad \vdots & \\
\alpha_{p1} y_{1i} + \ldots + \alpha_{pp} y_{pi} + \beta_{p1} x_{1i} + \cdots + \beta_{pq} x_{qi} &= e_{pi}
\end{aligned}
\tag{1.1}
$$

In these relations, then, the αs and βs 'parameterise' the linear hypothesis. Because we want to think of policy in a stochastic sense, further, we have attached an error term (e_{ji}) to each equation in order to express the notion that such things as hypothesis error and measurement error will cause these relations to fit the real world inexactly. These errors are usually taken as random with an expected value of zero. In Equations 1.1 we have also included the index i in order to identify the observation $(i = 1, \ldots, n)$. That is, there are i observations on each of the sets of variables denoted by y and x, with i varying over time, for example. When the model is applied to the data for any time period (that is, for any i), there will be an amount unexplained – a residual – that results for each structural relation. In this scheme, y, arbitrarily, represents the endogenous variables (e.g. income, consumption, investment) and x denotes the exogenous and predetermined variables. The latter are any lagged variables and any variables that are determined outside the system.[1] We will also refer to the αs and βs as the structural coefficients. As noted, the basic idea is that these equations are derived directly from economic theory (are, for example, consumption, investment and demand for money functions that we feel represent the results of individual (aggregated) decision-making).

Converting the system in 1.1 to matrix notation, we have

$$
YA = -X\beta + \varepsilon
\tag{1.2}
$$

where Y is nxp, A is pxp, X is nxq, β is qxp, and ε is nxp. If we attempt to estimate the relations in Equations 1.1 directly, for example by ordinary least squares, we will have problems because we will have endogenous variables on the right-hand side of the equation; consider Equation 1.3

with the i subscript dropped – for $\alpha_{11} = -1$, arbitrarily – as an example.

$$y_1 = \alpha_{12} y_2 + \cdots + \alpha_{1p} y_p + \beta_{11} x_1 + \cdots + \beta_{1q} x_q - e_1 \qquad (1.3)$$

In this event we have variables $y_2, \ldots, y_p$ that are themselves dependent on y_1 (that is, are jointly dependent by assumption). This being the case, they will, in general, be correlated with the error (e_i). The consequence of this correlation is that ordinary-least-squares (OLS) estimates of the coefficients of Equation 1.3 will be inconsistent (biased for large samples). In short, by ignoring the interaction (or 'feedback') between y_1 and $y_2, \ldots, y_p$ the coefficients will be wrong and so will any policy that is based upon them.

As a more satisfactory alternative we may try to estimate Equation 1.2 in its *reduced form*. This involves writing equations for each of the endogenous variables in terms only of the exogenous variables. Indeed, if we write

$$Y = -X\beta A^{-1} + \varepsilon A^{-1} = X\pi + U \qquad (1.4)$$

we have the reduced form of Equation 1.2, and we can successfully estimate by OLS for example – equation by equation – and obtain consistent estimates of the parameters of π. We can do this if the model is complete so that the inverse A^{-1} actually exists. Necessarily, this would be the case if the rank of A is the same as the number of equations (p) in the system. In the case of the reduced form we would then achieve consistent estimation of the parameters of Equation 1.4.

The equation system given in Equation 1.2 contains the structural coefficients while the equation system in Equation 1.4 contains the reduced-form parameters $(\pi = \beta A^{-1})$. In Equation 1.2 there are two sets of parameters in A and β, and they are $pxp + qxp$ in number. If Equation 1.4 is estimated directly, π, the estimated coefficient matrix, contains qxp coefficients to identify the components of A and β. Getting from the coefficient matrix of Equation 1.4 to that of Equation 1.2 – that is, solving for the values of the structural parameters from the estimates of the reduced-form parameters – is possible if we solve the *identification problem*. In particular, when we have as many estimates in Equation 1.4 as in Equation 1.2 and all of the coefficients in 1.2 can be calculated from those in 1.4, our model is exactly identified. We are over-identified if we have more coefficients in 1.4 than we need for 1.2, and we are under-identified if we do not have enough information in 1.4 to solve for the parameters in 1.2.

There is a second general issue we need to raise at this point and this concerns omitted variables. Data considerations (or conceptual errors) may cause us to omit variables that are actually relevant for the problem at hand. The consequence of this is that least-squares estimates will be biased. This is an issue in the policy literature because some monetarists (as we shall see in Chapter 6) are apparently inclined to recommend the estimation of simple reduced forms and thus there is the distinct possibility that in these cases some further relevant explanatory variables are omitted. This is, of course, a matter for statistical testing, and we shall go over this literature in Chapter 6, but for now it is important to point out that many of the basic policy models certainly appear to be reduced form (or, more accurately, 'simplified form') in this literature.

The consequences of omitting relevant independent variables can be seen in the following. Suppose that the *true* model, which is actually a simplification of the full model in 1.4, is that of Equation 1.5.

$$\tilde{y} = X\tilde{\beta} + \tilde{u} \tag{1.5}$$

On the other hand, suppose that we actually estimate

$$\tilde{y} = \overline{X}\tilde{\beta}^* + \tilde{u} \tag{1.6}$$

Under ordinary least squares the vector of coefficients for 1.6 would be given by

$$\hat{\tilde{\beta}}^* = (\overline{X}'\,\overline{X})^{-1}\overline{X}'\tilde{y} \tag{1.7}$$

and the properties of this estimator are what we wish to examine.

To see that $\hat{\tilde{\beta}}^*$ provides a biased estimate of $\tilde{\beta}$, substitute Equation 1.5 into 1.7 to obtain

$$\hat{\tilde{\beta}}^* = (\overline{X}'\,\overline{X})^{-1}\overline{X}'X\tilde{\beta} + (\overline{X}'\,\overline{X})^{-1}\overline{X}'\tilde{u} \tag{1.8}$$

Clearly, when we calculate $E(\hat{\tilde{\beta}}^*)$, we find that the term

$$(\overline{X}'\,\overline{X})^{-1}\overline{X}'X \neq I$$

and not $= I$ as is required to demonstrate unbiasedness. Indeed, we can calculate the sign of this bias (and the magnitude) in practical cases, and we will do so in Chapter 6, when we consider whether a popular monetarist model has a bias against fiscal policy. In addition, in this case the OLS estimates will be inconsistent and inefficient (the estimates of var $(\hat{\tilde{\beta}})$ will be too high). Whether or not these are practical concerns is, as we have pointed out, an empirical matter. It is surely enough to note that many macro models in use in the policy debate appear to be quite simple (or, if you wish, quite 'reduced' from some broader conception) in order to underscore the potential for problems here. Indeed, much of the empirical literature on the structural functions (e.g. on the demand for money) consists of just trying out other variables in what will certainly be a never-ending debate if that is the accepted standard of research. The problem is not that it is not a useful activity, because it is, but that the debate is often not sufficiently structured by theory to settle in on an area where disagreements can be put to the test.

1.3   A BASIC MACROPOLICY MODEL

Let us, then, set down a more specific version of the basic model of Section 1.2 in which the left-hand variables (the $\tilde{y}_t$) are macropolicy objective variables – the price level, the unemployment rate, etc. – and are expressed as dependent on three sets of independent variables. These last consist of the predetermined values of the dependent variables ($\tilde{y}_{t-1}$), truly exogenous variables ($\tilde{g}_t$), and a set of intermediate financial variables ($\tilde{m}_t$) that will be discussed further in a moment. This model is written in linear form as Equation 1.9 where the entries can be interpreted as vectors of the logarithms of the variables. Note that this model is, for the moment, specified in a non-stochastic form.

$$\tilde{y}_t = B_1 \tilde{m}_t + B_2 \tilde{y}_{t-1} + B_3 \tilde{g}_t \tag{1.9}$$

Also note that in this equation B_i defines a matrix of coefficients, with B_1 being $p x n_1$, B_2 being pxp, and B_3 being $p x n_2$, arbitrarily.

The expression just given could be interpreted as a reduced form, in the sense described in Section 1.2, in so far as the $\tilde{m}_t$ are truly exogenous. They are not, though, because in these sorts of models what is intended is that these variables are interest rates (e.g. the Treasury-bill rate) and monetary quantities (M1, etc.) which are themselves directly influenced by the authorities (and perhaps by other variables). If they are completely determined by the authorities, then, with a little more structure, we can arrive at a proper reduced-form system. To do this, we assume that when the authorities set their instruments ($\tilde{I}$) they determine these variables uniquely, as described in 1.10. By instruments we mean such entities as income-tax rates, central bank discount rates, or open-market operations in most of this discussion.

$$\tilde{m}_t = F \tilde{I}_t \tag{1.10}$$

Here the matrix F is $n_1 x p$. We can refer to these intermediate variables as proximate *targets* which are, then, hit by choosing values of the instrument vector.

With this determination, and taking the instruments as themselves truly exogenous (i.e. set by the authorities after reviewing the data for the economy), we can substitute Equation 1.10 into 1.9 to obtain the reduced-form model of the economy.

$$\tilde{y}_t = B_1 F \tilde{I}_t + B_2 \tilde{y}_{t-1} + B_3 \tilde{g}_t \tag{1.11}$$

Here the matrix $B_1 F$, which is $p \times p$, presents us with a set of scrambled coefficients, but, at least, this reduced form can be estimated consistently, if that is our intention. Note that the product $B_1 F$ must be defined (the number of columns in B_1 equal to the number of rows in $F = n_1$) for us to proceed. In words, there must be as many intermediate variables as there are instruments in this problem.

We may endogenise the macropolicy decision by assuming that the authorities have an objective function of some reasonable sort. A natural choice – although it is somewhat simplistic – is to assume that they attempt to minimise a quadratic loss function such as is expressed in Equation 1.12, which is not itself in matrix form (yet).

$$d_t = \sum_{i=1}^{P} w_i (y_{it}^* - y_{it})^2 \tag{1.12}$$

Here direct disutilities are attached to the authorities' not achieving their objectives while tradeoffs among the objectives are implicitly assumed, in the eyes of the authorities, in the sense that the weights in this function (the w_i) must sum to unity.[2] In Equation 1.12 the y_{it}^* are the desired values of the objectives, and the y_{it} are the actual (or predicted) values in the absence of a policy action. Thus, we have a discrepancy between desires and achievements, the elimination of which is, in effect, the general objective of macroeconomic policy.

The next step in the solution procedure is to expand Equation 1.12, still not converting to matrix notation, in which case we obtain

$$d_t = \sum_{i=1}^{P} w_i y_{it}^{*2} - 2 \sum_{i=1}^{P} w_i y_{it}^* y_{it} + \sum_{i=1}^{P} w_i y_{it}^2$$

This, written in matrix notation, is

$$d_t = \tilde{y}_t^{*'} W \tilde{y}_t^* - 2 \tilde{y}_t' W \tilde{y}_t^* + \tilde{y}_t' W \tilde{y}_t \tag{1.13}$$

where W is a $p \times p$ matrix of policy weights. The weights, as noted, sum to unity and can be thought of as representing the authorities' views as to how they should generally rank the objective variables (as guided, for example, by the political process or by their own prejudices, for that matter).

We may rearrange this system (a descriptive model and a disutility function) by substituting the model of the economy laid out in Equation 1.11 into the objective function to obtain

$$d_t = \tilde{y}_t^{*\prime} W \tilde{y}_t^* - 2[B_1 F\tilde{I}_t + B_2 \tilde{y}_{t-1} + B_3 \tilde{g}_t]' W \tilde{y}_t^* + [B_1 F\tilde{I}_t$$
$$+ B_2 \tilde{y}_{t-1} + B_3 \tilde{g}_t]' W[B_1 F\tilde{I}_t + B_2 \tilde{y}_{t-1} + B_3 \tilde{g}_t] \qquad (1.14)$$

The policy problem facing the authorities is to minimise their perception of social disutility by picking a vector of instrument settings (a set of values for $\tilde{I}_t$). The framework just laid out suggests that this choice is constrained by the model of the economy that the authorities use and by the authorities' perceptions of the weights that are attached to the objectives. To solve for this optimal vector of instruments we can further expand Equation 1.14 and then partially differentiate with respect to $\tilde{I}_t$; the result is Equation 1.15.

$$\partial d_t / \partial \tilde{I}_t = -2(B_1\ F)'\ W\tilde{y}_t^* + 2(B_1\ F)'\ W(B_1\ F)\tilde{I}_t$$
$$+ 2(B_1\ F)'\ WB_2 \tilde{y}_{t-1} + 2(B_1\ F)'\ WB_3 \tilde{g}_t = 0 \qquad (1.15)$$

By striking the common terms we can simplify this to Equation 1.16. We also bring the vector of optimal instrument settings over to the left-hand side and arrange the objectives, the predetermined variables and the exogenous variables, as right-hand variables.[3]

$$\tilde{I}_t = (B_1 F)^{-1} \tilde{y}_t^* - (B_1 F)^{-1} B_2 \tilde{y}_{t-1} - (B_1 F)^{-1} B_3 \tilde{g}_t \qquad (1.16)$$

This reduced-form equation is referred to in the literature as a 'reaction function', and it is frequently estimated in the form of Equation 1.16 with the addition of an error term and the omission of $\tilde{y}_{t-1}$ and $\tilde{g}_t$. Notice that because of the functional form chosen the authorities' opinions – the w_i – actually drop out of the solution so that (ignoring the other variables) the optimal setting reflects just the linkages between $\tilde{I}_t$ and $\tilde{y}_t^*$ which were expressed in Equation 1.11. In this sense one can use the *actual* results to judge what the authorities must have been thinking (it is, in effect, a 'revealed' preference formulation). The result is achieved, in effect, by substituting $\tilde{y}_t^*$ for $\tilde{y}_t$ in the basic model of the economy. It is, actually, as if the authorities can determine the value of the objectives uniquely and without fail by varying their instruments, but this does not seem to square with the facts. Nevertheless, as maintained above, this is the way many students of macropolicy visualise the problem (as we shall see), and it is certainly likely that much of the public believes that the authorities ought to announce and then hit their objectives, so that this simple model has an important place in the macropolicy debate, at least as a starting-point.[4]

1.4   STOCHASTIC AND DYNAMIC PROBLEMS IN THE BASIC POLICY MODEL

The following pages will present several basic and generally respected treatments of the macroeconomic policy problem in stochastic and dynamic-stochastic forms. The presentation of these basic results will provide the starting-point for their critique and extension in the rest of this study and, more positively, will provide what are essentially standard formulations that are still often employed in both formal and informal discussions of macropolicy. In addition some of the specific techniques that these models employ will be echoed elsewhere, and, more to the point, some of the broad findings are repeated in more recent efforts that find a role for monetary and fiscal policies.

1.4.1   A Simple Stochastic Model

By and large the literature discussed in this entire section makes use of variations of the basic model described in Section 1.3, but with different details in the representative model of the economy (in Equation 1.9). Our first example will be a discussion of what is known as the *instrument selection problem*; it is based on a paper by Poole (1970). Poole sets the problem as that of solving for the choice of optimal policy instruments – in this case either the money stock or the nominal interest rate – when the overall objective of the authorities is to minimise the variance of real income. The framework is the static *IS–LM* model with a single objective variable (real income) and, accordingly, a single policy instrument (either the interest rate or the stock of money). The model is taken in a stochastic form which means that each of the basic equations – *IS* or *LM* – is observed with error (u and v in what follows).

The following two equations represent stochastic – but static – versions of the *IS* and *LM* curves, respectively.

$$y = a_0 + a_1 r + u \tag{1.17}$$
$$M = b_0 + b_1 y + b_2 r + v \tag{1.18}$$

The variables are real income (y), the interest rate (r), and the money stock (M), with the latter two being the instruments and the level of real income being the objective variable. It is not obvious that either M or (especially) r can be taken to be exogenous in this way, but this is a conventional-enough procedure, at least at the textbook level, and this is the way much of the literature is written. Later on, in Chapter 6 particularly, we will attempt to assess the significance of the lack of 'reverse causation' (y on M, for example) that such an approach assumes. But for now we can proceed with the understanding that when we speak of an interest-rate instrument, we mean that the money-supply curve is horizontal, and when we speak of a money-stock instrument, the same curve is vertical. These results will be assumed to have been achieved by means of the appropriate open-market operations. Finally, we note that in Equations 1.17 and 1.18 u and v are the stochastic components and they have the properties that $E(u) = E(v) = 0$, $E(u^2) = \sigma_u^2$, $E(v^2) = \sigma_v^2$, and $E(uv) = \sigma_{uv} = \rho_{uv}\sigma_u\sigma_v$ where ρ_{uv} is the correlation coefficient between u and v. We are also assuming away autocorrelation in the residuals.

Now let us assume that the authorities attempt to minimise a quadratic expected loss function in this single objective framework, as described in Equation 1.19.

$$L = E[(y - y^*)^2] \tag{1.19}$$

Again, y^* refers to desired real income, and y is its actual level. The system of equations described in 1.17 and 1.18 has three variables and two equations. These equations are not symmetrical in that 1.17 has one potential 'control' variable (one instrument) while 1.18 has two; this will be a consideration in what follows.

Let us first consider the policy of using the interest rate (r) as the instrument. The ideal setting for r would be to use open-market operations to set it so that the variance of income (in Equation 1.17) is zero; this target value for the interest rate is clearly

$$r^* = a_1^{-1}(y^* - a_0)$$

That is, we pick a value for y^* and then find the r^* that reduces u to zero. Note that with r exogenous, if we determine y in Equation 1.17, then with that value plus r, we also determine M in 1.18. This system is, consequently, 'block recursive' so that we can discuss our solution for income entirely in terms of Equation 1.17. Note also that we use the desired value of $y(= y^*)$ in this expression; in words, we wish to minimise fluctuations of income around some desired value of real income. We are not permitting a tradeoff between y^* and its variance; we are simply selecting y^* and then finding the interest rate that produces the least variance (in y). Substituting the value of r^* just derived into Equation 1.17 we then have

$$y = a_0 + a_1 a_1^{-1}(y^* - a_0) + u = y^* + u$$

This directly gives us $y - y^* = u$ which can then be substituted into Equation 1.19. Taking expectations to calculate the expected loss of the policy of interest-rate control we then find that

$$L_r = \sigma_u^2 \tag{1.20}$$

That is, the expected loss of an interest-rate control policy comes entirely from 'shocks' to the IS curve. Monetary shocks (v) are irrelevant because they are contained in the monetary sector by virtue of the choice of an interest-rate stabilisation policy. This strategy is sometimes attributed to Keynesians.

To see the situation graphically, consider Figure 1.1. Here we draw an IS curve as a range (IS_1 to IS_2) whose width depends on the irreducible error (u) in the IS equation. If we assume that it is the money-demand curve that provides all of the explanation of the stochastic LM curve in Equation 1.19 – and that the money-supply curve is non-stochastic – then a monetary policy of controlling the interest rate will completely eliminate v in that equation as an influence on the LM curve. This can be verified easily and it has the consequence of providing a flat LM curve, as shown in Figure 1.1.

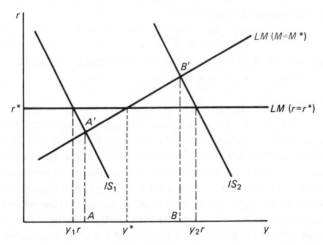

Figure 1.1   The loss associated with an interest-rate control policy

In this event the potential loss of the policy is defined by the distance $y_{2r} - y_{1r}$; it is clearly due to the irreducible error in the *IS* curve (due to u) that determines how far apart the two curves are. (Note that the second *LM* curve in Figure 1.1 will be referred to in a moment, when we are in a position to compare money-stock control with interest-rate control.)

Consider the alternative policy, that of controlling M. In this case, since r and y are now both endogenous variables, we will need to solve our entire system to find the irreducible loss associated with the optimal solution for the money stock; we proceed as follows. Substituting 1.18 into 1.17 we obtain a stochastic aggregate demand curve of

$$y = (a_1 b_1 + b_2)^{-1} [a_0 b_2 + a_1 (M - b_0) + b_2 u - a_1 v] \tag{1.21}$$

From Equation 1.21 we see that the variance-minimising strategy is to pick a value of M (call it M^*, the target value of the money stock) such that

$$y^* - (a_1 b_1 + b_2)^{-1} [a_0 b_2 + a_1 (M^* - b_0)] = 0$$

This we can see directly (we want $b_2 u - a_1 v = 0$, in effect). The value of y here can again be taken as the desired value (y^*), and it is again the value of y that would be reached in a non-stochastic setting for optimal monetary control. Our procedure, again, is to find the value of M that equates y to y^* and then to calculate the loss of this policy (we will call this loss L_m). Subtracting the expression for y^* just given, from y in 1.21, we arrive at the argument for the loss function. This, for $M = M^*$ for the vertical money-supply function, is

$$y - y^* = (a_1 b_1 + b_2)^{-1} (b_2 u - a_1 v) \tag{1.22}$$

This we may substitute directly into 1.19 to obtain

$$L = E[\{(a_1 b_1 + b_2)^{-1} (b_2 u - a_1 v)\}^2] \tag{1.23}$$

Expanding and taking expectations, then, we see that

$$L_m = (a_1 b_1 + b_2)^{-2} (a_1^2 \sigma_v^2 - 2\rho_{uv} a_1 b_2 \sigma_u \sigma_v + b_2^2 \sigma_u^2) \tag{1.24}$$

This expression provides the loss for a money-stock control approach. This loss clearly depends on both variances, that for the *IS* curve (σ_u^2) and that for the *LM* curve (σ_v^2). We note that these slopes and variances are observable in principle so that this is an empirically implementable framework although it is certainly a little on the Spartan side.

We may now effect a direct comparison between the losses of the two policies; an obvious way to do this is to compute the ratio of the two losses as in Equation 1.25.

$$\frac{L_m}{L_r} = (a_1 b_1 + b_2)^{-2} \left(a_1^2 \frac{\sigma_v^2}{\sigma_u^2} - 2\rho_{uv} a_1 b_2 \frac{\sigma_v}{\sigma_u} + b_2^2 \right) \tag{1.25}$$

This expression is arranged as a quadratic in the ratio of the two standard deviations with associated parameters; the following generalisations are available:

(a) Assuming that the two errors are uncorrelated (i.e. that $\rho_{uv} = 0$), then in the event that $\sigma_u^2 > \sigma_v^2$, i.e. in the event that our knowledge about the *LM* curve is better than it is about the *IS* curve, then a money-control policy is better than an interest-rate control policy in the sense of making the relative loss in 1.25 less than unity.

This situation is also shown in Figure 1.1 where it is assumed, for simplicity, that there is no variance in the *LM* curve. That is, if there is no variance in the money-demand curve, then a money-stock control policy will produce something like the *LM* ($M = M^*$) curve, with the traditional upward slope. It is non-stochastic, of course. Clearly, then, the loss from this policy ($B - A$) is less than the loss from the interest-rate control policy ($y_{2r} - y_{1r}$). This is an extreme example (assuming error only along the *IS* curve), but it does illustrate the basic point – this is that the state of knowledge about the economic system has something to do with the style of policy and, perhaps, on whether one adopts a Keynesian or a monetarist stance.

(b) Conversely, if $\sigma_v^2 > \sigma_u^2$, i.e. assuming that uncertainty about the *LM* curve exceeds that for the *IS* curve, an interest-rate control policy would be superior in that $L_m/L_r > 1$.[5]

To see this, we can redraw Figure 1.1 as follows in Figure 1.2 with no variation along the *IS* curve. Then an interest-rate stabilisation policy would produce an *LM* curve of *LM* ($r = r^*$) as before. The loss from this policy, assuming we set the curve as drawn in Figure 1.2, is zero.

On the other hand, a money-stock control policy will not succeed – in the event that there are irreducible errors along the money-demand function – in reducing the error in the *LM* curve. This will produce an *LM* curve lying between LM_1 and LM_2 as drawn in Figure 1.2. The result then is a loss of $y_{2m} - y_{1m}$, which is clearly greater than zero (the loss from the interest-rate control policy).

We should point out that this discussion could present the two strategies as either monetarist or Keynesian and that this is a typical way

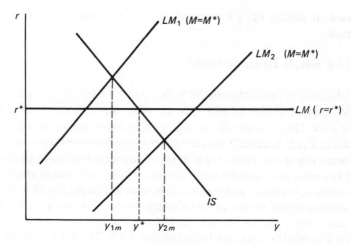

Figure 1.2　Interest-rate and money-stock control in the Keynesian case

of comparing these positions. Indeed, there is Keynesian writing (see Goodhart's survey, 1975) that emphasises monetary chaos and monetary irrelevance as elements of a coherent policy design. This point of view would be correct, then, under the presumed stochastic condition of $\sigma_v^2 > \sigma_u^2$. Of course, a monetary control policy would be better, assuming an income stabilisation objective in the converse case. We should label this last 'activist' rather than monetarist since, to anticipate the discussion later in this chapter and in Chapter 6, many Keynesians now accept monetary intervention while some monetarists reject any sort of stabilisation policy.

There is one final point often made about the foregoing, and that is that

(c) the steeper the slope of the demand for money the lower the expected loss from the money-stock policy.

To see this, at least provisionally, go back to Equation 1.25 and set $\rho_{uv} = 0$, $a_1 = b_1 = 1$, and $\sigma_u^2 = \sigma_v^2$.[6] Thus another dispute between Keynesians and monetarists over the interest elasticity of the demand for money is also an understandable one. That is, the flatter the demand-for-money curve, the more an interest-rate stabilisation policy would tend to be preferred over a money-stock control policy. We will return to this model in Chapter 3, under rational expectations, but for now it is enough to note that such strategy choices are still very much a subject of discussion at the policy level, and the model employed here still seems relevant in setting up a framework in which empirical work might flourish.

1.4.2 A Simple Dynamic Model

The objective of the authorities in Subsection 1.4.1 was to minimise the 'mean squared error' in real GNP in what was essentially a static framework. This is hardly the most general problem that we would want to look at if only because it does not relate to the business cycle – and the business cycle is our prime topic in this study. The first thing to do to work toward a more general result is to show how cycles might arise – by construction, in effect – and then to show what one might do about them in a policy context similar to that already discussed. As we proceed, we will move from the simple stochastic model of Subsection 1.4.1 to a dynamic stochastic structure in Subsection 1.4.3. The main purpose of these exercises is to lay out basic models which will be referred to repeatedly in this study; we also wish to establish some notation for later reference.

In order to keep the economic structure on the table, let us start with the model that is perhaps most typical of the cyclical models, the basic Samuelson (1939)–Hicks (1950) 'accelerator–multiplier' model. The purpose of this first part of the exercise is to show a simple 'equilibrium business cycle' model that, in itself, contains a justification for stabilisation policy. Assume, then, a consumption function of

$$C_t = \tau + \beta Y_{t-1} \tag{1.26}$$

where β is the propensity to consume *lagged* income and τ is a constant term. Assume, also, an investment demand function of

$$I_t = \alpha(Y_{t-1} - Y_{t-2}) \tag{1.27}$$

where investment depends on the *first difference* in lagged income. Equation 1.26 defines the multiplier and 1.27, with α as the incremental capital–output ratio, the accelerator. With an equilibrium condition $(Y_t = C_t + I_t)$ this system can be written as the second-order difference equation in 1.28.

$$Y_t - (\beta + \alpha)Y_{t-1} + \alpha Y_{t-2} = \tau \tag{1.28}$$

Here, it is obvious, there is a built-in serial pattern to Y_t that (as it turns out) could 'cycle' (if y were ever *jolted* (shocked) from its stationary value of $y_t = y_{t-1} = y_{t-2}$). Lags in responses, in decision-making, in the construction of capital equipment and in the adjustment of inventories are frequently mentioned as aggravating factors in modern business cycles; factors such as these lie behind the lags modelled in 1.26 and 1.27 and thus behind this standard 'explanation' of the business cycle.

Following Sargent (1979), let us consider the properties of a more general version of 1.28

$$Y_t = f_1 Y_{t-1} + f_2 Y_{t-2} + \tau + \delta M_t \qquad (1.29)$$

where M defines an exogenous variable (such as the money stock, which is taken below as a potential control variable). In this expression $f_1 = \beta + \alpha$ and $f_2 = -\alpha$ in the accelerator–multiplier model. Let us define the general lag operator (L) as

$$LY_t = Y_{t-1}, \ L^2 Y_t = Y_{t-2}, \ldots, \ L^n Y_t = Y_{t-n} \qquad (1.30)$$

where $n > 0$ defines backward lags and $n < 0$ defines forward 'lags'. What this operator does is shift any time-subscripted variable back a number of periods as defined by the exponent in L^n. We use it because it compresses the notation. A polynomial in the lag operator is given by

$$A(L) = a_0 + a_1 L + a_2 L^2 + \ldots = \sum_{j=0}^{\infty} a_j L^j \qquad (1.31)$$

where the coefficients a_j might represent weights attached to (in this case) historical data. If this way of writing the 'distributed lag' in income is applied to Y_t we get

$$A(L)Y_t = (a_0 + a_1 L + a_2 L^2 + \ldots) Y_t$$

$$= a_0 Y_t + a_1 Y_{t-1} + a_2 Y_{t-2} + \ldots = \sum_{j=0}^{\infty} a_j Y_{t-j} \qquad (1.32)$$

In actual work one takes $A(L)$ to be 'rational'; an example is the popular Koyck transformation in which the infinite series $1 + \lambda L + \lambda^2 L^2 + \ldots$ when summed is shown to be equivalent to $1/(1 - \lambda L)$ for $|\lambda| < 1$.[7] Equation 1.29, with the lag operators, is

$$(1 - f_1 L - f_2 L^2) Y_t = \tau + \delta M_t$$

which solves to

$$Y_t = \frac{\tau}{1 - f_1 L - f_2 L^2} + \frac{\delta}{1 - f_1 L - f_2 L^2} M_t \qquad (1.33)$$

and describes the time path of income. Note that we plan to treat M_t as exogenous and will ignore its time subscript in what follows. The expression $1/(1 - f_1 L - f_2 L^2)$ is an infinite distributed lag.

To see how actual business cycles might be built into the structure of a representative model let us examine the roots of this equation. We may factor the expression in the denominators of Equation 1.33 as in

$$1 - f_1 L - f_2 L^2 = (1 - \lambda_1 L)(1 - \lambda_2 L) \tag{1.34}$$

where $f_1 = \lambda_1 + \lambda_2$ and $f_2 = -\lambda_1 \lambda_2$. Then $1/\lambda_1$ and $1/\lambda_2$ can be interpreted as the roots z_1 and z_2 of the *characteristic equation* $1 - f_1 z - f_2 z^2$. Expressing the characteristic equation in standard form as $f_2 z^2 + f_1 z - 1 = 0$, the roots of this expression can be derived directly from the following standard equation.

$$s_i = \frac{-f_1 \pm \sqrt{f_1^2 + 4f_2}}{2f_2} \tag{1.35}$$

We can, returning to our economic model, write the *general solution* of Equation 1.33 as

$$Y_t = \frac{\tau}{(1 - \lambda_1 L)(1 - \lambda_2 L)} + \frac{\delta}{(1 - \lambda_1 L)(1 - \lambda_2 L)} M_t + c_1 \lambda_1^t + c_2 \lambda_2^t \tag{1.36}$$

where c_1 and c_2 depend on initial conditions.[8] The temporal behaviour of this dynamic system, then, depends on the value of the structural parameters. In particular, if both roots of this expression are negative and real then there are no cycles; on the other hand, if the term under the radical in Equation 1.35 is negative – so that we have complex roots – then the system oscillates. For $f_1^2 + 4f_2 < 0$ and $0 > f_2 > -1$ this will be a damped oscillation (a cycle that dies out) while for $f_2 < -1$ the cycle gets progressively larger (it explodes). In terms of our original coefficients, the condition producing oscillations is

$$(\beta + \alpha)^2 + 4(-\alpha) < 0$$

We have no right to pick values of β and α out of the air, as, for example, Hicks (1950) does, but, even so, it is certainly easy to generate cycles – even explosive cycles – for trial values of α and β (try $\alpha = 0.25$ and $\beta = 0.5$).[9] A useful diagram, for all possible values of f_1 and f_2 appears in Sargent (1979, p. 183). This model, in any case, provides an explanation of the business cycle in terms of natural reactions ingrained in the system. It is, also, an equilibrium model of the cycle.

1.4.3 Simple dynamic–Stochastic Models

The next thing to do is to move a step closer to the actual policy world by taking the dynamic model in a stochastic form. While we do so, we will stick a good deal closer to the policy literature than we have in much of this chapter. The point of departure is again the accelerator–multiplier model, but this time it will have a fiscal policy response function attached to it (as described by Turnovsky, 1977c).

Since the model of this section slightly extends that of Subsection 1.4.2 we will construct it almost from scratch; the originating paper is that of Baumol (1961). He starts with an accelerator–multiplier equation of

$$Y_t = \beta Y_{t-1} + \alpha(Y_{t-1} - Y_{t-2}) + \tau + G_t \tag{1.37}$$

in which β is the propensity to consume, α is the accelerator coefficient, τ is autonomous expenditure, and G_t identifies government spending (for fiscal policy, arbitrarily). For government spending we will assume the policy reaction function

$$G_t = \delta_1 Y_{t-1} + \delta_2 Y_{t-2} + B \tag{1.38}$$

where δ_1 and δ_2 are policy determined parameters (or reaction coefficients) and B is a constant. We are, of course, still assuming that the authorities wish to stabilise income. For purposes of later reference it is handy to have an explicit solution for this system. Thus, we can combine Equations 1.37 and 1.38 to obtain the second-order difference equation of

$$Y_t + (f_1 - \delta_1)Y_{t-1} + (f_2 - \delta_2)Y_{t-2} = B + \tau \tag{1.39}$$

Here $f_1 = -(\beta + \alpha)$ and $f_2 = \alpha$. As with Equation 1.36 the general solution of this equation is given by

$$Y_t = \frac{B + \tau}{1 - (f_1 - \delta_1)L - (f_2 - \delta_2)L^2} + A_1 \lambda_1^t + A_2 \lambda_2^t \tag{1.40}$$

where A_1 and A_2 are determined by the initial conditions (by setting starting values for Y_0, Y_1, for example). In this expression λ_1 and λ_2 define the roots of the characteristic equation

$$\lambda^2 + (f_1 - \delta_1)\lambda + (f_2 - \delta_2) = 0$$

Necessary and sufficient conditions for stability in this model, then, are that

$$1 - f_2 + \delta_2 > 0,$$
$$1 + f_1 + f_2 - \delta_1 - \delta_2 > 0$$
$$\text{and } 1 - f_1 + f_2 + \delta_1 - \delta_2 > 0$$

in which case Y_t would converge to the constant value in Equation 1.40.

In our previous example in Subsection 1.4.2 our stability conditions were determined entirely by the underlying parameters – by the f_i, in effect. In this model, though, where there is a government reaction function, obviously the policy parameters δ_1 and δ_2 are involved in the stability of the system. We may take δ_1 as a direct response and δ_2 as an indirect or 'echo' response; here two points seem worth emphasising.

(a) Given values for f_1 and f_2 that produce cycles (or explosions) after a shock, there exist values of δ_1 and δ_2 that would enable the authorities to eliminate this disturbance. This is the usual rationale for the use of macroeconomic policy.

(b) Government policy – even well-intentioned government policy – could add to instability if certain values of δ_1 and δ_2 are chosen. This has surely happened (see Friedman and Schwartz, 1963).

But with regard to the last point we do not have sufficient evidence to judge the severity of the 'natural' part of the cycle, so any surmises we might make about the role of governments in adding to or subtracting from instability in practice are just that – surmises – as things presently stand.

To close in on the stochastic version of the problem let us consider more explicitly the policy issue just raised. This issue concerns whether a feedback type policy might be preferred to a monetary rule (as, for example, recommended by M. Friedman (1959a)). The controversy is an old one in macroeconomics and involves a long-running debate over 'rules' versus 'authorities' in the management of the macroeconomy. Broadly speaking, Keynesians have favoured 'authorities' with discretionary policy controls while monetarists – or, at least, more conservative monetarists such as Friedman – have favoured rules. By a *rule* we mean such as a fixed rate of monetary growth (e.g. 4 per cent per year growth in M1); perhaps, to avoid later confusion, we could refer to this as a 'passive' rule.

Following Sargent and Wallace (1976) we can put the argument as follows. Suppose that the dynamic behaviour of national income is correctly described by a first-order difference equation of

$$y_t = \alpha + \lambda y_{t-1} + \beta m_t + u_t \tag{1.41}$$

where m_t is the rate of growth of the money stock, y_t is the deviation of GNP from the level of potential GNP, and λ provides the engrained persistence that the authorities want to deal with. If, as earlier, the objective is to minimise the variance over time of y_t around some desired level y_t^* then we can suppose that the authorities can do this by picking some δ_1 and δ_2 in the monetary reaction function

$$m_t = \delta_1 + \delta_2 y_{t-1} \tag{1.42}$$

assuming, of course, that they can control m_t (see Chapter 7 for a further discussion). Here δ_1 is the passive rule (recall that m is the rate of growth of the money stock) and δ_2 – itself clearly an 'active' rule – describes the feedback part of the proposed policy. We may substitute 1.42 into 1.41, producing

$$y_t = (\alpha + \beta\delta_1) + (\lambda + \beta\delta_2)y_{t-1} + u_t \tag{1.43}$$

This is a stochastic first-order difference equation describing the determination of the time path of GNP (relative to potential GNP) in the event there is a monetary policy. From Equation 1.43 we can calculate the steady-state solution for this system (by assuming $y_t = y_{t-1}$), which is

$$E(y) = (\alpha + \beta\delta_1)/[1 - (\lambda + \beta\delta_2)] \tag{1.44}$$

Here we assumed $E(u_t) = 0$, of course.

To move toward the stochastic part of the problem we should note that the variance of u_t is σ_u^2 and that this variance is assumed to be constant and finite. We may calculate a variance term for the steady state (for y around its steady-state value and thus around y^*); this expression, which comes directly from 1.43 with $y_t = y_{t-1}$, is

$$\text{Var } y = \sigma_u^2/[1 - (\lambda + \beta\delta_2)]^2 \tag{1.45}$$

The policy-makers, let us say, desire to minimize this variance by choosing their policy parameters, δ_1 and δ_2. Transparently, there is no setting of δ_1 that affects the variance of y because the value of δ_1 merely sets the constant in 1.43. Indeed, the correct strategy to minimise this variance is to choose δ_2 such that 1.45 is minimised; this could ideally reduce that expression to σ_u^2, which is the best that can be done. In this model this amounts to setting $\delta_2 = -\lambda/\beta$ such that the effect of the lag – that is, the effect of the persistence – in 1.44 is overcome. δ_1 can be set, of course, and this would be done using Equation 1.44 so that $E(y) = y^*$; the ideal value would be for $\delta_1 = (y^* - \alpha)/\beta$, assuming that $\delta_2 = -\lambda/\beta$ has already been chosen. Substituting the two policy settings for δ_1 and δ_2 into Equation 1.42 we have an overall monetary reaction function of

$$m_t = \frac{(y^* - \alpha)}{\beta} - \frac{\lambda}{\beta}y_{t-1} \tag{1.46}$$

The first part is the passive rule and the second is the (active) stabilisation component. This, in a simplified framework, equates y to y^* (plus an error) and, as long as $\lambda \neq 0$, presents a solution that is superior to the rule alone (which, in effect, sets $\delta_2 = 0$). As we shall see, though (in Chapter 3), this result generally does not hold up under rational expectations.[10]

The policy just described utilises a first-order difference equation and thus is inherently incapable of dealing with the business cycle. To extend the discussion in this respect, and to consider fiscal policy, we now, finally, consider an early paper by Howrey (1967); once again the presentation is that of Turnovsky (1977c). We begin by returning to Equations 1.37 and 1.38, but this time we make them stochastic.

$$Y_t = \beta Y_{t-1} + \alpha(Y_{t-1} - Y_{t-2}) = G_t + \tau + v_t \tag{1.47}$$

$$G_t = \delta_1 Y_{t-1} + \delta_2 Y_{t-2} + B + w_t \tag{1.48}$$

Combining the error terms as in $u_t = v_t + w_t$ and assuming that the individual errors are uncorrelated, we have a stochastic-difference equation that is the same as Equation 1.39 in form.

$$Y_t + (f_1 - \delta_1)Y_{t-1} + (f_2 - \delta_2)Y_{t-2} = B + \tau + u_t \tag{1.49}$$

Here $E(u_t) = 0$, $\mathrm{var}\,(u_t) = \sigma_u^2$ and $E(u_t, u_t') = 0$ for $t \neq t'$. Note that $f_1 = -(\alpha + \beta)$ and $f_2 = \alpha$ in this model.

As in Sargent, the general solution for Y_t in the case of Equation 1.49 is given by

$$Y_t = (\tau + B)/[1 - (f_1 - \delta_1)L - (f_2 - \delta_2)L^2]$$

$$+ A_1\lambda_1^t + A_2\lambda_2^t + \sum_{i=0}^{\infty} \alpha_i u_{t-i} \quad t = 1, 2, \ldots \tag{1.50}$$

where the set of new terms makes up the *stochastic component* of the solution and

$$\alpha_i = (\lambda_1^{i+1} - \lambda_2^{i+1})/(\lambda_1 - \lambda_2)$$

are weighted differences of the roots of the characteristic equation; the term

$$A_1\lambda_1^t + A_2\lambda_2^t$$

provides what is called the *transient component* of the disturbance. Note that if the system is stable, then Y_t converges to the steady-state value of

$$\overline{Y} = (B + \tau)/[1 - (f_1 - \delta_1) - (f_2 - \delta_2)]$$

Y_t will still fluctuate around $\overline{Y}$, of course, following shocks, and so there is a stabilisation role for fiscal policy. The job is, as before, to minimise the variance of income over time. This variance can be derived from Equation 1.49, following our previous procedure, and is

$$\sigma_y^2 = \frac{(1 + f_2 + \delta_2)}{[1 - (f_2 + \delta_2)]\{[1 + (f_2 + \delta_2)]^2 - (f_1 + \delta_1)^2\}} \sigma_u^2 \tag{1.51}$$

This is derived in the same way that we obtained the variance exhibited in Equation 1.45. It is necessary and sufficient for this to be finite for the stability conditions of the non-stochastic system (listed after Equation 1.40, above) to be satisfied.

The minimisation of this variance is, as before, the objective of policy. The best policy, then, would be to set the fiscal policy parameters δ_1 and δ_2 to $-f_1$ and $-f_2$ respectively, in which case the solution would be

$$Y_t = \overline{Y} + u_t \quad \text{and} \quad \sigma_y^2 = \sigma_u^2.$$

The optimal policy, in this case (provided we have overall stability), is clearly to offset the effect of the autoregressive structure of the system. There is, in short, a role for policy in this more general case, although plenty of difficulties remain.[11]

Baumol argues that 'plausible and reasonable' stabilisation policies could make matters worse and concludes that since the model presented here is a simple one, in the 'far more complex and unpredictable world of reality' there would be little ground for confidence about these 'reasonable' policies. Howrey, really, adds a stochastic component to the previous analysis and concludes that a policy that speeds up the rate at which the transient disturbance is damped could increase the variance of the time path of income. To both – but especially to Baumol – one should point out that more complex (and possibly more realistic) systems are not necessarily more unstable although it is certainly likely to be harder to set up a clear policy. This, of course, is a favourite neoclassical argument in which considerably more faith is put in what one might term the 'natural stability properties of the system'. These are given no significant role in the foregoing (which operates somewhat like a knife-edge model) and precious little in any of the literature that we will be looking at in this study (which drastically oversimplifies in this respect). But in any case all of this work is in the equilibrium business-cycle tradition in which cycles are embedded in the system on account of the consistent reactions of economic agents to changes in their circumstances.

2 The Natural-rate Hypothesis and Other Matters

> The hypothesis that there is a stable relation between the level of unemployment and the rate of inflation was adopted by the economics profession with alacrity.... But as the '50s turned into the '60s and the '60s turned into the '70s, it became increasingly difficult to accept the hypothesis in its simple form. It seemed to take larger and larger doses of inflation to keep down the level of unemployment. Stagflation reared its ugly head.
>
> M. FRIEDMAN, 1977, p. 469

2.1 INTRODUCTION

The main topic in this chapter is a general discussion of the evolution of ideas about the relation between inflation and unemployment. In the first instance the material we will look at is concerned with the possible existence of a relatively stable tradeoff between inflation and unemployment that can be exploited in some way by the macropolicy authorities. More generally, though, we will be interested in both the real and the nominal effects of monetary and (sometimes) fiscal policy especially as these effects occur in the short run. Of course we have already been working on this topic, but the standard *IS–LM* model that supported our discussion in Chapter 1 does not actually have a supply side of any depth and is, in any case, an awkward framework for many interesting questions about policy. Now we wish to bring in the labour market, as we must do in order to say something coherent about unemployment; we not only have to specify that market more carefully but also must deal with the (physical) capital market and its interaction with the labour market. The result is an aggregate supply theory that completes the standard macro model in a way that enables us to get a somewhat firmer grip on the nominal and real effects of monetary and fiscal policy.

Actually, we are going to divide our material on these topics into three partly overlapping sections in this and the next two chapters. In this chapter we will consider the development of the *natural-rate hypothesis* from its beginning as an extension of the Phillips curve to its current role as part of the modern theory of aggregate supply. But this discussion will not be complete because we will arbitrarily consider only *adaptive expectations* in this chapter, putting aside rational expectations until Chapters 3 and 4. The reasons, quite simply, are (a) that a good deal of the relevant material on the unemployment/inflation tradeoff predates (or does not employ) rational expectations and (b) that we will want to lay out rational expectations theory formally, with an amount of detail that would distract us somewhat from the basic policy problems at hand. Even so, Chapters 2 to 4 still do not contain the entire story because the context there is short run; the long run, and more on the natural rate, continues on into Chapter 5.

Specifically, in this chapter we will begin our discussion with some brief historical notes on the early Phillips curve and some of its theoretical or empirical rationalisations (e.g. those of Perry, Okun, Lipsey, etc.). This material was written mostly in the 1960s, although work at this level actually continues. Then we will discuss the development of the 'natural-rate' hypothesis. This theory employs labour market theory (involving the influence of changing expectations) in an effort both to provide some theoretical structure for the Phillips relation and to help explain the all-too-apparent shifts and loops in the actual empirical relation between inflation and unemployment. The remainder of the chapter considers the empirical implementation of natural-rate theory and the development of alternative and more detailed paradigms designed to link labour and spending markets. The culmination here is in the development of the early versions of the 'Lucas supply function' which do not make much use of rational expectations. We should note, though, that we will not be digging very deeply into labour market theory at any point in this study, settling, instead, for the minimum necessary to motivate certain well-known models.

2.2   THE ORIGINAL PHILLIPS CURVE AND SOME VARIATIONS

The story of the relation between inflation and unemployment could begin with the early papers by Phillips (1954, 1958) in which an empirical regularity formed the backdrop for some basically casual theoretical observations. Phillips looked at annual U.K. data for the period 1861–1957 and discovered a negative relation between the rate of change of nominal wages and the per cent of the labour force unemployed. Phillips's interest in this phenomenon was not entirely empirical, although this is the way his work is frequently represented. In fact, one of the things he had in mind was trying to bridge the gap between the newer Keynesian models of his time and the neoclassical models they sought to replace. That this was a major concern at the time is easily documented; it is certainly less obvious that Phillips had this in mind, but this reasonable argument is advanced in a survey paper by Lipsey (1976).

The argument, broadly, is that the neoclassical model is a long-run model with flexible prices in which full employment obtains; the Keynesian model, on the other hand, is a short-run one, in which there exists unemployment and in which there is a (relatively) fixed price level.[1] In these circumstances, then, an empirical relation between inflation (or wage inflation) and unemployment could provide the missing link. It would be better, no doubt, if a theoretical link could be forged, but failing that, an empirical regularity – such as the Phillips curve – could conceivably do, certainly for practical purposes.

Phillips's model, when stated formally, is nothing more than Lipsey (1960)

$$\pi_w \equiv \dot{W}/W = a + bU^{-1} \qquad \dot{W} = \frac{dW}{dt}, \quad b > 0 \tag{2.1}$$

This wage inflation (π_w) equation seems to fit the data that Phillips looked at and is set up as a hyperbola in order to capture an apparent upward curvature in the empirical relation between wage inflation and unemployment. But it was almost immediately noticed in the original Phillips scatter diagrams that there were also counter-clockwise loops in the relation. At the least this suggests omitted variables – and thus bias – in the estimates of the coefficients, particularly in view of the fact that the data loop serially and not randomly over the business cycle. A brute-force approach to this problem, in keeping with the empirical orientation of the material we are working with, is simply to amend Equation 2.1 as in

$$\pi_w = a + bU^{-1} + cU^{-2} + d(\dot{U}/U) \tag{2.2}$$

where the last term could capture the loops. This version of the Phillips curve is Lipsey's (1960). If we think of $\dot{U}/U$ as the 'variation' of the unemployment rate, then with $d > 0$, a higher variation is associated with more wage inflation than is a lower variation. If, in turn, this variation changes over the cycle – in particular, rising during upturns and falling during downturns – then we have an apparent explanation of the loops that accords well with the facts just mentioned, having the upper part of the loops during upturns and the lower part during downturns.[2] But some of this early work now seems beside the point, if only because the loops, since the early 1950s at least, have been clockwise in general and very 'unstable' in appearance (see H. I. Grossman, 1974).

The most obvious way to provide theoretical underpinnings for the Phillips curve is through some sort of labour market pressure theory in which the pressure of increased demand reduces unemployment and somehow 'pushes up' prices (more rapidly). There are indeed some early theoretical Phillips curve models that are in this tradition. One, the work of Lipsey (1960) that was in use for a time employed another apparent empirical regularity, this time between vacancies and unemployment ($UV = h$, a constant) to close the model (see Dicks-Mireaux and Dow, 1959). An alternative which fits more neatly into the stream of non-monetarist material uses a cost-push (or mark-up) equation to link inflation with labour market pressure. One version of this is also due to Lipsey, who describes it as a non-Walrasian model which in effect provides an early disequilibrium interpretation of the Phillips curve (1960, 1974, 1976). Assuming that the long-run demand for labour is measured by J and the supply by N, the excess demand for labour is, then, $J - N$. Let people leave jobs, voluntarily or not, at the rate αE where E is the level of employment. Workers also find jobs, and we will assume they do so at the *rate $\beta U(J - E)$* where $J - E$ defines the available vacancies in the market (with $\beta > 0$, presumably). Combining these ideas, *changes* in unemployment then would depend on the gap between 'quits' and 'hires'.

$$dU/dt = \alpha E - \beta U (J - E) \tag{2.3}$$

To obtain a Phillips curve, let $E = N - U$ and assume that $dU/dt = 0$ (that the level of unemployment is in equilibrium). This directly produces

$$J = \frac{\alpha}{\beta} N U^{-1} - U + N - \frac{\alpha}{\beta} \tag{2.4}$$

In this expression $(J - N)/N$ could represent pressure on wages. Employing a cost-push rationale we can then argue that wages adjust directly to this labour market pressure. The result is a Phillips curve of

$$\tau(w) = -\frac{\alpha}{\beta N} + \frac{\alpha}{\beta} U^{-1} - \frac{U}{N} \tag{2.5}$$

in which $\tau(w)$ represents the wage adjustment. This has the properties required of a Phillips curve (see Lipsey, 1974). Thus standard macro-theoretical interpretations of the empirical Phillips curve are available.[3]

An alternative explanation of this cost-push, adjustment scenario builds on the widely used price and wage equations; we follow the discussion of Turnovsky (1977c). In Eckstein (1964) the basic Phillips-style relation for *wage* inflation can be defined as

$$\pi_w = a_0 + a_1 U + a_2 \pi + a_3 \mu \tag{2.6}$$

where μ can be interpreted as a measure of the aggregate profit rate. The idea is that *actual* price inflation (π) would directly inflate money wages (via cost-of-living adjustments) while increases in profits would stimulate greater demand for wage increases (by, for example, unions).[4] Price inflation also needs to be explained, and so a second equation (the price equation) is included for that purpose.

$$\pi = b_0 + b_1(y - y_f) + b_2(\pi_w - \delta) \tag{2.7}$$

Here $y - y_f$ represents demand pressure (y_f is full-employment real output or real income) and $\pi_w - \delta$ represents wage pressure on prices (via cost-push); δ is a measure of the rate of change of labour productivity.

The two equations just described are structural and need to be taken as a pair (at least) since each has two other endogenous variables in it. A way to proceed is to write the 'reduced' form of the system (taking y as exogenous for the moment); this is the motivation for the following two expressions.

$$\pi = \frac{(b_0 + a_0 b_2) + b_1(y - y_f) + b_2 a_1 U + b_2 a_3 \mu - b_2 \delta}{1 - b_2 a_2} \tag{2.8}$$

$$\pi_w = \frac{(a_0 + b_0 a_2) + a_1 U + a_2 b_1(y - y_f) + a_3 \mu - a_2 b_2 \delta}{1 - b_2 a_2} \tag{2.9}$$

These equations, or some variant of them, appear often in large-scale econometric or forecasting models, and in these roles have established a decent empirical record. Even so, we should note that none of the right-hand variables is truly exogenous so that direct use of the equations, either separately or together, could run into some of the problems discussed in Chapter 1. Furthermore, as the model stands, *both* U and $y - y_f$ represent the demand-pressure hypothesis and one of them should be eliminated. That is, as explained by Turnovsky (1977c), there is also an implied linear relation between U and $y - y_f$ of the form[5]

$$U = \alpha_0 + \alpha_1(y - y_f) \tag{2.10}$$

Indeed, in this model if y_f is predetermined (or constant), then unemployment depends directly on y. This result is recognisable as Okun's Law (1970), yet another possible empirical regularity that, if true, rationalises the use of this pricing/mark-up Phillips model.

These basic Phillips curve models have generated a truly enormous empirical literature which has been surveyed on occasion (see Santomero and Seater, 1978; Rutledge, 1975). What seems to have been established is the following.

(a) A nonlinear and negative relation between either inflation or wage inflation and unemployment (however measured), especially on quarterly data, is a fairly standard result for most periods of time and for many countries.

(b) These tests regularly show instability in the sense of changes in the coefficients over time; testing of this instability is, however, not very frequent, especially in the early papers.

(c) Tests to try to explain the exceptions – the loops, the shifts, or whatever – are not easy to rationalise theoretically and are not often successful empirically.

A common approach in dealing with these problems has been to introduce other variables. Among these one finds the strongest aid from price-level changes, productivity indices, profits, and union power.[6] Usually there is an acceptable rationale attached to these efforts, but solid theoretical work, in the sense of setting up some deeper structure, is generally absent, or, when it is there, is 'unbelievable' (see Sims, 1980). But, as noted, the success of this literature is in its empirical record (in macroeconometric models) and the agnostic approach suits it very well, on the whole.

2.3 THE NATURAL-RATE HYPOTHESIS

As the preceding discussion has indicated, it is certainly possible to patch up the Phillips relation in order to bring it into closer conformity with the data. A more satisfying way to proceed, in contrast, is either to work with the Phillips curve part of a realistic 'rock-bottom' model (as explained in Lipsey, 1976, and Blinder and Solow, 1974) or to seek to build up a curve from some deeper structure, directly linking the supply side with the demand side (as is achieved through the use of the Lucas supply function, for example). The rock-bottom model approach makes one thing perfectly clear: the Phillips relation can reasonably be used in a fully specified macro model to work on questions of policy effectiveness (Lipsey, 1976, p. 9):

The comparative statics of the macro model closed by the Phillips curve are exactly those of the neo-Classical model: there is a unique level of real income and a unique price level for any set of values of the parameters and the endogenous variables. What the Phillips curve does for the model is to provide a possible explanation, absent from the dichotomized model, of the division of impact effects between real and monetary variables when the model is in disequilibrium.

This is yet another way to provide the 'missing equation' in a standard macromodel. On the whole, however, there is more interest in deeper structure, particularly because of the promise of developing a better empirical grip on policy problems, and so we will move in that direction, beginning with the *natural-rate* hypothesis.

The reason we are interested in natural rates at all is that the Phillips curve represents a potential short menu of opportunities to the macropolicy authorities who may desire to establish 'unnatural' rates of interest or unemployment because, in their view, they can (via policy actions) improve things. We will not discuss the welfare aspects of the problem, but we will certainly turn to broad concerns over the objectives of policy in Chapters 4 and 7. Here, though, our concern is whether the Phillips curve represents a well-behaved choice set from which the authorities can select attainable (and desirable) combinations of un-employment and inflation.

The initial work on the natural-rate hypothesis belongs to Phelps (1967) and M. Friedman (1968). What is involved, basically, is a theory that links revisions in expected inflation rates, as they affect labour market activity, to actual inflation rates. The result is an *expectations augmented Phillips curve* that, in effect, shifts whenever inflationary expectations are revised. If we dig a little deeper we see that what underlies both the original policy effect and its revision is a distinction between money prices (as measured by the general price level) and relative prices. That is, economic agents will want to make their optimising decisions in real terms (at relative prices), using the price level in order to make adjustments in any nominal magnitudes (e.g. their bond and money holdings) in their environment. It is here that macropolicy enters the picture. If policy alters nominal prices, economic agents who will be forecasting prices (both nominal and real) will generally revise their expectations in order to arrive at correct decisions. If they cannot make such revisions – if they have nominal contractual obligations, if they are slow to react, or if they make errors in their responses (simply confusing nominal and real, for example) – then policy will have an effect, at least in the short run. It is obvious, then, that the Phillips curve tradeoff could come from this source. In the long run, contracts are revised, reactions have to occur and errors may well be corrected. In this event the tradeoff that defined the Phillips curve tends to disappear.

2.3.1 The Natural Rate of Interest

The foregoing is based on the notion of a *natural rate* of unemployment that is itself the result of some sort of equilibrium in the labour market. In particular, in this theory it is argued that macropolicy can successfully lower the actual rate of unemployment in the short run – lower it even below the natural rate – but in the long run such a policy will produce only inflation, and unemployment will return to its equilibrium (natural) level. We need to devote more space to actual labour market material to make all this clear, and we will certainly do so later in this chapter, but for now we will take advantage of the strategy that M. Friedman employed in his 1968 paper and consider further what happens when the authorities try to control the *natural rate of interest*. As it turns out this material is parallel to the labour market discussion and arrives at similar conclusions about the role of macropolicy. Indeed, the simple dynamics which unfold in the capital markets case are easy to visualise and can be presented without the encumbrance of the *ad hoc* labour market theory that is usually added to the model when that market is included. Furthermore, there is a basic distinction made here – between nominal and real interest rates – which is essential if we are to make sense of actual macropolicy strategies. In particular, we will find that both fiscal and monetary policy are worked through capital markets and that there is a tendency, not always in the interest of stability, to monitor financial rates of return either as the targets or as the indicators of monetary policy.

The discussion of what happens when the policy authorities attempt to drive the nominal rate below its equilibrium level (in order to stimulate the economy) begins with the well known 'Fisher effect' of I. Fisher (1898). What Fisher proposes is a distinction between the nominal and the real rate of interest in the form of [7]

$$i = r^e + \pi^e \tag{2.11}$$

Here i is an observed market rate of interest; r^e is an expected real interest rate, measuring real marginal rates of interest on, for example, consumption and investment activity; and π^e, measuring the expected rate of inflation, is an inflationary correction. This correction is applicable because, in general, the securities whose returns are measured by i are nominal instruments and, as such, will deteriorate in value at the rate of inflation.[8] In particular, participants in capital markets, realising that inflation will erode the value of their financial instruments which are denominated in nominal terms, will arrive at a consensus opinion as to the premium which should be attached to the expected real rate of return to account for expected inflation.

It is important to realise that the right-hand terms in Equation 2.11 is directly observable since both are expected (that is, *ex ante*) concepts. This has produced quite a variety of empirical procedures. These include

(a) direct estimates of expectations (either π^e or r^e) by means of, for example, sample surveys,
(b) the construction of real rate of interest indices taken from corporate or other sources,
(c) the use of weighted averages of the past values of the variable being predicted,
(d) the use of weighted averages of the past values of variables which *cause* the variable being predicted.

But none of these proves to be entirely satisfactory in practice although certain series (notably the money stock and the price level) have been pretty easy to predict, using (c) or (d).

An important policy issue that immediately arises concerns the potential interaction between the two right-hand variables in Equation 2.11. This is an issue, quite simply, because a lack of interaction implies that expected inflation could just be tacked on to the nominal rate (and would explain it, *ceteris paribus*). With such a result, as we will see, nominal interest-rate stabilisation policies basically have no chance of being successful. The more general view of this interaction, though, is that these two variables are part of the general structure of the economy and, as such, are both subject to influences from all parts of the economy. Sargent notes (1973, p. 430):

> Only in the special case in which the *LM* curve is vertical, the *IS* curve is horizontal or the short-run Phillips curve is vertical . . . does an increase in expected inflation produce an immediate equivalent jump in the nominal interest rate. These special sets of parameter values obviously impart a very monetarist or classical sort of behaviour to the model.
>
> On this interpretation of Fisher's theory, all of the parameters influencing the slopes of the *IS*, *LM*, and Phillips curves are pertinent in evaluating its adequacy.

While this generalises the interaction problem, it hardly settles the basic empirical question of how much interaction there really is.

At this reading it seems as if the empirical evidence largely runs in the direction of independence. Fama (1975), in particular, argues that US Treasury-bill rates actually exhibit *rational* predictions of inflation (and so r^e and π^e are unrelated) although in a later paper (Fama and Gibbons, 1980) he concedes that there is a positive relation. Even so, nominal rates appear to be dominated by changes in expected inflation rates. This being the case, the neoclassical policy–inflation interaction which we are about to discuss is certainly relevant to present conditions. We should note, though, that we will return to the Fisher equation in Chapter 4 when we consider what effects monetary and fiscal policy might have had on real and nominal rates in recent years.

The policy, let us assume, is an attempt to control the nominal rate of interest by, for example, open-market operations. An early and lucid explanation of the effects of trying to drive the nominal interest rate below the natural or equilibrium rate (by means of an expansion of the money supply) is seen in Wicksell (1898, 1936, in English). Wicksell interested in explaining why interest rates and prices are both pro-cyclical series, a problem that once preplexed economists unequipped with Equation 2.11.[9] In order to push the interest rate below its equilibrium level, money is pumped into the system; this, in turn, forces up prices. Then (1936, p. 94–5):

> a fall in the rate of interest, even though it is casual and temporary, will bring about a perfectly definite rise in prices. . . . if the rate of interest remains at a low level [below the natural rate of interest] for a considerable period of time, the influence on prices must necessarily be cumulative.

As noted, while the actual interest rate is below the natural rate and is maintained there by the open-market policy of the monetary authorities, money is pumped into the system. If the actual rate is permitted to rise (for whatever reason), this 'inflationary gap' persists although it steadily narrows as the two rates converge.

The next question concerns what happens if the authorities do not permit the two rates (their target rate and the natural rate) to converge but, instead, try to maintain the gap between them.[10] Keynes has the answer in his *General Theory* (p. 198).

> It is evident, then, that the rate of interest is a highly psychological phenomenon. We shall find . . . that it cannot be in equilibrium at a

level below the rate which corresponds to full employment, because at such a level a state of true inflation will be produced, with the result that M1 will absorb ever-increasing quantities of cash.

M1 here is, of course, transactions balances, and so Keynes is suggesting that ever-increasing changes in the price level will occur, especially at full employment. In other words, to borrow a later phrase, Keynes postulates an 'accelerationist hypothesis' and a direct link between the natural (equilibrium) rate of interest and the equilibrium (natural, full) employment rate. Note that we need to explain more carefully why inflation accelerates rather than dies out; this will be done below.

2.3.2 The Natural Rate of Unemployment

The labour market version of the natural-rate hypothesis utilises the same pressure (monetary or fiscal policy) but at a different point in the economy. M. Friedman (1968) begins by assuming the existence of a 'natural' rate of unemployment that represents equilibrium in the labour market in the sense of a solution to a Walrasian general equilibrium of labour and commodity markets. This rate is not necessarily constant cyclically and should be taken, presumably, to be the result of the decisions of economic agents on their labour-force participation rates, decisions which reflect worker mobility, the quality of available information on labour markets and the like. By analogy this version of the natural-rate hypothesis then argues that attempts to drive the unemployment rate below its natural rate (by means of a monetary or a fiscal expansion) produce increased inflationary expectations which themselves shift the Phillips curve to the right. Attempts to hold an actual unemployment rate below its natural level, as before, produce successively larger percentage increases in the money supply and, therefore, in the price level.

The initial mechanism for producing a lower unemployment rate by means of a policy stimulus involves an error in the calculations of workers who do not realise that the real effect of the rise in nominal wages is cancelled by an accompanying rise in the price level. Having incorrectly calculated a rise in real wages, workers initially offer more labour services; this accounts for the basic negative tradeoff between π and U (along the Phillips curve). As correct information comes in, though, workers revise their offers. This produces a reversal of the initial effect – and a 'shift' of the Phillips curve – and a return of unemployment toward its natural level. As M. Friedman puts it (1968, p. 10), 'As in the interest rate case, the "market" rate can be kept below the "natural" rate only by inflation. And, as in the interest rate case, too, only by accelerating inflation.' Furthermore, even though it may appear to be possible, the correct policy, says Friedman, is not to try to use macropolicy to set unemployment at the natural rate – since that rate will be hard to measure and will also be variable – nor to attempt to smooth out the market rate (which would be subject to all sorts of temporary fluctuations), but to adopt a monetary rule. A rule (for example, a steady 4 per cent rate of growth of the nominal money stock) would keep the authorities from attempting the 'impossible' – which for Friedman is stabilising the economy with discretionary policy – and would have the important by-product of making it easier for economic agents to form correct expectations. We have already considered rules in Chapter 1 and will return to the subject at several later points in this study (notably in Chapter 3); the informational aspects of adopting a rule are also considered in that chapter and in Chapter 7.

The foregoing does not explicitly show why the policy pressure has to be stepped up to maintain a target i or U below their natural levels. The answer, broadly, is that the policy runs into diminishing returns as economic agents speed up their reactions. It is, that is to say, a result of 'curvature conditions' which seem reasonable in the face of a pressure that is both persistent and, really, easy for economic agents to monitor. The following discussion, drawn from Phelps (1967), makes this clear.

The model that Phelps uses is necessarily dynamic. Let us, first, rewrite Equation 2.11 as

$$i = r^e - x \tag{2.12}$$

where $x \equiv -\pi^e$ is the expected rate of *deflation*. We can suppose that the real rate of interest depends on the marginal product of capital as in

$$r^e = r^e(y) \qquad r' > 0, \quad r'' \geqslant 0 \tag{2.13}$$

Here y is the incremental 'utilisation rate' of the capital stock (it is the incremental output–capital ratio). From a golden-age model (see Phelps, 1966) in which the supply of labour grows at the rate τ – and is improved in quality by technological change (is augmented) at the rate λ – we know that all variables that grow will grow at the rate $\tau + \lambda$. The capital stock is one such variable and so, too, is the level of real income (both, therefore, grow at $\tau + \lambda$ along the golden-age path). In this case the utilisation rate is clearly constant if we are growing at the natural rate of growth. Note that the real interest rate (equal to the marginal product of capital) will also be constant over time under golden-age rules.

Phelps then argues that the *actual* inflation rate (π) depends on the utilisation ratio (y) and on the expected inflation rate ($= -x$).

$$\pi = f(y) - x \tag{2.14}$$

Here $f(y)$ is a supply pressure (or cost-push) expression in which attempts to raise the utilisation ratio produce increased inflation; the expected inflation rate is just added on as a second causal factor. Equation 2.14 is graphed in Figure 2.1.

Here we have a series of augmented quasi-Phillips curves (the function $f(y)$ is the quasi-Phillips curve, and $-x$ augments it) with the required positive slope and upward curvature (representing the hypothesis that attempts to achieve a higher utilisation rate (y) are bought at the cost of an increasing inflation rate). In Figure 2.1 $\bar{y}$ represents a technical upward limit on the utilisation ratio. Note that we can transform this to the more familiar Phillips relation between U and π by means of Okun's Law (which ties together unemployment and high-employment real income). For y^* representing the level of the utilisation ratio at which inflationary expectations are just equal to actual inflation, we find that there is one

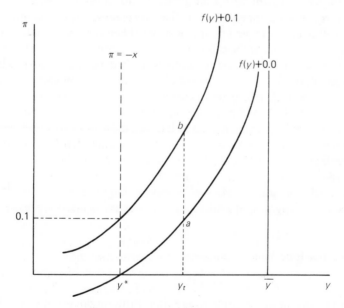

Figure 2.1   Quasi-Phillips curves

$f(y) - x$ curve that is consistent with zero inflation; this is the one that is labelled as $f(y) + 0.0$ in Figure 2.1. In this sense all points along the vertical y^* dashed line are equilibrium points (in having $\pi = -x$).

To illustrate the dynamics, consider the case in which there is overutilisaton ($y_t > y^*$) on account of the use of a fiscal or monetary policy. We can visualise this as a movement along $f(y)$ to point a. Expectations of inflation ($-x$) will adjust here, and if $-x = \pi$ the result will be a new curve at $f(y) + 0.1$. The 'equilibrium' for this curve would be at a utilisation ratio of y^*, but so long as the policy is maintained and the overutilised y_t is achieved, the rate of inflation will continue to increase (to b in the next stage). Indeed, on account of the curvature restrictions here ($f'' > 0$), the point b represents an increase in the rate of increase of prices. This formally represents the accelerationist hypothesis.[11]

2.3.3   Monetary Policy and Natural-rate Theory

In the material discussed so far in this section the basic idea is that economic agents produce real responses to inflation because they cannot correctly divide observed price-level changes into nominal and real components. That is, they monitor the data, calculate an expected price, sign a contract of some sort and then deliver the goods (or labour services) whatever the actual *real* reward they receive. If they underpredict the inflation rate, they will oversupply, and in this way an underestimated inflation will produce a stimulus to the economy. The authorities can take advantage of this situation–rational expectations aside–in so far as they can produce inflation that produces under-prediction and hence stimulation (or the converse). We can, indeed, motivate this effect by assuming some form of habit-persistence (not further specified) that gives the authorities their leverage. This is what we will do in the remainder of this section, where we follow the work of Sargent (1979). What we are after here is a basic generalisation of Section 2.3.2 as a starting-point for the criticism and extension of the natural-rate approach.

A textbook model of the economy might have a stochastic expectations-augmented Phillips curve (*where all variables are in logs*) of

$$y_t = \tau(p_t - p^*_{t-1}) + \lambda y_{t-1} + u_t \tag{2.15}$$

with a portfolio balance equation of

$$m_t - p_t = y_t + e_t \tag{2.16}$$

This expression arises from equilibrium in the money–bonds market. The stimulation hypothesis is contained in the coefficient τ (> 0) and in a third relation that assumes that inflationary expectations are formed adaptively.

$$p^*_{t-1} = V(L)p_{t-1} = \sum_{i=0}^{\infty} v_i p_{t-i-1} \tag{2.17}$$

The notation is the same as that employed at the end of Chapter 1. Note that we omit the interest rate in order to simplify and that the error terms u_t and e_t are uncorrelated.

Let us assume, still following Sargent, that the authorities seek to minimise the following loss function by setting the monetary quantities in a manner to be described in a moment. d, here, refers to the 'mean square error'.

$$d = E(y_t - y^*)^2 \tag{2.18}$$

This function is in the spirit of those studied in Chapter 1. We may square the terms on the right-hand side of Equation 2.18 and then rearrange to get the following:

$$d = E[(y_t - Ey)^2] + (Ey_t - y^*)^2 \tag{2.19}$$

where the first term is σ_y^2 and the second is generally referred to as the 'bias squared' (around y^*); it describes the disutility that comes from missing the target (squared), given the variance in y.

To pick the optimal time path of m_t, given u_t and e_t, we need to solve for the time path of real income expressed as a function of these three exogenous influences. Note, though, we will be assuming in what follows that m_t will be set *before* u_t and e_t are known. If we combine 2.15, 2.16 and 2.17, looking at backward lags, we have

$$y_t = H(L)m_t + G(L)e_t + F(L)u_t \tag{2.20}$$

where

$$H(L) = \frac{\tau(1 - LV(L))}{(1 + \tau - (\lambda + \tau V(L))L)} = \sum_{i=0}^{\infty} h_i L^i = -G(L) = -\sum_{i=0}^{\infty} g_i L^i$$

$$F(L) = \frac{1}{(1 + \tau - (\lambda + \tau V(L))L)} = \sum_{i=0}^{\infty} f_i L^i$$

What the authorities will do in this scenario is pick their m_t based on the following linear feedback rule, where the lagged errors are known to them.

$$m_t = k + A(L)e_{t-1} + B(L)u_{t-1} \tag{2.21}$$

Note again that they are setting m in t based on an arbitrary lag in their information. The expressions $A(L)$ and $B(L)$ are, of course

$$A(L) = \sum_{i=0}^{\infty} a_i L^i \quad \text{and} \quad B(L) = \sum_{i=0}^{\infty} b_i L^i$$

The authorities, then, are assumed to know, at time t, all of the parameters of the model and the values of all of the data up to and including $t - 1$. They will pick k (which is, in effect, Friedman's rule), $A(L)$ and $B(L)$ assuming that the structure just laid out remains unchanged.

To see what happens when they operate their policy in this way we can substitute 2.21 into 2.20 to get

$$y_t = kH(1) + [G(L) + \Phi(L)]e_t + [F(L) + \Theta(L)]u_t \tag{2.22}$$

where for simplicity

$$\Phi(L) = \sum_{i=1}^{\infty} \Phi_i L^i = H(L)A(L)L$$

$$\Theta(L) = \sum_{i=1}^{\infty} \Theta_i L^i = H(L)B(L)L$$

Here, assuming a Phillips relation and adaptive expectations, the policy authorities can alter the time path of income by picking suitable values of k, $\Phi(L)$ and $\Theta(L)$. The latter are achieved by picking the a_i and the b_i, of course. They will do this in an attempt to minimise the contributions of the two variances e and u to the time path of income. To see this procedure and its limitations more explicitly, still following Sargent, we can calculate the variance of y_t directly from Equation 2.22 – assuming, as we are, that e_t and u_t are uncorrelated. This produces

$$\text{var } y_t = \text{var } e_t[g_0^2 + \sum_{j=1}^{\infty}(g_j + \Phi_j)^2] + \text{var } u_t[f_0^2 + \sum_{j=1}^{\infty}(f_j + \Theta_j)^2] \tag{2.23}$$

whereby a setting of the parameters such that

$$\Phi(L) = -\sum_{i=1}^{\infty} g_i L^i \quad \text{and} \quad \Theta(L) = -\sum_{i=1}^{\infty} f_i L^i$$

will clearly reduce the variance of y_t in Equation 2.19 to its minimum $(= g_0^2 r_e^2 + f_0^2 r_u^2)$. This formulation is, of course, similar to that described in Chapter 1. This value is the result of irreducible current noise that the authorities are not in a position to recognise (by assumption); the upshot is clearly that any recognisable cycle in y_t is completely eliminated. Of course this strong result is questionable in practice since the approach ignores rational expectations and assumes that the authorities know the exact structure of the economy and that this structure does not alter in response to the policy itself.

The actual policy also includes a setting for the constant term (k) in Equation 2.21 which we interpreted as Friedman's rule. Our decomposition of the objective function in Equation 2.19 should now be recalled. The exercise that produces the rules for $\Phi(L)$ and $\Theta(L)$ actually reduces the variance of that expression to its minimum; this leaves the 'bias squared' term

$$(Ey_t - y^*)^2$$

We may calculate Ey_t from Equation 2.22 directly. Indeed, since $E(u_t) = E(u_t)$ for all t we have that

$$Ey_t = kH(1) \tag{2.24}$$

Thus, by setting $kH(1) = y^* = Ey_t$ the authorities can reduce the bias to zero. This is the Friedman component of the total policy that produces a final result of

$$y_t = y^* + g_0 e_t + f_0 u_t \tag{2.25}$$

when monetary policy is applied to a world in which an expectations-augmented Phillips curve exists. Thus, natural-rate theory, taken by itself, implies a stabilisation role for monetary policy beyond the simple rule of Friedman, provided, of course, that Friedman's concerns about poorly working models (etc.) are not important. Rational expectations results also should be considered as qualifications here, if only because of the simple adaptive expectations structure that we have employed in the telling of this story.

2.3.4 Some Empirical Notes on the Natural-rate Model

We really do not have the space to discuss more than a small sample of the empirical work that has been done on the basic expectations hypothesis. The place to begin is with the single-equation studies that insert an expected inflation variable – or an expected wage inflation variable – directly into the basic Phillips curve (usually with an adaptive expectations rationale). In one thorough test on semi-annual US data, Turnovsky and Wachter (1972) compared five specifications of a wage equation and found results marginally in favour of the standard formulation of Eckstein (1964) (as is described above). Not performing quite as well were various lagged versions of the theory (extrapolative, adaptive, general distributed and Phelps-type models). When an error-learning version is tested (using the popular Livingston data on expected wages and prices) price and wage expectations are found to affect wages as the theory predicts. This effect is interactive with the profit rate (a standard variable in such functions) and, in any case, has a sufficiently weak response over the six months horizon to suggest a strong role for policy in the US economy. This is judged by whether the coefficient on expectations is significantly less than unity (with unity being the prediction of the natural-rate theory).

The price-expectations coefficient obtained by Turnovsky and Wachter is both significant and low (at around 0.2); similarly, the error-learning hypothesis produces an effect (around 0.4) that is significantly different from zero. R. J. Gordon (1971), in a parallel paper using the Livingston data, confirms the first of these results but not the second. In an attempt to reconcile the difference, Lahiri (1977) proposes that the correct way to write out all of the structural equations – including the *ad hoc* expectation equations – is with error terms on each and with the use of a three-stage least-squares estimation technique on the problem. He also proposes adding a combined 'regressive-adaptive' model to the menu of *ad hoc* price-expectation hypotheses; this is attributed to Frenkel (1975). In the event Lahiri finds that the combined model outperformed the three standard models (adaptive, extrapolative and unrestricted) in terms of its explanation of the Livingston data; it also produces a coefficient on expectations of around 0.4 in an OLS test. Using 3SLS, Lahiri raises the coefficient to 0.536, but it is still significantly different from unity and so the 'policy effectiveness' result of Turnovsky and Wachter survives this retesting (*on data up to* 1970).

Looking at *Canadian* experience, Turnovsky (1972) covers pretty much the same ground as the Turnovsky–Wachter study just discussed, but with the general result that while short-run estimates show a role for policy, long-run estimates do not. Heroically, in this Canadian study, the same Livingston (US) data are employed for price and wage expectations in several tests for Canada. An *Australian* study, with comparable methodology, but with 'reduced-form' expectations generating mechanisms (involving price and productivity changes) is by Parkin (1973). Parkin finds a weak short-run and no long-run tradeoff. But Parkin's work is questioned by McDonald (1975) on various econometric grounds (see below) and on the grounds that the Parkin study assumes that the labour market is in equilibrium. (McDonald argues that the

Phillips relation seems to require disequilibrium.) McDonald's overall point, approximately, is that the Parkin study is so badly specified that on his evidence no judgements can be made as to the effectiveness of policy.

On the quarterly data for *Japan*, covering the period 1956 to 1968, Toyoda (1972) uses a first differencing technique to link past price-level changes to what he calls the expected price level. This produces an expectations coefficient of around 0.5, which he regards as a contradiction to the 'strict' expectations hypothesis. Finally, a study of sixteen Latin American countries by Bomberger and Makinen (1976), taking them one at a time and using a measure of capacity utilisation to measure the short-run tradeoff, finds a variety of results covering all of the possibilities from a strong Phillips curve (both short and long run) to no relationship at all. At least a short-run Phillips curve occurs in eleven of the sixteen countries, and most of these have a long-run relationship as well. What are basically data corrections were made to this study by Sheehey (1979) and the effect is that many of the results can no longer be claimed to be significant. The 'policy effectiveness' result of Bomberger and Makinen is the chief casualty of this retest.

The studies just described are not really very carefully specified, and there does not seem to be any really good reason for suspecting that a short-run tradeoff has been firmly demonstrated to this point. In some ways the most obvious problem refers to the expectations themselves. Thus, we can question the expectations data as either inaccurate or improbable and we can doubt that Koyck, Almon or similar lag schemes for past prices effectively capture all of the information relevant for predicting those prices. Furthermore, following a list considered by Cargill and Meyer (1974, p. 99)

(a) It is unrealistic to assume the absence of feedback between wages and prices,
(b) the accounting for serial correlation produces inefficiency (and, when there is feedback, inconsistency) and
(c) the frequent use of moving averages or smoothed data for wages can produce inefficiency and inconsistency.

The empirical result in the Cargill and Meyer test of US data is broadly indeterminate and more readily suggests that the US wage equation might be unstable (and hence useless). The Australian study by McDonald (1975) that we referred to above is in broad agreement with these principles for the Australian situation.

2.4   OTHER THEORIES OF THE PHILLIPS CURVE

In a loose sense the inclusion of other variables – taxes, productivity, etc. – implies other 'theories', and so we have already looked at a number of suggested variations on the basic themes in this chapter. In this section we want to look at material that generally extends the model by laying out more structure, usually, but not inevitably, in the labour market. We will begin by considering several attempts to derive the basic Phillips curve by means of a distinction between short-run and long-run Phillips curves or by means of policy-on versus policy-off curves. Then we will turn to the search-theory literature which explains the existence of an unemployment–inflation tradeoff in terms of the optimising actions of economic agents in labour markets. These are, if a general term is needed, equilibrium theories involving economic agents who do not have full and costless information, yet who must decide whether to work or not. When this survey is completed we will then be in a position, in Section 2.5, to construct a basic aggregate supply theory along the lines laid down by Lucas.

2.4.1   The Short-run Phillips Curve

The conclusion that the Phillips curve is at most a short-run phenomenon is now pretty widely accepted. A Keynesian view, for example, comes from Tobin's 1972 riposte to Friedman's 1968 paper on the natural-rate hypothesis. Tobin calls the Phillips curve 'an empirical finding in search of a theory', and since (p. 9) 'Unemployment is . . . a disequilibrium phenomenon. . . . The overall balance of vacancies and unemployment is determined by aggregate demand, and is therefore in principle, subject to control by overall monetary and fiscal policy.' In particular (p. 10) 'wage inflation will be greater the larger the variance among markets in excess demand and supply' and, since dispersion is potentially inflationary, one can construct a link strong enough to support a Phillips curve in unemployment and inflation rates. Indeed, 'Phillips tradeoffs exist in the short run, and the time it takes for them to evaporate depends on the lengths of the lags with which today's actual wage gains become tomorrow's standards.' For a long-run tradeoff, says Tobin, we would require downward rigidity of wage changes in markets that show an excess supply of labour.

   To see how a theory might be constructed to represent these observations (we briefly discussed the dispersion hypothesis earlier), consider the following adaptive expectations approach, as described by

Turnovsky (1977c). Assume a short-run expectations augmented Phillips curve of

$$\pi_t = a_0 + a_1 U_t + a_2 \pi_t^e \qquad (2.26)$$

where all variables are as defined above. Now assume that the expected inflation rate is equal to the *lagged* inflation rate, so that it represents the adaptive expectations hypothesis. Substituting this into Equation 2.26 we have a first-order difference equation in actual inflation rates that describes how prices evolve.

$$\pi_t = a_0 + a_1 U_t + a_2 \pi_{t-1} \qquad (2.27)$$

This equation, in the steady state (for $\pi_t = \pi_{t-1}$) converges to

$$\pi = a_0/(1 - a_2) + [a_1/(1 - a_2)]U \qquad (2.28)$$

This, for $a_2 < 1$, implies that the short-run curve is flatter than the long-run curve (i.e. $a_1 < a_1/(1 - a_2)$). This pretty much captures what Tobin has in mind in the paper already quoted from.

Phelps (1970b) motivates the short-run/long-run distinction in terms of lags in the wage (and price) setting behaviour of firms. An interesting empirical paper which employs a similar strategy on British data is by Lipsey and Parkin (1970). They use the price-and-wage equation approach that we described above, with per capita output and imports in the price equation (along with wages) and unemployment and trade-union strength (along with prices) in the wage equation. The result is a Phillips curve that appears to have two distinct and well-defined shapes, depending on whether incomes policy is on or off (an incomes policy is, broadly, a set of wage and price guidelines that are enforced to some extent). Thus, when policy is 'on', the curve is flatter than when it is 'off' (although in the latter case the curve is just badly determined in their tests). This accords well with the discussion to this point, especially in that when 'on', an incomes policy could introduce a shock that has a short-run (or disequilibrium) interpretation when prices and wages are themselves not free to adjust by virtue of the incomes policy.[12] Of course, if the structure itself alters when policy is imposed, it is still not easy to judge the impact of tax policy (unless the shift is itself stable). In any case the shift here makes policy more effective in the sense that a given change in unemployment comes at the expense of less inflation (in the short run) at least when prices and wages are not (legally) free to adjust.

2.4.2 Search Theories

Cost-push theories of inflation are eternally popular, and they lead directly to a Phillips relation, but there is sufficient dissatisfaction with them to have provoked a literature that concentrates on firm–worker behaviour of a different sort. The dissatisfaction, first, is related to three broad stylised facts:

(a) a cost-push mechanism does not lend itself to an explanation of *sustained* inflation (it is, in other words, hard to credit as a dynamic theory);
(b) explanations involving unions are not much use in situations – like that in the United States – where unions are not very powerful; and
(c) Phillips curves can be established on data that show little or no union strength.

Much of the remaining literature on the inflation–unemployment tradeoff – rational expectations aside – then focuses on imperfections and market failures, information costs or differences, indivisibilities, contracts and various (other) kinds of transactions costs. As it turns out, the representative papers in this literature are the search-theory explanations of the Phillips curve in which the costs of making a job search, borne either by the firm or by the worker, can motivate the tradeoff between inflation and unemployment. These models are then reinforced by assuming that workers are slow to adapt to changes in actual wages or prices.

Speaking first at the most general level there are, of course, a variety of different types of aggregate supply theory, from simple notions involving the summation of firms' supply functions to the more recent 'expectations augmented' versions associated with rational expectations theory. Broadly speaking, what we do to construct a basic aggregate-supply theory is to begin with a complete specification of the labour market and then tie it up with an aggregate production function to produce an aggregate supply function. If we then assume money illusion in the labour supply function, so that it depends directly on the price level, it is but a short step to the Phillips curve. Such an interpretation is common in the literature and is derived explicitly by Lucas and Rapping (1969b). The purpose, of course, is to 'force' a policy effect. In this case demand management policy (resulting in a shift of the aggregate demand curve) will have an effect comparable to that modelled by the negatively sloped Phillips curve.

Moving away from the *ad hoc* money illusion framework, it is useful to present the important Lucas–Rapping (1969a, 1969b) search model in some detail. The problem we are interested in is a dynamic one, in which workers voluntarily resign their jobs in order to search for employment opportunities. Since the reason for doing so is the perception (whether accurate or not) that a job is available somewhere at a higher wage, the decision necessarily involves tradeoffs between future work–consumption–leisure and present work–consumption–leisure. For example, when a worker decides to become unemployed, he gains a shot at future employment (at a better wage) and a shot at current leisure, but he loses command over current resources. In contrast, when the wage rate rises solely because of inflation, he may misread this signal and accept a job in the belief that he has achieved the gain he is after; this belief will be revised as he becomes aware of the fact that his real wage is not higher in the new job.

To capture all this, Lucas and Rapping suggest a standard two-period goods–leisure dynamic consumption model in which the household maximises utility. They begin with an aggregate labour supply function of

$$\bar{N} = F\left(W, \frac{W^*}{1+i}, P, \frac{P^*}{1+i}, \bar{A} \right) \tag{2.29}$$

where the asterisk indicates a future variable and A is the fixed nominal value of initial assets. Assuming that the function is homogeneous of degree zero in all five variables (so that we can deflate by the price level), that future goods and leisure are substitutes for current leisure (which is, itself, not inferior), and that the asset effect is small, it can be established that $\partial F/\partial(W/P) > 0$ and that $\partial F/\partial(W^*/P(1+i))$, $\partial F/\partial(P^*/P(1+i))$, and $\partial F/\partial(\bar{A}/P) < 0$, as one might expect.[13] We may assume a log-linear form for 2.29 in per capita form (M is population). Then, after rearranging, we obtain

$$\log(N_t/M_t) = \beta_0 + \beta_1 \log(w_t) - \beta_2 \log(w_t^*) + \beta_3 [i_t - \log(P_t^*/P_t)]$$

$$- \beta_4 \log(a_t/M_t) \qquad \beta_i > 0; \quad i = 1, \ldots, 4 \tag{2.30}$$

Here w_t, w_t^*, and a_t are the same variables as above, but this time are expressed in real terms and $i_t - \log(P_t^*/P_t)$ approximates the real interest rate (using the fact that $\log(1+i)$ is approximated by i). We may, further, think of the expected wage (w_t^*) as the *permanent* real wage (and P_t^* as the permanent price level) and the other elements producing price, nominal wage and asset effects as *transitory* components of the labour response mechanism.[14]

What remains is specifying how expectations are formed for the real wage and for the price level. An *adaptive expectations* formulation for wage expectations is

$$\frac{w_t^*}{w_{t-1}} = \left(\frac{w_t}{w_{t-1}^*}\right)^{\lambda} e^{\tau_1} \tag{2.31}$$

After taking logs of this expression we obtain

$$\log w_t^* = \lambda \log w_t + (1-\lambda) \log w_{t-1}^* + \tau_1 \tag{2.32}$$

Here τ_1 identifies the trend. Assuming the same adjustment parameter for prices (of λ) but a different trend (τ_2) and after applying a Koyck transformation and deleting i_t and a_t for simplicity, we can solve 2.30 along with the expressions for $\log w_t^*$ and $\log p_t^*$. In that case the result is Equation 2.33, which is in observables on account of 2.32, and the comparable expression for prices and hence wages can be directly estimated.

$$\log\left(\frac{N_t}{M_t}\right) = \alpha_0 + \alpha_1 \log w_t + \alpha_2 \log w_{t-1} + \alpha_3 \log\left(\frac{P_t}{P_{t-1}}\right) \tag{2.33}$$

Here, for example, $\alpha_1 = \beta_1 - \lambda\beta_2$, and $\alpha_3 = (1-\lambda)\beta_3$, from our original aggregate supply function.

Equation 2.33 is an aggregate labour supply function with the property that $\alpha_3 > 0$ (since $\beta_3 > 0$ above). This condition, that labour supply increases with current prices, would produce a positively sloped short-run aggregate supply function. Note that it is adaptive expectations that has produced this result, essentially as it affects optimal search in labour markets, and that we have not here relied on money illusion. This is true even though the aggregate labour supply function is non-homogeneous in P_t and w_t as if it were so due to the *ad hoc* assumption of money illusion. That is, the positive response to inflation results from a (partial) revision of expectations that convinces the worker that he has made a (partial) gain in his real conditions. Indeed, to push on a little further, the worker facing this imperfect information must evaluate his participation rate, and he must decide whether or not to search for a better situation. In this decision-making process he uses p_t^* and w_t^* as if they were normal prices and wages. But the decision is voluntary and this is an *equilibrium* interpretation of both labour-market activity and the Phillips relation.

The next step, still following Lucas and Rapping (1969a, 1969b), is to construct a Phillips curve in this context. Using a variant of Equation

2.30, as simplified, we have an aggregate labour supply function of

$$\log\left(\frac{N_t}{M_t}\right) = \beta_0 + \beta_1 \log\left(\frac{w_t}{w_t^*}\right) + \beta_2 \log (w_t^*) - \beta_3 \log\left(\frac{P_t^*}{P_t}\right) \quad (2.34)$$

Here $\beta_1 > 0$ since a rise in the wage induces an offer of more current employment. Further $\beta_3 > 0$ since a rise of future expected prices will induce a substitution of current leisure for future consumption and produce a negative effect on current employment. β_2 cannot be signed. Let the normal (that is, equilibrium) labour supply (N_t^*) function (for the anticipated normal wage w_{t-1}^* equal to w_t and p_{t-1}^* equal to p_t) be

$$\log \frac{N_t^*}{M_t} = \beta_0 + \beta_1 \log w_{t-1}^* + (\beta_2 - \beta_1) \log w_t^* - \beta_3 \log\left(\frac{P_t^*}{P_{t-1}}\right). (2.35)$$

From Equations 2.34 and 2.35 we can then calculate the difference between $\log (N_t/M_t)$ and $\log (N_t^*/M_t)$ – between the *actual* labour supply and the *normal* labour supply – and this calculation would produce something like the *normal* unemployment rate. This is done directly, of course, and produces

$$\log(N_t^*/N_t) = \beta_1 \log (w_{t-1}^*/w_t) + \beta_3 \log (P_{t-1}^*/P_t) \quad (2.36)$$

Assuming, then, that U_t is proportional to $\log (N_t^*/N_t)$ and solving the difference equation that results when Koyck lags are applied to expected prices and wages, we obtain a Phillips curve from this search-theory model. This is

$$U_t = \tau_1 - \tau_2 \log\left(\frac{w_t}{w_{t-1}}\right) - \tau_3 \log\left(\frac{P_t}{P_{t-1}}\right) + (1 - \lambda)U_{t-1} \quad (2.37)$$

Here τ_3 is positive (it depends on β_3 and on the proportionality between U_t and N_t^*/N_t). Lucas and Rapping note that this model, because it is built on adaptive expectations, has the significant defect that households (assuming that the elasticity of expectations is less than unity) systematically underpredict the inflation rate (in both P and w) and so even the long run Phillips curve in this model is not vertical. But in any event it is an equilibrium Phillips curve that stands in contrast to the disequilibrium versions discussed earlier, and it does not rely on an unspecified money illusion to motivate the tradeoff between inflation and unemployment.

It is the fashion in this literature to specialise the labour market a little more than Lucas and Rapping do in order to gain realism and/or increased leverage on empirical testing. Mortensen's basic papers (1970a,

1970b) are of this genre and are generally taken as part of the micro-foundations of this broad topic. Mortensen (1984) notes that a common underpinning to these theories is the use of 'optimal stopping' theory. By this he means that the worker decides when to *stop* working and when to *stop* searching for a new job based on

(a) the flow of information on jobs that he receives (Barron, 1975),
(b) the rates at which offers arrive and/or are terminated (Wilde, 1977), and
(c) any liquidity constraints that he faces (Danforth, 1979).

All of this is contingent on the explicit expected costs and benefits from the overall strategy (as already discussed in connection with the Lucas–Rapping studies).

In the basic version of this theory (in Mortensen, 1984), the probability that a worker will stop searching and take a job is

$$\Phi = \lambda[1 - F(w^*)] \tag{2.38}$$

where w^* is the reservation wage, $1 - F(w^*)$ is the probability that a random offer is acceptable, and λ is the (random) rate at which offers arrive. The financial constraints mentioned can then be introduced by making w^* time-dependent (as one runs out of resources his reservation wage drops). These factors would then be expected to have cyclical patterns that would generate exploitable inflation/unemployment tradeoffs for policy purposes, at least under certain conditions.

In the first of Mortensen's early papers (1970a) the position is taken that because the worker has to sample job information and incur search costs, the individual firm faces a labour supply curve that is not perfectly elastic at a given wage. This provides the firm with monopsony power that it can exploit. The reason for an employment response to nominal wage changes – and hence the reason for a Phillips curve tradeoff – is basically that workers respond with a lag, with the lag providing the time for workers to get sample information. It is, thus, a short-run tradeoff which we achieve here. The natural, or long-run, rate of unemployment, then, depends on the following parameters:

(a) the flow of new participants into the market,
(b) the costs of search, and
(c) the frequency with which current employees consider the quit decision (they would not do this at every moment because of the various sorts of costs that are involved).[15]

In his second paper (1970b) Mortensen has workers suffering *involuntary* unemployment on account of their encountering a skill requirement in a prospective job that is greater than they actually possess. The problem is again a lifetime consumption one in which the job seeker balances the expected gains from employment against the costs of search.[16] In Mortensen's model (p. 847): 'During periods of excess demand for . . . labor, each employer simultaneously attempts to raise . . . his own money wage offer relative to the general level and to lower . . . the level of skill he requires of new employees.' This produces the effect – in a period of unexpectedly rapid inflation – of a fall in the level of unemployment (and vice versa for a period of excess labour supply). The worker, in his turn facing an uncertain distribution of skill requirements and wages, must choose his acceptance wage and the expected duration of his search. Again in Mortensen's words (pp. 848–9), 'the best choice of the acceptance wage is that which equates at the margin the value of the time spent searching to the present value of the future benefits attributable to search'. It is, in other words, a problem in the optimal investment of human capital where the investment is, in effect, the value of the time spent in search.

In one extension of this approach, workers actually accept such jobs – in ignorance of the actual skill requirements – and then continuously re-evaluate their positions (Mortensen, 1984, p. 43): 'As more information about the job characteristics is acquired, the decision to stick with it is continually reconsidered. A quit in this framework results as a consequence of a decision that a job is "not a good fit" relative to alternatives available.' Both quits and layoffs are then part of the fallout from previous decisions, in effect. Jovanovic (1979) discusses job productivity in this context while Viscusi (1979) considers the non-pecuniary characteristics of jobs. The description of Jovanovic's model by Mortensen (1984) explains the details of this intensely microtheoretic material.

Models of this general sort, emphasising a search rationale for unemployment, suffer from conceptual and data problems and have been pretty thoroughly criticised thereby. For one thing the models do not construct *a priori* frameworks for certain conceivable types of unemployment if only because most (but not all) imply that unemployment is voluntary. For another, they often model one sort of tradeoff producing behaviour (e.g. workers' search behaviour) and ignore others. Building 'combined' models often escalates the complexity, but a case in which this does not happen is the integrated consumption, labour supply and job-search model of Seater (1977) in which individuals can simultaneously pick leisure, labour and search (in a context of perfect certainty). An important set of criticisms of these models also involves data problems introduced by drop-outs (Perry, 1972) or, especially, by layoffs (Tobin, 1972). The latter is a serious matter because the search models do not readily comprehend either non-wage rationing or implicit constraints on workers (who, indeed, may be willing to accept the implied wage cut).[17] The application of these types of constraints can suggest the consideration of either sticky prices and wages (that is, disequilibrium theory in the sense of Barro and Grossman (1976)) or contract theory. The latter (as in papers by D. F. Gordon (1974), Azariadis (1975), H. I. Grossman (1977) and by Kihlstrom and Laffont (1979)) involves the formation of a contract, whereby employers reduce the risk to workers of fluctuating incomes in return for the ability to adjust hours of work or to increase (or decrease) layoffs. Of course, since the contracts are themselves voluntary in some sense, it can be argued that the expected unemployment that results is also voluntary and thus fits the search framework reasonably well since workers can search better while they are laid off (see Barro, 1977b).

Another quarrel with the basic search model suggests that workers adopt what is in effect a Bayesian approach to deal with uncertainty, in effect learning about the distribution of wages and skill requirements after they quit, using a trial-and-error method (Rothschild, 1974). This consideration would require a more complicated model than we have used here. Still others argue against the empirical potential of these search models (with adaptive expectations). That is, these models imply that workers will quit when a recession starts in the erroneous belief that their relative wages have fallen, whereas the data show that quits actually fall in recessions. A reason, simply, could be that as perceived vacancies fall, workers actually reduce their quit rates. In effect the real wage they perceive is not the only data they process if only because experience has taught them that labour markets are subject to cycles, and in this environment they have learned how to read the cycle to some extent. The search models described so far are not really very good on these points.[18]

Finally, we should consider some of the arguments against both the natural-rate and equilibrium-search hypotheses or various of their component parts or implications. Tobin has been most outspoken in his criticism and his 1972 paper is the standard counter-argument to Friedman's 1968 paper, both having been presidential addresses to the American Economic Association. Tobin's position rests on three propositions. First of all, he argues that workers may actually accept price inflation rather than nominal wage cuts (to reduce their real wages) because of contracts, because of trade-union monopolies, and because of their desire to maintain their position relative to other workers in terms of *nominal* wages. While there is a potential semantic confusion here, Tobin insists that this implies that unemployment is essentially involuntary and is therefore the result of disequilibrium dynamics. Indeed (p. 4), 'The resistance of money wage rates to excess supply is a feature of the adjustment process rather than a symptom of irrationality.' It is, that is to say, a part of the institutional structure of the system.

For his second objection, Tobin quarrels with an implicit condition in the equilibrium-search theories that workers *voluntarily* accept unemployment in order to conduct efficient job searches. Tobin, in contrast, doubts that workers actually do this voluntarily (and cites some evidence).[19] Furthermore, while he accepts the idea of money illusion by workers – in that they accept more employment (in the short run) because they overestimate their real wage – he feels that they would overestimate *all* wages, of the job they hold as well as all jobs they might hold, if they quit in order to search. Hence, although it does have an (unsignable) income effect (p. 6), 'As a first approximation, inflation illusion has no substitution effect on the margin between working and waiting.'

Tobin, though, does accept the argument that 'search theory' explains why *some* unemployment is voluntary. Finally, for his third objection, he argues that the natural rate of unemployment is actually itself too high from a social point of view because it contains (a) some involuntary unemployment, (b) some unemployment unnecessary for optimal job search, and/or (c) some unemployment in excess of the vacancy rate. The appeal here is generally to the facts, using a 5 to 6 per cent unemployment rate as a typical natural rate. We will return to this topic in Section 3.4.

2.5 TOWARDS RATIONAL EXPECTATIONS – THE LUCAS SUPPLY FUNCTION

In the Lucas and Rapping model described above, the labour-supply function was derived from a two-period consumption – leisure model in which the consumer has precise but not necessarily correct expectations of future prices. The result is a labour supply function which relates quantity supplied to current and expected future prices and wages. This, in turn, implies a distinction between the labour supply response to permanent wage and price changes compared to transitory changes, and – via a production function – an aggregate supply function of the form of

$$y_t = a(p_t - p_t^*) \tag{2.39}$$

This is a simplified version of the Lucas – Rapping model in which all variables are expressed in logs and p_t^* represents an index of expected future prices. We have simplified here in order to make it clear wherein the Lucas supply function differs from the foregoing. Equation 2.39 is an aggregate supply function, but it is not in observables since it contains the expected price level. Of course, under stable prices, as a condition of rationality, we would have that $E(p_t - p_t^*) = 0$.

To make this theory operational, as above, we might specify the expectations generating mechanism lying behind the variable p_t^*. One way to proceed is to utilise an adaptive expectations hypothesis as in

$$p_t^* = \lambda p_t + (1 - \lambda)p_{t-1}^* \tag{2.40}$$

This, with a single-factor production function and with a Koyck transformation, produces an aggregate supply function in observables of

$$y_t = a(1 - \lambda)(p_t - p_{t-1}) + (1 - \lambda)y_{t-1} \tag{2.41}$$

This function has the property that for a rise in inflation in the short run, since $a(1 - \lambda) > 0$, there is an increase in y_t. This is the inflation–output tradeoff implied by the Phillips curve. In the long run, further, there would be no effect from a once-for-all increase in the price level. On the other hand, as discussed by Lucas (1972a), the function suggests that by a suitable choice of short-run inflations (via monetary policy, for example) we can always obtain short-run gains in output (never, in effect, reaching the long-run). Indeed, one can also obtain a permanent gain in output for a sustained inflation. Finally, we note that this or any model purporting to explain an actual inflation–output tradeoff must also include an aggregate demand hypothesis if it is to refer to actual experience. Lucas (1973) makes the aggregate demand curve unit-elastic so that this last is not really required.

In a widely used and tested extension of the foregoing, Lucas (1973) proposes what is now known as the 'Lucas supply function', based *loosely* on the Lucas–Rapping model. As Lucas notes (p. 326), 'All formulations of the natural rate theory postulate rational agents, whose decisions depend on *relative* prices only, placed in an economic setting in which they cannot distinguish relative from general price movements.' This leads him to suggest a theory of the natural rate based on the notion that individuals operate in widely scattered markets over which demand is distributed unevenly. That is, in terms of the labour market problem we are considering here, workers operate in widely scattered 'markets', where the markets are to be understood as different employers. The geographic isolation is thus an analytical convenience (proxying for 'informational isolation') and is not meant to suggest an immobility theory of unemployment, although such a theory might be an interesting one.

To begin with, let us assume that supply in market z has a normal component (y_{nt}) and a cyclical component $(y_{ct}(z))$ as in

$$y_t(z) = y_{nt} + y_{ct}(z) \tag{2.42}$$

The normal component is assumed to follow a trend, as in $y_{nt} = k + \beta t$, while the cyclical component is assumed to vary with relative prices and with its own past values. By relative prices we mean that economic agents will compare their own prices $(p_t(z))$ with their estimate of what the general price level is $(E(p_t:I_t(z)))$. This last is conditional on the information set $I_t(z)$ that is specific to the local market. This information, of course, is that which is relevant to predicting the general price level. These ideas generate the following expression for the cyclical component of output in z.

$$y_{ct}(z) = \tau[p_t(z) - E(p_t:I_t(z))] + \lambda y_{c,t-1}(z) \tag{2.43}$$

Note, about this expression, that all variables are measured as logs, that we can refer to the price difference as a *'relative'* price (since it describes the cyclical response in z that results from mistakes in estimating the price level compared to the local price), and that we are building in an arbitrary cycle in the last term in 2.43. The information set, finally, consists of two components: information about past y_t – about shifts, the normal level, etc. – as it bears on p_t, and information about deviations of the actual price from the economy wide average.

The problem facing traders in this set-up is that of bringing the correct amount of 'produce' to the other markets when they have incomplete information on the general price level. It is, of course, the same problem workers have when they decide whether to work or search for a better job, so we are obviously working over an analogy here. In any event the information about y_t, as it bears on p_t (the log of the price level in question), can be assumed to produce a 'prior' or *objective distribution* on p_t with mean $\bar{p}_t$ and variance σ^2. Economic agents also have information on the local price, some of which will help them in predicting the general price level, and thus there is also a prior distribution for that. Let us assume that this second or *subjective distribution* is independent of that for p_t and that the price $p_t(z)$ differs from p_t by z (this is a normalisation, essentially) in which case it has a mean of zero and a variance of σ_z^2.[20] In this event the process by which agents form their expectations of the price level required in Equation 2.43 is to do so conditional on p_t and on the additional information that is provided by the systematic difference z (with its own prior distribution). This provides us with

$$E(p_t : I_t(z)) = E(p_t : p_t(z), \bar{p}_t) = (1 - \Theta)p_t(z) + \Theta \bar{p}_t \qquad (2.44)$$

an expression that divides the information set used to predict the price level into a local component and an overall component (with attendant weights). The variance of this distribution is $\Theta \sigma^2$ where $\Theta = \sigma_z^2 / (\sigma^2 + \sigma_z^2)$.

The expression just derived can be described as the projection of p_t on $p_t(z)$ and $\bar{p}_t$ or it can be described as the regression of the same variables. In the latter case, remembering that we are operating in log form, the weights $(1 - \Theta)$ and Θ can be interpreted as elasticities. The formulation adopted here assumes that the two independent variables are independent sources of information and that they are the only sources of information. Furthermore, these weights depend only on the relative variances in this 'errors in variables' format and do so in the following way.[21] If the (expected) variance of p_t is zero, then $\Theta = 1$ and all of the weight is placed on the information provided by that low-variance term; that is, if the price level 'prior' has no variance in it, it will provide a more useful part of the overall projection on which to base a forecast of the price level. Conversely, if the *prior* distribution on $p_t(z)$ is perfectly tight, all of the weight would be put on that information in forecasting the general level ($\Theta = 0$). These are limiting cases, of course, and all we are saying is that we would apportion the weight in our projection (prediction) based on the series that we think we can measure most accurately, other things being equal.

To arrive at the aggregate supply curve Lucas takes the following approach. First of all, combine Equations 2.42, 2.43 and 2.44 to produce a reduced form for the supply response of economic agents in market z.

$$y_t(z) = y_{nt} + \Theta \tau [p_t(z) - \bar{p}_t] + \lambda y_{c,t-1}(z) \qquad (2.45)$$

We have, in this expression, a normal component, a weighted relative price (or, in another context, an inflation) component and an arbitrary cyclical component. Averaging across all markets (all z) the aggregate supply function is then given as

$$y_t = y_{nt} + \Theta \tau (p_t - \bar{p}_t) + \lambda (y_{t-1} - y_{n,t-1}) \qquad (2.46)$$

The slope of this function, then, varies directly with Θ, itself the ratio of relative price dispersion across markets (σ_z^2) to total dispersion.

To see the policy implications of this formulation we can begin by noting that Θ, which conditions the response to inflation shocks, can take on different values depending on relative variances. That is, the policy response is small (the aggregate supply curve is nearly vertical) for a small σ_z^2 or for a large σ^2. Further, as Lucas notes (1973, p. 328), 'At the other extreme when general prices are stable (σ^2 is relatively small) the supply curve approaches the limiting value of τ.' At this limit there is a policy tradeoff along the lines of the Phillips curve. Then, as Barro (1976, p. 1) puts it, linking inflation to the behaviour of the money stock, 'It also follows here that an increase in the variance of the monetary growth rate . . . induces individuals to attribute a larger fraction of observed price movements to monetary forces, and thereby leads to a reduced responsiveness of output to a given monetary disturbance.' They do this since (p. 12), 'when the money growth is less predictable, individuals are more inclined to associate observed price fluctuations in their markets with (aggregate) monetary movements'. This, of course, is under the condition of a relatively large σ^2 and thus for Θ near zero. Barro also notes that in Lucas's model, if the authorities have the objective of trying to reduce the variance of output around some desired value (some y_t^*) by increasing their monetary activity, then, since increased money variance 'clouds the real picture and reduces the value of observed prices as allocative signals' (Barro, 1976, p. 19) such activity may actually *increase* the variance of y_t around y_t^*.[22] In this case, for both Lucas and Barro, the optimal policy is to have $\sigma_m^2 \to 0$, although Barro's result is contingent on the structure of the economy having a particular form. In the condition $\sigma_m^2 \to 0$ we can recognise Friedman's monetary rule once again. Because this begins to raise the question of rational expectations we will drop the discussion at this point and leave the further development of this type of model of Chapters 3 and 4 after we have brought in rational expectations explicitly.

It is obvious that we can readily deduce a Phillips curve from this model and that such a device would tend toward the vertical (showing no policy response) in the event that $\Theta \to 0$. To see a simple derivation of the Phillips curve, we can begin with a stripped-down version of the aggregate supply function given as Equation 2.46

$$y_t = y_{nt} + \alpha(p_t - p_t^e) + e_t \tag{2.47}$$

where the variables are expressed as logs and y_{nt} is the natural rate of output. Very simply, a labour market alternative to this, with inflation rates rather than the log of prices (achieved by subtracting p_{t-1} from both price terms in 2.47), is

$$U_t = U_{nt} - \beta(\pi_t - \pi_t^e) + e_t \qquad (2.48)$$

This is a standard expectations-augmented Phillips curve with U_n representing the natural rate of unemployment and π_t, π_t^e defining actual and expected inflation rates. Its rationale is the same as that of 2.46 with informational discrepancies (or lags) providing a discrepancy between π and π_t^e. This discrepancy is eliminated (at the rate β) in the form of a change in the quantity of labour supplied and hence in the actual rate of unemployment. For purposes of the discussion in this chapter we assume that π_t^e is formed adaptively, and leave the discussion of rational expectations versions of 2.47 to Chapter 3.

Above we noted that the Lucas supply function – as derived by Lucas – is based *loosely* on the Lucas–Rapping model; we now need to make that qualification more precise. Following Bull and Frydman (1983) we see the problem is that the Lucas supply function is based on the island paradigm (where agents exist in geographically scattered markets) while the Lucas–Rapping model is in the search theory tradition of a single labour market. Of course, informational difficulties motivate aggregate supply responses in both cases, but in the case of the Lucas supply function the problem is determining the wage *today* while in the Lucas–Rapping model the problem is the intertemporal one of comparing today's wage with (the present value of) tomorrow's expected wage. In the island-paradigm model in which no time elapses and markets clear within each island, such search is, strictly speaking, impossible. Bull and Frydman propose a version of the island paradigm in which the islands are *informationally isolated* rather than geographically isolated and in which individuals are randomly scattered about the 'islands' each period (so they need only forecast the overall real wage level and not individual ones). Individuals then engage in search (i.e. accept unemployment) if they find themselves in a market where their actual wages are lower than they expected.

The difference this makes to the Lucas supply function result about the variance of expected inflation depends on the role of inflationary expectations in the Bull and Frydman model. If the expected nominal interest rate does not *fully* reveal the economy-wide expected inflation rate then (Bull and Frydman, 1983, p. 84) 'the coefficient on price expectation error in the Lucas supply function for the individual market . . . is not independent of the variance of aggregate demand shocks'. Thus, the direct link between the variance of expected inflation and the supply response is complicated by a cross-equation effect, and (p. 89, my italic) 'the Lucas supply function cannot be treated as a structural equation. In fact, *it appears to suffer from the* difficulties pointed out by *Lucas . . .* in his *critique* of the equations in standard econometric models'. This conclusion is derived using an exogenous interest rate, it not being possible to obtain a 'closed form' solution to such a system with an endogenous interest rate (Barro, 1976). The reader should note, finally, that the exercises are carried out here in terms of rational expectations – partly because the Lucas supply function is often embedded in rational expectations models. The next section contains a similar amendment to the Lucas model by Hercowitz (1981), but in this case the amendment is accompanied by an empirical test of, roughly, the stability of the Lucas inflation-variability coefficient.

2.5.1   Empirical Tests Involving the Lucas Supply Function

Lucas himself (1973) provided the first tests of his model in a cross-country framework using eighteen countries in his sample (of annual data, 1951–67). The structure of the model is essentially that of the Lucas and Rapping paper (1969b) with the motivation for short-run supply responses coming from economic agents having a 'lack of information on some of the prices relevant to their decisions' (p. 326). With the rather heroic assumption that the aggregate demand curve is unit elastic, the real or 'rigidity' effects will have to come from the supply side. In effect, nominal income is determined on the demand side (exogenously) in this model and the supply side determines the division between the nominal and real that we are interested in. Finally, expectations are formed 'optimally', but not rationally (although, according to Minford and Peel (1980), this makes little difference to the results).

Lucas combines his supply function with the unit-elastic demand function and, for his sample, looks at the fit of the model *within countries* and at the effect of different inflation rates *across countries*. The model estimates λ and a reduced-form coefficient π $(\pi = \Phi\tau/(1 + \Phi\tau))$. Judged by the R^2 with the log of real output as the dependent variable, the fits are quite uneven with an especially poor fit coming in the high inflation country of Argentina and with the United States showing a good fit (but see below). Across countries, Lucas warns that the variance of inflation is high in two countries and low in the other sixteen, giving him just two 'observations' for his cross-country test. Even so, he finds that in the two volatile inflation countries there is no real output effect while in the other sixteen stable-inflation countries there appear to be short-run tradeoffs.

This, of course, is what his supply theory predicts, as discussed above. Hanson (1980) extends Lucas's test to a third data point (moderate inflation South American countries) and broadly confirms Lucas's findings.

We have mentioned that Lucas assumes that aggregate demand is unitelastic in order to concentrate the potential for expectational effects on the supply side. Arak (1977) questions this procedure, pointing out that if the true elasticity is not unity, Lucas's method will return biased estimates of the supply response. In her retesting of the US curve, Arak finds the elasticity in question to be greater than unity and finds (therefore) a seriously overstated supply response. This is damaging, certainly, but the real point of Lucas's exercise is the cross-country comparison referred to above. In this connection Froyen and Waud (1980) propose to rerun the tests, motivated in part by the fact that Lucas's set of countries has only two data points and in part by the desire to examine a more recent (and more volatile) data set. Accepting the modifications to the theory proposed by Cukierman and Wachtel (1979), Froyen and Waud uphold Lucas's important result on the role of the inflation variance (it is negatively related to the inflation–unemployment tradeoff). On the other hand, two other important implications of Lucas's model

(a) that the tradeoff be negatively correlated with the variance of nominal income changes and
(b) that the variance of inflation and the variance of nominal income changes be positively related

are not confirmed on the ten countries tested. The countries, incidentally, are advanced-industrial and do not include any South American 'outliers'.

Another direct way to approach the Lucas natural-rate hypothesis is to embed it in a small econometric model and then to adopt a simultaneous-equations methodology to evaluate the performance of the model, either in comparison with other models or in terms of the significance of the model's identifying restrictions. Fair (1979), Sims (1980) and Cuddington (1980) do this with little success on US data; Leiderman (1979) produces a satisfactory result for the Lucas hypothesis on post-war Italian data; while Koskela and Viren (1980) produce mixed results for a set of five Scandinavian countries. A simultaneous-equations test on British data by Dwyer (1982a), covering the period 1870–1913, is also generally successful, particularly in fit and in the satisfaction of the cross-equation restrictions. The Lucas rational expectations, the basis of this test, was also supported. Among other reasons, the 1870–1913 period was selected because of the uniformity of its financial institutions.

At the end of Section 2.5 we discussed a paper by Bull and Frydman (1983) which suggests that the Lucas supply function should not be interpreted as a structural equation since it (when properly derived) has demand-side variances in it. We could there have added another theoretical amendment by Hercowitz (1981) that runs along similar lines. The reason we did not is that the Hercowitz paper presents empirical results that make sense only after the earlier tests are explained. Hercowitz is motivated by the thought that inflation variance will also affect the *frequency* of transactions (increasing it) and thus the frequency with which price level 'samples' will be drawn by economic agents. This, in turn, should have a supply effect, in particular in providing another reason why higher inflations (and, perforce, variance of inflations) might be associated with lower supply responses (and Phillips curves closer to the vertical). Hercowitz's model, which is developed in the island-economy framework, is quite complicated; his theoretical work concludes that in his model (p. 14) 'the shorter the trade period, the more information agents possess about the price level and thus the more accurate their estimations of the current value of the money stock'. The result is 'a more neutral effect of monetary disturbances'. In the empirical part of the paper he looks to see if in the Lucas cross-country test the coefficients of a regression of the Phillips curve on the variance of income are themselves dependent on the level of inflation across countries (taken as an additional variable). They are, in both the Lucas sample and in a broader set of countries (43) put together and Lucas-tested by Alberro (1980).[23] In any event the neutrality result is actually strengthened in this case, at least in the event of (recent) increases in the level and variance of inflation.

Above we mentioned that Tobin (1972) thinks that inflation will be greater the greater the variance among the markets in disequilibrium. This is basically the dispersion hypothesis that we discussed briefly before, but it does raise a question about how *inflation variance* itself might directly affect the Phillips relation. At the same time, by the mid-1970s, macroeconomists were busy with a new empirical finding: empirical Phillips curves had become positively sloped, and this, it seems, was associated with considerable cross-country evidence to the effect that the variance of inflation was the culprit (e.g. M. Friedman, 1977, Azariadis, 1981).

The Tobin dispersion hypothesis could, loosely, explain this association, but what has become the strongest theoretical position is actually due to M. Friedman (1977). The Lucas model suggests that as the variance of inflation increases economic agents rely less and less on price-level data and therefore are less liable to be tricked. The Phillips curve, then, approaches the vertical. To tie this to a positive slope Friedman suggests (1977, p. 467, my italic)

> The more volatile the rate of general inflation, the harder it becomes to extract the signal about relative prices from the absolute prices: the broadcast about relative prices is, as it were, being jammed by the noise coming from the inflation broadcast. At the extreme, the system of absolute prices becomes nearly useless, and economic agents resort either to an alternative currency or to barter, *with disastrous effects on productivity.*

The negative effect on productivity, then, can be associated with higher unemployment. Friedman does not leave it at this, though, and mentions other ways in which inflation variability might decrease efficiency (and 'plausibly' raise unemployment). The most obvious of these ways arises because of the existence of long-term contracts, indexing arrangements, and legal restrictions which, if unchanged, impose welfare costs on the economy as inflation rates vary. If the institutional arrangements are altered, then there are the explicit costs of change itself (including such things as labour strife and accounting changes). In the long run, though, this effect might disappear as institutions would tend to adapt to whatever inflation situation the economy forces upon them.[24]

Since all this is essentially an empirical judgement at this stage (and M. Friedman does provide some reasons why increased inefficiency might lower unemployment),[25] it is just as well to mention some other conclusions in this literature. The Friedman proposition boils down to the idea that the positive relation between inflation and unemployment is the result of the costs of increased inflation-*uncertainty*. That is, there is a positive link between the *level* of inflation and inflation-uncertainty (with, in naïve models, the variance of inflation).[26] The level of inflation is readily measured, and we may proxy uncertainty with the variance of inflation under certain conditions. There are, then, several empirical questions raised in this literature:

(a) Is the inflation-variance–unemployment connection robust?
(b) Is increased expected inflation-uncertainty itself associated with increased inflation-variance or, more usually, with a higher level of inflation?

This last would give us an explanation of the results after 1970, since inflation and inflation-variances generally increased after that date (into the early 1980s).

With regard to the effect of inflation-variance on unemployment (or real output) US empirical results generally run in the direction proposed by M. Friedman. Mullineaux (1980) embeds variances of expected inflation into a standard natural-rate model with the correct (and possibly 'rational') Livingston data of J. Carlson (1977); a Granger causality framework is employed (as discussed in Chapter 6). The result is a positive effect for inflation-expectation variability on unemployment. Similarly, tests by Mullineaux for the effect of increased inflation-uncertainty on industrial production show the expected negative effect. These results (on y or U) are confirmed in studies by Levi and Makin (1980), who also use the Livingston data, by Blejer and Leiderman (1980) and by Evans (1983). Also on British data Froyen and Waud (1984) separate the Friedman proposition (on allocative efficiency) from the Lucas one (on informational confusions) and find the former, but not the latter, effect (they also controlled for supply shocks). These results are repeated in a separate US study (1985). For cross-country studies the evidence is not so clear, with Logue and Willett (1976) and Foster (1978) among those finding in favour and Logue and Sweeney (1981) and Katsimbris and S. M. Miller (1982) finding against. For a recent summary of this real effect literature and some further cross-country results running against the view that inflation variability has real effects, see Katsimbris (1985). Katsimbris also records only modest success for the connection between inflation and its variability (as discussed at greater length in the next paragraph).

With regard to proposition (b) above, there is considerable evidence to the effect that high inflation is associated with a high variance of inflation; an early cross-country example is by Logue and Willett (1976) and an intertemporal paper is by Parks (1978). With respect to the link between the variance of inflationary expectations and the variance of inflation, Cukierman and Wachtel (1979) find such a relation on US data (using the Livingston data), although both their theoretical model and their empirical results have come under fire by Mitchell and H. E. Taylor (1982, but see their reply and Cukierman and Wachtel, 1982). For a survey of the evidence on these two issues – and some further reservations – see Holland (1984). We should, finally, note that there is also some evidence to the effect that inflation-variance is linked to, and possibly caused by, *relative* price dispersion so that (if the link is causal) relative-price variation provokes both real adjustments and more inflation-variance (roughly the opposite of the high-variance/low-real-effect finding of Lucas). This argument and some evidence are advanced by Vining and Elwertowski (1976) and challenged by Cukierman (1979) on the grounds that some (real) common shocks could produce both results without weakening the Lucas hypothesis. Pagan, Hall and Trivedi (1983) formalise Cukierman's proposition (without reference to his paper) in a study devoted mainly to econometric issues and produce an 'Australian test' that broadly supports the Lucas interpretation of the connection between relative prices and inflation-variance.

We can close this chapter, then, with another result by Alogoskoufis (1983) that argues that wages are less volatile than prices because workers have poorer information about price-level changes than do firms. That is, since workers make more errors, they also make larger supply responses which (thus) tend to stabilise the level of real wages; something like this is discussed in an earlier paper by Block and Heineke (1973), who argued against the idea that wage inflation-uncertainty (variance) necessarily has a disincentive effect on labour-force participation. This question is studied by Alogoskoufis in a rational expectations context, but is, in any event, a Phillips curve result since under these conditions we can establish a Phillips curve tradeoff and a role for demand-management policy (see H. I. Grossman, 1981). We also can provide a rational expectations/equilibrium explanation of relative wage-level 'stickiness' in this manner although the full explanation of such a result must await later chapters in this survey.

3 Rational Expectations I: Basic Theories

The hypothesis asserts three things: (1) Information is scarce, and the economic system generally does not waste it. (2) The way expectations are formed depends specifically on the structure of the relevant system describing the economy. (3) A 'public prediction' ... will have no substantial effect on the operation of the economic system (unless it is based on inside information). This is not quite the same thing as stating that the marginal revenue product of economics is zero. . . .   J. F. MUTH, 1961, p. 316

3.1 INTRODUCTION

In this chapter we will look at some of the basic results for rational expectations, with the emphasis placed on the general policy and 'natural-rate' debates which were introduced in Chapters 1 and 2. We will also extend our discussion to a consideration of the causes of business cycles, as they are explained in this new literature and to a consideration of fiscal and monetary policies under the assumption of rational expectations. Rational expectations is the subject of both Chapter 3 and Chapter 4, but in the remaining chapters of this book we will try to remain conscious of the results of our exercises here, even in cases in which there is no formal 'rational' material to describe. We should note, too, that the development in this chapter will generally not be econometric although something obviously needs to be said on those topics since we are, really, dealing with stochastic processes. In Chapter 4, though, where we will devote some space to the rapidly growing literature on the empirical record of rational expectations, we will venture into the econometrics to a greater extent, although the policy results and not econometric niceties are the object of that part of the survey.

Broadly speaking, the macroeconomic versions of rational expectations theory have arisen by analogy with the analysis of efficient capital markets. An efficient capital market determines the prices of the securities that are traded in it in such a way that the market price of each security embodies all of the information relevant to the future economic performance of the entity that issued the security. For example, for an

65

individual stock, economic agents in the securities markets will assess the expected relative performance of the company in question and determine the relevance of that information for the future behaviour of the stock's price. These agents will then lay their bets, and in the process the stock price will come to reflect their convictions. Since they are playing with their own money or their jobs are on the line, these agents will tend not to make systematic (and recognisable) errors. They will also process the market information available to them in such a way as to line up the marginal cost of acquiring information with the marginal net expected benefit derived from using that information as part of their investment strategies; the benefit, ultimately, is a gain in expected utility.

The description just provided leads naturally to a provisional definition of rational expectations that fits easily into the macroeconomic framework of this study. In particular, *rational expectations* assumes that economic agents, using information in an economically optimal way, attempt to forecast and use in their dynamic plans, those events (and variables) which are relevant to their own situations. Put this way, about all rational expectations adds to existing notions of rationality in the economics literature is the reference to a kind of 'optimal information' as if this, too, were part of the decision-making process.[1] This is a simplification, possibly, but the consequences of specifying the informational aspects of individual and aggregate decision-making – and of introducing rationality into the markets that monetary and fiscal policy affect – are very unsettling to much of the standard macropolicy literature (such as that described in Chapters 1 and 2). Rational expectations also shapes the Keynes-versus-the-Classics debate (as we shall see in Chapter 6). Of course, all of this has a practical dimension which we shall certainly attempt to document in the following pages.

Under rational expectations individuals do not knowingly make systematic errors in their predictions. They also act on the basis of their predictions, for this is no ivory-tower exercise that we are describing. The predictions of economic agents are not always correct, of course, but they are the best individuals can manage under particular circumstances. If, for example, it is expected that macropolicy is about to unleash another of its bolts and if economic agents have a clear idea of how the event might affect them, then they will do their best (considering the costs of action and the constraints that bind them), to try to profit from – or avoid any losses from – the policy. In practice this task is lightened by those – the 'press' and the stock market gurus, for example – who manufacture information that is relevant to economic agents and, further, by those who have products to sell that will help agents carry out their strategies. This last includes supplying equities and bonds as well as such items as 'money market deposit accounts' which provide both liquidity and an interest rate that varies with market interest rates.

The consequences of the foregoing for macroeconomic policy are far-reaching, to the extent that the necessary qualifications are not important. The qualifications we have in mind include the possibilities that agents might be irrational, that prices might be inflexible and that useful information might not be available cost-effectively. The consequences are the following:

(a) Monetary (and sometimes fiscal) policy, if correctly anticipated and acted upon by economic agents, may not be effective, even in the short run.

(b) The macroeconomic models used for forecasting or policy simulations may

(1) work poorly because they model expectations in nonrational ways (for example, adaptively) and

(2) simulate and forecast inaccurately because they do not incorporate the actions that rational economic agents take either after the policy has been applied or even in anticipation of the policy effects.

(c) A policy designed to have an effect by tricking economic agents may, if the systematic component is correctly foreseen, merely raise costs and uncertainties without having the intended effect and may, in the event that it is sustained, deteriorate quickly in effect as the credibility of the policy-makers diminishes.

Among the new costs introduced by this last point would be those incurred as political processes work to replace the authorities whose policies have been discredited.

On net, then, rational expectations offers a set of new theoretical and empirical findings as a result of the natural extension of expectations theory to consider states of the economy akin to perfect competition. At the very least it offers a theoretical benchmark against which to judge alternative frameworks, and at the most it presents us with a whole range of new material on how fiscal and monetary policy might (or might not) affect the economy. As the literature has unfolded, many apparent exceptions to rationality have been produced. Similarly, the econometric tests pro and con have generally been of a rather weak sort, mainly because it is necessary to compose a test of joint hypotheses; these hypotheses concern (a) propositions about the economic structure and (b) propositions about how expectations are formed. This is not a new problem in macroeconomics, at least since the development of the permanent income hypothesis (in which *ad hoc* expectations generating mechanisms are jointly tested along with consumption theory), but it certainly does present econometric difficulties. Even so, with all of the qualifications it is likely that the broad effects suggested by rational expectations theory are relevant in practice; if this is correct it means that policy-makers (and other economic agents, of course) will need to incorporate this into their strategies, at the very least.

The plan of this chapter is as follows. In Section 3.2 we attempt to provide a more rigorous definition of rational expectations that will, at the same time, bring its stochastic and empirical dimensions to the surface. With this in hand we will jump right in, in Section 3.3, and consider the policy issues that have attracted the most attention. These are the 'Lucas critique', which is point (b) above, and the 'policy ineffectiveness' result, which is point (a). That having been done we will present yet another view of the 'instrument selection' problem of Chapter 1, but this time from a rational expectations perspective (in Subsection 3.3.3). The material in the first half of the chapter is pretty well-worn, on the whole, and much of the controversy has been wrung out of it in the ten or so years it has been around, but from Section 3.4 until the end of Chapter 4 we will look at material that picks up the themes from the basic results and is still in motion as these words are being written. This material begins, in Section 3.4, with explanations of the real business cycle, in essence continuing a topic that we first presented in Chapter 1. The results of this section extend basic equilibrium business cycle models to the case of rational expectations and make it perfectly clear that we do not have to think of trade cycles as disequilibrium phenomena but can visualise them as 'rational' events in an equilibrium (and neoclassical) world. Finally, Section 3.5 looks at some basic results for the scope of fiscal policy under rational expectations. This material is justified as a distinct topic because fiscal policy is different from monetary since its operation involves directly altering the relation between the private and the public sectors. At this point our survey of what we are arbitrarily calling the *basic rational expectations* results will be finished; in Chapter 4 we will continue with rational expectations, but most of the material will be in the nature of extensions or refinements – or will consist of empirical tests of the models in Chapters 3 and 4.

3.2 SOME BASIC PROPOSITIONS

Before launching our discussion of rational expectations we should introduce some notation and some basic results about expectations themselves; we are following Sheffrin (1983) in this. We define an *expected value* for x to be $E(x)$ in

$$E(x) = \sum_{i=1}^{n} p_i x_i$$

where the p_i are the probabilities that agents assign to each of the uncertain events x_i. A *conditional expectation* for some variable x at time t_i is described by

$$E[x_t : I_{t-1}]$$

where the expectation is conditional on (i.e. depends on) the information available in the period $t - 1$. Normally, when using this notation, we will assume that the expectation is formed in $t - 1$ and that it concerns the value of x in some future period (in this case, the immediate future (t)). An *error in prediction* arises when the realisation of a variable (x_t) is unequal to the previous prediction, as in

$$\varepsilon_t = x_t - E[x_t : I_{t-1}]$$

As we will show below, under rational expectations (or in the efficient-markets theory) this error will have an expected value of zero (you would not plan to make a mistake) and will be uncorrelated with any other information available at $t - 1$ (you would not leave out any useful information). These propositions are the fundamental building-blocks of all that is to come in this and the next chapter.

We may work toward a more precise definition of rational expectations by setting down a set of rules. Begg (1982) argues that the central insight of the rational-expectations approach is that individuals do not make systematic errors. Thus, on average, their forecasts will be as accurate as possible; these forecasts will concern all future periods and involve all of the past data relevant to effective prediction. Furthermore, in particular applications, if it is legitimate to visualise the variables in the economic system as being generated by a macroeconomic model, then (p. 30), 'Individuals are assumed to know the structure of the entire model and observe past values of all relevant variables.' When the model has stochastic elements, indeed, they are assumed to know the statistical properties of the distributions of the stochastic variables. They do all this, of course, in the context of a plan of action that will maximise their expected utility over time.

We can formalise our loose definition of rational expectations considerably – following Begg (1982) and Sheffrin (1983) – by putting down three sets of more precise rules. Our first set concerns the prediction errors of rational economic agents, which we will now redefine as

$$y_{t+1} - E(y_{t+1}:I_t) = \varepsilon_{t+1}$$

where the first term on the left is the realisation and the second is the prediction (conditional on the information set I_t) itself presumably made in period t. The first rule, then, states that the errors will be assumed to be serially uncorrelated with themselves over time, with an expected value of zero.[2]

$$E(\varepsilon_{t+1}) = E(y_{t+1} - E(y_{t+1}:I_t)) = 0 \qquad (\varepsilon_t, \varepsilon_{t+1}) = 0 \qquad (3.1)$$

Furthermore, ε_t will be uncorrelated with any information available at time t. Formally, that is to say, ε_{t+1} will be 'orthogonal' to I_t so that no useful (i.e. error-reducing) information is untapped by economic agents bent on achieving optimal forecasts.

It is obvious that the rationality just described establishes a kind of *consistency* for economic agents. This idea can be firmed up by detailing a second set of rules; these are that (a) when the same variable is being predicted for different future periods or (b) when different $(t, t + 1)$ forecasts for a particular future variable are being compared, these forecasts will be consistent with one another. To make the second of these ideas more precise, let us assume that economic agents, in predicting some economic variable y for period $t + i + j$, where t is the present, have as their best guess *now* of what they will be predicting (for the same variable) any period before $t + i + j$ (e.g. in period $t + i$) what they thought about the variable in t (the present). To do otherwise is to build in a deliberate error and that would be irrational. Formally,

$$E\{ [E(y_{t+i+j}: I_{t+i})]: I_t \} = E(y_{t+i+j}: I_t) \qquad (3.2)$$

where y is the variable being forecast, I_t is the information set of all relevant information presently available, and I_{t+i} is the set of information assumed to be available in the future period $t + i$. Equation 3.2, then, states that the best guess of what agents would be predicting (in $t + i$) for y_{t+i+j} conditional on information available in $t + i$ (itself conditional on information available in t) is what they expect today. That is, if they expect to have information available in $t + i$ that they do not have today and if they know it is going to affect y_{t+i+j}, then they will already have incorporated it as information in the set I_t, and they will have acted upon it.

There is a derivative property of this second set of propositions that is known as the 'chain rule of forecasting'. The basic idea here is that since forecasts (from time t) of all future values of a variable must be consistent (as in 3.2), then in principle one can build up general expressions for the future variables in terms of relations already known at t. Thus the predictions,

$$E(y_{t+i}:I_t), E(y_{t+i+1}:I_t), E(y_{t+i+2}:I_t), \ldots$$

all conditional on I_t, are assumed to be consistent in such a way that we can build up general expressions for future forecasts (since only factors unexpected at t will influence these forecasts). For example, if $E(y_{t+1}:I_t) = ay_t$, then

$$E(y_{t+2}:I_t) = E(ay_{t+1}:I_t) = aE(y_{t+1}:I_t) = a^2 y_t = \ldots$$

and so on, dropping the implicit random term in each expression. We can build up a general expression for any forecast, then, say in the form $a^n y_t$ for $E(y_{t+n}:I_t)$, by application of this chain rule of forecasting.

A third set of rules leads us into the area of econometric tests of the rational-expectations hypothesis. Two of these are suggested by Sheffrin (1983) as follows:

(a) In an econometric test the predictor x_t^* should be an *unbiased* expectation of x_t. For example, in the expression $x_t = a + bx_t^* + u_t$ we should find $a = 0$ and $b = 1$.

(b) The predictor x_t^* should use information about the past history of x_t in the same way as x_t actually evolves through time (Sheffrin refers to this as *efficiency*).

We will find that (b) is important in our discussion of policy effectiveness in the next section and that (a) has figured in the direct implementation of rational expectations on (for example) the consumption function (see the discussion in D. Fisher, 1983).

Finally, in this last set we note a consideration emphasised by Begg; this is that any relevant pieces of information – that is, relevant to predicting some future variable – will be incorporated into the full information set used for forecasting the variable. This being the case, no subset will improve one's forecast. Formally, the rule is that

$$E\{[y_{t+i} - E(y_{t+i}:I_t)]:S_t\} = 0 \tag{3.3}$$

where y_{t+i} is the realisation and $E(y_{t+i}:I_t)$ is the forecast of y_{t+i} at t (an earlier period than $t+i$) based on the full information set I_t. S_t is a subset of I_t. Thus the error in the prediction of y (in square brackets in 3.3) is not affected – and still has an expectation of zero – when one uses a subset of the full available information set so long as individuals are rational and actual economic variables incorporate their projections. This rule, then, provides a testable implication of the theory since one can try out subsets (e.g. the phases of the moon). Indeed, a considerable part of the testing of the efficient- (equity-) markets hypothesis has been of this sort, sometimes with limited contradiction to the rationality hypothesis.

We should, at this point, since we are on the topic of econometric problems, underscore a serious problem with rational expectations models: they have acute identification problems, having to do with the joint nature of the hypothesis. In particular, as we have already noted, rational expectations is a specialised hypothesis about how expectations are formed and is often embedded in structural equations (e.g. those for consumption and for investment spending). An example of a structural hypothesis is that consumption is affected by expected (permanent) income and *jointly* that expectations of income are themselves rational. Unless one has an expectations proxy that is direct and is known to be formed rationally, the two (joint) hypotheses will have to sink or swim together, and rationality cannot easily be broken out and tested separately, at least in this simple framework. We do have some direct expectations data (the Livingston data in the United States, for example), but the debate goes on concerning the usefulness of this data. The most popular alternative method of modelling expectations is that of using the lagged values of the variable that is being predicted. This, however, does not break the identification deadlock since, obviously, the simple distributed lags that result would leave one hard put to construct tests that distinguish rational expectations from both adaptive expectations and/or permanent income style expectations. This results because both of the latter exist in versions that employ lagged variables, essentially as proxies for expectations. This is basically a problem of *observational equivalence* and, says Begg (1982, p. 77) in those cases when either adaptive or rational expectations could apply 'Only when the relevant economic theory suggests that the lag patterns . . . are very different will it be possible to identify separately the two sets of parameters.' This is not the usual task of economic theory, which has generally not taken a position about the exact shape of lag distributions. We shall return to these econometric issues in Chapter 4.

3.3   THE EFFECTIVENESS OF MACROECONOMIC POLICY

The best way to come to grips with how rational expectations changes the face of the policy debate is to consider the main result in the literature, that on the effects of macroeconomic policy when rational expectations is assumed to hold. The proposition, quite simply, is that macropolicy will be (a) inefficient and/or (b) ineffective in the event that economic agents operate with rational expectations.

One way of describing policy, as we have seen, is that which appears in Chapter 1. This is a set-up in which the authorities construct and estimate a model, generally a large-scale econometric model, which they then use to forecast alternative paths of the endogenous variables in the system, contingent on various assumed settings for their control variables (their fiscal and monetary instruments). The authorities then implement the best policy by selecting actual values for their instruments. Revisions in the policy then would come in the event that results did not correspond to the anticipations of the authorities; this process, though, may only involve trying new data or new instrument settings and may not involve re-estimating or rethinking the basic model.

In fact, non-governmental economic agents also build their 'models' of the economy, and they include the government and its projected policy actions in their models. The result is that either the policy is correctly anticipated, so that individuals will avoid – to the extent that they can – the real effects of the policy *or* the policy is a genuine surprise, in which case it will affect economic agents until they are able to discern and act on any systematic elements in the policy. In either case, but particularly in the first, the parameters of the authorities' model will actually change as individuals react to the policy. For an example look back to the discussion of the Phelps model of the natural-rate hypothesis (in Chapter 2). There we saw that the Phillips curve shifted whenever inflationary expectations were revised; inflationary expectations would, of course, be based on private sector guesses as to what the authorities are doing and are going to do with the money supply. Thus the government's forecasts (based on simulations in a model with fixed parameters) will be in error, at least if the forecasts use a Phillips curve that does not shift with expectations. It is important to appreciate, here, that individuals would have an incentive to act in this fashion whenever macropolicy is enacted.

So far in the discussion there have really been two points which need to be underscored. The first of these is that in a world in which individuals employ rational expectations, the government cannot simply operate the basic policy models of Chapters 1 and 2. They will, in short, miss their targets because of the structural changes. This occurs because the parameters of those models will change since, in effect, individuals' rational expectations about policy are part of the structure of the model. The second point, to which we shall return in Subsection 3.3.2, is that conventional demand management policy may actually not work at all.

3.3.1 The Lucas Critique

The first point is now a very familiar one and is often referred to as the 'Lucas critique'. An effective general statement of the critique has been put forward by McCallum (1980); we will state the most obvious result using McCallum's version before considering some specific results by Lucas (1976). Assume an *IS* curve of

$$y_t = a_0 + a_1 [i_t - E(p_{t+1} - p_t)] + w_t \tag{3.4}$$

in which the term in brackets is the real interest rate (all variables except the nominal interest rate (i_t) are in log form). Assume, also, an *LM* curve of

$$m_t - p_t = c_0 + c_1 y_t + c_2 i_t + v_t \tag{3.5}$$

and a Lucas (aggregate) supply function of

$$y_t = \alpha_0 + \alpha_1 (p_t - p_t^*) + \alpha_2 y_{t-1} + u_t \tag{3.6}$$

Finally, let the policy rule be specified as a combination active and passive sort as

$$m_t = \mu_0 + \mu_1 m_{t-1} + \mu_2 y_{t-1} + e_t \tag{3.7}$$

In this model we will assume rational expectations for $E(\cdot)$ and for p_t^*. We will also assume that the authorities use this (correct) model to produce an explanation of the time path of the log of real income in the general form of

$$y_t = \Phi_0 + \Phi_1 y_{t-1} + \Phi_2 m_t + \Phi_3 m_{t-1} + \varepsilon_t \tag{3.8}$$

The parameters of this model are assumed to be fixed and simulations are run for the effect of varying the parameters in 3.7 in order to arrive at the best policy (interpreted as that which smoothes the time path of y_t the most). The Φ_i are reduced-form parameters, of course, but they ought not to be taken as constants in the fashion just described since they contain the μ_j. That is, for example,

$$\Phi_0 = \alpha_0 - \mu_0 \left[\frac{\alpha_1 \left(\dfrac{a_1}{a_1 c_1 + c_2} \right)}{\alpha_1 + \dfrac{a_1}{a_1 c_1 + c_2}} \right]$$

and so alterations in μ_0 (etc.) – a policy parameter – will actually cause the coefficients of the reduced form (Φ_i) to change as economic agents revise their expectations about the log of the price level. That is, as long as α_1 and a_1 are not equal to zero – and α_1 will not be equal to zero under rational expectations since it would not be rational to ignore a mistaken price prediction – the policy will induce changes in the economy which would cause the econometric model (summarised in Equation 5) to provide incorrect estimates of the policy effect in future periods. Further, as discussed by McCallum (1980), techniques to deal with this are not particularly easy to implement.

We should also consider the examples provided by Lucas (1976) in order to see the role of rational expectations in all of this more clearly. The basic macro functions in the structure of the economy – e.g. consumption, investment, money demand – can be assumed to depend on permanent income, itself a construct of the general form of

$$y_{pt} = (1 - \beta) \sum_{i=0}^{\infty} \beta^i E(y_{t+i}:I_t) \tag{3.9}$$

where β is a subjective discount factor (incorporated as a weight) and where the forecasts of income are conditional on the information set I_t which is available at t, the time the forecast is made. (In the actual consumption decision other variables are also forecast, of course, but we are abstracting from them here.) The dependence of consumption on permanent income may simply be

$$c_t = k y_{pt} + u_t \tag{3.10}$$

where u_t is an arbitrary random error. A simple distributed lag – which is also a minimum variance estimator – could describe how $E(y_{t+i}:I_t)$ might be calculated by consumers; we will assume that this is correct. This would be

$$(1 - \lambda) \sum_{j=0}^{\infty} \lambda^j y_{t-j}$$

where the λ^j provide a set of weights on past incomes. Combining this expression with 3.9 and 3.10 we then derive a consumption function in observables

$$c_t = k(1 - \beta)y_t + k\beta(1 - \lambda) \sum_{j=0}^{\infty} \lambda^j y_{t-j} + u_t \qquad (3.11)$$

It is this 'permanent income' consumption function which the government inserts into its macro model.

Now consider what happens when there are deliberate policy actions in some future period T (and beyond) that were not in the original information set I_t. It does not matter, here, what the policy is, but the prototype is, of course, one that attempts to fool consumers. To the extent that the policy is announced and/or that the policy is apparent to consumers, they will recognise the policy (or predict it), and when they do, they will recompute their permanent income. If the policy adds (or subtracts) a constant increment ($= x$) to their permanent income over all periods beyond T, then the change in consumption in any period t is kx, using Equation 3.10. This includes periods before the policy comes into effect (before T). The government, however, will forecast consumption by using the slowly adjusting distributed lag in Equation 3.11 in which case it estimates that the *change* in consumption for any time t is

$$dc_t = k\bar{x}\left[(1 - \beta) + \beta(1 - \lambda) \sum_{i=0}^{t-T} \lambda^i \right] \qquad (3.12)$$

That is, whether the consumer knows the policy or not (p. 113), 'the theory of economic policy prescribes the *same* method for evaluating its consequences: add x_t to the forecasts of y_t for each $t > T$, insert into 3.6, and obtain the new forecasts of c_t'. For periods before T the government does not realise that agents have adjusted their behaviour (rationally) and for $t > T$ the authorities stick with 3.11, with its initially defined and slowly adjusting weights, in spite of the fact that the equation produces a bias in its predictions that can be eliminated only by adjusting the weights. Predicted consumption is in error (in opposite directions) both before and after the policy is laid on, even though the government has the correct model of permanent income. In this event any policy that is based on these predictions will also be in error.[3] Of course, in this demonstration we have made only a limited use of rationality because we have utilised the adaptive expectations measure of permanent income rather than a rational expectations one. The reason for this is that we have to provide some motive for policy for, as we will see, under pure rational expectations policy is ineffective.

Lucas (1976) also works his point on the expectations-adjusted Phillips curve model which we looked at in Section 2.5. There we concluded, in a two-market economy with informational discrepancies, that

$$E[p_t : p_{it}, I_{t-1}] = (1 - \Theta)p_{it} + \Theta \bar{p}_t \qquad (3.13)$$

where i is an index that runs over markets and Θ depends on price dispersion across the 'islands' of informationally separated markets (see Equation 2.44); the ps are, again, the log of the price level. This estimate of the price level will be unbiased but will not be perfectly accurate, in general. When errors in prediction occur, supply responses will result according to the expression

$$y_t = y_{pt} + \Theta \beta (p_t - \bar{p}_t) \qquad (3.14)$$

Here, following Lucas, we have put 'permanent' output in place of the normal output of Equation 2.47. It is this expression that captures the mechanism that produces Phillips curve tradeoffs in the short run.

The question, of course, is whether the existence of such a tradeoff gives the policy-maker a reasonable shot at a productive stabilisation policy. Whether this is so will, in the first instance, depend on the stability of the parameters β and Θ over time. This, in turn, will depend on whether economic agents know these parameters and, of course, whether they actually change. In fact, σ^2 – the variance of the general price level that is included in Θ – is itself likely to change when policy is conducted. Possibly of a more serious nature, the authorities could perceive a tradeoff between y_t and changes in prices and act on this understanding even though the tradeoff does not really exist. To see this (still following Lucas), suppose that prices actually evolve by the rule

$$p_t = p_{t-1} + \varepsilon_t$$

which is a random walk. Then if we assume that ε_t is $N(\pi, \sigma^2)$, we can take expectations of this expression and replace $E(\varepsilon_t)$ with its expectation (π). When we substitute the resulting expression into 3.14 for $\bar{p}_t (= E(p_t))$, we obtain a correct reduced form for the log of real output of

$$y_t = y_{pt} + \Theta \beta (p_t - p_{t-1}) - \Theta \beta \pi \qquad (3.15)$$

Here, clearly, the actual inflation rate (in parentheses) enters twice, with opposite signs. Assuming that π and y_{pt} are both constant, a regression of y_t on $p_t - p_{t-1}$ will produce the appearance of a tradeoff that actually does not exist (because it is cancelled by agents' reactions – since they do not make mistakes). That is, $p_t - p_{t-1} = \pi$ describes the actual evolution of

Monetary and Fiscal Policy

prices which, we assume, private agents know and act upon (the Phillips curve simply jumps up at the natural rate of unemployment). As long as monetary policy does not alter the parameters β and, especially, Θ, it will be ineffective even though a precise tradeoff can be estimated.[4] It is clear, then, that policy designed to exploit a tradeoff that does not really exist can only cause confusion if we grant the assumptions of this analysis. We should note, before pressing on with the second part of the 'policy ineffectiveness' discussion, that policy may work and large-scale models may predict 'well enough' to be used as a basis for policy, in practice. That is, the empirical dimensions to the problems raised here have not yet been considered, nor have the theoretical objections, for that matter.

3.3.2 Policy Effectiveness under Rational Expectations: The Basic Result

At this point in the discussion we should attempt to be more precise about the 'ineffectiveness' proposition itself, putting aside the errors in policy theme discussed above. Let us assume that aggregate supply is explained by the following, in which output (y_t) depends on the normal level of output and the difference between the price level in t and that expected in $t-1$ to rule for t; the variables are in log form.

$$y_t = y_n + \alpha(p_t - p_t^e) + \varepsilon_t \tag{3.16}$$

This is the Lucas supply function (as discussed in Chapter 2), and the term $p_t - p_t^e$ is the error in the prediction of the log of the price level. Here policy affects aggregate supply by causing workers (for example) to make errors (they have to forecast the price level when contracts are drawn up). In particular, if they underpredict the price level workers will end up providing additional labour services for which they did not originally plan, and actual output will, accordingly, be higher. That is, they will be offering their services at a lower real wage, in effect, and so more of their services will be demanded and used.

In a moment we will add the demand side to this model in order to consider the possibility of a demand-management type of policy, but for now let us look at a simple result which comes directly out of the supply side (and has a great deal to do with the neutrality theorems in this section). Because we are assuming rational expectations we can jump ahead to our solution for the price level after applying the property (discussed above) that individuals do not make systematic mistakes. That is, rational expectations implies that actual prices can be described by

$$p_t = p_t^e + \mu_t \tag{3.17}$$

where the error reflects random elements wherever they arise in the model. When we substitute Equation 3.17 into 3.16 we obtain

$$y_t = y_n + \alpha \mu_t + \varepsilon_t \tag{3.18}$$

Thus, under rational expectations, at least as we have specified the model (a supply-side model only), output deviates from its natural rate only because of the random shocks μ_t and ε_t. Clearly, the scope for policy is not going to be considerable.

Now let us create a somewhat richer structure by including an aggregate demand equation as in

$$y_t = -\beta_1 p_t + \beta_2 m_t \tag{3.19}$$

This has as right-hand variables the log of the price level and the log of an unspecified and exogenous policy variable (in m). If we solve for the price level across both aggregate demand 3.19 and aggregate supply 3.16, we then obtain

$$p_t = \frac{1}{\alpha + \beta_1} (\alpha p_t^e + \beta_2 m_t - y_n - \varepsilon_t) \tag{3.20}$$

which describes the path of the price level in this richer model. Since price expectations, if they are assumed to be rational, should be based on the same model that actually generates prices, we directly have that the unspecified price expectation in 3.20 is

$$p_t^e = E \left[\frac{1}{\alpha + \beta_1} (\alpha p_t^e + \beta_2 m_t - y_n - \varepsilon_t) \right] \tag{3.21}$$

Taking expectations of 3.21, then, we have the result that price expectations are given by

$$p_t^e = \frac{1}{\alpha + \beta_1} (\alpha p_t^e + \beta_2 E m_t - y_n) \tag{3.22}$$

We define the error in the prediction of prices as the difference between p_t and p_t^e; this calculation produces

$$p_t - p_t^e = \frac{1}{\alpha + \beta_1} [\beta_2 (m_t - E m_t) - \varepsilon_t] \tag{3.23}$$

When this expression is substituted into the aggregate supply equation 3.16 we have

$$y_t = y_n + \frac{\alpha}{\alpha + \beta_1} [\beta_2 (m_t - E m_t) - \varepsilon_t] - \varepsilon_t \tag{3.24}$$

Thus, fluctuations of real output around its natural level depend on the shocks in the aggregate supply curve (we could also have shocked the demand curve) and on errors in predicting the policy variable(s). This last would have an expected value of zero under rational expectations.

To see the role of the authorities in a more concrete way, we can now specify a rule for the money supply. Let this rule be the following policy reaction function.

$$m_t = \tau_1 m_{t-1} + \delta_t \tag{3.25}$$

Here policy can take the form of a change in the reaction coefficient τ_1 or it can take the form of a random shock (a change in δ_t). If it is the former, rational (and observant) individuals will recognise it and re-solve the system for a new p_t^e; in that event p_t will also change. If they get it right, and we are making it part of a systematic (and very naïve) passive feedback policy that is easily recognisable (because the policy is in the coefficient on m_{t-1}), then Equation 3.17 will still hold. So, too, will 3.18 so that the policy will be ineffective, in the sense of not affecting y_t or (unemployment).[5] If they get it wrong, on the other hand, then there will be a temporary effect which will disappear as soon as individuals recognise the systematic error they are making. Once again policy is ineffective, although not in the short run.[6]

The second policy alluded to in this design is that of a change in the shock component in Equation 3.25; this is a monetary surprise of a non-systematic nature. The effect of such a shock will be to make prices more unpredictable, randomly, and thus to make y_t fluctuate more. In this event y_t will also fluctuate more around its mean value (which is the value of y_n in this case). This is certainly 'having an effect', but it has to be random and unpredictable. In any event, all one gets if y_n is truly independent of policy is increased variation in y_t. It is hard to see the point of such a policy.

As suggested in Chapter 2 and earlier in this chapter, the labour-market alternative to Equation 3.16 is a Phillips curve in the form of

$$U_t = U_{nt} - \beta(\pi_t - \pi_t^e) + \varepsilon_t \tag{3.26}$$

where errors in the prediction of the rate of inflation produce deviations of unemployment from its natural level. The term in parentheses in Equation 3.26 is basically the forecasting error in the prediction of inflation rates; this term could then be based on Equation 3.17, the rational-expectations solution for the log of the price level, in which case the forecasting errors would have an expectation of zero. In this event only unexpected and presumably unsystematic factors would have an influence on unemployment, unless U_n itself varies over time.[7] Thus the analysis of the previous model goes through and monetary policy, if systematic, will have at best a short-run effect on U_t (if it is perceived incorrectly). Policy, if random, will merely increase the fluctuations of U_t around U_n, possibly producing the impression of a statistical Phillips curve since a positive error in the money-supply equation will produce a positive error in the inflation prediction and an increase in employment (a decrease in U_t).

3.3.3 Policy Effectiveness and Instrument Selection under Rational Expectations

In Chapter 1, following Poole, we compared two alternative policy strategies – interest-rate stabilisation and money-stock stabilisation – in terms of their respective potential for stabilising fluctuations in real output. The model we used there was basically *IS–LM*, and the conclusion offered was that either type of policy could be correct (ignoring problems of nominal/real interest rates) under certain conditions. The conditions were that the interest-rate policy was better when the *LM* curve was unpredictable relative to the *IS* curve and that the money-stock-control policy was better when the *IS* curve was unpredictable compared to the *LM* curve. Under rational expectations, as we have seen, monetary policy is just plain ineffective, but it is interesting, none the less, to compare the two ways of setting the instruments partly because the comparison helps in explaining the theory and partly because there actually is a difference between the two styles, even in the 'ineffective' context. The work is that of Sargent and Wallace (1975).

Assume, then, the following version of the Lucas supply curve (all variables but the interest rate are again in logs).

$$y_t = a_1 k_{t-1} + a_2 (p_t - p_t^e) + u_{1t} \tag{3.27}$$

Here k defines a measure of productive capacity (it comes from a homogeneous production function) which itself depends on its own lagged value, the real interest rate, and a vector of unspecified exogenous variables (z_t).

$$k_t = d_1 k_{t-1} + d_2 [i_t - (p_{t+1}^e - p_t^e)] + d_3 z_t + u_{2t} \tag{3.28}$$

Note that the expectations on prices for t and $t+1$ are assumed to be taken at $t-1$. We can describe the demand side of the model by an *IS* curve as in

$$y_t = b_1 k_{t-1} + b_2 [i_t - (p_{t+1}^e - p_t^e)] + b_3 z_t + u_{3t} \tag{3.29}$$

and an *LM* curve of

$$m_t = p_t + c_1 y_t + c_2 i_t + u_{4t} \tag{3.30}$$

where the coefficients (in both equations) have the traditional signs. All that then remains to complete the model is specifying an objective function for the authorities (Sargent and Wallace use a quadratic). Again note that price expectations are defined at $t-1$ in these expressions.

If the expectations of (the logs of) the price level are formed adaptively rather than rationally, then the Poole result goes through; that is (p. 246): 'Which policy is superior depends on which delivers the smaller loss, which in turn depends on all of the parameters of the model, including the covariance matrix of the disturbances. Which rule is superior is therefore an empirical matter which is completely consistent with Poole's analysis'. However, there is no neat set of results comparable to Poole's (as laid out in Chapter 1). If we assume rational expectations, things are different, though. In this case, expected prices come from

$$p_{t+i, t-j}^e = E_{t-j} p_{t+i} \tag{3.31}$$

where the second subscript on p^e identifies the period in which the expectation is formed. E is the expectations operator. It is, of course, conditional on all information available up to the end of $t-j$.

To proceed to analyse the effect of a change in the log of the money stock, we can solve Equations 3.27, 3.29 and 3.30 for y, i and p (given m) to produce a 'reduced' form for p. This is

$$p_t = J_0 E_{t-1} p_t + J_1 E_{t-1} p_{t+1} + J_2 m_t + X_t \tag{3.32}$$

where the J_i are composed of the parameters of those equations, X_t consists of linear combinations of the exogenous, predetermined (k_{t-1}), and stochastic parts of those equations, and E is the expectations operator. The procedure to show that monetary policy does not work here is the following. We can calculate $E_{t-1} p_t$ from Equation 3.32 and then subtract that from 3.32 to produce 3.33. This is the error in the prediction of p_t.

$$p_t - E_{t-1} p_t = J_2 (m_t - E_{t-1} m_t) + X_t - E_{t-1} X_t = X_t - E_{t-1} X_t \tag{3.33}$$

Note we are assuming that $m_t = E_{t-1} m_t$ because the authorities are following a deterministic rule that is readily discernible by rational economic agents. Putting this expression together with Equation 3.31 for expected prices, we can produce another version of the aggregate supply function (Equation 3.32) of

$$y_t = a_1 k_{t-1} + a_2 (X_t - E_{t-1} X_t) + u_{1t} \tag{3.34}$$

If we then substitute the right-hand side of 3.34 into the *IS* curve (Equation 3.29) we get the real interest rate as a function of k_{t-1} and exogenous processes. If we then substitute this new function into Equation 3.30, the *LM* curve, we get a difference equation in k, driven by exogenous processes. Thus k is an exogenous process, and so is y, via Equation 3.34. In this event, no matter what the deterministic rule, monetary policy is ineffective (in influencing y_t).

Sargent and Wallace do show a 'positive' role for a deterministic money-supply rule in the case in which the authorities' quadratic loss function contains quadratic terms in the price level. In that instance the rule is to set the monetary parameters such that the expected value of next period's price level is equal to the target values (in the loss function). That is, they should ensure that (rational) expectations are confirmed. With respect to the issue raised by Poole – that there is an empirically-interesting difference between money-stock stabilisation and nominal interest-rate stabilisation – they conclude that there is a difference under rational expectations in that (p. 242) 'a unique equilibrium price level does not exist if the monetary authority pegs the interest rate period by period, regardless of how the value varies from period to period'. Of course (McCallum, 1981) if a more reasonable rule were adopted, such as tying the interest-rate rule to the amount of money that can be absorbed by the demand for money, then a measure of interest-rate smoothing can be achieved without runaway inflation.[8]

3.4 THE REAL BUSINESS CYCLE

Up to now we have taken the business cycle as 'given' in that we have simply built it into the structure in some obvious way, mainly in order to provide a rationale for the use of monetary and fiscal policies. In so doing we were able (a) to provide an explanation of the basic reasoning behind the use of activist policies and (b) to explain how the consideration of rational expectations might undermine the argument for these policies. There is, though, considerably more work available on the cycle itself and so in this section we will discuss mostly recent efforts to construct business-cycle theories (generally with rational expectations) which are themselves consistent with the broad cyclical experiences of Western economies. Note that in this section a 'real' cycle will have both real and nominal causes.

We should pause for a moment and consider just what the 'cyclical experiences' just referred to might be. Since the early 1800s, at least, fairly irregular fluctuations in real income and employment (and other variables) have occurred across the Western economies. Somewhat remarkably, with the exception of the Great Depression of the 1930s, these events have been fairly similar both across countries and across time. As Lucas (1980, p. 706) puts it:

> If the magnitude of the Great Depression dealt a serious blow to the idea of the business cycle as a repeated occurrence of the 'same' event, the postwar experience has to some degree restored respectability to this idea. If the Depression continues, in some respects, to defy explanation by existing economic analysis (as I believe it does), perhaps it is gradually succumbing to the Law of Large Numbers.

The regularities concern the coincident swings of real variables (comovements) and the relatively comparable magnitude of these swings. The length of the cycles, though, is definitely not the same from event to event (and from country to country), and the causes – the precipitating shocks that set the cycle in motion – are probably numerous and, worse, both small and large in size (Blanchard and Watson, 1984). In any case the repetitions and comovements are sufficiently obvious so that reasonably successful efforts have been made to 'model' cycles empirically. Indeed, a large number of economic time series are currently classified as coinciding with, leading or lagging the general cycle, and thus a profile of the cycle – its 'proximate causes', its nature and extent and its 'proximate consequences' – has been built up (see Zarnowitz, 1985). This profile is what one encounters in popular discussions of actual business cycles.

A major problem with the statistical build-up of data on business cycles is that it has become somewhat of an encumbrance for the theorist, since he is frequently held to the standard that his cycle model should conform to this reality, if such it is. The problem is not that the theories should predict the data for, of course, they should. It is, first, that the data themselves seem to suggest and condition the theories and, second, that specific theories are often discarded (or ridiculed) for not having one or more of the important features of the 'standard profile' of the real cycle embedded in them. The most common way this occurs, and certainly the most controversial, is in the assumption that cycles are basically best studied as disequilibrium $(S \neq I)$ phenomena as if the existence of sustained unemployment is *in itself* evidence of disequilibrium. For an example of the disequilibrium approach the reader could look back to the Lipsey (1960, 1974) explanation of the Phillips curve, as discussed in Chapter 2. One can also recall McDonald's (1975) complaint about the Parkin 'natural-rate' model for Australia as an example of the insistence on putting disequilibrium into the structure, perhaps directly.[9] An alternative exists, though, and it has appealing theoretical properties; this alternative is to model the equilibrium business cycle. This is the subject of this section.

We should emphasise, at the start, that the equilibrium-cycle theories we will be describing here generally make use of inflexibility of some sort – especially in the form of price stickiness – in order to motivate the *persistence* that is a common feature of cyclical experiences. It was once thought that price stickiness was inconsistent with the equilibrium approach – and required a disequilibrium structure – but, as we will see, it is actually perfectly consistent with the existence and stability of equilibrium under rational expectations. R. J. Gordon (1981, p. 493) puts the case as follows:

> Because prices do not carry the full burden of adjustment in the short run, quantities must by definition carry part of the load. In this sense the phenomenon of gradual price adjustment is at the heart of fluctuations in output and employment and of the related debate over activist stabilization policy to control such fluctuations.

But we need not abandon the equilibrium–rational-expectations approach in doing so. Thus, a major issue in the policy debate is 'disequilibrium versus equilibrium' but not necessarily price stickiness; another, indeed, is rational versus adaptive expectations.

Now, of course, there are many views on how monetary policy could have an effect, even if rational expectations holds. We have, so far, argued that expectational errors can produce effects, for example, if the inflation rate is incorrectly perceived. But what if it is correctly perceived? One such effect occurs because changes in the rate of inflation affect financial contracts that are written in nominal terms (e.g. bonds). Most such contracts could, in principle, contain explicit or implicit inflation forecasts, but most do not; if they do not, then economic agents will experience price-induced wealth effects whenever the price level changes. One important asset for which no contract exists is cash. In this case, whether inflation is expected or not, agents will be taxed by inflation as long as cash is at all useful (presumably for transactions purposes). However its effect is rationalised, this operation of a wealth effect will tend to alter the rate of capital formation in the economy and thus, presumably, employment and output. As a variable tax (see Section 3.5) it will also tend to have real effects by altering real marginal tax rates.

In the remainder of this section we will undertake a review of recent attempts to explain the real business cycle and the accompanying role of monetary policy under the assumption of rational expectations (see Barro, 1981b, for a recent survey). To begin with, we will consider the main explanations that have been produced by – or are consistent with the assumptions of – rational expectations theorists. This begins with Lucas (1972b). We take it as understood that policy under non-rational assumptions has been sufficiently discussed in Chapters 1 and 2 – and will be returned to in Chapter 5 – so that the material here can be discussed as a reworking of that analysis with some basic alterations in the structure (mostly of expectations). We will, though, present some of the material that is critical of these models in order to explore the range of the theory completely.

The first rational expectations paper on the equilibrium business cycle is that of Lucas (1972b); it is an extension of the island-economy paradigm of Phelps (1970a). Phelps proposes (p. 6) 'to picture the economy as a group of islands between which information flows are costly: to learn the wage paid on an adjacent island, the worker must spend the day traveling to that island to sample its wages instead of spending the day at work'.

To amend this search theory rationale Lucas suggests the use of the 'overlapping generations' dynamic model in which one of two segments of society (the 'young' in this case) possesses an informational disadvantage over the other (the 'old'). This disadvantage arises because they receive information on the money stock, which they need in order to sort out relative from absolute price effects in their environments, with a time lag. This information lag, of course, is an arbitrary device, but it is one that produces the necessary response. That is, since current prices only imperfectly reflect the necessary information, agents must (1972b, p. 103) 'hedge on whether a particular price movement results from a relative demand shift or a nominal (monetary) one. This hedging behavior results in a nonneutrality of money, or broadly speaking a Phillips curve'. But the system retains classical neutrality in the long run.[10]

In the system just discussed, a change in the quantity of money (a shock) has a real effect that persists as long as the shock itself persists. This result provides a start on explaining an important problem – the role of money in propagating or perpetuating cycles – but it does not provide a monetary explanation (under rational expectations) of how the cycle persists after the monetary shock is turned off. That is, this model does not really provide an effective explanation of the real business cycle. In a follow-up paper (1975) Lucas extends the island-economy paradigm in order to model the persistence of the policy shock. The amendment involves introducing the inherited capital stock – the accelerator, in effect – along with information lags of the imperfectly linked island economy. With these devices a monetary explanation of real cycles is provided that holds up under rational expectations. A paper of the same vintage by J. B. Taylor (1975) has a similar rationale but builds on a possible informational discrepancy between the public and the central bank; in this case Taylor employs adaptive expectations. Here monetary policy has its effect in the 'transition to rational-expectations equilibrium'.

The Lucas (1975) rational-expectations cyclical model is embedded in a standard neoclassical growth model, similar to the sort discussed in considerably greater detail in Chapter 5. Assuming that output is produced by a linear homogeneous production function $F(K_t, N_t)$ and is divided among real consumption, government spending and capital (at the end of the period), we have that

$$C_t + G_t + K_{t+1} = f(K_t, N_t) + (1 - \delta)K_t \tag{3.35}$$

Here δ is the depreciation rate of the capital stock. Assuming that the labour-supply function is perfectly elastic (hence the N, for labour, in Equation 3.36, below) and that households own the capital stock (K) and all nominal money balances (M), then, when the factor markets are in equilibrium, households will be constrained by

$$P_t(C_t + K_{t+1}) + M_{t+1} \leqslant P_t f(K_t, N) + P_t(1 - \delta)K_t + M_t \tag{3.36}$$

Notice that this function is in nominal terms and that end-of-period money balances are included among the expenditures on the left-hand side of the equation. For the government, finally, we will provide a combined fiscal–monetary policy in the form of a dynamic budget constraint of

$$P_t G_t = M_{t+1} - M_t = \mu M_t \quad \text{or} \quad m_{t+1} - m_t = \mu \tag{3.37}$$

Here nominal government expenditures are financed by money creation. μ is, in effect, the monetary policy parameter. The second expression in Equation 3.37, with lower-case letters, reflects recasting the problem in logarithms (since $\log(1 + \mu)$ is approximately μ).

Along with the three equilibrium constraints just described, the system needs to be completed by specifying the representative household demands for assets (for capital and for money holding). Lucas shows no interest in deeper structure here and simply lays out an *ad hoc* log-linearisation of these demand functions as in

$$k_{t+1} = \alpha_0 + \alpha_1 r_{kt} - \alpha_2 r_{mt} + \alpha_3 k_t \tag{3.38}$$

$$m_{t+1} - p_t = \beta_0 - \beta_1 r_{kt} + \beta_2 r_{mt} + \beta_3 k_t \tag{3.39}$$

Here $\alpha_i, \beta_i > 0$. To construct rates of return for these expressions, we note that with money being non-interest-bearing, its 'own rate' (r_{mt}) is merely the rate of deflation.

$$r_{mt} = p_t - p_{t+1} \tag{3.40}$$

For the capital stock the rate of return is calculated by taking the real rate of return next period – which is simply the marginal product of capital $f_k(K_{t+1}, N)$ – and deducting the rate of depreciation from it. Since this depends only on capital, Lucas approximates it with the following *ad hoc* linearisation (in logs)

$$r_{kt} = \delta_0 - \delta_1 k_{t+1} \qquad \delta_1 > 0 \tag{3.41}$$

Thus 3.40 and 3.41 define the *expected* rates of return needed for the asset demand functions. Since these rates depend on future prices and the future capital stock (of course), these terms have to be predicted by economic agents. Lucas assumes that agents do this rationally.

Lucas does not solve this first-order difference equation system in the usual way (see Chapter 5 for examples) but suggests an alternative. At time t the parameters in Equations 3.37 to 3.41 and the two variables m_t and k_t describe the state of the system. A solution, if it exists, for k_{t+1} (or m_{t+1}) and p_t can then be expressed as

$$k_{t+1} = \pi_{10} + \pi_{11}k_t + \pi_{12}m_t \tag{3.42}$$

$$p_t = \pi_{20} + \pi_{21}k_t + \pi_{22}m_t \tag{3.43}$$

where the solution is in log-linear form (since the underlying equations are also log-linear). Then by a *solution* of the system we mean finding expressions for π_{ij} in terms of the parameters in expressions 3.37 to 3.43. The technique is simply to substitute Equations 3.37 and 3.40 to 3.43 into 3.38 and 3.39 and then to equate coefficients across the resulting expressions (for k_{t+1} and p_t) with those in 3.42 and 3.43. This produces

$$\pi_{10} = \alpha_0 + \alpha_1\delta_0 - \alpha_1\delta_1\pi_{10} + \alpha_2\pi_{21}\pi_{10} + \alpha_2\pi_{22}\mu$$

$$\pi_{12} = -\alpha_1\delta_1\pi_{12} + \alpha_2\pi_{21}\pi_{12}$$

$$1 - \pi_{22} = \beta_1\delta_1\pi_{12} - \beta_2\pi_{21}\pi_{12}$$

and expressions for π_{11}, π_{20} and π_{21}.

Comparing the second and third of the equations just given, we see that a viable solution for these is $\pi_{12} = 0$ and $\pi_{22} = 1$. Since, as it turns out, overall stability requires that $\pi_{21} < 0$, this is actually the only solution for the two equations. Looking back at Equation 3.42, $\pi_{12} = 0$ implies that the *level* of real money balances has no real effect – that is, has no effect on capital formation in the model – while 3.43 shows, for $\pi_{22} = 1$, that 'classical neutrality' results for changes in m_t. But monetary policy does have real effects in this system for it also enters by means of μ, the *rate of growth* of the real-money stock; consequently 'super neutrality' does not hold. The parameter μ represents the government's policy response, and it enters into the solved value of π_{10} used in Equation 3.42. Indeed, for $\pi_{22} = 1$, the effect of an increase in μ is stimulatory on k_{t+1} (that is, on capital along its time path and at its stationary point). As Lucas notes, this is the famous 'Tobin effect' (1965) that works through the rate of return on money as in

$$r_{mt} = \pi_{21}(k_t - k_{t+1}) - \mu$$

In the stationary state ($k_t = k_{t+1}$), finally, r_{mt} is merely the inverse of the rate of monetary expansion.

In the foregoing a clear description of real-business cycles does not emerge since traders are able to judge the price level in t and, using their knowledge of the structure of the economy, correctly estimate m_t. As Lucas puts it (1975, p. 1120), 'there is "too much" information in the hands of traders for them ever to be "fooled" into altering real decision variables'. Policy, in this definite form, would be ineffective under rational expectations. Lucas, then, proposes tacking on the island paradigm of Phelps to this accelerator model. This paradigm, it will be recalled, uses the analogy of geographic isolation to motivate informational discrepancies across markets. In this scenario traders are assigned to markets randomly and form forecasts of the real rates of return r_{kt} and r_{mt} from known distributions depending on the model just laid out (where, in contrast, r_{kt} and r_{mt} were simply known). These markets are then shocked (by, for example, an unsystematic monetary policy) after the traders have set up shop.

Assuming that the markets are indexed by z, the asset demand functions can now be written as

$$k_{t+1}(z) = \alpha_0 + \alpha_1 r_{kt}(z) - \alpha_2 r_{mt}(z) + \alpha_3 k_t(z) \tag{3.44}$$

$$m_t^d(z) - p_t(z) = \beta_0 - \beta_1 r_{kt}(z) + \beta_2 r_{mt}(z) + \beta_3 k_t(z) \tag{3.45}$$

We now wish to have a variable money supply to provoke an equilibrium real-business cycle, and this is done by assuming that money changes according to

$$m_{t+1} = m_t + x_t \tag{3.46}$$

Here x_t is itself distributed as $N(\mu, \sigma^2)$. Note that we are still operating in logs.

Equation 3.46 describes the overall production of money; its distribution across each market is assumed to be given by

$$\Theta_t(z) = \tau \Theta_{t-1}(z) + \varepsilon_t(z) \quad 0 < \tau < 1 \tag{3.47}$$

where $\Theta_t(z)$ describes the deviation of the increment in market z from the average increment x_t defined in 3.46. Thus there is an overall shock and a market specific shock similar to the price shocks discussed in Chapter 2 when we first considered the Lucas supply function.

In the situation discussed here, then, equilibrium in the money market requires that

$$m_t^d(z) = m_t + x_t + \Theta_t(z)$$

The two rates of return needed for 3.44 and 3.45, then, are

$$r_{mt}(z) = p_t(z) - \bar{p}_{t+1}^e(z)$$

$$r_{kt}(z) = p_{t+1}^e(z) - \bar{p}_{t+1}^e(z)$$

where, as noted earlier, both require forecasts. Note that $r_{mt}(z)$ is still interpreted as the negative of an inflation rate and that $r_{kt}(z)$ is still an expected real yield. For the latter the expected price is, in effect, deflated by the expected average price, over all islands, conditional on information available in z. The forecasts, of course, are still assumed to be rational.

We do not have the space to follow Lucas further than this in describing his solutions, but a few words about this work are certainly in order. Economic agents begin with accurate knowledge of the structure (the means and variances). After being assigned to their respective markets, they get new information on the price level (and on $P_t(z)$), and thus they can form a posterior distribution on the variables of interest to them $(k_t, m_t, x_t, \theta_t(z), \mu)$. They use their new information to update their model and to calculate their expected yields. An unsystematic monetary shock (x_t) introduced into this system (a 'pulse') causes a deviation in the real variables (k_t, m_t) which, because we have set things into a difference equation, persists as 'an extended, distributed lag effect'. Specifically, the time paths of the real variables consist of a deterministic part (essentially the same as in 3.42 and 3.43), which shows no policy effect, and (p. 1131) of 'autocorrelated deviations from this path, determined by the shocks and their lagged effects . . .'. This, then, is a standard rational expectations approach to the real cycle where the shocks that set the real-cyclical engine humming are monetary in origin. Lucas then considers several special cases:

(a) If σ_ε^2 is zero, all markets are essentially identical, and the island paradigm collapses to the case in which trade occurs in a single market. This system has no monetary induced cycles and this shows how something like informational discrepancies are needed to motivate business cycles.

(b) If $\alpha_1 = \alpha_2 = 0$ so that money does not affect capital formation (which is itself a random walk), then, in this model, the cycle disappears and the effects of monetary shocks just die out, monotonically.

Lucas develops several other cases in his paper along with some conjectures as to both empirical testing and the realism of his model.

In some ways more promising approaches than islands of information would seem to lie in studying the behaviour of inventories, in recognising the lags inherent in the durability of consumption goods (in addition to the investment goods considered by Lucas) or even in utilising real balance effects (Minford and Peel, 1981). In the model just discussed, Lucas introduced the inherited capital stock in such a way that a shock produces both a labour-supply and an investment-demand response. The effect persists, then, as long as the desired capital stock is less than the actual; this adjustment could take several periods. The same thing happens in a model with inventories in it (see Blinder and Fischer, 1980) in which several periods are needed to restock or run down inventories following a shock. This mechanism is motivated partly by a dislike of letting policy effectiveness depend on an inability to predict the price level; after all (Blinder as quoted in Klamer, 1983, p. 157), 'Everybody who cares to know, knows what the money supply is within a small margin of error. This can't be why we have business cycles.' Rather, inventory behaviour, with a natural-embedded lag in it, provides a device that is, in fact, widely observed in contemporary cycles. Indeed, an inventory cycle has a broad appeal even, as in this case, when the cause of the cycle is monetary and the inventory build-up, for example, merely evidence that the slowdown (whatever its cause) is under way.

An 'informational-advantage' approach to price setting is another way to proceed while still operating under rational expectations. For example, Phelps and Taylor (1977) consider the case in which firms set their prices in one period $(t-1)$ in advance of the period (t) in which they expect to sell their products.[11] Firms, in this instance, are assumed to know the structure of the economy, including the role of the monetary authorities. The monetary authorities, however, have an informational advantage in that they can reset the money supply in period t, based on new information available in t (they know firms' prices, for one thing). Firms, having bound themselves to contracts, cannot react, and monetary policy thereby acquires some leverage. Phelps and Taylor rationalise the use of these contracts in terms of reducing information costs, of keeping customer loyalty and of bearing some of the risk of price fluctuations (for whatever reason). They then work out a detailed model and consider specifically how changes in various policy rules influence the real variables in the model.

In the Phelps and Taylor paper the original Sargent–Lucas rational-expectations framework is somewhat altered in order to achieve the contradiction to policy ineffectiveness. In particular Phelps and Taylor drop the Lucas supply function

> replacing it with an output equation that involves the value of p_{t+1} expected as of $t-1$. It is the combination of this equation with the predetermined price level that provides their result: the money supply for t – which has an influence on p_{t+1} – is set *after* the price for t is fixed, hence with additional data available. (McCallum, 1977, p. 630)

In effect, then, the authorities have an informational advantage that leaves a stabilisation role for monetary policy even assuming rational expectations and flexible, market-clearing prices. On the other hand, says McCallum (1977), if we simply retain price stickiness itself – and the authorities have no built-in informational advantage – then the Sargent–Lucas results go through and policy is actually ineffective. Price stickiness – *per se* – will not do the job by itself in this case. Indeed, we can also build a model in which the information advantage of the authorities gives them no ability to control real variables, but in which real variables respond to money-stock announcements because these contain information (Siegel, 1985). That is, assuming the government has more timely information, when the money stock is announced, the private sector, too, is let in on the secret and makes the appropriate real adjustments. So money has a real effect – that is, is part of the real-business cycle – because of its information content, but policy itself is still ineffective. This seems an important distinction.

A second paper of the same vintage as Phelps and Taylor and with roughly the same structure is by Fischer (1977). This paper provides a more accessible model for purposes of elaboration on the basic point. Fischer assumes that labour contracts run for two periods so that there is a kind of stickiness to wages. Here we assume monetary policy can be changed more frequently than wages and so once again the authorities have an informational lead which they can take advantage of. The rationale for entering into such contracts is essentially that of cost-saving and/ or risk-sharing. In period t workers form expectations for $t + 1$ and $t + 2$ and sign binding nominal wage contracts. In $t + 1$ a new set of workers will sign contracts (running to $t + 3$); these are referred to in the literature as 'staggered contracts'. At any time, then, there is a stock of contracts, some in their first year and some in their second. At t, both 'new' workers and the central bank face the same information set; under rational expectations there is nothing the central bank can do to affect output since they have no leverage over workers' decisions. Presumably, both years of the contract initiated at period t will contain rational expectations of the real conditions workers will face in $t + 1$ and $t + 2$. In $t + 1$, however, there will be new, stochastic, information available to the central bank. At that point the bank will be able to produce a change in the money stock, based on the new information, that will affect the real conditions of workers in the second year of their contracts. This, in turn, implies an effect on real output and employment. Thus, even under rational expectations, as long as there are still good reasons for setting up long-term contracts, monetary policy works in the sense of providing a short-run tradeoff between monetary expansion and employment.[12]

The foregoing is vulnerable for various reasons (agents do not have rational expectations, prices are not flexible, etc.) and is not completely general because there is a sense in which long-term contracts are not optimal. As Fischer points out (p. 200), 'the stabilization is achieved by affecting the real wage of those in the second year of labor contracts and thus should not be expected to be available to attain arbitrary levels of output – the use of too active a policy would lead to a change in the structure of contracts'.

Indeed, such a structural change would be a 'rational' development. One such change would be to have indexed wage contracts where the nominal wage is indexed to the price level *and* to an index of firm profits (because of real-wage changes). In this event monetary policy would again be ineffective (in altering real output and employment). Such contracts are generally not observed in practice, possibly because the computations involved would be difficult (part of the difficulty in any such case are the costs of negotiating complicated contracts) and even price-indexed contracts (COLA) are relatively infrequent. Fischer conjectures that if workers prefer stable real wages, no indexing is better than COLA indexing (under rational expectations); the reason is that the variance of the real wage is higher under the latter procedure. In any event in this scenario we see that even under rational-expectations monetary policy works, and works without tricking workers. This literature has been extended in recent papers (by J. B. Taylor, 1980, and Fethke and Policano, 1981) and the economics of staggering itself has been examined by Fethke and Policano (1984, 1985). This last is required because (a) in the Fischer model staggering is just 'given' and (b) across countries one observes different types of staggering and synchronisation of labour contracts (Japan and Germany have synchronised contracts, while the United Kingdom has shorter staggered contracts (one year, generally) than the United States (three years).

The Lucas real-cycle model described a few pages back provides one way in which real cycles can be given an equilibrium interpretation under rational expectations. The cycles can be generated by monetary shocks really, and thus the possibility of an active monetary policy is embedded in the model. Lucas's work on cycles has inspired further work along the same lines – that is, in the equilibrium–rational context – that promises to leave us with a rich collection of alternative paradigms when this work has finally run its course. One of the characteristics of the cycle literature, taking the whole hundred-odd years of it in at once, is that much of it is based on specific institutional structures (e.g. long-term contracts) or on imperfections in the economic system. Even the Lucas model just discussed requires an informational discrepancy to motivate persistence.

In an interesting recent paper Long and Plosser (1983) attempt to reduce this sort of specialisation, offering, if you can believe it after what has passed so far in this discussion, an explanation of the cycle in which the following hold:

(a) rational expectations, complete information, stable preferences;
(b) no long-lived commodities, no frictions or adjustment costs;
(c) no technological change, no serial dependence in stochastic elements of the environment;
(d) no government and no money.

As we have pointed out in this section, one or more of these (in (b) to (d)) are prominent features in most recent real business-cycle models.

Long and Plosser build their cycle model on two main stylised facts that most economists would accept. These are

(a) that individuals (rationally) want to spread any unanticipated wealth over both time and commodities and

(b) that a general view of production possibilities implies that there is a wide range of both contemporary and intertemporal substitution possibilities.

The second of these is an idea similar to that employed in the 'equilibrium-cycle model' of Kydland and Prescott (1980, 1982); their device was to suppose that it takes multiple periods to build new capital equipment. In any event the two conditions just stated provide the incentive and the opportunity for the persistence of cycles and for the correlated movements among the real variables of the economy following shocks to the system. The implication is, in their framework, that cycles are, in effect, chosen by private economic agents who *prefer* to smooth their consumption stream – and, by construction, have the opportunity to do so – and reject life without the cycle because it represents a suboptimal solution if intertemporal decisions are taken. Let us go through the basic example of Long and Plosser.

Assume that individuals have the following single-period utility function where, for purposes of exposition, an additive form is adopted.

$$u(C_t, Z_t) = \Theta_0 \log Z_t + \sum_{i=1}^{n} \Theta_i \log C_{it} \quad \Theta_i \geq 0 \tag{3.48}$$

Here Z_t defines leisure 'consumed' at time t. This function may be thought of as a specialisation of the following (dynamic) intertemporal function

$$U = \sum_{t=0}^{\infty} \beta^t u (C_t, Z_t) \tag{3.49}$$

in which β identifies a discount factor. For the representative firm a Cobb–Douglas production function describes the transformation of j inputs (X_j) and labour into outputs (i of them).

$$Y_{i,t+1} = \lambda_{i,t+1} L_{it}^{b_i} \prod_{j=1}^{n} X_{ijt}^{a_{ij}} \quad i = 1, \ldots, n \tag{3.50}$$

In this expression (see 3.52 below) labour is measured in the number of hours needed to produce the output. Note that persistence is guaranteed by the assumption that inputs in t are transformed into outputs in $t+1$. Note also that outputs are drawn from the same list as the inputs so that both Equation 3.49 – for outputs – and the product operator Π in 3.50

are defined over the n commodities. Indeed a separate resource constraint makes this relationship clear.

$$C_{jt} + \sum_{i=1}^{n} X_{ijt} = Y_{jt} \qquad j = 1, \ldots, n \tag{3.51}$$

There is a second resource constraint, also defined at t, which organises the 'day' between leisure and labour activities.

$$Z_t + \sum_{i=1}^{n} L_{it} = H \tag{3.52}$$

These constraints make it clear, if it was not already, that the representative economic agent here is both a producer and a consumer. Note, in Equation 3.50 – the production possibilities curve – the existence of a vector of multipliers in λ_{t+1}. This is actually a random vector whose value is realised at $t + 1$. It is assumed by Long and Plosser that the vectors in the sequence $\{\lambda_t\}$ are independent and identically distributed. This, effectively, rules out technological persistence (as suggested in (c), above).

The consumer–producer's problem, then, is to maximise 3.49 – specialised by 3.48 – subject to the production-possibilities function 3.50 and to the two resource constraints in 3.51 and 3.52. The solutions for optimal consumption, worktime and output at time t are then given by the following:

$$C_{it}^* = (\Theta_i/\tau_i)Y_{it} \qquad i = 1, \ldots, n \tag{3.53}$$

$$X_{ijt}^* = (\beta\tau_i a_{ij}/\tau_j)Y_{jt} \qquad i, j = 1, \ldots, n \tag{3.54}$$

$$L_{it}^* = \beta\tau_i b_i (\Theta_0 + \beta_j \sum_{j=1}^{n} \tau_j b_j)^{-1} H \qquad i = 1, \ldots, n \tag{3.55}$$

where τ comes from an expression for welfare.

There is also an expression for Z_{it}^* in the Long and Plosser paper. These functions respond to their arguments and parameters in the following general ways.

(a) The use of a stock of a commodity in a given employment (or consumption) is an increasing function of its productivity in that use.
(b) The amount of a commodity (or time) allocated to each of its employments (and consumption) is an increasing function of the total available amount of a commodity (or time).

The last result implies that a shock to one commodity demand, for example, spreads itself across all its inputs (in the same direction) at the same time and into the future for itself and, via the input markets, for all other outputs. Thus, in this simple model, consumption, inputs and output will all move in the same direction, and such effects will persist (depending on the discount factor). Long and Plosser also deduce that

(a) the real wage moves in the same direction as output, and
(b) labour employment is constant (in the face of commodity output fluctuations).

This last is certainly not a desirable feature of the model, although it can be improved upon by adopting a less restrictive utility function (this is an example, after all).

The model described to this point makes no use of the rational-expectations framework and is little more than an arbitrary general equilibrium-over-time model. It generates 'spatial' and 'temporal' inter-action, then, by building these elements directly into the structure, but, of course, we have not *explicitly* showed the nature of the real cycle in the model. To see the basic dynamics here we can return to the dynamic production function in Equation 3.50. When we substitute the two optimal vectors in Equations 3.54 and 3.55 into 3.50 and rewrite in logarithmic form, we produce the following system

$$y_{t+1} = Ay_t + k + \mu_{t+1} \tag{3.56}$$

where A is an $n x n$ matrix of 'production coefficients', k is a vector of constants and μ_{t+1} is an $n x 1$ stochastic vector $\{\log \lambda_{i,t+i}\}$. Here, as already noted, it is clear that the matrix A provides a useful, if somewhat unexciting, explanation of cyclical interaction.

Assuming, then, that the λs are independent and identically distributed, Long and Plosser show that all cyclical behaviour works through A and that the various output series follow autoregressions of order greater than one. These restrictions on the λ are consistent with *rational expectations*. Long and Plosser summarise by noting that (p. 67): 'Of particular importance is the manner in which the model transforms and amplifies serially uncorrelated and cross-sectionally independent shocks to production in each sector into output series that exhibit positive serial correlation (persistence) and a significant amount of positive cross-sectional correlation (comovement).' Indeed, they warn, these cycles are basically Pareto optimal, and (p. 68) 'Efforts to stabilise this economy can only serve to make consumers worse off'. This neatly disposes of the policy issues surrounding this particular model.

The Lucas model described several pages back has the desirable feature of explaining real-business cycles in terms of monetary (or other) shocks and the undesirable feature of being based on the rather unconvincing 'island paradigm'. The Long and Plosser model, on the other hand, while utilising a standard intertemporal general equilibrium framework, introduces neither money nor the government into the problem. What it does do, though, is provide a very general business-cycle model. A recent paper by R. G. King and Plosser (1984), then, adds to the (simplified) general equilibrium framework of Long and Plosser by putting in an internal monetary sector (producing transactions services) and then considering various shocks, including that of a monetary policy. As noted, this is in the context of a model of the real-business cycle.

In the King and Plosser model (1984, p. 367) 'a positive correlation (comovement) of real production, credit, and transaction services arises from the general equilibrium of production and consumption decisions by firms and households.' In particular, bank deposits in their model turn out to be positively correlated with real output. While this is a 'roughly coincident' pattern, King and Plosser argue that a 'higher than average' shock to the output production function would increase transactions, especially in the factor markets, without having much effect on consumption or leisure. This would generate (intermediate) money-balance responses before final output responses and thus produce a *lead* of money over real activity even though the cause in this instance is a shock to the real production function. Such a lead is a 'stylised fact' in the business-cycle literature and has been the subject of much discussion between the Keynesians (e.g. Tobin, 1970) and the monetarists (e.g. M. Friedman and Schwartz, 1963).

The results just described are produced with no role for the government in the model. What we can do to involve the government is to have it provide an alternative 'transactions service' commodity – currency – that is *not* a perfect substitute for bank deposits. When the banking system is completely unregulated, then, when the authorities fix the supply of currency, they will fix the price level; in this event once-for-all changes in the money stock are neutral, as they are in the Lucas (1975) model. Similarly, Lucas's result for changes in the growth rate of currency hold and there are real (cyclical) effects. Indeed, transactions time increases (recall that in Lucas it produced more information) and (p. 370), 'Since an increase in real transactions services involves the use of real resources, the economy is made worse off by sustained inflation.' But this effect, King and Plosser feel, still does not preclude a kind of empirical 'superneutrality' in that there is no effect on real general equilibrium.[13] These results hold for an unregulated banking system, in general, but when there are regulations (for example, reserve requirements), then the central bank can determine the price level in the market for high-powered money (currency plus bank reserves) and not in the market for currency; thus, both neutrality and superneutrality go through. In any event this model (and Lucas's (1975)) has the implication that a rise in real activity produces a fall in the inflation rate. Not all observers find this an appealing property although it is always possible to impose a policy behaviour on the authorities in order to restore the traditional positive correlation.

3.5 RATIONAL EXPECTATIONS AND FISCAL POLICY

Up to this point we have concentrated our discussion of rational expectations on the role of monetary policy as a device for controlling the levels of output and/or employment and, of course, for controlling the rate of inflation. As we will discuss further in Chapter 5, fiscal policy is not necessarily a parallel case, and various authors have set up frameworks in which it has short-run and sometimes even long-run effects. This is generally most obvious when expectations are not rational, but, actually, there is a potential influence from fiscal policy even under rational expectations. It will be the task of this section to add fiscal policy to the basic discussion of policy effectiveness featured in this chapter.

Begg (1982) considers fiscal policy in a model that we have already used. Thus, let the labour force be held constant so that the goods-supply curve is

$$y_t = \alpha_0 + \alpha_1 k_t \qquad \alpha_1 > 0 \tag{3.57}$$

where k_t is the log of the capital stock (measured at the beginning of the period), and y_t is the log of real income. If there is a proportional consumption function of $c_t = \beta y_t$, with no role defined for the interest rate, then aggregate demand would be $(y_t = c_t + I_t)$

$$y_t = \beta y_t + (k_{t+1} - k_t) \tag{3.58}$$

From this formulation the *IS* equation (using 3.57) would be

$$k_{t+1} = \alpha_0(1-\beta) + [\alpha_1(1-\beta)+1]k_t \tag{3.59}$$

which is a first-order difference equation in the capital stock; it describes the time path of the log of the capital stock. Notice that since there is no interest rate in the consumption function (and none in the demand for money) the role of the real-interest rate here is, implicitly, to equate the supply and demand for investment.

Let us, then, compare fiscal and monetary policy in this framework. Suppose, then, that we have a *monetary policy* (we could add a money-demand curve and a rule for monetary policy to effect this). In this case, since the time path of the capital stock is completely determined by Equation 3.59, and Equation 3.58 – given 3.59 – completely determines real national output (with the interest rate bringing aggregate demand in 3.58 into line with aggregate supply), monetary policy is ineffective in both the short and the long run. This, indeed, is the Sargent and Wallace (1975) model – and their result – that we considered above. Now suppose that we have *fiscal policy* in the form of changes in (the log of) government expenditures. In this case the *IS* curve must be amended to

$$\alpha_0 + \alpha_2 k_t = \beta(\alpha_0 + \alpha_2 k_t) + (k_{t+1} - k_t) + \Phi k_t + g_t \qquad (3.60)$$

The results depend on whether or not policy is anticipated and differ in the short and long run. At time period t an unanticipated fiscal policy (a sudden jump in g_t) will alter total spending but not the capital stock. Thus, Equation 3.57 will hold and fiscal policy is powerless to affect y in the short run. It will, however, affect the composition of aggregate demand toward a reduction of private investment by means of the crowding-out effect. In the long run, though (Begg, 1982, p. 146), 'The shift in fiscal policy will affect future capital stocks and, in general, future values of all real variables.' On the other hand, if fiscal policy is correctly anticipated, in this model it will have neither a short-run nor a long-run effect.

A parallel topic is, naturally, an unexpected change in income-tax rates. A paper by R. E. Hall (1978) considers this policy in a rational expectations context. Hall's model is quite specific (using a Cobb–Douglas production function) because he is interested in obtaining empirical results; we may, however, paraphrase his results as follows. Assuming that the *modus operandus* is an unexpected income-tax cut, then the immediate response is for consumers to re-evaluate their permanent income. If consumers expect a cut in future government expenditures, such that the resources will be available for present and future consumption, then they will increase their current consumption outlays.[14] If there is no consumption effect then there will be no effect of fiscal policy; therefore, in order to justify continuing, we should assert such an effect here. Assuming that economic agents have entered into binding contracts covering the short and medium run, then aggregate supply will not be perfectly price level inelastic. Hall (1978, p. S73) says,

As time passes after the tax cut, more and more contracts are renegotiated, and the demand shift is gradually offset by shifts of the labor supply schedule. When the process reaches its conclusion, the expansion has no lasting real effect within the labor market – it is translated entirely into increases in the nominal wage.

This period of effect, Hall feels, could be as much as five years, and it is over that length of time that fiscal and monetary policy would have real effects.

The actual size (and direction) of the effect in Hall's model depends on the extent of crowding out and on the interest elasticity of the investment demand function. This is not surprising, of course. As Hall puts it (p. S73)

If money demand is highly interest elastic, real output rises by more than the increase in consumption because of an induced increase in investment. . . . If money demand is totally unresponsive to the nominal interest rate . . . at first, increased consumption is exactly offset by decreased investment, and real output remains unchanged, but in later years real output is decreased by the tax reduction because of the shortfall in the capital stock.

Hall feels that the actual results (he applied his model to actual data in a loose way) lie in a middle range where there is some effect of fiscal policy mainly resulting from alterations in the nominal, but not necessarily the real interest rate. This result affords conclusions exactly similar to those for a monetary expansion (whose effects are on nominal variables).

Another popular sort of policy is the 'investment tax credit' which some early studies have suggested can be used to influence investment directly; the studies of Hall and Jorgenson (1967, 1969) come to mind.[15] Lucas includes this work in his 'critique' paper (1976), concluding that 'The forecasting method used by Hall and Jorgenson . . . cannot be expected to yield even order-of-magnitude estimates of the effects of explicitly temporary tax adjustments.'

The forecasting method used is by the 'rational' distributed lag that has the same properties as were discussed for consumption (when we first considered the Lucas critique above). The thing to do, then, is to model the investment tax credit under rational expectations, and that is just what Kydland and Prescott (1977) do, employing a Jorgenson-style investment function along with the assumption of rational expectations on the part of business firms (who employ econometricians!). Kydland and Prescott construct examples in which policy-makers use optimal control to determine their policy, given an observed investment function (and other objectives). After a given policy is implemented, because the econometricians have estimated a new function contingent on the new policy, a new 'equilibirum' investment function is determined. This is recognised by the authorities who then re-solve their control problem with the new structure . . . – and so on. This is obviously a dynamic 'game' which will tend to show short-run policy effects and which will lean toward policy ineffectiveness (if the authorities are slow and obvious) and will lean toward policy effects as long as there are exploitable lags in the economy. In their simulations, however, for some choices of weights in the authorities' objective function, the economy tended to diverge from its desired position. That is, in those instances, even the reasonable practice outlined above could produce more rather than less instability in the objectives. As Kydland and Prescott say (p. 473), 'The reason for this apparent paradox is that economic planning is not a game against nature but, rather, a game against rational economic agents.' As such it must endogenise the reactions of economic agents, or it is likely to go seriously astray in practice.

In a second paper, Kydland and Prescott (1980) tackle the problem of the effect of fiscal shocks in an economy whose persistence comes from the fact that capital equipment takes time to put into place. To avoid a problem of 'time inconsistency' (see below), they suggest that only fiscal rules can be analysed in this context. The system they build is subject to technological shocks and the authorities' attempt to set things right with counteracting fiscal 'shocks' – by operating stabilising rules. Under the assumption of rational expectations, Kydland and Prescott show that (p. 169) 'tax rates should remain constant or nearly constant over the cycle with the budget being balanced on average. This does not minimize fluctuations but does minimize the deadweight burden of financing government expenditures.' This exceeds the benefits, even, of cyclical stabilising via fiscal policy (in their model). Their reasoning with respect to the cycle is somewhat similar to that of Long and Plosser (see above) and is cast in terms of a dynamic version of a Pareto-optimal world with no informational discrepancies. Indeed, they explicitly do not justify their rule the way Friedman does his, even though they agree that sometimes fiscal policy will smooth and sometimes will exaggerate the cycle. Friedman's rationale for a rule, it may be recalled, was stated in terms of the lack of information, poorly fitting models, and long and variable lags, none of which (lags aside), Kydland and Prescott rely on. This is, to repeat, a justification of a fiscal rule in terms of a 'principle of effective taxation'.

Kydland and Prescott's earlier work on the investment tax credit (a form of 'capital taxation') is actually embedded in a paper concerned with what has become a major theoretical topic. This is the 'time inconsistency' problem first identified by Strotz (1956); there is also a second paper by Kydland and Prescott (1980) on this topic. The problem is that when a government levies a tax (or grants a credit) that is currently 'optimal', it may create an environment that future, even similar, governments will dishonour. The policy could be one of a high tax (low credit) on *current* capital – that is designed to take advantage of the fact that in-place capital cannot be reduced by current taxation (so that the tax is neutral in its impact on capital formation) – coupled with the promise of a *future* cut in such taxes so that plans for important capital expansion are not reduced. The trouble is that future governments will also have the same incentive – and so would cancel the legislation requiring them to ease the tax burden – and impose a tax of their own on the then currently in place capital stock. The result would be a suboptimal pattern of capital growth over time, in so far as (cynical) economic agents could foresee that future governments would surrender to their successive temptations. Incidentally, an inflationary tax on private bond and money holding is subject to the same considerations.

To see suboptimality more clearly, let us consider the simple example of Kydland and Prescott (1977). Suppose that the social utility function is

$$U(x_1, x_2, \delta_1, \delta_2) \tag{3.61}$$

where x_1 and x_2 are private economic agent's 'policies' in periods 1 and 2 and δ_1 and δ_2 are the government's tax policies for the same two periods. There is no structure here, to avoid confusing the issue, and the instruments are entered directly into the social utility function (which we assume is defined over the two sets of instruments). Let the government pick δ_2 so as to maximise (3.61) subject to private agents' past reaction to the whole announced tax policy in period 1:

$$x_1 = f(\delta_1, \delta_2) \tag{3.62}$$

and in period 2

$$x_2 = g(x_1, \delta_1, \delta_2) \tag{3.63}$$

A consistent policy, then, would be a value of the tax policy δ_2 that maximises 3.61 subject to 3.62 and 3.63.

If the authorities ignore the effects of δ_2 on x_1, then the consistent policy can be defined in terms of the necessary condition that

$$\frac{\partial u}{\partial x_2}\frac{\partial g}{\partial \delta_2} + \frac{\partial u}{\partial \delta_2} = 0 \tag{3.64}$$

δ_2 is, to achieve consistency, set to account for private sector reactions in period 2 but not in period 1. The effect of the first term in 3.64 is akin to the promise to lower taxes later so that private sector investment plans (x_2) are not adversely affected. But the consistent policy is not optimal in view of the fact that when period 2 arrives, the government has the temptation to ignore its previous promise. The optimal policy actually has a first-order condition of

$$\frac{\partial u}{\partial x_2}\frac{\partial g}{\partial \delta_2} + \frac{\partial u}{\partial \delta_2} + \frac{\partial f}{\partial \delta_2}\left[\frac{\partial u}{\partial x_1} + \frac{\partial u}{\partial x_2}\frac{\partial g}{\partial x_1}\right] = 0 \tag{3.65}$$

which is the necessary condition for the full system 3.61 to 3.63, with the new term reflecting the complications produced by the consideration of private reactions to the two taxes proposed in Equation 3.62. Thus, clearly, consistency and optimality will occur simultaneously if either $\partial f/\partial \delta_2 = 0$ or if the term in square brackets is zero. The first case just asserts that current private sector plans are unaffected by whatever tax plan the government announces in the future so, in effect, the government can do whatever it wishes. This consideration makes it look as if 'time inconsistency' is the general case. The reader will note that in this material we are providing a variation on the theme of the 'Lucas critique' as this was described above. The implication is that a policy that is a commitment, whereby future governments are tied to a rule (or a constitutional amendment), will be optimal and time-consistent as long as agents have any knowledge about how the government operates. Indeed, say Kydland and Prescott (1977, p. 473), 'there is *no* way control theory can be made applicable to economic planning when expectations are rational'. This discussion is continued in Subsection 4.4.1, with reference to monetary policy, and not just fiscal policy.

4 Rational Expectations II: Extensions and Empirical Tests

> There are 500 crazy people down there [in Washington] with
> worries about getting reelected; they don't know what they want,
> they don't know what will work or how it will work. God knows
> what they will do.   attributed to R. SOLOW in KLAMER, 1983

4.1 INTRODUCTION

We have two broad tasks in this chapter; these are (a) to go over the
empirical record concerning the effectiveness of monetary and fiscal
policy and (b) to consider some of the recent extensions and criticisms of
the basic rational expectations results of Chapter 3, in so far as they
directly involve macroeconomic policy. The empirical debate is dominated by Barro's early results (1977a, 1978), which establish neutrality
empirically on the US data, but in recent years there has been a tendency
to use other methods and to find in favour of the non-neutrality of
money (i.e. to find 'policy effectiveness') especially in the short run.
Among the recent work that runs against neutrality, we will look at
empirical material that we could describe as in the Keynesian-rational
tradition. Blanchard, Blinder, Fischer, Taylor and many others have
established this promising line of research which seems to lead to an
activist solution of the questions about how macropolicy might work
and what effects actual past episodes of policy might have had. In this
discussion we will also be looking at problems of 'observational
equivalence' – that is, problems of identification; in addition, we will in
later sections extend the 'policy effectiveness' search to financial markets.
This chapter will also consider theoretical work on sequential (rather
than once-for-all) policy choice and on 'credibility'. In some of these
areas there are empirical tests to go over, although not all of these topics
have an empirical counterpart. It should be noted here, though, that
most of the material in this chapter – whether empirical or theoretical – is
in the process of being developed and so what is reported here is more in
the nature of a selective progress report than a complete survey.

105

At this point, before considering actual policies, we will stop and consider just what the government might hope to achieve with an active monetary policy, assuming rational expectations. Taking the policy to be, for example, an inflationary one, the authorities may expect to create benefits for the private sector and/or the government (that is, the 'public' sector). More inflation, of course, will have private losses associated with it, but there will also be benefits, mostly related to the possibility that lower unemployment would be likely to follow a bout of inflation (that is policy-induced). A case in which this is obvious occurs when the natural rate of unemployment is, itself, perceived to be too high – perhaps on account of suspected distortions in the private sector – so that benefits would accrue to the private sector from what is, in effect, an offsetting (and often temporary) policy-induced 'distortion' that drives the actual rate below the ('unnatural') natural rate (Kydland and Prescott, 1977). The original distortions relevant here include the tax system (e.g. double taxation of corporate profits) and such programmes as unemployment compensation, welfare, and the like, which reduce the incentive to work or to produce. Private sector distortions – e.g. monopoly and monopsony – are also relevant.

In addition to the possible benefits just described, the government can also 'profit' from macropolicy at least when the economy is being stimulated by a monetary expansion. This is the case of 'inflationary finance' which arises from the existence of government liabilities – money and bonds – which are fixed in nominal terms. The bonds are the main item here, and (Barro and D. B. Gordon, 1983a, p. 103) 'Surprise inflation, $\pi_t - \pi_t^e$, depreciates part of the real value of these bonds, which lowers the government's future real expenditures for interest and repayment of principal. In effect, surprise inflation is . . . a source of revenue to the government'. Furthermore, as long as this 'tax' is unexpected it will not affect private incentives, at least in the first instance (before private agents using rational expectations extract usable information from the policy action). The government is more likely to engage in this kind of activity when the private sector is thought to be in trouble (whatever the cause) and when the government badly needs revenues (as in wartime). Thus, some relation in the actual data – e.g. between government deficits and inflation – might be expected although the evidence for this is just not that strong, and certain theoretical results, too, are not particularly encouraging for this hypothesis as we shall see below.

In the foregoing, both economic agents and the government have what seem to be 'correct' and equal perceptions of how the economic system works. Taken literally, this is ridiculous, and so it is interesting to look further into what would be a more reasonable position to take and to see how sensitive the results are to an alteration of this assumption. Part of the objection is simply that it is not a reasonable scenario – and nobody believes it – to describe policy as a policy rule plus a random term as we have generally done in Chapter 3. Indeed, the public may well take the view that the government is just not competent and structure their plans accordingly. The public, that is to say, may well form its expectations rationally, but it certainly may not be rational to expect much consistency from the policy-makers. This is all the more likely in the event that the authorities follow neither passive rules (a constant monetary growth rate) nor active feedback policies, but operate policy in such a way that it impresses the public as basically being incoherent. Such 'policies', loosely, tend to be operated until they cease to produce any 'results' and then are 'shifted'. But (Sheffrin, 1983, p. 16) even so

> Sargent and Wallace (1976) argue that it is difficult to even talk about shifts in the conduct of policy. If individuals can assign probabilities to potential policies, then any actual policy is just a realization from the probability distribution over policies. The actual policy chosen may have had a low probability of occurring but should this be seen as a 'shift' in policy? The question can best be left to professional philosophers.

Then there is the question of what happens when economic agents start off on the wrong foot, with the wrong model or with erroneous data (perhaps data 'planted' by a devious government). In this all-too-likely event it would be difficult (and certainly expensive) for agents to correct their forecasting errors since their actions produce results that cannot be interpreted correctly either by them or by the government. Under these circumstances having the 'correct' model in some sense would not be much help either (B. Friedman, 1979, and DeCanio, 1979). In this case, though, recent work suggests that such a system would tend to converge to its rational expectations equilibrium, even if it starts off on the wrong foot, especially in the event that learning itself is also an economic activity guided by rational expectations, as it surely is (Feldman, 1982; Bray and Kreps, 1981). In any event, the misinformation provides some leverage for monetary and fiscal policy to have an effect in, let us say, the short run (Turnovsky, 1977c).

The authorities, too, need to be given a more intelligent role to play in any extension of the basic rational expectations model. As long as we are admitting rational expectations into one side of the game – and we can certainly think of it as an economic game – the authorities are being put at an arbitrary disadvantage which may not correspond to their operation of policy. In particular, the authorities may actually assume, in effect, that individuals have rational expectations and reset their policy variables after each episode in full realisation of the fact that the parameters of the model have changed. Indeed, the authorities can do this implicitly in the same way that we often argue the public builds its model of the economy. This possibility does away with the Lucas critique, on the whole, although a suboptimal policy may still occur as we shall see below. Furthermore, the authorities could have an effect on the real variables in the economy, under rational expectations, as long as they have some other leverage. Indeed, to go one step further, it is not unreasonable to argue that individuals have a kind of implicit contract with the government in which they do not bother to build models or construct 'contingent contracts' – such as wage-indexation schemes – but instead rely on the government to deal with aggregate disturbances at a lower cost and with greater expertise than individuals themselves can manage. As Fischer puts it (1980, p. 212):

> The case for active monetary policy is that it is more efficient for the Fed to offset aggregate disturbances than it is for the private sector to do so. The efficient division of labor between the private and public sectors leaves it to macroeconomic management to deal with aggregate disturbances.

This implies that there could well be an effect for the *anticipated* part of policy settings, as a voluntary matter. However, it is certainly clear that private agents can cheat on this implicit contract, and as they do so (and they certainly have the incentive) policy ineffectiveness again becomes an issue.

4.2 THE BASIC EMPIRICAL TESTS OF THE RATIONAL HYPOTHESIS

Our first empirical concern is, of course, over how well the basic rational-expectations model does in direct empirical tests. There have actually been a large number of empirical tests of the rational-expectations hypothesis in what is a very rapidly growing literature. In this section (and the next) our primary interest is in direct tests that were produced in the context of policy itself – let us say with an explicit money supply or tax rule – and not in the many varieties of tests which concern themselves with expectations formation or with the testing of the theory itself (say, by imposing and testing the restrictions inherent in the theory).[1] To some extent the issue at hand involves the type of policy rule that the authorities should adopt under rational expectations. As described in Chapter 1, M. Friedman (1959a), for example, has favoured the adoption of a non-feedback-type policy rule (e.g. 4 per cent growth in the money stock per year); earlier we pointed out that this produces a policy that could be inferior to the feedback-style policy rule to the extent that the effect of endogenous business cycles could also be counteracted successfully.

The question we are now raising concerns whether *anticipated* money is neutral in its effects in the short run (and, of course, in the long run). On the one hand, we have had no real problem showing how *un*anticipated money changes create effects that can be exploited. On the other hand, there is the implication that unless anticipated money growth (or anticipated inflation) also affects real variables, the resulting policy is, at least as Barro and D. B. Gordon discuss it (1983a, 1983b), a somewhat unsavoury affair, involving the maintenance and exploitation of the stock of credibility of the policy-makers when it is not simply based on the ignorance of economic agents and/or on inefficient institutional arrangements. But inflation surely has real effects and so it is just as well to look at *Fischer's Catalogue* of anticipated inflation effects before considering the empirical record, such as it is.

Dealing first with non-institutional factors, Fischer (1980) argues that there are *wealth effects*, arising because, in effect, there are forms of money that do not pay interest (and so they simply deteriorate at the rate of inflation). With this weapon the government could employ monetary policy to alter the distribution of wealth (for whatever reason). This, in turn, would affect saving (and thus capital formation), and labour *supply* would be directly affected (in a dynamic consumption-leisure frame-work). Furthermore, if there are assets other than money and if portfolios are diversified, then the rates of return on these assets will be affected by changes in the real yield on money, and there will be a whole conglomeration of cross-wealth effects.[2] In sum (Fischer, 1980, p. 216), 'Lower real balances may imply more transactions and less resources available for production; they may also produce wealth effects that will affect spending on goods and services and labor supply . . .'. There are direct tests of wealth (and/or real balance) effects running back to the days of Pigou. Patinkin (1965) has an early survey that is updated in D. Fisher (1978) and, especially, Grice (1981). Grice concludes his survey by noting that (static) wealth effects can be demonstrated empirically and that they involve more than just liquid assets. This is not a topic to be explored explicitly in this study, but note that the wealth-effect literature is scattered around this study with perhaps the largest chunk appearing later in this chapter. Returning to Fischer, we note his feeling is that here the issues are more theoretical than empirical, especially since the arrival of more competitive interest payments on the various forms of money.

Fischer's second group of anticipated inflation effects are essentially institutional and thus can be expected to vary from situation to situation; they are also potentially of greater magnitude, he argues. We have already mentioned the fact that the 'inflation tax' is often part of the structure of taxes and can be expected to have real effects, depending on the nature of the tax structure. The effects, generally, arise because taxes themselves affect incentives at the margin. For example, when inflation occurs individuals are pushed into higher tax brackets (in a progressive structure); for another example, to the extent that private sector accounting systems use historical costs for purposes of calculating depreciation, and hence tax deductions, there will be effects. Both of these could adversely affect capital formation (as noted by Feldstein and Summers, 1978). In addition, there are interest ceilings on many types of loans which can easily be responsible for real effects – and are by some accounts the major reason that monetary policy affects the economy – in so far as interest rates are unable to clear these markets. So-called 'credit rationing' is often mentioned in this context. In particular, increased anticipated inflation that takes the equilibrium nominal interest rate past the ceiling rate could tend to be associated with what is sometimes called a 'credit crunch' in the housing market. But while we may suspect that these factors have been important in the past, the evidence here is not very strong – generally lacking causal testing, for one thing – and recent deregulation and the like have made this response to anticipated inflation less likely, somehow, although the debate goes on.

4.2.1 Barro's Tests

The first standard direct tests in this literature are those by Barro (1977a, 1978). In the first of these papers Barro uses a two-stage procedure. First, he proposes to find out what the systematic proximate causes of changes in the money stock are and then, assuming that the systematic part is 'knowable' on the part of economic agents, to assess whether the *prediction* (the anticipated part) or the *residual* (the unanticipated part) of the money stock change affects real economic variables.

$$\Delta M_A = f(\Delta M_{t-1}, \Delta M_{t-2}, F_t, U_{t-1}) \tag{4.1}$$

In this paper, with US data from 1941 to 1973, the predicted change in the money stock is assumed to be dependent on current federal fiscal policy (F_t) relative to its normal level, lagged unemployment and several lagged money-growth terms. In this form it is basically a policy reaction function (see Chapter 1). Note that the 'normal' fiscal variable is, somewhat inconsistently, measured by an adaptive expectations format and is dated at time t. When the second stage is tested, using the employment rate as the real (dependent) variable, the unanticipated part is successful.[3] This unanticipated part is the residual from the first-stage equation. When the total change in M is added to the regression, the result worsens, at least as judged by the usual statistical tests. These results accord well with the results of the strong form of the rational expectations theory we have been discussing in this study. In the second paper (1978) referred to above, Barro adds the rate of growth of real output to the list of dependent variables and extends the model to consider the inflation rate; the data in this case run to 1977. In this attempt both prices and output are shown to respond to unanticipated money growth, but the primary response of prices is to the anticipated changes in the money stock (again as the natural-rate/RE model predicts). Tests on the data of other countries – using the same methodology – have often shown results similar to Barro's (in favour of neutrality),[4] although there are many dissenters on all sorts of data sets.

The Barro model may seem pretty simplistic and the econometrics pretty naïve, on the whole, and it is readily attacked in these terms, although it has been hard to generate firm empirical contradictions, in practice. For example, Germany (1978) argues that Barro's working assumption that expectations are known exactly is an unreasonable one. Further, Fischer (1980) argues that Barro's assumption that the authorities only operate with a one-period information advantage is too restrictive in the current environment (where meaningful data revisions come long after the original series is published). Then, too, there is a potential problem of 'reverse causation' in the model that is not dealt with. That is, there needs to be causal testing of the direction of influence assumed in Barro's study (from M to P, y and U) because even an apparent lead of money over the other variables does not establish that money causes them. Indeed, while Barro finds a *stable* money supply process, Fischer (1980, p. 221) argues that this is implausible because it is measured 'over a period during which the Fed moved from a policy of supporting interest rates to one in which it claims to pay attention to monetary targets'. These are doubts rather than the results of tests, though, and so is Fischer's concern with Barro's omission of interest rates in his tests. We will have more to say about the causality issue later in this chapter and, especially, in Chapter 6 where some formal definitions are attempted.

There have been, of course, a considerable number of direct empirical challenges to Barro. Small (1979), for example, reworks the basic US test on the grounds that some of what Barro regards as unanticipated money may, in fact, have been anticipated. He introduces an additional federal fiscal variable in this context (because Barro's measure left 'predictable' elements in the errors, especially during periods of war finance) and, especially, criticises Barro's set-up of the determinants of the unemployment variable. He claims support for the 'anticipated-money' hypothesis in his reworking of the data. Barro (1979d), acknowledging that his own analysis of the *real* determinants of unemployment is flawed, still rejects Small's result on the effectiveness of anticipated money, after rerunning the tests. The dating of the fiscal variable (F_t) is also questioned by Pesaran (1982), who compares Barro's model to a Keynesian alternative. The problem with the fiscal variable is that it is dated at the same time as the dependent variable and could not be known to agents at that time. Barro argues that it was well-enough publicised in advance, but Pesaran substitutes a *predicted* fiscal policy variable for the actual one. While this adjustment does not seem to make much difference, the Keynesian alternative which Pesaran uses appears to outperform the Barro model. Recall that Barro does not attempt any comparisons of this sort. Finally, Sheehan, in a recent paper (1985b), argues that it is wrong to use the entire data set in a regression (as Barro and so many others do) rather than to generate expected variables as they become known to economic agents at the time they do their forecasting. That is, Sheehan, in effect, argues that most such studies use revised data when the revisions apparently add a significant amount to economic agents' information sets. In his experiment on US data Sheehan finds short-run unanticipated and anticipated (non-neutral) effects.

These simple tests are not very powerful, however, because of a basic problem of 'observational equivalence' that confuses the issue considerably. That is (Sargent, 1976a, p. 631),

there are always alternative ways of writing the reduced form, one being observationally equivalent with the other, so that each is equally valid in the estimation period. . . . Therefore, estimates of reduced forms alone will not permit one to settle the difference between Friedman and advocates of rules with feedback. Given any set of reduced-form estimates, there is an invariance assumption that will permit a member of either camp to make his point.

Barro's tests are not immune to this objection, as we will demonstrate, and this rules out the most obvious direct tests.

In order to see the observational equivalence problem more clearly, consider the following simple demonstration (Minford and Peel, 1983). Assume that the *true* reduced-form equations for an economy are the Lucas supply function

$$y_t = \alpha(m_t - Em_t) + \lambda y_{t-1} + u_t \tag{4.2}$$

and a monetary policy reaction function with a systematic component (τ) and a random component (e_t).

$$m_t = \tau m_{t-1} + e_t \tag{4.3}$$

This is approximately how Barro sets up the problem. Barro, then, tests Equation 4.2 directly, putting in prediction errors in the form $m_t - Em_t$, finding that they affect y_t. Barro's test is a logical one, of course, but we can organise our test a little differently by taking expectations of Equation 4.3, as economic agents would do, and then substituting the result into 4.2. The result is the reduced-form equation 4.4.

$$y_t = \alpha m_t - \alpha\tau m_{t-1} + \lambda y_{t-1} + \varepsilon_t \tag{4.4}$$

This equation seems to show that actual *and known* changes in m_t and m_{t-1} affect y_t when, by Equation 4.1, only *unanticipated* changes in m are supposed to do so. Thus 4.3 is an implication of 4.1 and 4.2 – a rational-expectations model. It is also, potentially, a Keynesian – let us say 'habit-persistence' – model. Thus, successful tests that include m and lagged m will not refute either theory and will not discriminate between the rational and the non-rational hypotheses. In summary, Sargent notes, there is generally a way to write the rational model, adhering to its underlying conditions, so as to obtain a reduced form consistent with the rival (non-rational) hypothesis; a further elaboration of the econometric issues involved appears in a paper by Buiter (1983).

4.2.2 Other Tests of The Basic Hypothesis

Partly in response to these and other doubts, Barro and Rush (1980) extend the basic model and employ a cross-equation estimation procedure. They also work on a quarterly data in addition to the annual data used in Barro's two earlier studies. In this case the lags are short (one to two *quarters*), and the anticipated part of money stock changes still has no effect. Another version of this test is that of Attfield, Demery and Duck (1981a) as explained in their later survey (1985). The problem these studies address is that in the simultaneous equations framework the same parameter appears more than once in the model; to be estimated efficiently, such values should be restricted to be equal, or we face 'over-identified' coefficients. Suppose, just to simplify, that the first stage is

$$DM_t = \alpha_1 DM_{t-1} + \alpha_2 F_t + DM_{Rt} \qquad (4.5)$$

while the second stage is

$$y_t = \beta_1 DM_{Rt} + \beta_2 DM_{Rt-1} + v_t \qquad (4.6)$$

We may calculate DM_{Rt}, DM_{Rt-1} using 4.5 and substitute these expressions into 4.6, in which case we obtain

$$y_t = \beta_1 DM_t - [\beta_1 \alpha_1 - \beta_2] DM_{t-1} - \beta_2 \alpha_1 DM_{t-2}$$
$$- \beta_1 \alpha_2 F_t - \beta_2 \alpha_2 F_{t-1} + v_t \qquad (4.7)$$

There are, then, four distinct parameters, $(\alpha_1, \alpha_2, \beta_1, \beta_2)$ but five coefficients to be estimated (call them π_i) for the right-hand variables in the reduced form in Equation 4.7. We can successfully obtain estimates of β_1, β_2, and α_1 from the first three terms, but once we have calculated β_1, and β_2, the other two terms (π_4, π_5) give us two, potentially inconsistent, estimates of α_2. In short, there is an identification problem which can be resolved by imposing the implied restriction (in this case that the estimate of α_2 from π_4 is equal to that obtained from π_5, given β_1 and β_2) in effect estimating the system simultaneously. Attfield, Demery and Duck (1981a) do this on annual UK data and confirm the Barro hypothesis. In an extension to quarterly UK data (1981b) they continue to confirm the Barro result. We should note that when Attfield and Duck apply this model to a set of eleven countries (1983), the results are not as strong and include a test of the Lucas variance hypothesis (that increased variance reduces the effectiveness of policy). There are underdeveloped countries (e.g. El Salvador and Argentina) in this set.[5]

There is a related problem with the Barro test, which was first dealt with in this context by Leiderman (1980). As already noted, tests of expectations models are inevitably joint hypotheses of a structural relation (e.g. economic agents smooth their consumption over time) and an expectations hypothesis (e.g. rational expectations). When all goes well, as Barro's tests seem to suggest for the United States, both hypotheses are supported, but when there are recorded failures, then we are inevitably interested in which component of the hypothesis fails to hold up. In the case of Barro's work the joint hypothesis tested involves both 'monetary neutrality' and 'rational expectations'. It is, then, of interest to specify a framework for separating the two elements if only because we are especially attracted to the general idea of expectational rationality (because it extends standard consumer theory in a reasonable direction) while monetary neutrality can fail for a variety of institutional and other reasons which both neoKeynesians and neomonetarists might be willing to accept.

What Leiderman points out is that neutrality, which has a very specific implication in Barro's test, provides one with a testable restriction across equations; we follow the discussion of this in Attfield, Demery and Duck (1985). Beginning with a simplified unemployment equation, neutrality implies that

$$U_t = \beta_1 (DM_t - DM_t^e) + v_{1t} \tag{4.8}$$

The coefficients on DM_t and DM_t^e are equal and of opposite sign $(\beta_1, -\beta_1)$. If, instead, they are different, we do not have neutrality (that is, we have real effects). This we can write as

$$U_t = \beta_{11} DM_t - \beta_{12} DM_t^e + v_t \tag{4.9}$$

but in this case we can still assume rational expectations. That is, assume that the expected change in the money stock is based on all available information, as in

$$DM_t^e = \alpha_1 DM_{t-1} + \alpha_2 DM_{t-2} + \alpha_3 F_t \tag{4.10}$$

and that actual changes in the money stock are merely those anticipated plus a random term

$$DM_t = DM_t^e + DM_{Rt} \tag{4.11}$$

This is a simplified Barro model.

We may combine Equations 4.9, 4.10 and 4.11 to form a test for rational expectations *without* neutrality; the result is separate equations for DM_t and U_t as in

$$DM_t = \alpha_1 DM_{t-1} + \alpha_2 DM_{t-2} + \alpha_3 F_t + DM_{Rt} \tag{4.12}$$

$$U_t = (\beta_{11} - \beta_{12})(\alpha_1 DM_{t-1} + \alpha_2 DM_{t-2} + \alpha_3 F_t) + \beta_{11} DM_{Rt} + v_t \tag{4.13}$$

Ignoring the error term $(\beta_{11} DM_{Rt} + v_t)$ in the second equation, we see that there are six variables and only five coefficients in this sytem $(\alpha_1, \alpha_2, \alpha_3, \beta_{11}, \beta_{12})$. If this were directly estimated (as a reduced form) there would be six coefficients (π_i). These equations can be estimated, though, without neutrality, in effect, by imposing a restriction on the reduced form, using an appropriate estimation technique. This is a test of rational expectations only. To test for neutrality in addition to that we compare results with and without $\beta_{11} = \beta_{12}$ (a likelihood-ratio test). Leiderman argues that both parts of the hypothesis succeed on the US data. A paper by Driscoll *et al.* (1983) points out that Leiderman's neutrality test is nested within his rationality test so that if the former fails the latter will too, without implying that neutrality itself has failed. Because both succeed, this does not matter to Leiderman, but on British data Driscoll *et al.* find a rejection of the rationality restrictions and thus a rejection of the rational expectations-neutrality package. The authors candidly point out that all of these sorts of test are very model specific.

A cross-equation procedure motivated by Leiderman's test is also used by Mishkin (1982a), who argues that identification of the money forecasting equation is achieved – and Sargent's (1976b) observational equivalence problem avoided – if the set of arguments in the forecasting equation includes the lagged values of at least one other variable besides money growth, which itself does not enter independently of the forecasting error. This provides a cross-equation restriction. For short lags the joint hypothesis of 'rational expectations' and 'monetary policy neutrality' are accepted, but with long lags (twenty quarters) it is decisively rejected. With regard to these results Mishkin argues that (p. 33), 'it appears that the shorter lag models are more favorable to the MRE hypothesis only because misspecification yields incorrect test statistics'. Indeed, both sets of restrictions – those associated with rationality and those associated with neutrality – are part of this rejection. But the point just raised is not exactly logical since failure of rationality implies that neutrality will not hold (it actually implies that the model is inapplicable) as explained above and by Attfield, Demery and Duck (1985). In an extension of these results Mishkin (1982b) considers aggregate *nominal* demand shocks and inflation shocks as alternatives to the monetary shocks. For the former (p. 795), 'the data do not reject the rationality of expectations. The culprit behind the joint hypothesis rejections is the neutrality proposition. These neutrality rejections are exceedingly strong. . . . .' When inflation is the agent of surprise, rationality again fares well, compared to neutrality; in addition, the Lucas supply function used in this test does not itself appear to perform well.

Strong rejection is also obtained in a study by Boschen (1985), who returns us to the question of data revisions raised (above) in a paper by Sheehan (1985b). Boschen argues, in a test he claims is not subject to observational equivalence, that on US data non-neutralities are roughly equivalent for observed and unobserved (that is, revised) money growth. On British data Alogoskoufis and Pissarides (1982) also reject neutrality in a model that attempts to estimate price 'sluggishness' as compared to market-clearing. The test involves identifying these competing adjustment mechanisms, and the result actually favours the dominance of price sluggishness. Price sluggishness carries with it the implication of short-run non-neutrality. In a recent paper, to continue with the parade of evidence, a vector auto-regression model dealing with observational equivalence and non-stationarity (see Nelson and Plosser, 1982) is proposed and tested on US data by McGee and Stasiak (1985). They, too, find short-run non-neutrality for anticipated money, although in the long run monetary neutrality is upheld. In sum, the results of recent retests of the basic Barro model – at least when neutrality restrictions are also tested – seem to run pretty much against the neutrality proposition in the short run. This is believable, although this work has hardly begun.

There are, to be sure, other direct tests available. If one can locate points at which policy changes dramatically (and, presumably, as a surprise to the public), then inspection of the standard macro models should show some effect of the surprising changes in the policy regime. This was the case, apparently, for US data in 1929 and 1964, as discussed by Neftci and Sargent (1978). Another way to proceed is to see if there are readily obtainable data sets that actually do seem to affect real variables, when they should not (and do not affect real variables, when they should). A good example is provided by Boschen and H. I. Grossman (1980), who look at the first preliminary announcement of a money-stock change (on postwar US data) and find that it does affect *contemporaneous* aggregate output. It should not, since it is readily available data. On the other hand, revisions in this series, which could be thought of as unexpected and hence effective, actually do not produce any effect on aggregate output on the same data set. (Below, however, we will look at results which suggest that such revisions actually may have had some effect on certain financial variables; see also Barro and Hercowitz (1980).)

4.3   THE EFFECT OF MONETARY POLICY ON THE FINANCIAL MARKETS

Another type of empirical test that might be conducted is to look at financial markets to see if (apparently) unexpected shocks are at work there. The obvious place to do this research, and practically the only candidate so far, is in the capital (bond and equity) markets. In the case of bond markets there is a considerable literature that goes back, if one wants to push that far, to the neoclassical concern with the effect of monetary expansion on interest rates (e.g. to Wicksell or I. Fisher) as described in Chapter 2. From Keynes until 'efficient markets' theory, the macroeconomic literature on bond-market effects concentrates on the direct effect on interest rates, and the list of effects emphasises the value of the slopes of the demand for money and the investment-demand function. Bond markets are always in these models, but the use of Walras's Law or a private sector budget constraint (with individuals dividing their wealth between a conglomerate saving asset and a representative money) makes it possible to analyse the system with just goods and a money market. Indeed, this is the way Chapters 1 and 2 above are organised and the policy effects shown there are typical of what is found in the literature.[6]

There are, of course, numerous studies of the effect of 'tight' money – and occasionally 'easy' money – on practically every conceivable financial market,[7] and while this material is an important part of the macroeconomist's tradition it does not seem uncharitable to say that much of this material has been rendered irrelevant by improvements of an econometric and theoretical nature. Rational expectations has only a part in this story, but in this chapter it is the whole story. In Chapter 7, in any case, we will flesh out the capital markets material a little more and refer to a more traditional literature on the use of intermediate variables as potential targets and indicators of monetary policy.

With regard to equity markets the scope of the older literature is equally broad although here we find an early awareness of the possibility that the equity market is efficient (and investors rational). After Keynes, for a time, it was often argued that monetary policy had little effect, since equities operate as a hedge against price-level movements (i.e. corporate earnings and therefore corporate equity prices would be expected to keep up with changes in the price level, at least on average). But two events in the 1970s really set the academic paper mills churning.

(a) Equities have, in general, performed relatively poorly among the broad sets of financial assets (as, indeed, have corporate profits).
(b) Savings have appeared to increase sharply after any large (apparently unexpected) bouts of inflation.

To explain (b), that is assuming that our measures of savings are at all reasonable, a popular explanation is that of the 'restocking' of the financial portfolio, as if consumers have a target real wealth (see Howard, 1978, and Carlino, 1982). A second explanation is that additional savings have been required because of increased financial uncertainty (see Juster and L. D. Taylor, 1975, Deaton, 1977, and Howard, 1978); this effect is exacerbated by the increasing variances in practically everything financial following the shifts in the style of monetary policy and the deregulation and general financial innovation across Western economies. With regard to point (a) – the effect on equity prices – it seems that the empirical finding that inflation reduces equity prices is not in doubt (although causal testing has not been frequent). The explanations cover the gamut from 'inflation accounting' – that inflation leads to understated costs and overstated profits (and hence to overdistributed dividends and bonus payments) – to the increased generalised uncertainty that adds variation to stock prices and, in an efficient market, suggests that equity prices will be lower under these conditions (Friend and Hasbrouck, 1982). We will dig a little further into this empirical literature in Subsection 4.3.2, but mostly we will be interested in tying this material firmly to the macroeconomic 'policy-ineffectiveness' debate in the subsections that follow.

4.3.1 Monetary Policy Effects on Bond Markets

In this subsection we will consider bond-markets effects, a topic we will interpret to mean that we will be looking at the effects of policy on interest rates. When we look to interest-rate effects we must begin by considering whether the unanticipated effect proposed is

(a) a *nominal* interest-rate response to a money-stock announcement that is the result of agents revising their prediction of inflation, for example, upward, or

(b) a response that is in *real* rates because agents expect the authorities to, for example, tighten up soon (producing an effect on employment and output).

Let us start with the brief literature on (b) before discussing (a).

With respect to the control of the real rate of interest, we can return to a topic introduced in Subsection 2.3.1 with the discussion of the distinction between nominal and real interest rates. The question is raised in an empirical context by Fama (1975), who argues that r^e is actually constant in the United States (since the Second World War). In subsequent studies, though (Nelson and Schwert, 1977; Garbade and Wachtel, 1978; Fama and Gibbons, 1980; and Hafer and Hein, 1982), this is not confirmed, although 'relatively constant' would not do too badly to describe the post-war behaviour of the real rate. In a recent discussion of this literature Shiller (1980) suggests that the relative constancy of the real rate since the war may be the result of deliberate Federal Reserve action (especially since the Accord of 1951) which boils down to r^e control, whether or not the authorities used r^e as a target variable. In particular, Shiller argues that the authorities can influence the real rate and that there is some indirect evidence they have, since a strong seasonal in the real rate disappears after 1951 (and appears in the money stock at the same time). It should be pointed out that after the founding of the Federal Reserve in 1914 a strong seasonal in *nominal* interest rates disappeared (Miron, 1985). This definitely was a deliberate policy decision taken at that time as part of the notion of providing an elastic currency. On the other hand, a more direct test by Hafer and Hein (1982) finds no strong evidence that monetary policy has a lasting effect on US real interest rates in the 1955–79 period. In any event, Shiller's point might easily not hold after the 1979 shift in the style of policy although, apparently, the seasonal is still out of the nominal rate and in the money stock.

After 1979 both *ex-post* and *ex-ante* measures of the real rate of interest seem relatively high, compared with any other post-Second World War data, and this result has provoked some discussion, to say the least. There was also a sharp increase in interest-rate volatility, as noted in Chapter 2. The most obvious hypothesis about the higher real rate is that the tighter monetary (and even fiscal) policies instituted at that time by the United States and several other major countries were 'un-believable' and did not succeed in dampening inflationary expectations. Considering that these expectations are usually calculated using short moving-average processes, it is at least conceivable that a measurement error was introduced, at least for a time, in actual real rates. But the relatively high (*ex-post*) real-interest rates have continued well past 1982 in generally prosperous economies and so this point is clearly not the entire story.

A second major hypothesis is also policy-related – this is that large deficits crowd out capital markets, as we have discussed at various points in this survey. With regard to this possibility, Blanchard and Summers (1984) point out that indeed in the United States, since even before 1983, there has been a rapid 'fiscal expansion', but this is not the case across the rest of the major OECD countries, although they, too, have experienced high real rates. Putting together both monetary and fiscal policy, Blanchard and Summers suggest that the period until 1982 might have been dominated by tight money across the OECD but that since 1982 they suggest either a

(a) loose US fiscal – tight European money or a
(b) loose US fiscal – tight anticipated European money

explanation. It should be pointed out that Blanchard and Summers also find evidence in favour of a non-policy influence: a rise in anticipated profits from investment that produces a boom in investment goods (and in their finance). This last proposition neatly brings in several other facts about this period, the most important of which is the prevalence of stock-market booms that continued into the mid-1980s.

One frequently cited test of interest-rate effects is that of J. Grossman (1981), who looks at private-sector forecasts collected from money market dealers who are sampled two days *before* the money stock announcement and then again on the day of the announcement itself. Looking first to see if the forecasts and the revisions were unbiased and used all available relevant information (and hence are rational),[8] Grossman concludes that the expectations and the weekly revisions are efficient (the prediction errors are orthogonal to an arbitrary but broad set of available information) and that they provide a better forecast of the money stock than an arbitrary extrapolative autoregressive money-stock forecasting equation. With regard to the interest-rate effect of such monetary surprises Grossman suggests a direct test (assuming that the Fed has no informational advantage over the public with respect to the announcement) in which he hypothesises a *positive* effect of a monetary surprise on interest rates. While both (a) and (b) above should provide such an effect, his rationale is in terms of (b). He finds his sign expectation confirmed along with some evidence of non-linearity and asymmetry (different responses of interest rates to positive and negative surprises). He concludes that interest (p. 423) 'rates respond *only* to monetary surprises, in a way which correctly incorporates the policy rule in operations. Thus the paper lends . . . support to the rational expectations monetary models.' With a similar approach on the US data Urich and Wachtel (1981) and Urich (1982) also find a positive effect. Huberman and Schwert (1985) on Israeli data (which has an indexed bond and greater inflation variance) find that the bond market assimilates the news on price-level changes as it occurs (before the CPI is announced) with only 15 per cent of the reaction to unanticipated inflation coming after the announcement (one day after the announcement). This strongly suggests that agents (in bond markets) do a good job in collecting and acting on new price information.[9] Since indexed bonds are a direct bet on the inflation rate they make an especially good data set on which to study this question.

Other theoretical studies of this sort of effect on interest rates provide, at least, some potential warnings about the results just described. In one paper without a test, Nichols, Small and Webster (1983) point out, partly with reference to Grossman's test, that the money-stock announcement has an effect because it contains new information; as such (p. 383, my italic) 'The announcement provides the same, possibly surprising, information about the quantity of money *demanded* as it does about the quantity supplied.' That is, if the authorities hold to a money growth rule (as they may have been doing with the United States after 1979 for a time) and if the demand for money increases unexpectedly, then this tightens the money market and pushes interest rates up. This explanation (p. 383, my italic) 'is consistent with the Keynesian view that, in the short run, the way to bring down interest rates is to *expand* the money supply'. This work is extended by Small and Nichols (1984) with particular reference to the mechanics of the US 'federal funds' market, again without an empirical test attached. The demand for money is also involved in an explanation of greater interest-rate volatility after 1979. In particular, Walsh (1982a) thinks this increase may be the result of shifts in the parameters of the demand for money as those parameters are adjusted rationally to the change in the policy rule after 1979. This is work, of course, that recognises the potential of the Lucas critique; the critique, it is generally argued, applies to any structural relation except those for the underlying preferences or technology.[10]

We have mentioned changes in policy regimes as having the potential for springing surprises on economic agents, and this notion has been extended to a consideration of the 'money-stock announcement' effect both before and after the October 1979 policy-regime change in the United States. The studies referred to above (J. Grossman, 1981, Urich and Wachtel, 1981) find a positive response to money-announcement surprises just on pre-October 1979 data. In one of these tests looking at pre-and-post-1979 data, P. Evans (c. 1982) finds that the 1979 shift may have created a 'surprise' for the public, as judged by the behaviour of the bond market. Roley (1983), noting that the variances of both interest rates and announcements increased dramatically since October 1979 and that the authorities seem to have been more committed to a firm and coherent policy thereafter, suggests that a different and nonlinear model may help to control for the apparent instability of a Grossman-style test on pre- *and* post-1979 data. He concludes that (p. 353) 'the change in policy regimes has significantly affected the behavior of the three-month bill yield. . . . This change in behavior apparently reflects the market's assessment that the Federal Reserve will respond more vigorously to deviations in money when money growth is outside of the long-run range'. All of this, of course, refers to tests in which *anticipated* money-stock changes do *not* affect interest rates.

Cornell (1983) noticed that *long-term* interest rates (the above tests all use short-term rates) also show the effects of a regime change with a larger response to money-supply announcement surprises appearing on the post-1979 data; this is interpreted by Cornell in terms of (a), above, primarily as the 'inflationary expectations' effect of the surprise. Roley and Walsh (1983), on the other hand, attempt to separate (a) from (b) using a term-structure framework, concluding that the 'policy-anticipations hypothesis', i.e. (b), is consistent with the response of the entire term structure of interest rates in both pre- and post-1979 data. The 'expected-inflation hypothesis' is also consistent with the data.[11]

4.3.2 Monetary Policy Effects on Equity Markets

In an obvious way, as applied to macroeconomic problems, rational expectations theory is a natural extension of the 'efficient markets theory' of behaviour in equity markets. Returning to our earlier discussion of monetary policy effects on equity markets, we will begin this section with a further tabulation of the empirical record before we consider recent attempts to formalise the connection between equities and money, assuming rational expectations. We take things in this reverse order because (a) the literature was written this way and (b) there is no obvious way that the empirical 'results' could be taken as evidence on the appropriateness of the particular models themselves. The results, though, are included here because they hold up pretty well by themselves – and they set some interesting questions – and the theory is here because it suggests a path one could take to firm up this literature.

Early studies (Keran, 1971, Homa and Jaffee, 1971, and Hamburger and Kochin, 1972) find that money-supply increases (*and their lags*) are associated with higher equity prices. This suggests a trading strategy that is contrary to efficient-markets theory. These studies, however, were soundly taken apart on econometric grounds and on account of their failure to deal with risk (the studies only considered the *level* of equity prices) by, for example, Pesando (1974). Pesando shows that 'out-of-sample' forecasts are generally poor for these early tests. In the event later empirical studies show that money-stock changes simply do not have useful information for investors. Representative papers in this literature are by Cooper (1974), Rozeff (1974) and Rogalski and Vinso (1977); the last cited provide results from causality tests which firmly reject unidirectional causality from money to stock prices.[12] Going a bit further, even, studies by Bodie (1976), Nelson (1976) and Fama and Schwert (1977) have indicated that inflation in the post-war period has had a *negative* effect on the equity market. Some of the reasons advanced for this (Feldstein, 1980b; Pearce, 1982) are that

(a) inflation causes the real value of depreciation to fall and real *taxable* profits to increase so that real net profits vary inversely with inflation;
(b) inflation imposes an additional tax on nominal capital gains;
(c) inflation increases the return on assets that are alternative to equities (e.g. on houses); and
(d) inflation confuses economic agents as to the true value of their equity investments.

These factors may be influential, but this sort of work smacks of *ex-post* rationalising, and some alternatives need to be considered. Fama (1981), for one, argues that the negative effect of M on stock returns is really a spurious result that appears because the process has several stages to it. That is, stock returns and anticipated real growth rates are positively correlated (or ought to be) while inflation (if unanticipated) affects real activity adversely. Thus, stocks may still be a good hedge against inflation, *ceteris paribus*, but impounded in the *ceteris paribus* is the unpleasant real-world result that inflation affects real activity adversely, and *that* is why stock returns and inflation have a (derived) negative correlation (see Canto, Findlay and Reinganum (1983) for another explanation).

Students of the equity market have, of course, a traditional interest in evaluating the efficient-markets hypothesis, and so it is not surprising to find doubts about the wisdom of using *actual* money-supply changes rather than unanticipated changes as the theory requires (e.g. Pesando, 1974). One early study by Tanner and Trapani (1977) does make this distinction and finds that only the unanticipated change in the money-stock matters (and it is quickly assimilated as the efficient-markets theory predicts). Following this line, Bonomo and Tanner (1983) use the capital asset pricing model along with three different methods of distinguishing the unexpected from the expected money supply. Their results show broad confirmation of the rational-expectations theory but with one qualification: forecast *revisions* seem to have relative price effects. They conclude that (p. 343) 'Such a result is consistent with the Keynesian rational expectations theory that the U.S. is characterized by contracts permitting a minor role for discretionary policies.' There could easily be problems with the data that Bonomo and Tanner use, of course, and so a natural extension is to try an application of the money-announcements approach that we have already considered to be a useful test of both the Barro model (loosely) and the effect of policy on interest rates. In one such paper, Berkman (1978), who also looks at interest-rate effects, finds that only unexpected increases in the money-supply work and that they actually lower equity prices in the United States. These findings are confirmed in a separate study by Pearce and Roley (1982), who also find that revisions in the money stock have an effect and that revisions of the authorities' long-term goals do not affect the situation. In any case the equity-price response appears to be non-linear. Furthermore, again on a topic we introduced above, there is some evidence in the Pearce–Roley study that the switch of policy in 1979 to 'reserve targeting' altered the equity-price response mechanism in favour of a *smaller* response to small surprises and a *larger* response to large surprises.

A study by Blanchard (1981a), using Tobin's 'q' theory of investment (1969) in an *IS–LM* framework, represents the most comprehensive recent attempt to pull equity prices directly into the standard macro-policy debate. In Tobin, q is defined as the ratio of the capital stock to its replacement value. It also depends directly on the value of the firm as determined in the equity market – since investors are, in effect, valuing the firm's capital stock in that market – and so we can write

$$q = V/P_k K$$

where V is the value of the firm (as determined in the equity market) and $P_k K$ is the replacement cost of existing capital. In the short run, with K fixed and $P_k = 1$, we can treat changes in q as synonymous with changes in the value of the firm. Blanchard makes these assumptions, in effect.

Let us, then, assume that total real spending (d) consists of investment (aq), consumption (βy) and government spending (g); this would produce an *IS* curve of

$$d = aq + \beta y + g \tag{4.14}$$

Let us further assume that output adjusts to spending over time according to

$$\dot{y} = \tau(d - y) = \tau(aq + g - by) \qquad \tau > 0, \, b = 1 - \beta \tag{4.15}$$

This *ad hoc* adjustment equation can be justified with reference to the slowness of actual spending to adjust to desired spending; it can also be justified with reference to the existence of explicit costs of adjustment.

For the financial markets, Blanchard assumes three non-money assets that are aggregated, in effect, by the assumption that all are perfect substitutes. Their common – marginal – rate of return is then taken to be the short-term nominal interest rate (i). The *LM* curve, then, can be written as

$$i = cy - h(m - p) \tag{4.16}$$

and the nominal rate is explained by the Fisher equation with inflationary expectations determined rationally.

$$r^e = i - \pi^e \tag{4.17}$$

As already pointed out, there are three non-money assets in this problem – short-term and long-term bonds, and equities – and, since $\dot{q}$ represents changes in the market valuation of the firm, the expected real rate of return on equity holding is simply

$$\dot{q}^e/q + \sigma/q$$

Here σ measures real profits. This expression catches both earnings and capital gains/losses since the equity market includes these in its valuation of q. If we then arbitrarily assume that profits increase with output (income) as in

$$\sigma = \alpha_0 + \alpha_1 y \qquad \alpha_1 > 0$$

and that, as noted, short term bonds and equities are perfect substitutes, we directly have

$$\frac{\dot{q}^e}{q} + \frac{\alpha_0 + \alpha_1 y}{q} = r^e \tag{4.18}$$

This expression links the stock market with the bond market (through which monetary policy operates).

For his first experiment Blanchard assumes that prices are fixed. For this case we would use Equations 4.15, 4.16 and 4.18, with r replacing i in 4.16. In the steady state, for $\dot{y} = \dot{q} = \dot{q}^e = 0$, we then have

$$q = \frac{\sigma}{r} = \frac{\alpha_0 + \alpha_1 y}{cy - h(m - p)} \tag{4.19}$$

and the value of equities is equal to the ratio of steady-state profit to the steady-state interest rate. Here, clearly, $\partial q/\partial r < 0$ while $\partial q/\partial y$ could be positive or negative depending on the parameters. If the money supply increases in this system, then, both output and equity prices will increase (Blanchard, 1981a, p. 135): 'The higher money stock lowers the real interest rate and thus the cost of capital. This lower cost leads to a higher stock market value, higher spending, higher output and profit'. But in the transition to the steady state, before output begins to adjust, the short-term rate shoots down and equity prices shoot up. This jump is an unanticipated one. The reaction may even involve an overshooting in that, for example, interest rates could decline sharply and then rise somewhat as they move to equilibrium.[13] On the other hand, if it were known in advance that policy is involved, the effect will have occurred earlier, and when the announcement of policy comes, there will be no observed effect. Blanchard notes that fiscal policy, which takes considerably longer to unfurl, is especially subject to this consideration and thus is especially hard to evaluate fairly.

With flexible prices we get a more realistic framework, of course, but at the expense of added complexity. Obviously, perfect flexibility is of no interest here since money changes would be neutral and stock prices and output would not be affected by policy (under rational expectations). With partial adjustment – justified by inertia or nominal contracts and not by money illusion – the steady-state real values of output and equity prices are unaffected by money-stock changes. An unanticipated increase in money will, though, have an effect in the transition to the steady state. Since prices do not adjust instantly, real money balances $(m - p)$ are higher; this, by Equation 4.16 will decrease the nominal interest rate. At the same time inflation is now expected to increase (π^e) which, for a given nominal rate, will decrease the real rate (in Equation 4.17).[14] Consequently, real rates in 4.17 will fall, and there will be a short-run stock-market boom – the cost of capital having fallen. But as we increase price flexibility we decrease the potential for this effect. Of course, correct anticipations of policy also rob the enactment of policy of any effect at the time of the policy and favour an effect distributed over the periods before the policy (although it may run past the actual enactment date, undiscernibly). This framework, it seems, rationalises either no effect (rational expectations) or a positive effect of a monetary expansion on equity prices. Since much of the empirical literature suggests that inflation damages equity prices, this standard macroeconomic derivation represents an interesting challenge to the usually looser empirical record on this matter. Naturally, not all tests concur in this; Ciccolo (1978), for example, finds (on US quarterly, interwar data) that (p. 61) 'no intertemporal relationship between stocks prices and money was found'.

This test uses the Sims test of Granger causality (see Chapter 6) and so puts the relation between money and stock prices to the test.

4.4.1 Rational Expectations and Sequential Policy Choice

There is a puzzle in all of this material which involves the rationale for monetary policy in a world dominated by rational expectations. We can always take the neo-Keynesian line that neutrality does not exist (in the short run) but, at the same time, this may not be correct and Barro's view that 'anticipated money' (in the United States) actually does not affect real variables may be. If Barro is correct, then we still have to explain why the authorities actually conduct policies, although we may be happy to say that while any attempt at macroeconomic policy is itself economically irrational (on the part of the authorities), political realities dictate its use. The question is: assuming rationality and neutrality, can we explain the existence of policy by designing alternative models which will open up some scope for policy, without making it seem totally irrational in an economic sense.

An answer, according to Barro and Gordon (1983a, 1983b), is to abandon the assumption that policy follows a fixed rule and instead adopt a framework in which (1983a, p. 591) 'policy is sequentially chosen, [so that] the equality of policy expectations and realizations is a characteristic of equilibrium – not a prior constraint'. In this scenario, then, policy is ineffective *in equilibrium*, but because of its sequential nature it appears to economic agents and the government to be reasonable to have a policy. Policy, that is to say, 'works' in the short run when, to use the term in the literature (Kydland and Prescott, 1977), the authorities are *uncommitted* (i.e. untied) to a course of action. As we will see, this policy may well be suboptimal when compared to a *committed* policy, but (Barro and Gordon, 1983a, p. 592), 'Given an environment where this type of policy commitment is absent – as appears to characterize the United States and other countries in recent years – the results constitute a positive theory of monetary growth and inflation.' We will explain exactly what form this commitment might take in the following. Note that this material continues the discussion of 'time inconsistency' first introduced in Section 3.5 with reference to fiscal policy. Here, though, we consider only monetary policy.

Following Barro and Gordon (1983b) we will adopt a natural-rate/rational-expectations framework. The Phillips curve is

$$U_t = U_{nt} - \alpha(\pi_t - \pi_t^e) \qquad \alpha > 0 \tag{4.20}$$

with an undefined *cycle* built into U_{nt} in the form of a shock that persists according to the parameter λ in

$$U_{nt} = \lambda U_{n,\,t-1} + (1-\lambda)\overline{U}_n + \varepsilon_t \tag{4.21}$$

This formulation is roughly compatible with both the monetary and real-cycle theories discussed in Chapter 3. A usable objective function which can be assigned to the authorities is the quadratic-loss function that appears as Equation 4.22.

$$Z_t = a(U_t - kU_{nt})^2 + b(\pi_t)^2 \qquad a,\, b > 0 \tag{4.22}$$

Here k $(0 \leqslant k \leqslant 1)$ embodies the assumption that the natural rate of unemployment could exceed the efficient rate (i.e. the private-sector optimum rate). We considered this rationale for policy at the beginning of this section. We also assume explicit costs to inflation which are picked up by b. The objective of the authorities, then, is to minimise the expected present value of the loss Z, given the initial state of information.

In this framework both private agents and the government have full information about each other. The problem facing us, then, is a 'game-theoretic' one. The authorities set the growth rate of money in t (based on information in $t-1$) in order to minimise Equation 4.22; this rate is μ_t and the information set is I_{t-1}. Private agents form expectations of π_t^e based on the *same* set of information (i.e. on I_{t-1}) as well as on the information that the authorities are operating by means of Equation 4.22. Private agents must live with the selected π_t, obviously, but they know that the government is setting π_t given I_{t-1} (which *includes* the π_t^e of private agents).[15] The multi-period problem for the government collapses to a single period one of picking π_t (i.e. μ_t) to minimise $E_{t-1}Z_t$.

Inflation expectations by the public under these conditions are given by

$$\pi_t^e = h^e(I_{t-1}) \tag{4.23}$$

where $h^e(\cdot)$ is a private sector 'reaction function' which is part of the solution for the authorities (they will set $\pi_t = \pi_t^e$ once they have $h^e(\cdot)$). Note that this function changes over time, in line with the 'Lucas critique'. We may combine 4.20, 4.21 and 4.23 to yield

$$U_t = \lambda U_{n,\,t-1} + (1-\lambda)\overline{U}_n + \varepsilon_t - \alpha[\pi_t - h^e(I_{t-1})] \tag{4.24}$$

By substituting U_t and π_t^e into 4.22 we then have the costs (i.e. disutility) to the authorities implied by this model as in

$$Z_t = a\{(1-k)[\lambda U_{n,\,t-1} + (1-\lambda)\overline{U}_n + \varepsilon_t]$$
$$- \alpha[\pi_t - h^e(I_{t-1})]\}^2 + b(\pi_t)^2 \tag{4.25}$$

The authorities, then, minimise $E_{t-1}Z_t$ by picking the control variable $\hat{\pi}_t$ (by setting μ_t) in what is now a single equation framework. This value is

$$\hat{\pi}_t = (a\alpha/b)\{-\alpha[\hat{\pi}_t - h^e(I_{t-1})]$$
$$+ (1-k)[\lambda U_{t-1}^n + (1-\lambda)\bar{U}_n]\} \tag{4.26}$$

an equation which, under our assumptions, the public fully appreciates and uses in its calculations of $h^e(I_{t-1})$. The public, then, will set $h^e(I_{t-1}) = \hat{\pi}_t$ so that

$$\pi_t^e = h^e(I_{t-1}) = (a\alpha/b)(1-k)E_{t-1}U_{nt} \tag{4.27}$$

This just comes directly from 4.26.

The authorities at full (Nash) equilibrium will have to satisfy the first-order condition for 4.25; this will require setting $\hat{\pi}_t = \pi_t^e$ as defined in 4.27. This is, of course, at a non-zero inflation rate. In this case $U_t = U_{nt}$. Of course (Barro and Gordon, 1983b, p. 598):

> The policymaker is not required to select an inflation rate that equals the given expected inflation rate. However, people also realize that the policymaker has the power to fool them at each date. Since the formation of expectations takes this potential for deception into account, a full equilibrium will ultimately involve $\pi_t = \pi_t^e$.

Barro and Gordon also point out that a rule such as $\pi_t = 0$ would be superior (would have the same U_t and a lower inflation rate) but would not occur in the sequential model because of the implicit tradeoff established between the costs of inflation and unemployment in the original loss function.

Finally, Barro and Gordon consider some other results obtained with their model.

(a) A system with rules (e.g. the Gold Standard) as commitments could show lower inflation rates than one without.
(b) If the natural rate rises (as in the United States and the United Kingdom recently), then there will be greater benefits to unexpected inflation and the policy-makers will tend to produce more inflation.
(c) If government grows, then so may k, the distortion parameter in Equation 4.22. This would widen the gap between U_{nt} and the target rate, increasing the benefit to a higher inflation rate: 'more government is inflationary in the model' (p. 600).
(d) A positive shock to U_t persists over time and thus provides 'policy temptation' in the next period similar to that described in Point (b).

(e) If inflation is not very costly in Equation 4.22, then in this model we would end up with more inflation, perhaps even considerably more inflation.[16] This may well describe the situation in certain under-developed countries which have somehow developed the institutions to deal with variable inflation rates.

But still there is no equilibrium policy effect on U_t, and none of these results refer to the long run.

4.4.2 Credibility and Reputational Equilibrium

Another way we might look at policy effects is to think of the government as operating a sequential policy that is constrained by the government's *credibility* as a policy authority. To paraphrase L. H. Meyer and Webster (1982), if the authorities have complete credibility, then the public will expect money growth to be equal to the growth announced by the government, and so none of the actual changes in money growth will be unanticipated. Under (pure) rational expectations, then, there are no real effects, and the desired rate of inflation can be achieved with minimal costs. If, on the other hand, the authorities have no credibility at all, then the public simply monitors all present and past actions of the authorities. In this case there will be real effects of policy since unanticipated changes in the money stock will occur, and so the cost of operating a policy could be considerably larger. Indeed, if the point of the policy is to affect real output, the policy will work at first (if the authorities start with complete credibility), but it will be less and less effective, with costs increasing, as the credibility of the authorities diminishes. Meyer and Webster (1982) and Webster (1982) model this situation, using as a parameter the 'probability that the policy has not changed' since the previous period.

There is another aspect to the credibility problem, and this concerns the facts that economic agents are also voters and that governments which create policy effects by springing unpleasant surprises (such as an unanticipated inflation) run the risk of being turned out of office, especially if, after agents have caught on, the net long-run effect is readily seen to be negative. This also brings up the question of a government's establishing its credibility. Presumably, as noted above, we are speaking of the government's attempting to create a net social gain (or, more narrowly, a gain to the government in power) by the use of their policy, and so the use of their reputation (their political 'chits') would be a reasonable thing to do if only there were no costs. There are costs, though, because institutional structures are strained, political empires lose credibility (and elections cost money), and credibility itself (or, broadly, faith in government as an institution) declines. There are also explicit costs to the policy, of course, as already discussed.

'Open mouth', 'jaw bone', or 'moral suasion' have long been part of the arsenal of the macropolicy authorities. There have been times when such announcements have seemed to work directly, at least when institutional structures have made it difficult to disguise a contradictory policy response (as in the United Kingdom before the policy known as 'competition and credit control' was implemented in 1971). Indeed, it is obvious that *if* people believe the government when it says, for example, that the inflation rate is coming down *and if they act accordingly* this action will help to reduce inflation. But the faith many observers seem to have in self-fulfilling prophecies is not justified on the evidence and is, in any case, not well enough understood to serve as the basis of an effective policy under present conditions. On net, we could well accept the judgement that (J. B. Taylor, 1982, p. 81) 'the simple *announcement* by policymakers of an intention to change policy will not establish credibility. Rational individuals need more to go on than mere announcements'. They will insist, that is to say, on a level of analysis and evidence that is consistent with their 'models' of the economy. But credibility itself clearly has some role to play in this policy scenario as we shall see.

Barro and Gordon, in their second paper on these topics (1983a), explore the nature of the 'reputational equilibrium' that might arise when governments need their credibility to maintain leverage over the economy; the context again is that of monetary policy. As we have just seen, the *equilibrium* result for discretionary monetary policy, when economic agents can and do adjust their expectations, is for higher inflation (and costs of inflation) and no net gain in real terms. *Rules*, in contrast, will lower these costs, but when they are in operation, the authorities will be tempted to cheat each period. This cheating will drive the economy toward the *inferior* discretionary equilibrium. But (p. 102) 'Because of the repeated interactions between the policy-maker and the private agents, it is possible that reputational forces can support the rule. That is, the potential loss of reputation – or credibility – motivates the policymaker to abide by the rule'. It does so by 'disciplining' the officials, particularly if they (or their appointors) have to face the ballot box. The result is an equilibrium that 'looks like a weighted average of that under discretion and that under the ideal rule'. Indeed, the authorities drift toward the (better) fixed monetary rule when the interest rate is low and toward the discretionary policy when the interest rate (really, the rate of discount) is high. In this model, as before, if inflation shocks have larger benefits (due to wars or larger deficits, for example) then the model predicts a higher rate of growth of money and prices.

Assume that the authorities have a simple objective function of

$$Z_t = (a/2)(\pi_t^2) - b_t(\pi_t - \pi_t^e) \qquad a, b_t > 0 \qquad (4.28)$$

in which the *benefit* parameter b_t on the 'surprises' is permitted to vary over time (it is distributed randomly with a mean of b and a variance of σ_b^2). This is done to capture the idea, just referred to, that the benefit to inflation appears stronger at some times than at others. The rationale (a 'finance motive', a war, etc.) for this effect and that for the cost-of-inflation term (the quadratic) is the same as those discussed earlier in this section.

Under the game-theoretic model of the earlier Barro and Gordon paper (1983b), discretionary policy can be described as a non-co-operative game between the authorities on the one hand and economic agents on the other. If we assume that the policy-makers cannot predict either interest rates or benefits for time period t when they set π_t, then, under a discretionary policy, they will pick

$$\hat{\pi}_t = \overline{b}/a \qquad (4.29)$$

which is the result of minimising EZ_t in 4.29. In turn, private agents will try to predict inflation with their knowledge of the authorities' model; in this case they will expect $\pi_t^e = \overline{b}/a$ presumably. We will have inflation in overall equilibrium ($\hat{\pi}_t = \pi_t^e$ where there is no benefit to inflation and where costs are $\hat{Z}_t = \frac{1}{2}\overline{b}^2/a$). Both of these results come directly from Equation 4.28.

Under a rule, on the other hand, the policy-makers will, in effect, choose π_t and π_t^e together; their incentive, indeed, is zero inflation under this setup, and thus it carries a zero cost ($Z_t^* = 0$). A comparison of Z_t and Z_t^* shows the superiority of the rule. But, as we noted, under a rule the authorities are tempted to cheat (because of the benefits from inflation in the short run). In period t, the appropriate setting of π_t is the same as in Equation 4.29, clearly–i.e. $\tilde{\pi}_t = \overline{b}/a$ under *cheating*. This policy has an expected loss of

$$E\tilde{Z}_t = -\frac{1}{2}\overline{b}^2/a \qquad (4.30)$$

This comes directly from 4.28 with the (additional) assumption that $\pi_0^e = 0$. This expression is negative, of course, so the *temptation*, to continue with Barro and Gordon's colourful terminology, is

$$T = E(Z_t^* - \tilde{Z}_t) = \frac{1}{2}\overline{b}^2/a > 0 \qquad (4.31)$$

That is, there is a positive incentive to cheat in this framework. A cheating/rule strategy dominates the rule itself, in the short run, *when people expect the rule.* When they need to be convinced by some actions, then the cheating/rule strategy lies in between the rule and the discretion policy.

There are various sorts of enforcement possible which could increase the costs of cheating to the authorities. Political and legal methods suggest themselves, but Barro and Gordon (1983b) consider factors that result from the loss of reputation. In particular, if the authorities cheat on a rule (and are detected), private agents will revise their expectations of inflation and adopt the discretionary solution (producing the maximum loss to the policy). The authorities are then 'punished' for each transgression by not achieving any gains in the period(s) following the 'crime'. What happens in a model from this point depends on the rate of credibility loss and, since time is involved, the interest rate (future losses of credibility need to be discounted). As Barro and Gordon put it (p. 110), 'The rules that can apply in equilibrium are those that have enough enforcement to motivate the policymakers to abide by them. . . . Then, the equilibrium satisfies two properties . . . the expectations are rational . . . [and] the policymaker's choice π_t, maximizes his objectives, given the way people form expectations'. In the simple case that we are considering, when future interest rates and b_t are unobservable, the inflation rate that is best lies between zero and b/a and is a weighted average of the two. The weights, then, depend on the interest rate, with higher interest rates (lower value on future penalties for crimes) implying a larger weight on discretionary policy. Barro and Gordon (1983b) have an interesting diagram of the situation as well as a list of empirical conjectures that is not unreasonable. These are that a higher b – which induces higher π^* – is motivated by war needs, a big debt, a weak tax system (as in underdeveloped countries), monetary policy effectiveness (for whatever reason) and any secular rise in the natural rate of unemployment itself.

The credibility hypothesis is not without its critics, of course, with the main line of attack coming from those who basically argue in favour of the traditional Phillips curve approach to policy formulation (as if loss of credibility has nothing to do with whether a policy works); representative papers are by B. Friedman (1982), R. J. Gordon and S. R. King (1982) and, especially, R. J. Gordon (1984). Whether this is a valid line to take depends on whether the Lucas critique of the Phillips curve is invalid, among other problems and is, at this stage, an unsettled issue. A discretionary policy (in the Barro–Gordon framework described above) is one that is inferior to a rule in that some inflation occurs (none of which is expected inflation); this is because the authorities 'gain' by such a strategy. In the case where the authorities' 'reputation' is also on the line (the authorities announce an inflation target and then lose credibility to the extent that they miss it) there is less inflation than in the 'discretionary case' but more inflation than under a rule. J. B. Taylor (1983) argues that this undesirable state of affairs will be eliminated by co-operation among the players of the game (the Congress and the Federal Reserve, for example), but at least in the United States such co-operation is not part of the policy design; in reality the (US) authorities do not announce their objectives but are quite evasive about their intentions. In this event the 'discretionary' game is the correct way to think about policy effects and, perforce, we generally get more unanticipated inflation than we need (under a fixed rule). In any case, all of these views are theoretical conjectures at this stage although empirical support for the fixed Phillips curve certainly exists, and some recent estimates of the cost of 'disinflationary' policy are, accordingly, very high (in terms of unemployment); see Okun (1978).

4.5 EMPIRICAL ASPECTS OF THE ROLE OF FISCAL POLICY

This section continues the discussion of Section 3.5 with respect to topics that refer mainly to fiscal policy. The purpose of this chapter is to consider both extensions and empirical tests concerning the basic material in Chapter 3, and this purpose is continued in this section. There are two major topics that will be covered here. The *first* of these concerns the *net wealth controversy* as it has been applied to the existence of, and alterations in, the value of government debt. What we are looking for here is a 'real bond effect' similar to the 'real balance effect' of the monetary literature. The literature on 'tax-discounting' – i.e. on whether or not individuals regard debt issue as a promise to levy future taxes and adjust their dynamic plans accordingly – is also relevant in this first part of the discussion. The *second*, related, topic concerns the real and nominal effects of a growing deficit. While a somewhat different framework for this is provided in Chapter 5, we will here consider a recent literature that is often expressed in the short-run tradition of Chapters 1 to 4. It is worth noting, at the outset, that there is little empirical agreement as to the magnitude of these effects, at least as the literature presently stands. The effects we have in mind are real (on output, employment, etc.) and nominal (mainly on nominal interest rates and on inflation rates).

Well-known basic results in the macropolicy literature suggest that just like real (outside) money balances, bonds issued by a government agency can be perceived as net wealth by the private sector so that anything that changes their value (broadly interest-rate and price-level changes) will tend to produce wealth effects on, for example, consumption, investment, and money-holding decisions. These are real effects, ultimately brought on, for example, by changes in the supply of nominal money balances which change the rate of inflation and/or the interest rate, in the first instance. The 'real-balance effect' relevant here has a long theoretical pedigree – for example, it provides the link between monetary theory and value theory in Patinkin's (1965) classical integration of the two – and there is certainly a measure of empirical support for the proposition. But for the 'real-indebtedness effect' we are presently considering, although standard financial models consistently demonstrate its potential power, both theoretical and, especially, empirical support is not particularly abundant.

Bailey (1962, 1971) is perhaps the first modern economist to state the issues clearly with regard to how deficit financing might *not* affect real-spending decisions (1971, p. 156).

> Besides valuing government expenditures as income, households may regard deficit financing as equivalent to taxation. ... If a typical household were to save the entire amount that was made available to it by a switch from current taxation to deficit financing, the interest on the saving would meet the future tax changes to pay interest on the government bonds; the amount saved would be available to meet possible future taxes imposed to repay the principal of the government bonds.

This, broadly, is a statement of what is now called the 'Ricardian equivalence theorem' in honour of an early and lucid statement of it in David Ricardo's *Principles* (see Buchanan, 1976, and O'Driscoll, 1977). In Bailey's version an increase in government *consumption* spending financed by a bond issue would have the effect of substituting public consumption for private consumption and of shifting actual tax from the present to the future. Indeed, if the private sector correctly (rationally) foresees the future tax liability, then the effect of fiscal policy financed by either method is identical (Bailey, 1971, p. 158). It is nil: 'the behavior of the community will be exactly the same as if the budget were continuously balanced ... additional government consumption replaces private consumption and has a multiplier effect of zero'. Of course, if the government has no intention of paying off the debt and the public understands this, it is very likely that changes in this 'permanent' debt will have real effects (see Cox, 1985, for a survey).

Barro (1974) provides us with the basic recent theoretical paper on the debt problem. Allowing that individuals have finite lives would seem to allow a wealth effect for debt issue because government, with an infinite life, would be able to pass the tax on to unborn generations. Similarly, if capital markets are imperfect, in particular with tax liabilities having a higher discount rate applied to them than future interest payments, then there will be a gain in present wealth brought about by using debt issuance rather than a tax levy (to finance current expenditure). This argument applies even if individuals have infinite lives. Barro deals with the first problem by adopting an intergenerational transfer model (old to young or young to old). In this case the net-wealth effect disappears since, in effect, individuals plan to live forever through their children. Barro also argues that changes in social security payments are analogous to changes in government debt and have no real effects in the basic intergenerational model. On the other hand, if there are capital market imperfections, in particular if

(a) the government is more efficient than the private sector in carrying out the loan process between generations or
(b) the government acts like a monopolist in the production of the liquidity services associated with (money and) debt issue,

then there is a positive 'net-indebtedness' effect.

Turning to the empirical record we consider, first, the effect of the deficit on real variables. The reader should note, however, that this is a literature still very much in motion and that we will not attempt to run it all to earth. Note, further, that we will limit ourselves to a rational-expectations format here, taking up 'non-rational' material in Chapters 5 and 6. One direct way to proceed is to insert the real value of the government debt into the consumption function and to see if, as the theory predicts, it has a zero coefficient or, as the net-wealth theory predicts, a positive coefficient. Recent results employing such a method in favour of complete discounting are by Tanner (1979a, 1979b), Kormendi (1983), and Mariano and Seater (1985), and there is a separate study in which discounting is almost complete (there are effects of a deficit on non-durable consumption) by Seater (1982). In addition, the Kormendi study finds a difference between how government consumption (which is arguably non-wealth-creating) and government investment are evaluated by the consumer. Alternative studies with incomplete or even no discounting are by Kochin (1974), Yawitz and L. H. Meyer (1976) and Feldstein (1982). These latter studies have been criticised (mostly on econometric grounds) and reworked by Seater (1982), Aschauer (1985) and Mariano and Seater (1985) to the disadvantage of the net-wealth position.[17] Aschauer notes that the idea that government spending is a close substitute for private spending is *rejected* in his tests, while rational expectations and Ricardian equivalence are not. Mariano and Seater suggest that Feldstein's work suffers from misspecification and, when this is corrected, tends to show no fiscal effect. But Mariano and Seater find an effect from transitory income on consumption which, they argue, is not due to a liquidity constraint (because there is full tax-discounting). Liquidity constraints on individuals (due to credit-rationing or the inability to borrow against future income) are an important part of the net-wealth position (but see W. P. Heller and Starr, 1979). At any rate, enough loose ends remain to permit us to judge this as a set of preliminary results in favour of the existence of, but not the dominance of, tax discounting.

Barro himself includes what might be termed 'empirical speculations' in a number of his studies that bear on these questions. In his 1979 paper on the public debt (1979a) Barro finds that government debt in the United States (1917–76) may well have grown primarily in order to level (approximately) the tax burden of government spending over time. As Barro notes (p. 940): 'This behavior implies a positive effect on debt issue of temporary increases in government spending (as in wartimes), a counter cyclical response of debt to temporary income movements, and a one-to-one effect of expected inflation on nominal debt growth.' Roughly speaking at least, these predictions seem to be upheld in that (Barro, 1980) in the United States

(a) there is more deficit financing during recessions in order, possibly, to stabilise the tax burden cyclically;
(b) blips in expenditures are generally financed by debt issue; and
(c) permanent government expenditures are matched by permanent taxes.

If all of these observations are correct, they are readily perceived by individuals, and they make it possible for economic agents to ignore the size of the debt in their current consumption plans and to concentrate instead on their permanent tax burden.

Underlying the discussion to this point is a somewhat hot topic these days – this is the effect of the deficit on interest rates.[18] Perhaps the most straightforward way to look at this effect is in terms of the short-run

IS–LM model as is done by Evans (1985). The *IS–LM* model basically asserts that under the usual slope conditions an increase in the deficit will, first, shift the *IS* curve outward (with spending constant and current taxes *falling* to balance the government's budget) and, second, will raise nominal interest rates. A reduced-form equation for the nominal rate from such a simple structure is

$$i = a_0 + a_1 g + a_2 d + a_3 m + a_4 \pi^e + a_5 u_{IS} + a_6 u_{LM} \qquad (4.32)$$

Here we would expect the coefficient on the deficit (d) to be positive; the variables g and m are real government spending and real-money balances; the last two terms are errors on the *IS* and *LM* curves, respectively. If π^e is not exogenous, its reduced form could be defined in terms of the same variables as

$$\pi^e = b_0 + b_1 g + b_2 d + b_3 m + u_\pi \qquad (4.33)$$

Then, eliminating π^e between 4.33 and 4.34 we would have a reduced-form coefficient on d of $a_2 + a_4 b_2$. This is the *a priori* effect of the deficit on *nominal* interest rates (the effect on real interest rates is a_2, of course). But these estimators, in the reduced form

$$i = c_0 + c_1 g + c_2 d + c_3 m + u \qquad (4.34)$$

are probably inconsistent because of feedback among the variables. Evans adopts various procedures (notably two-stage least-squares and monthly data) to remove the correlation between the independent variables and the error term in 4.34 and finds on several sets of US wartime data that growing deficits did *not* produce higher interest rates; this repeats a result obtained by Dwyer (1982b). Evans's explanation generally runs in terms of an increase in private saving that offsets the changes in the deficit. This is basically Barro's (1974, 1979b) Ricardian equivalence theorem (P. Evans, 1985, p. 85): 'Households will so react if capital markets are perfect, if they understand the intertemporal budget constraints they face, and if they have operative altruistic intergenerational transfer motives. They will then know that the current deficit equals in present value the taxes to service the extra debt.' Hence an increase in saving occurs because the increased deficit is, for all practical purposes, just a tax.

Our last empirical topic concerns the effect of the deficit on the inflation rate. To begin with, the equivalence theorem we are working under implies that there is no effect of a growing deficit on inflation rates; indeed, an 'a-structural' test by Dwyer (1982b) arrives at just that conclusion (on US data). As we have pointed out, the issue is basically that of the *permanence* of the deficit; an alternative way of putting it concerns whether (or, rather, to what extent) the deficit is *monetised* by the central bank. With regard to the monetisation of the deficit, one position that has been taken is that the Federal Reserve really has little choice but to monetise the debt in view (partly) of the potentially explosive effect of the interest payments on the debt. As Sargent and Wallace (1981) put it, the choice is whether to increase the money stock at the time of the deficit or later; independent monetary policy is thus not possible (in the case in which a deficit is already established). One way to study this is to see if the *monetary base* (consisting, roughly of hand-to-hand currency and bank reserves) is affected by the deficit; if so, the actual process of monetisation is demonstrated. Another procedure is to look at a key interest rate (such as the US Federal Funds rate) which the authorities might actually be controlling (via open-market operations).

From the point of view of permanence it is conceivable that a large part of the American debt is thought by the public to be permanent and never expected to be paid off. This is the conjecture of Cox (1985), who uses an *ad hoc* inflation equation to show that money creation and (59 per cent of) the deficit 'Granger-cause' the US inflation rate. Looking at the monetary base in the United States, Levi (1981) finds an effect of the deficit while Hamburger and Zwick (1981) do not. Sheehan (1985a) compares the money stock (not the 'base') with the Federal Funds rate as the channel of influence of the deficit. He finds that from 1958 to 1970 debt influenced the money stock, but that after 1970 it did not. Conversely, after 1971, when (he argues) the money stock was being used as a policy target, Sheehan finds that the deficit effects are transmitted to the uncontrolled variable (the Federal Funds rate). He concludes, reasonably, that the specific influence of the deficit depends on what rule the authorities are following and that their ability to control their target is not (empirically) hampered by the deficit (up to 1984); a separate study by Thornton (1984) agrees. One should note, though, that data problems abound in this area, that causality testing is infrequent and that adherence to the rules of rational expectations is rare.[19] Consequently, at this writing we really do not known the answer to the deficit-inflation question or, for that matter, to any of the empirical questions raised in this section.[20] Perhaps, although it is a little on the provocative side, we should at least record Dwyer's judgement (based on vector-autoregressive tests) that (1982b, p. 320), 'This preliminary analysis turns up no evidence that is inconsistent with a very strong hypothesis: predictable changes in government debt do not affect any other variable in the economy.'

5 Monetary and Fiscal Policy in the Long Run[1]

> We quite shamelessly assume that the economy is always in equilibrium, that the prices observed at any instant clear all the markets we study. In particular, inflation and deflation never occur because the economy is in disequilibrium and is searching for the price level. In this model, inflation or deflation indicates a continuously changing equilibrium price level.
>
> FOLEY and SIDRAUSKI, 1971, pp. 2–3

5.1 INTRODUCTION

The literature addressed in this chapter concerns a small but important set of material that is concerned with the extension of the macropolicy debate in the direction of more explicit dynamics. The papers discussed are mostly on the topic of 'money-growth', but the context is one in which fiscal policy gets a full treatment, as well, although not at the beginning (in Section 5.2). For readers interested only in short-run policy questions the material in this chapter is no more than a footnote to what we have already discussed although we have a section at the end of this chapter that explicitly considers short-run results. On the other hand, as recent speculation on the long-run consequences of a 'runaway' deficit suggest, there is considerable interest in certain limiting cases of fiscal and monetary policy. The dynamic context of this chapter is explicitly suited to that task. There are, in addition, some other interesting results that can only be hinted at in the short-run discussions that are available.

In the first section of this chapter we will lay out and examine the steady-state solution of a basic money-growth model in which the only important financial commodity is money. This is the basic money-growth model in the literature and is, in particular, the appropriate place to begin in order to make the approach clear with respect to both the economics and the mathematics that are employed. In this model we will assume a household that allocates its income between saving and consumption and divides its wealth between money and the claims to the physical assets of business firms. That is, there is both a flow and a stock dimension to the consumer-choice problem. Firms, in this model, will be assumed to produce an output – itself used for both consumption and investment purposes – and to accumulate physical capital. The firm, too, will have both a stock and a flow decision although in the early going we will trivialise its stock decision. The final agent in this model, the government, will exist solely to issue money to the household. Thus only monetary policy, essentially of the 'helicopter' variety, is possible here. Even so, the analysis of the properties of this model will be very detailed in order to achieve a full illustration of the state of the art of this type of dynamic modelling. In later sections we will then be able to economise somewhat on the explicit mathematics and concentrate more on the interesting policy issues.

In such models we really do not have a meaningful analogue to the real-policy world until we allow for fiscal policy, so in Section 5.3 we extend the basic model by expanding the role of the government. Indeed, by permitting endogenous government expenditures and taxes and admitting of a non-trivial government budget constraint, we will permit the government to create an active policy role in the long run. The focus of this section is on the comparative equilibrium effects of changes in government expenditures and taxes on capital intensity, on money balances and on the rate of inflation.

In Section 5.4 we will extend the basic model in yet another direction, this time by broadening the asset-choice problem. In Sections 5.2 and 5.3 there are only two stocks – money and physical assets (that is, the claims to physical assets). In Section 5.4 we will add a government bond and then examine the effects on both the structure of the model and its steady-state properties when the government has this additional security with which to finance its expenditures. This permits us to get a grip on interesting problems of debt management – that is, on the sales or purchases of government securities – as they affect the steady state. We are not only interested in the properties of this solution here, of course, and so we will not neglect to dwell on the possibilities for monetary and fiscal policy in this reasonably general long-run framework.

The last section in this chapter actually presents results from a short-run 'money-growth' model. The reasons it is attached here are (a) that it is 'backed out' of the long-run model and hence employs the same methodology and notation and (b) that it rationalises and generalises certain familiar short-run policy themes. For the latter, the results do differ from those of the standard short-run models; indeed, the differences seem worth considering in view of the fact that the model used here is somewhat more general than the typical *IS–LM* construction (for example).

5.2 A BASIC MONEY-GROWTH MODEL

The purpose of this section is to lay out the structure of what is currently the basic money-growth model. The main early contributions to this literature are contained in important and still often-cited studies by Tobin (1955, 1965), Sidrauski (1967a, 1967b), Levhari and Patinkin (1966) and Hahn (1969). As already noted, the model will contain a household sector and a business sector along with a trivial government sector (the government here just issuing 'outside' money).[2]

Our procedure, in this rather long section, is as follows. We will start by laying out the structure of the model (in Subsection 5.2.1). This involves setting down the flow demands and constraints of households, business firms and the government. As already noted, some of these relations are uninteresting. In Subsection 5.2.2 we will begin to analyse the model by looking at short-run equilibrium. There are two major results here, one involving the characterisation of Walras's Law in our framework and the other involving the nature of short-run equilibrium. We are, though, more interested in the existence, uniqueness and (local) stability of the *steady state* since this discussion will document the range of this sort of model and so in Subsections 5.2.3 and 5.2.4 we will go over this ground. Finally, in Subsection 5.2.5 we consider the only interesting policy experiment in this model. This is a monetary policy – typified by an increase in the rate of growth of money – and what we want to know is how this affects the rate of inflation and capital intensity in the steady state. The latter is, of course, a potential real effect (since the rate of growth of real output is connected directly to capital intensity).

5.2.1 The Structure of the Model

Beginning with households, the first task is to describe their *flow* constraint. The following relation describes how *income* arises and is distributed across household consumption and saving activities.

$$C^d + S^d = \frac{W}{P} N^s + r K_f + \left(\frac{\dot{M}}{P} - \pi^e \frac{M}{P} \right) \tag{5.1}$$

In Equation 5.1 the flows of real consumption and savings demands are financed by real labour income (N^s is labour supply), by real income from claims on financial business assets ($r K_f$), and by changes in real money balances. The latter are adjusted by the expected deterioration of existing money balances because of expected inflation. Note that, as usual,

$\dot{M} = dM/dt$, etc., while $\pi^e = \dot{P}^e/P^e$ is the expected rate of inflation in the price of the single product in this model.

The next task is to consider the *stock* constraint of individuals. As already noted, individuals derive real 'returns' from money and from equities. We will assume only equity financing (for convenience) and we will do so with the following rationale. We will assume that the corporation can actually finance its physical capital expenditures by means of an equity issue (entirely), by a bond issue (entirely) or by a combination of the two at a *fixed* debt–equity ratio. This eliminates any interest we might have in the corporate capital structure in this problem and enables us to work only with the equity without (further) loss of generality. This, essentially unspecified, financial commodity is, under the circumstances, a perfect substitute for the firm's physical capital, a fact we will make use of in what follows. Furthermore, since the price of physical capital is identical to the price of the firm's product (the good is both a consumption good and an investment good), then the price of the financial commodity – 'shares', for example, since the firm is assumed to be entirely equity-financed – is *also* identical to the product price (Turnovsky, 1977a). What this yields is an overall wealth constraint for individuals of the following form:

$$\frac{M^d}{P} + K_f^d = \frac{M}{P} + K_f \tag{5.2}$$

Here, in effect, we equate real-stock demands to real-stock 'supplies'.

Returning to Equation 5.1, let us simplify the notation by combining the terms there. Thus, we define $y = (W/P)N^s + rK_f$ as individuals' real income derived from firms and $Z = y + \dot{M}/P - \pi^e(M/P)$ as individuals' *disposable* real income. This last treats the inflation-adjustment term as a kind of tax, which it is. Also, by this arrangement, we line up our terms so that consumption plus saving equals disposable income. The two household constraints in 5.1 and 5.2 must be consistent with each other, of course. Indeed, full consistency between the stock and the flow constraint is guaranteed by the fact that

$$S^d = \frac{\dot{M}^d}{P} - \pi^e\frac{M^d}{P} + \dot{K}_f^d = \frac{\dot{M}}{P} - \pi^e\frac{M}{P} + \dot{K}_f \tag{5.3}$$

Since saving occurs as desired additions to both money holding (as adjusted) and equities and since demands for these assets are forced into equality with the available supplies (in 5.2) we have the consistency just described in Equation 5.3. All we are saying is that in this problem, for consistency to hold, individuals must take up into their savings all new equity (issued by firms) and money (issued by the government) in *real* terms. We will use this definition of saving below. So much for the household's constraints.

The next step is to set down our demand functions. Again we must keep track of both stocks and flows. Utilising our definitions, then, *consumption demand* – a flow – is given by the simplified

$$C^d = (1 - s)Z \tag{5.4}$$

where s is the fixed marginal (and average) propensity to save. The demands for the two stocks, in turn, following conventional asset-demand theory, will be assumed to depend on wealth and on rates of return. The *demand for nominal money* balances, in its typical form, then, is

$$M^d = J(Py, PA, r + \pi^e) \qquad J_1 > 0, 0 < J_2 < 1, J_3 < 0 \tag{5.5}$$

and the *demand for* nominal *securities* is

$$PK_f^d = n(Py, PA, r + \pi^e) \qquad n_1 < 0, 0 < n_2 < 1, n_3 > 0 \tag{5.6}$$

where A is real wealth ($\equiv M/P + K_f$). Here we employ the nominal value of income (Py) in these functions to identify a transactions (or flow) demand, in effect. It therefore represents the link between the flow and the stock decisions as it affects money and equity holdings. Note, especially, that the nominal rate of return ($r + \pi^e$) affects the two demands in opposite ways. That is, $r + \pi^e$ is the nominal rate of return on equity and so is the direct return on equity and the opportunity cost for holding money.[3]

For the individual sector, two further relationships are necessary to complete its structure; these involve labour supply and price expectations. For labour supply we will assume that this is fixed at each time period so that $N^s = N$, a stock of labour. *Over time*, in contrast, we will assume that the labour supply grows at the rate δ, with $0 < \delta < \infty$, such that

$$\dot{N} = \delta N, \quad \text{with } N_0 > 0 \tag{5.7}$$

This rate ($\dot{N}/N = \delta$) is, presumably, the augmented rate of growth of labour (as in Phelps, 1966); we note, for later reference, that along the 'golden-rule' path the capital stock will also grow at the rate δ. With regard to individuals' expectations of the product price, we will assume the *adaptive expectations* mechanism in Equation 5.8.

$$\dot{\pi}^e = \beta(\pi - \pi^e) \qquad 0 < \beta < \infty \tag{5.8}$$

Here, as before, π defines the rate of product price inflation. We will retain the assumption of adaptive expectations for the bulk of this chapter, considering only briefly the rational expectations alternative as a criticism. Therefore, in effect, this chapter is more logically an extension of Chapter 2, above, than of Chapter 3. In this study, as we have already noted, the complexity and tentativeness of rational expectations versions of the models of this chapter make inclusion of that material too expensive for the potential value added by the effort.

With household behaviour in hand, we next consider the *business firm*. Business firms will be conceived of as operating a production function of $y^s = F(K, N^d)$ which defines the supply of output in terms of existing physical capital and labour; F has the usual properties.[4] For the firm, the appropriate *flow* constraint equates the proceeds from production, in real terms, with the payments to the factors. We write this as

$$0 = F(K, N^d) - \frac{W}{P} N^d - rK_f \tag{5.9}$$

Here we are saying that all revenues in excess of the payments to labour are paid out to the firm's owners – that is, to households (as in Sargent and Henderson, 1973). Referring to our argument above, on the nature of the financial claims on the firm, we now take advantage of the situation that the financial claim (K_f) is assumed to be a perfect substitute for physical capital. In particular there is the further *stock* constraint, one that we have trivialised, of course, that $K_f = K$. This disposes of a potentially messy problem that would detract from the basic points we wish to make about policy in our framework (but see Feldstein, Green and Sheshinsky, 1978, 1979).

There are further conditions that essentially link the firm to the household (as the supplier of capital and labour); these are the usual marginal conditions. Thus, we assume that labour is paid its marginal product, as in

$$F_N = W/P \tag{5.10}$$

This condition, plus our assumption that the two factor production function $(F(\cdot))$ is homogeneous of degree one, implies that the marginal product of capital is equal to the real rate of return as in

$$F_K = r \tag{5.11}$$

Note that because we are only interested in the steady state here we will not specify an investment function although it would be appropriate for certain short-run questions. That is, an investment function would enable us to deal with the path the economy takes as firms approach their desired capital stocks. It would capture the role of adjustment costs, in effect, but, so long as we deal solely with the steady state, this is not an issue. A further discussion of adjustment costs in money–growth models, however, occurs below. Investment is defined implicitly, of course, as we will see in the next section. It also figures in the discussion of short-run policy choices in Section 5.5.

Finally, we consider the simple role of the *government*, the remaining economic agent in our problem. In our model the sole activity of the government is to issue money and transfer it to households. Thus the following condition fully characterises the government.

$$\dot{M}/P = \Theta(M/P)$$

This expression, in effect, defines the proportionate rate of growth of *nominal* money balances ($= \Theta$) as a policy-determined parameter.

5.2.2 Short-run Equilibrium

In this section we will pull the model together in such a way that we can simultaneously characterise Walras's Law and specify the nature of short-run equilibrium in this set-up. Speaking of Walras's Law, first, we note that the only non-trivial stock constraint in the model is that for the household because this sector is assumed to hold all of the assets (equities and money); if this is not obvious, look back at Equation 5.2. From that condition we see that equilibrium in the money market implies equilibrium in the share market and thus we have already provided a statement of Walras's Law *for* the *stocks* in the model.

There is also a *flow* constraint in these continuous-time models that provides a second dimension to Walras's Law. To derive this, we combine Equations 5.1 and 5.9 with $N^s = N$, so that

$$C^d + S^d = \frac{W}{P}(N - N^d) + y^s + \frac{\dot{M}}{P} - \pi^e \frac{M}{P}$$

Then, utilising the definition of saving that we established in Equation 5.3, we have that

$$C^d + \dot{K} = \frac{W}{P}(N - N^d) + y^s$$

Finally, since $\dot{K} = I^d$ (where I^d is the real-investment demand that is implicit in this model) and since, by definition, $C^d + I^d = y^d$ (where y^d is aggregate demand) we have the following constraint.

$$y^d - y^s = \frac{W}{P}(N - N^d)$$

This is Walras's Law for flows (in this model) and says that equilibrium in the product market also implies equilibrium in the labour market. Thus, in continuous-time models, there is a Walras's Law for stocks and a separate one for flows. In addition, we should point out that our statement that $\dot{K} = I^d$ itself actually guarantees product-market equilibrium. This, of course, is the condition that rules out adjustment costs in the investment function. Finally, we can observe that our four-market model actually reduces to a two-market model by application of the two constraints. That is, while we have product, labour, capital and money markets specified, equilibrium in two of these is sufficient to establish equilibrium in the remaining two, by application of the two Walras's Law constraints. This enables us to concentrate our analysis on just two markets, and so, following tradition, we choose to deal with the product and money markets in what follows.

When we set out our short-run equilibrium conditions it is convenient to convert the model into per capita (labour-intensive) terms. The product-market equilibrium, still in its original form, is

$$(1-s)Z + \dot{K} = F(K, N)$$

Taking this, employing the definition of disposable income and expressing the model in per capita terms, we then have as our *product-market equilibrium*

$$(1-s)[f(k) + m(\Theta - \pi^e)] + \dot{k} + \delta k = f(k) \tag{5.12}$$

Here we have defined $k = K/N$, $f(k) = F(k, 1)$, $m = M/PN$ and $\dot{k} \neq 0$ in the short run. For the *money market*, then, *equilibrium* is contained in the statement that the per capita demand is equal to the per capita supply.

$$L(k, f' + \pi^e) = m \qquad L_1 > 0, L_2 < 0 \tag{5.13}$$

To get to this expression we have defined $M^d/PN = J(Py/PN, PA/PN, r + \pi^e) = j(f(k), m + k, f' + \pi^e)$ from Equation 5.5; this makes use of the following substitutions: $y/N = f(k)$, $r = f'$, and $a = A/N = [(M/P) + K]/N = m + k$ (recalling that $K_f = K$). To get 5.13, since $j(f(k), m + k, f' + \pi^e) = m$, we solve this equation for m.

Equations 5.12 and 5.13 are sufficient to solve for two variables. In particular, if we are given M, N, K and π^e, then we can determine P and k. Furthermore, at overall equilibrium, there is equilibrium in the labour market (by application of Walras's Law) so that W/P is determined. Then, since M is given in the short run, we can also solve for the nominal wage. This is all that we need to point out about the short-run equilibrium properties of our model.

5.2.3 The Existence and Uniqueness of the Steady State

Our interest in this chapter is, of course, the analysis of monetary and fiscal policy in the steady state. To get there, we need to establish certain properties of the steady state. In the steady state, by definition, we would have the following conditions: $\dot{k} = \dot{m} = \dot{\pi}^e = 0$. We will begin our analysis of the steady state by investigating m from the equilibrium condition in the money market. To begin with, we have defined m in per capita terms as $m = M/PN$. This implies that $\dot{m}/m$ would be composed of the time paths of the real-money supply, adjusted by both the rate of inflation (to put it into real terms) and the rate of growth of the labour supply (to put it into per capita terms); we express this idea as follows.

$$\dot{m} = m(\Theta - \pi - \delta) \tag{5.14}$$

Looking next at the money-market equilibrium we differentiate that expression with respect to time to obtain

$$\dot{m} = L_1\dot{k} + L_2(f''\dot{k} + \dot{\pi}^e) \tag{5.15}$$

Note that we have employed an adaptive expectations form for $\dot{\pi}^e$, as described in Equation 5.8.

From Equation 5.8 we know that $\dot{\pi}^e = \beta(\pi - \pi^e)$. From 5.14 and 5.15 we have the result that

$$\pi = -\frac{L_1\dot{k} + L_2(f''\dot{k} + \dot{\pi}^e)}{m} + \Theta - \delta$$

Substituting this expression into 5.8 and defining the *capital elasticity of money balances* as

$$\frac{\partial m}{\partial k}\frac{k}{m} = \frac{L_1 k}{m} + \frac{L_2 f'' k}{m} \equiv \varepsilon$$

we have the result that

$$\dot{\pi}^e = \frac{\beta\left(-\frac{\dot{k}}{k}\varepsilon + \Theta - \delta - \pi^e\right)}{1 + \beta\frac{L_2}{m}} \tag{5.16}$$

We will assume that $\varepsilon > 1$ and that the expression in the denominator of 5.16 is non-zero.[5] Then, in the steady state (with $\dot{\pi}^e = \dot{k} = 0$) we have the result that $\pi^e = \Theta - \delta$. In this event the actual rate of inflation (with $\pi = \pi^e$) is equal to the rate of growth of the money stock (Θ) less the rate of growth of output (δ). This is a standard result which is certainly what we would expect here, in the steady state.

Our other market is the product market whose equilibrium we will now examine in the steady state. Briefly, the equilibrium condition is described by

$$m^r = \frac{sf(k^r) - \delta k^r}{(1-s)\delta} \equiv w^r(k^r) \tag{5.17}$$

This expression is derived directly from the short-run equilibrium, using both the result that $\pi = \Theta - \delta$ in the steady state and the assumption that $\dot{\pi}^e = \dot{k} = 0$. The superscript r is just notation designed to distinguish this condition from later results for the money market (designated t) and for steady-state equilibrium (designated s). Equation 5.17, then, shows the relationship between real per capita money balances (m) and capital intensity (k) in product-market equilibrium (in the steady state). Clearly $w^r(0) = 0$ and $w^r(k^u) = 0$, where k^u is the solution of

$$0 = \frac{sf(k^u) - \delta k^u}{(1-s)\delta}$$

which corresponds to a steady-state barter system (in which $m = 0$). With $m^r > 0$ in the steady state, then $k^s < k^u$ and so we have just established the important result that if money balances are held in the steady state then the capital intensity in a monetary economy is *less* than it is in a barter economy. We shall return to this result when we consider the effect of an *increase* in the rate of production of money in the steady state.

The slope of $w^r(k^r)$ is readily found by differentiating 5.17 with respect to k^r.

$$\frac{dm^r}{dk^r} = \frac{sf' - \delta}{(1-s)\delta}$$

This expression is positively sloped for smaller values of k and becomes negatively sloped for larger values. A possible shape is illustrated in Figure 5.1.

From the money-market equilibrium in the steady state we have the result that

$$m^t = L(k^t, f'(k^t) + \Theta - \delta) = w^t(k^t) \tag{5.18}$$

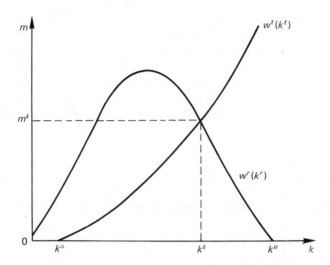

Figure 5.1   The steady state in the basic model

This expression is derived directly from Equation 5.13 with $\pi^e = \Theta - \delta$. The slope dw^t/dk^t can be established by looking at the differential for the money-market equilibrium in Equation 5.18, with $\pi^e = \pi$ in the steady state. The slope is

$$dm^t/dk^t = L_1 + L_2 f''$$

and it is strictly positive ($L_1, > 0$, L_2, $f'' < 0$). We will then find it convenient to assume that there exists a $k = k^\alpha > 0$ such that $0 = L(k^\alpha, f'(k^\alpha) + \Theta - \delta)$. That is, we have established that there exists some rate of return on shares that is so high that individuals do not want to hold money balances. We have also drawn $w^t(k^t)$ in Figure 5.1. Because $w^t k^t$ starts at $k^\alpha > 0$ and is monotonically increasing, while $w^r(k^r)$ begins at the origin and ends at k^u, there exists an equilibrium. Moreover, because the capital elasticity of money demand exceeds unity, $w^t(k^t)$ can only intersect $w^r(k^r)$ once. Thus we have established that the steady-state equilibrium (k^s, m^s) exists and is unique in this basic model. We now consider monetary policy in this framework.

5.2.4   Monetary Policy in the Basic Model

The next question concerns the effects on capital intensity and on per capita money balances when Θ, the rate of growth of the money stock, is changed. We may rephrase this question – in the steady state, at least – as follows. Since $\pi = \pi^e = \Theta - \delta$ in the steady state, it follows that $d\pi^e/d\Theta = 1$ so that an increase in Θ actually corresponds to an increase in the rate of inflation. In a nutshell, then, our simple result implies that in the steady state we can analyse the effect of a change in the inflation rate on k and m as if the inflation rate is controlled by Θ.

From the product- and money-market equilibrium conditions in 5.12 and 5.13, with $\dot{k} = \dot{m} = 0$ and $\pi^e = \pi = \Theta - \delta$, we have the result that in the steady state

$$-s(f(k) + \delta m) + \delta(k + m) = 0 \tag{5.19}$$

$$L(k, f'(k) + \Theta - \delta) - m = 0 \tag{5.20}$$

For an increase of the rate of supply of nominal money balances in this system we obtain the following result

$$\frac{\partial k}{\partial \Theta} = \frac{L_2 \delta(1 - s)}{H_1} > 0 \tag{5.21}$$

Here $H_1 = -[(\delta - sf') + \delta(1 - s)(L_1 + L_2 f'')]$ and must be negative for the steady state to be locally stable. To get this we assume $\delta - sf' > 0$ — i.e., we assume a positive slope for $w^s(k^s)$ in Figure 5.1. Then $H_1 < 0$ and $\partial k/\partial \Theta > 0$ for $L_2 < 0$. Thus an increase in the rate of inflation increases capital intensity in the steady state. This result occurs because the increase in π^e reduces the demand for money and so k must increase in order to restore equilibrium to both the product and money markets. In effect, an inflationary monetary policy spills over into the product market in the steady state. Money, clearly, is not neutral in this model.

Considering next the influence of Θ on the holding of real per capita money balances we begin by calculating Equation 5.22.

$$\partial m/\partial \Theta = (L_1 + L_2 f'')\partial k/\partial \Theta + L_2 \tag{5.22}$$

In this instance we identify two effects of an increase in the rate of inflation on equilibrium money balances. The first of these effects is positive and is adjusted by the positive effect of inflation on capital intensity (itself also positive as we demonstrated in Equation 5.21). But the second effect (L_2) is negative since the resulting increase in π^e makes money holding less attractive. In this case we are unable to establish a sign for $\partial m/\partial \Theta$.

Monetary expansion – inflation in this model – also affects per capita consumption (c) unless we are operating under 'golden rules'; to see this, consider the following. Because it increases capital intensity, an increase in Θ clearly increases output, but since $c = f(k) - \delta k$ in the steady state (recalling that both capital and labour grow at the rate δ), then

$$\partial c/\partial \Theta = (f' - \delta)\partial k/\partial \Theta \qquad (5.23)$$

Equation 5.23 argues that the effect of monetary expansion on consumption is directly related to the difference between the marginal product of capital and the rate of growth. Indeed, if $(f' - \delta) \gtreqless 0$, then $\partial c/\partial \Theta \gtreqless 0$, as 5.23 is written. We should note, then, that if we have the 'golden-rule' case in which $f' = \delta$, there is no effect of inflation on consumption in this simple growth model.[6]

We may calculate a result for the effect of monetary expansion on real disposable income (Z) in this model. It turns out that in the steady state, per capita real disposable income is given by

$$Z = f(k) + m\delta > f(k)$$

In this event real disposable income actually exceeds output. It follows, then, that in a barter economy with the same technology and rate of growth of labour as the monetary economy which we have been analysing, consumption will be lower and capital intensity will be higher. The introduction of money has the effect of raising capital intensity in this model.

Finally, turning to per capita real wealth (a) in the model, we note that since capital intensity and per capita real money balances could move in opposite directions, it is not possible to determine uniquely the sign of the effect of a monetary expansion on the household's per capita real wealth. Since $a = k + m$, we can combine Equations 5.21 and 5.22 to get

$$\partial a/\partial \Theta = a(f' - \delta)L_2/H_1 \qquad (5.24)$$

in which case $\partial a/\partial \Theta \gtreqless 0$ as $(f' - \delta) \gtreqless 0$. The effect, then, of the monetary expansion on wealth depends on the relationship between the marginal product of capital and its golden-rule level.

5.3 FISCAL POLICY IN THE BASIC MODEL

To introduce fiscal policy into the basic model we will have to respecify the role of the government – giving it expenditure and tax powers – and to rewrite the constraints for the private sector to allow for personal and corporate income taxes. An important and immediate generalisation is that the inflation rate becomes endogenous. Fiscal policy, here, will be typified by either a change in government expenditures or a change in the corporate tax rate (we omit the possibility of changing the personal income-tax rate for brevity). In Subsection 5.3.2 we will show that an increase in government expenditures 'crowds out' private spending in the steady state, thus reducing the capital intensity of the economy; furthermore, this policy raises the inflation rate. In Subsection 5.3.3 we will show that a change in the corporate tax rate does not have symmetrical effects to an expenditures policy. In particular, while a rise in the corporate tax rate will lower capital intensity, the same change will have an ambiguous effect on the rate of inflation. Indeed, because of this result, it is impossible to say in which direction wealth will change after a tax policy. Finally, as noted above, we point out in passing that given a fiscal policy, there is no additional role for an independent monetary policy, essentially because of the budget constraint of the government. That is, the inflation rate is endogenous in this model in the event that there is an active fiscal policy already in place. In these days of large budget deficits and rising interest bills for the accumulating debt, this is an interesting topic although a model without bonds is not going to take us very far along this road. In Section 5.4, however, we extend the model to include bonds and to consider the options that a more reasonable facsimile of a modern government might have in the presence of relatively large deficits and debts.

5.3.1 The Structure of the Fiscal Policy Model

The first task before us is rewriting the basic model to allow for tax and expenditure variables. Beginning with *households* we can describe their new income constraint, in net (of taxes) incomes as

$$C^d + S^d = \frac{W}{P} N^s (1 - u_w) - \pi^e \frac{M}{P} + r(1 - u_p)K_f \tag{5.25}$$

where u_w is a fixed tax rate on wage income and u_p is a fixed tax rate on portfolio income with $0 < u_w$ and $u_p < 1$.[7] Equations 5.2, 5.3 and 5.4, for a new value of Z (see 5.32), are retained, but we need to rewrite the financial demand equations to allow for the presence of taxes on portfolio income and for the fact that taxes are paid in money form (that is why we have put $P(y + T_c)$ in what follows).

$$M^d = L[P(y + T_c), r(1 - u_p), -\pi^e, PA] \tag{5.26}$$

$$PK_f^d = n[P(y + T_c), r(1 - u_p), -\pi^e, PA] \tag{5.27}$$

Here L and n have the same properties as were assumed in connection with Equations 5.5 and 5.6, and T_c represents real corporate income-tax payments. The new derivative values are $L_2 < 0$ and $L_3, n_2, n_3 > 0$; $-\pi^e$ is, of course, the expected rate of deflation and measures the increase in the value of nominal assets (M and PK). Note that Equations 5.7 and 5.8 are also carried over from the earlier model into this section.

For *firms*, with the indicated changes, the flow constraint now becomes

$$0 = \left[F(K, N^d) - \frac{W}{P} N^d \right](1 - u_c) - rK_f \tag{5.28}$$

where u_c is a fixed tax rate on corporate income (with $0 < u_c < 1$). Equation 5.28 should be compared with Equation 5.9. Here actual taxes (T_c) paid by the corporation in real terms are given by the expression

$$T_c = u_c \left[F(K, N^d) - \frac{W}{P} N^d \right]$$

where we ignore the interest deduction available to corporations on the grounds that our assumption – that corporate debt and equity are indistinguishable – renders this provision irrelevant.[8] Then, utilising the homogeneity property of the production function and continuing to work with Equation 5.10 – which was the standard marginal condition for labour – we have in place of Equation 5.11 the following marginal condition.

$$F_k(1 - u_c) = r \tag{5.29}$$

Thus, in this model, we could refer to our real rate (r) as the post-corporate tax (but pre-personal tax) rate of return to equity-holders. For business firms, we will continue to assume that investment demand equals capital accumulation, making the investment decision a trivial one, as before.

Finally, we need to reconstruct the role of the government since it is no longer just a money-producing and -transferring agency. Let us assume, for convenience, that government expenditures are proportional to output.

$$G = \tau y^s \tag{5.30}$$

With this expression we can rewrite the budget constraint for the government (where R_T is tax revenues) as

$$\dot{M}/P = \tau y^s - R_T \tag{5.31}$$

The tax revenues, then, looking back at the expressions derived in this section, are

$$R_T = u_c \left(y^s - \frac{W}{P} N^d \right) + u_w \frac{W}{P} N^s + u_p rK_f$$

5.3.2 Equilibrium in the Fiscal Policy Model

For this model, as in the basic model in Section 5.2, we can show that there are separate Walras's Laws for stocks and for flows. These restrictions permit us to eliminate two markets, and, as before, we choose to eliminate the equity (i.e. bond and equity) and labour markets. Our interest in this model is not in establishing the existence and uniqueness (or stability) of the steady state, but rather in investigating the effects of fiscal policy on capital intensity, on the rate of inflation, and on per capita money holdings. That is, we have set up the ground rules for such topics, but to conserve space and to concentrate on the policy themes that are the purpose of this study, we will jump right into the equilibrium conditions of this new structure.

In order to write out the equilibrium conditions for the steady state, we first need to collect the model and then to write out the resulting system in per capita terms. For product-market equilibrium we will use Equations 5.28 and 5.29 and the fact that real disposable income should now be written as

$$Z = \frac{W}{P} N^s (1 - u_w) - \pi^e \frac{M}{P} + r(1 - u_p) K_f \qquad (5.32)$$

This last is merely our former expression adjusted for income-tax payments. The result, which should be compared to Equation 5.12, is

$$(1 - s)[(f(k) - kf')(1 - u_w) - \pi^e m + f'(1 - u_p)(1 - u_c)k]$$
$$+ \dot{k} + \delta k + \tau f(k) = f(k) \qquad (5.33)$$

The differences involve the tax rates, the addition of government expenditures (in $\tau f(k)$), and the elimination of Θ in view of the fact that given an established tax policy, monetary policy is endogenous in this model. The money market equilibrium, in turn, is basically the same as before (see just after Equation 5.13) except for the netting out due to the tax rates. The result is

$$L[f(k), f'(1 - u_c)(1 - u_p), -\pi^e, m + k] = m \qquad (5.34)$$

Earlier, we imposed an adaptive structure on the revision of inflationary expectations; we will continue in this vein here. We repeat Equation 5.8 for reference, as 5.35:

$$\dot{\pi}^e = \beta(\pi - \pi^e) \qquad (5.35)$$

There is an additional 'accumulation condition' for changes in money balances that is required in this model because the money stock is now endogenous. This expression is

$$\dot{m} = \tau f(k) - u_c kf' - u_w(f - kf') - u_p kf'(1 - u_c) - m(\pi + \delta) \quad (5.36)$$

and it replaces the simple government budget constraint of $\dot{M}/P = \Theta(M/P)$ that we used earlier. Here, to take the terms in order, money balances are recirculated by expenditures, run off by tax receipts and absorbed by the private demand for money.

In the steady state, with $\dot{k} = \dot{m} = \dot{\pi}^e = 0$, we can rewrite the equilibrium conditions given as Equations 5.33 to 5.36 in the following way (at the steady-state values of k, m and π^e).

$$-s[f(k)(1 - \tau) + \delta m] + \delta(k + m) = 0 \quad (5.37)$$

$$L[f(k), f'(1 - u_c)(1 - u_p), -\pi^e, m + k] - m = 0 \quad (5.38)$$

$$\tau f(k) - u_c kf' - u_w(f - kf') - u_p kf'(1 - u_c) - m(\pi^e + \delta) = 0 \quad (5.39)$$

This system corresponds to 5.19 and 5.20 above.

Equation 5.37 is the product-market equilibrium condition in the steady state. It says that in the steady-state savings equal investment plus the growth in real-money balances. Note, about this expression, the presence of government spending (in $\tau f(k)$). Equation 5.38 is the money-market equilibrium condition. Equation 5.39, then, is the government budget constraint in the steady state. Here we can observe that the real per capita *deficit* – that is, the difference between the expenditure and tax terms – equals $m(\pi^e + \delta)$ and is positive in the steady state. The term $m(\pi^e + \delta)$ represents the real per capita rate of monetary expansion in the economy. We may regard $m\pi^e$ as the inflation tax in this model and $m\delta$ as the growth 'tax' (i.e. the money needed to finance growth; see Foley and Sidrauski, 1971). In effect, then, the government deficit in this model is financed by higher prices or by larger output. We can also think of $\pi^e + \delta$ as the *nominal* rate of growth in the economy and thus we may also put it that the real per capita deficit is financed by the nominal growth of real per capita money balances, if that is not too much of a tongue-twister.

Equations 5.37, 5.38 and 5.39 comprise the three equilibrium conditions in the steady state; there are also three unknowns here, k, $\pi^e (= \pi)$ and m. Clearly, as already pointed out in this revision of the basic model, not only are the capital intensity and real-money balances endogenous, but so, too, is the rate of inflation. The reason for this is simply that the government is assumed not to control the rate of growth of nominal money balances. Instead, the government controls tax and expenditure rates and must, to stay within its constraint, let the money supply go. Clearly, we cannot have an exogenous (and independent) monetary policy in this model, and so certain important real-world possibilities are not available to us. We will not leave it at that, though, and with a government bond in the model (of Section 5.4, below) we will be able to achieve a more complete perspective on fiscal and monetary policies and their interactions.

5.3.2 Fiscal Policy I: An Increase in Government Spending

Suppose now that the government increases its expenditures by increasing τ, which was defined in Equation 5.30 as G/y^s, a proportionality factor. We should think of this policy parameter as essentially increasing the deficit (*ceteris paribus*) although what is going on is that the government is increasing its expenditures as a percentage of total output. First of all, looking at the crowding-out (real) effects on *capital intensity* (k), we can differentiate Equations 5.37 to 5.39 with respect to τ.

$$\frac{\partial k}{\partial \tau} = \frac{-sf(k)}{H_2} \left[L_3\left(\pi^e + \frac{\delta}{s} \right) + m(L_4 - 1) \right] \tag{5.40}$$

where

$$\begin{aligned} H_2 = {}& (\delta - sf')[L_3(\pi^e + \delta) + (L_4 - 1)m] + \delta(1 - s) \\ & [L_3(-u_c(f' + kf'') + u_w kf'' - u_p(f''k + f')(1 - u_c)) \\ & - m(L_1 f' + L_2 f''(1 - u_c)(1 - u_p) + L_4)] \\ & + sf'\tau \left[L_3\left(\pi^e + \frac{\delta}{s} \right) + (L_4 - 1)m \right] \end{aligned}$$

For stability it is necessary that $H_2 < 0$. Assuming, then, that this is so[9] and assuming that the term in square brackets in the numerator of Equation 5.40 is negative, then it follows that $\partial k/\partial \tau < 0$.[10] In other words, an increase in the real per capita deficit brought about by an increase in government expenditures decreases the capital intensity of the economy. This is the familiar crowding out (presented, in this case, in dynamic form) caused by fiscal policy. This contrasts with our earlier result in which there was an increase in k that occurred as the result of an expansionary monetary policy (in Equation 5.21).

Consider next the effect of the change in government expenditures on the *rate of inflation*, the second endogenous variable. In the basic model above we established that the rate of inflation and the rate of capital intensity move in the same direction, but, as it turns out, this result does not necessarily carry over to the present situation where π^e is now an endogenous variable. Indeed, while k falls, an increase in government expenditure raises inflation, as the following calculation spells out (assuming, still, that $H_2 < 0$).

$$\frac{\partial \pi^e}{\partial \tau} = \frac{f(k)}{H_2}(L_4 - 1)(\delta - sf') - \frac{f(k)}{H_2}(s\pi^e + \delta)[L_1 f' + L_2 f''(1 - u_c)$$

$$(1 - u_p) + L_4] - \frac{sf(k)}{H_2}(L_4 - 1)[-u_c(f' + kf'') + u_w kf''$$

$$-u_p(f' + kf'')(1 - u_p)] > 0 \tag{5.41}$$

The sign here is achieved by utilising the restrictions listed in note 9, above, themselves sufficient to establish that $H_2 < 0$. That is, the set of these conditions on the coefficients of H_2 which is sufficient to establish that it is negative is also sufficient to establish a sign for Equation 5.41; this was also the case for Equation 5.40, as seen in note 10, above. The result, then, is that a rise in the 'government expenditures percentage' increases the inflation rate in the steady state.

For real per capita *money holdings* we would certainly expect that the effect of an expansion in government expenditures (as a per cent of output) would contract these because capital intensity – and therefore output – declines on the one hand, while the rate of inflation rises, on the other. The fall in output, clearly, implies fewer transactions, and the other effect represents the negative effect of the own rate of return on money. Performing the calculations on Equations 5.37 to 5.39 we have

$$\frac{\partial m}{\partial \tau} = L_3 \frac{f(k)}{H_2}(\delta - sf') - \frac{sf(k)}{H_2}\{L_3[-u_c(f' + kf'') + u_w kf''$$

$$-u_p(f' + kf'')(1 - u_c)] - m[L_1 f' + L_2 f''(1 - u_c) + L_4]\} < 0 \tag{5.42}$$

which is readily signed, as noted, without further restrictions.

There are several other effects that we can tack on here to complete the illustration of the effects of an increase in government expenditures in the basic fiscal policy model. For one thing it is obvious that since k and m fall as government expenditures increase, then this increase in the share (in total expenditures) of the government is associated with a fall in *real per capita wealth*. Furthermore, a similar result obtains with per capita consumption since $c = (1 - s)Z$ as it was in our basic monetary model. To see this, note, first, that

$$\frac{\partial c}{\partial \tau} = (f'(1 - \tau) - \delta)\frac{\partial k}{\partial \tau} - f(k) \tag{5.43}$$

What we need, to establish that $\partial c/\partial \gamma < 0$, is the condition that $f'(1 - \tau) - \delta \geqslant 0$. If we are operating under a 'golden-rule' condition, then, indeed, this is so because the golden-rule condition is simply that $f'(1 - \tau) = \delta$. In particular, what we are saying is that the marginal product of the capital that is supplied to the private sector must be equal to the rate of growth of the capital stock. The reason for this is simply that only the private sector in the model accumulates capital and so the government's contribution to the marginal product must be netted out.

5.3.3 Fiscal Policy II: An Increase in the Corporate-tax Rate

In this section we will conclude our basic work on fiscal policy with a discussion of the effects of a change in u_c, the corporate income-tax rate, and leave to the reader the task of working out the effects of changes in the other taxes (those on wage income and on portfolio income). The results, in any case, are similar to those that will be presented in this section. In what follows it turns out that the effect of an adjustment in the corporate income-tax rate is not exactly the mirror image of the effect of a change in government expenditure. While we are mainly trying to document the effects of tax policy here, the comparison is interesting in its own right since economists (and governments) often debate the relative advantages of expenditure versus income-tax policies. We will set this comparison up, then, as that of an increase in taxes compared with an increase in government expenditures. We will do it in this way because in either case the government is, in effect, taking resources from the private sector and thereby forcing an adjustment in private wealth.

The basic result, then, is easily stated: when the government increases the corporate income-tax rate, capital intensity falls. To see this we differentiate Equations 5.37 to 5.39 with respect to the rate u_c.

$$\frac{\partial k}{\partial u_c} = \frac{\delta(1 - s)f'(1 - u_p)(L_3 k - m L_2)}{H_2} < 0 \qquad (5.44)$$

This, of course, is the same sign we obtained for Equation 5.40 for the government expenditures effect. Where the symmetry fails, though, is when we calculate the effect of a change in the corporate tax rate on the endogenous rate of inflation in the model. This result turns out to be unsignable (it was positive for $\partial \pi/\partial \tau$) because while the increase in u_c renders money balances more attractive than the claims on physical capital (and is thereby inflationary), in this case the rate of return on portfolio income increases, and this alters the relative attractiveness of the components of wealth-holders' portfolios. Indeed, the latter effect is clearly deflationary in that a movement away from money occurs. This result does not carry over to the calculation for real per capita money balances for in this case we find that

$$\frac{\partial m}{\partial u_c} = \frac{[\delta - sf'(1-\tau)]f'(1-u_p)(mL_2 - L_3k)}{H_2} > 0 \qquad (5.45)$$

Finally, combining Equations 5.44 and 5.45, we may calculate the effect of a change in taxes on per capita wealth. In this case we have no definite result, but an effect that depends on the relationship of the marginal product of capital to the golden rule. In particular, our calculation yields

$$\frac{\partial a}{\partial u_c} = \frac{s}{H_2}(\delta - f'(1-\tau))f'(1-u_p)(mL_2 - L_3k) \qquad (5.46)$$

and so if $f'(1-\tau) - \delta \lesseqgtr 0$, then $\partial a/\partial u_c \lesseqgtr 0$. That is, if the marginal product of capital exceeds its golden-rule level (if $f' > \delta(1-\tau)^{-1}$), then the capital-intensity effect dominates the money-balance effect in Equation 5.46. However, for a capital intensity sufficiently high to produce a sufficiently low marginal product of capital, the money-balance effect dominates, and the sign of the result given in Equation 5.46 is reversed. This completes our work on the pure fiscal policy model.

5.4   MACROPOLICY IN A MODEL WITH MONEY AND GOVERNMENT BONDS

Obviously the economically interesting case in all of this involves neither a pure fiscal nor a pure monetary model, but a situation in which there is a possibility of running them both (but not, necessarily, at the same time). This is the task of this section. In this discussion we will be drawing on the work of Turnovsky (1980), Christ (1978, 1979), Infante and J. L. Stein (1980) and Feldstein (1980a), but some of the derivations in this section are original, particularly when we come to consider a non-trivial, three-asset selection problem. The problem, again, is to lay out the policy choices open to a government in the long run when the development of the economy is governed by its capital intensity, the rate of inflation and the real-interest rate. The formulation which we present here is still continuous time and still concerns three agents (consumers, producers and the government), but it now considers five markets (product, labour, bond, shares and money). The model, therefore, now has a general portfolio-selection framework since there are three assets which will not be treated as perfect substitutes in any combinations. The model also has wealth effects in it and these provide it with some of its more interesting predictions.

Drawing on the potential richness of detail in our framework, we will analyse four types of policies here (and there are several others that are readily solvable in the same framework). The first of these policies is that of fixing the *real* rate of interest on government bonds. This is a kind of price-control policy that is sometimes discussed in the policy literature although it is not always clear exactly how this control can be achieved in practice. In this case, if we could figure out how to do it, we would find that an increase in the real rate causes capital intensity in the economy to fall and inflation to rise (when the government is already running a deficit). This result occurs because the fiscal policy forces individuals out of money and shares and into bonds. In the second policy experiment the government is assumed to run a deficit while at the same time it attempts to target a *fixed* rate of growth of *nominal money balances*. In this case the rate of inflation is constant, and thus the burden of the deficit policy falls entirely on the level of capital intensity in the sense of a crowding-out of private investment. Clearly, a monetary rule is not always the best policy although the reader will note that our perspective is adaptive expectations here. For our third policy experiment we will examine the possibilities that arise when the government fixes real per capita government *debt*, while at the same time it runs a deficit. In this case we produce a higher rate of inflation, but, at the same time, there is no crowding-out effect. Finally, in a fourth experiment we will examine the situation that arises when the government runs a deficit and at the same time fixes the *real* rate of *monetary expansion*. In this case there is a distinct possibility of instability in the steady state (via interest-rate effects on the demand for money); we also will show that in this context an increase in the deficit will produce a lower capital intensity and a higher rate of inflation. Curiously, in this fourth experiment, we also discover a case in which an increased deficit is consistent with a lower capital intensity and a lower rate of inflation. This finding possibly has implications for the current debate over the size of the deficit (in, for example, the United States).

5.4.1 The Structure of the Model

The purpose of this subsection will be to lay out the changes in the structure of our three-sector dynamic model which are induced by our broader perspective. As before, there is both a stock and a flow constraint for households; we will begin with the latter in Equation 5.47. This expression should be compared with Equations 5.1 and 5.25; the new element here, of course, concerns the government bond (B) that households can hold in their portfolios.

$$C^d + S^d = \frac{W}{P}N^s(1 - u_p) + i_b\frac{B}{P}(1 - u_p) + rK_f(1 - u_p) - \pi^e\left(\frac{M}{P} + \frac{B}{P}\right)$$

(5.47)

In this version of the flow budget constraint the flows of desired real consumption (C) and savings (S) are financed by real-wage (W/P) earnings (net of personal income-taxes), net earnings on bonds and net earnings on shares. Note that B/P and K_f are the net real value of bond and share holdings, respectively, and i_b is the nominal interest rate on the bond (the price of the bond is £1); as before, r is the real rate of return on equities. The last term in Equation 5.47, then, represents the expected deterioration of real money and bond balances due to expected inflation. There are no further changes with respect to the capitalisation of the firm, as this sort of elaboration – for example, in the form of a variable debt/equity ratio – would be bought at the cost of considerable complexity. As the reader will soon appreciate, we have enough complexity as it is.

The stock (wealth) constraint appropriate for households in this problem is now

$$\frac{M^d}{P} + \frac{B^d}{P} + K_f^d = \frac{M}{P} + \frac{B}{P} + K_f$$

(5.48)

With bonds added into the problem, disposable income now becomes

$$Z = y + i_b\frac{B}{P} - \pi^e\frac{(M + B)}{P} - T_p$$

where T_p defines real tax payments (of $u_p[(W/P)N^s + i_b(B/P) + rK_f]$), and all other income comes from firms in the form of

$$y = (W/P)N^s + rK_f$$

As before, the two constraints in 5.47 and 5.48 can be reconciled (as in Equation 5.3) as long as $C^d + S^d = Z$. The formal statement of this resolution is

$$S^d = \frac{\dot{M}^d}{P} + \frac{\dot{B}^d}{P} - \pi^e\left(\frac{M^d}{P} + \frac{B^d}{P}\right) + \dot{K}_f^d = \frac{\dot{M}}{P} + \frac{\dot{B}}{P} - \pi^e\left(\frac{M}{P} + \frac{B}{P}\right) + \dot{K}_f$$

(5.49)

Finally, we will retain Equation 5.4 in which consumption is assumed to be proportional to disposable income.

There are now three distinct assets in the portfolio of individuals and the following represent the asset-demand equations of the representative wealth-holder. These should be compared to the two-asset case above in Equations 5.5 and 5.6, which were for money and a composite corporate security (K_f).

$$M^d = L(P(y + T_c), r(1 - u_p), i_b(1 - u_p) - \pi^e, -\pi^e, PA) \qquad (5.50)$$

$$B^d = g(P(y + T_c), r(1 - u_p), i_b(1 - u_p) - \pi^e, -\pi^e, PA) \qquad (5.51)$$

$$PK^d = n(P(y + T_c), r(1 - u_p), i_b(1 - u_p) - \pi^e, -\pi^e, PA) \qquad (5.52)$$

As in Section 5.3 we write these functions as dependent on gross nominal income (where T_c measures corporate-tax payments) and PA represents the nominal value of private wealth. These functions are also assumed to be homogeneous of degree one in $P(y + T_c)$ and PA, and, along with the usual differentiability and adding-up conditions, we also assume that

$$L_1, L_4, L_5, g_1, g_3, g_5, n_2, n_4 > 0$$
$$L_2, L_3, g_2, g_4, n_1, n_3 < 0$$

and $n_5 \geqslant 0$. Thus we are assuming that money and government bonds are transactions complements $(L_1, g_1 > 0)$ while money and equities are transactions substitutes $(L_1 > 0, n_1 < 0)$. In addition, we assume that decreases in the rate of inflation, *ceteris paribus*, increase the demands for money balances and shares and decrease the demand for bonds. Finally, given the adding-up conditions, the negative effect of inflation on bonds can be shown to exceed the positive effect on money. This, Feldstein (1980a) claims, is a plausible condition and, consequently, forms part of the stability conditions of our model.

We will retain many of our earlier relations, but considerations of space prevent us from repeating them here. First, for *individuals* we will retain our assumptions on the growth of the labour force (at rate δ) and on adaptive expectations (with adjustment parameter β); these relations appeared as Equations 5.7 and 5.8. For the representative *business firm* we will retain the production function $\Phi(K, N^d)$ and the first-order conditions described in 5.10 and 5.11; we will also utilise the flow constraint for firms that appeared as Equation 5.28. For the *government* we will still permit an expenditures policy–as described (by τ) in Equation 5.30–but we need a new budget constraint to reflect the new source of revenue (B) and its service costs (i_b). This equation is

$$\frac{\dot{M}}{P} + \frac{\dot{B}}{P} = \tau y^s + i_b \frac{B}{P} - u_p \left(y + i_b \frac{B}{P} \right) - u_c \left(y^s - \frac{W}{P} N^d \right) \tag{5.53}$$

All of this produces a model with five markets and two constraints: an economy-wide stock constraint and an economy-wide flow constraint. Since there is, in effect, a Walras's Law for stocks and one for flows, we may again eliminate one stock and one flow market. Again we choose to eliminate the equity market and the labour market primarily to enable us to present explicit results for the money and bond markets where monetary and fiscal policy are applied.

Gathering our results, we find that we must account for three equilibrium conditions (product, money and bonds) and 'accumulation' equations for the inflation rate (Equation 5.8), the rate of physical capital growth $(\dot{k} + \delta k)$, and the rate of government debt accumulation (see 5.57, below). With Equations 5.4 and 5.30 and the new definition of disposable income (after 5.48), we can now write the product-market equilibrium condition (in real per capita terms) as

$$(1-s)\left[(f(k) - kf' + i_b b)(1-u_p) + f'(1-u_c)(1-u_p)k \right.$$
$$\left. - (m+b)\pi^e \right] + \dot{k} + \delta k + \tau f(k) = f(k) \tag{5.54}$$

Here, as before, $k = K/N$, $f(k) = F(k, 1)$, $m = M/PN$ and $b = B/PN$. The money-and bond-market equilibrium conditions that go with this structure are, accordingly,

$$L[f(k), f'(1-u_c)(1-u_p), i_b(1-u_p) - \pi^e, -\pi^e, m+b+k] = m \tag{5.55}$$

$$g[f(k), f'(1-u_c)(1-u_p), i_b(1-u_p) - \pi^e, -\pi^e, m+b+k] = b \tag{5.56}$$

They replace Equation 5.34 in the fiscal policy model. Finally, our new government debt-accumulation equation is actually a dynamic government budget constraint:

$$\dot{m} + \dot{b} + m(\pi + \delta) + b(\pi + \delta) = \tau f(k) + i_b b$$
$$- u_p \left[f(k) - kf' + kf'(1-u_c) + i_b b \right] - u_c kf' \tag{5.57}$$

5.4.2 The Steady State in the Combined Model

The steady state is, of course, defined by the condition that $\dot{k} = \dot{m} = \dot{b} = \dot{\pi}^e = 0$. At this solution we can evaluate Equations 5.54 to 5.57 and 5.8

to produce

$$-s[f(k)(1-\tau)+\delta(m+b)]+\delta(k+m+b) = 0 \qquad (5.58)$$

$$L[f(k), f'(1-u_c)(1-u_p), i_b(1-u_p)-\pi^e, -\pi^e, m+b+k]-m = 0 \qquad (5.59)$$

$$g[f(k), f'(1-u_c)(1-u_p), i_b(1-u_p)-\pi^e, -\pi^e, m+b+k]-b = 0 \qquad (5.60)$$

$$\Delta - (m+b)(\pi^e+\delta) = 0 \qquad (5.61)$$

where

$\Delta = \tau f(k) + i_b b - u_p [f(k)-kf'+kf'(1-u_c)+i_b b] - u_c kf'$ conveniently describes the government's deficit and the rest of 5.61 shows how the deficit is financed. In this model, then, the government is assumed to be able to set τ, u_c, u_p, and the size of the deficit. In fact, the government deficit, in the steady state, is financed by an inflation tax, $(m+b)\pi_e$, and a growth tax, $(m+b)\delta$, as before.

The system of four equations just laid out actually has five endogenous variables, k, m, b, π^e, and i_b. The reason this underdetermination arises is that we have only assumed relationships on the fiscal aspects of the behaviour of the government. Indeed, fixing the size of the deficit merely specialises the manner in which the variables under government control interact and does not fix any particular variable. What has not yet been specified is the manner in which the government controls its stock behaviour (that is, its financial policy). Normally in basic money-growth models the government just fixes money balances via open-market operations or it fixes the interest rate in the same fashion (as, for example, described in Chapter 1). This, indeed, given the simple structure of those models, is really the only manner in which the system can be closed. In the present structure, though, there are a number of alternative rules that the government can employ when it sets up its financial policy. Thus, the authorities may (noting that $\pi_e = \pi$)·

(a) set m or set $m(\pi_e+\delta)$,
(b) set b or set $b(\pi_e+\delta)$,
(c) set $m+b$,
(d) set $\dot{M}/M$ (or $\dot{B}/B$) which, in the steady state, is equivalent to setting π_e,
(e) set $i_b(1-u_p)$, the after tax *nominal* rate of interest or
(f) set $i_b(1-u_p)-\pi^e$, the *real* rate of interest.

In what follows we will consider cases (f), (d), (c) and (a) – in that order – and will neglect (b) and (e). We will drop (b) since consideration of the other cases makes it clear how that might go. For (a) we will take the per capita form $(m(\pi^e + \delta))$ since fixing m is basically a simplification of the per capita case. We will neglect (e) since fixing the nominal rate of return on government bonds is not a policy actually followed by governments as our discussion in Chapter 2 suggested (see Yohe and Karnovsky, 1969, and Feldstein and Summers, 1977). In any event the consideration of cases (f), (d), (c), and (a) gives us a rich menu of actually conceivable policies whose properties we can examine in this dynamic framework. Note, though, that we will be considering these monetary policy choices under the assumption of a particular fiscal policy (an increased deficit). This is, of course, not the only conceivable fiscal policy, but it is one that is of great interest in the current situation in the United States (for example).

5.4.3 Interest-Rate Policy under an Increasing Deficit

Suppose, then, that $i_b(1 - u_p) - \Pi^e = \Phi$, where Φ is a fixed positive constant. This rule, if adopted, would set changes in the rate of inflation equal to changes in the after-tax nominal rate of interest on government bonds. Assume, also, that the government increases its deficit (Δ)–and that the other fiscal parameters τ, u_c, and u_p are held constant. Under these conditions the growing government deficit must come at the expense of capital intensity (k) in the economy and, further, at the cost of an increased inflation rate. To see all this, we can substitute Φ for $i_b(1 - u_p) - \pi^e$ in Equations 5.59 and 5.60 and differentiate all four equations with respect to Δ. When we do this, we obtain the following system.

$$
\begin{bmatrix}
\delta - sf'(1-\tau) & \delta(1-s) & \delta(1-s) & 0 \\
L_1 f' + L_2 f''(1-u_c)(1-u_p) + L_5 & L_5 - 1 & L_5 & -L_4 \\
g_1 f' + g_2 f''(1-u_c)(1-u_p) + g_5 & g_5 & g_5 - 1 & -g_4 \\
0 & -(\pi^e + \delta) & -(\pi^e + \delta) & -(m+b)
\end{bmatrix}
\begin{bmatrix}
\dfrac{\partial K}{\partial \Delta} \\[2mm]
\dfrac{\partial m}{\partial \Delta} \\[2mm]
\dfrac{\partial b}{\partial \Delta} \\[2mm]
\dfrac{\partial \pi^e}{\partial \Delta}
\end{bmatrix}
$$

$$
= \begin{pmatrix} 0 \\ 0 \\ 0 \\ -1 \end{pmatrix} \tag{5.62}
$$

A necessary condition for the local stability of the steady state here is that the determinant of the matrix in Equation 5.62 be negative; this determinant (H) is

$$H = (sf'(1-\tau) - \delta)[n_5(m+b) + n_4(\pi^e + \delta)] + \delta(1-s)(m+b)$$
$$[n_1 f' + n_2 f''(1-u_c)(1-u_p) + n_5 - 1] \qquad (5.63)$$

A sufficient condition for $H < 0$ is that $sf'(1-\tau) - \delta < 0$ which corresponds to a generalised version of the stability condition in the barter model discussed above.

The system just described provides the basis for evaluating the effects of changing the deficit. For the effect on capital intensity and real-money balances we find that

$$\frac{\partial k}{\partial \Delta} = \frac{\delta(1-s)}{H}\, n_4 < 0 \qquad (5.64)$$

$$\frac{\partial m}{\partial \Delta} = \frac{\delta(1-s)}{H}\, [L_4(g_1 f' + g_2 f''(1-u_c)(1-u_p))$$

$$- g_4(L_1 f' + L_2 f''(1-u_c)(1-u_p)] + (\delta - sf'(1-\tau))\frac{L_4}{H}$$

$$- sL_4\frac{g_5}{H}(\delta - f'(1-\tau)) + sg_4\, L_5\left(\frac{\delta - f'(1-\tau)}{H}\right) \qquad (5.65)$$

Here it is clear in 5.64 that capital intensity must fall when the deficit increases, $H < 0$ and $n_4 > 0$; the latter describes the effect of inflationary expectations on the demand for shares (in nominal terms) and is a crowding-out effect similar to that described above. Furthermore, if the marginal product of capital attributable to the demand from the private sector does not fall below its golden-rule level (δ), then the increased real per capita deficit also decreases real per capita money balances (i.e. the right-hand side of 5.65 is negative). With regard to real per capita bond holdings, though, there is some ambiguity when the deficit changes. Indeed, from 5.62

$$\frac{\partial b}{\partial \Delta} = -\frac{\partial m}{\partial \Delta} - \frac{n_4}{H}(\delta - sf'(1-\tau)) \qquad (5.66)$$

and so if $\partial m/\partial \Delta \leqslant 0$, then $\partial b/\partial \Delta > 0$. Thus the enlarged deficit is financed by government bonds, and the increase in bonds exceeds the decrease in money balances. This occurs since, as the rate of inflation rises (which implies that the after-tax nominal rate of interest must rise to keep the real rate fixed), individuals move out of money and shares and into bonds. In this case bond holdings must absorb the fall in m and k. Finally, the effect of the deficit on expected inflation (π^e) is that this variable also rises, as the following calculation makes clear.

$$\frac{\partial \pi^e}{\partial \Delta} = -\frac{n_5}{H}\left(\delta - sf'(1-\tau)\right) + \frac{\delta(1-s)}{H}$$

$$[n_1 + n_5 - 1 + n_2 f''(1-u_c)(1-u_p)] > 0 \qquad (5.67)$$

Thus, in this case, with a real interest-rate rule such as that described in case (f), we find that an increased deficit is inflationary. This, at least, provides one theoretical scenario in which this popular supposition holds true.[11]

Finally we should note that there is also an implied inverse relationship between the inflation rate (in Equation 5.67) and capital intensity (in 5.64). That is, the inflation induced in this framework is associated with the crowding-out effect of the larger deficit. This is not a causal relation exactly, but it certainly is something that many observers have suggested is an undesirable side-effect of the deficit.

5.4.4 A Fixed Rate of Growth of Nominal Money Balances

In this subsection we will undertake a brief analysis of a second policy rule, that of fixing the rate of growth of nominal money balances by means of open-market operations. We will define this policy in terms of the setting of the parameter Θ, where $\dot{M}/M = \Theta$. It is clear that with a particular value of Θ, in the steady state, the rate of inflation is constant and equal to the difference between the growth rates on money and on output ($\Theta - \delta$). Should the government then attempt to run a deficit there would be no inflationary tax available to moderate the crowding-out effect, and thus the entire burden of the government deficit falls on capital intensity. In addition, government *debt* must rise, not only on account of the larger deficit, but also on account of the need to absorb the decrease in the demand for corporate claims brought about from the financial effects of the fiscal crowding-out. It is clear, also, that both the rising deficit and rising debt will cause the nominal interest rate on government bonds to rise.

The assumption of the rule that $\dot{M}/M = \Theta$ drastically simplifies the analytics of our problem because $\pi^e = \Theta - \delta$ in long-run equilibrium. From the government budget constraint we now have $(m + b)\Theta = \Delta$ and so $\partial (m + b)/\partial \Delta = 1/\Theta > 0$. Furthermore, substituting Δ/Θ for $m + b$ in the product-market equilibrium condition–which was given above as Equation 5.58–we obtain the following effect on capital intensity as a result of a change in the deficit.

$$\frac{\partial k}{\partial \Delta} = \frac{-\delta(1-s)}{\Theta(\delta - sf'(1-\tau))} < 0 \tag{5.68}$$

Thus, the effect of a general deficit is to lower capital intensity when a monetary rule is already in place.

To show that the nominal interest rate on bonds (i_b) will rise under the circumstances assumed in this section (that is, with a rising deficit), we first note that when the rate of growth of nominal money balances is fixed at Θ, then in the steady state $\dot{B}/B$ will also grow at the rate Θ. In this event private portfolio decisions are not relevant (they will accommodate themselves to this reality); the same applies to the composition of the government's debt (between bonds and money). Then, combining Equations 5.59 and 5.60 with 5.68, we are able to determine the effect of an increased deficit on the nominal interest rate. This is

$$\frac{\partial i_b}{\partial \Delta} = \frac{-1}{n_3(1-u_p)}\left[n_1 f' \varepsilon' + \frac{n_5}{\Theta} - (1-n_5)\varepsilon' \right.$$

$$\left. + n_2 f'' \varepsilon' (1-u_c)(1-u_p) \right] > 0 \tag{5.69}$$

Thus for $k = \varepsilon(\Delta)$ as was defined in Equation 5.68 and for $\varepsilon' < 0$ we clearly have a rise in the interest rate. The upshot is that in the case of a fixed rate of growth of the nominal money stock – that is, with a simple monetary rule, in effect – when the government runs an increasing deficit there is pure crowding-out in Equations 5.68 and 5.69, in exchange for the constant rate of inflation.

5.4.5 A Policy of Fixing the Debt

Another policy that might be adopted is that is of fixing the *real per capita* national debt by imposing some sort of financing requirement on the central government. The debt would be fixed in per capita terms in order to permit it to grow as population expands; it would be fixed in real terms so that it could alter automatically as prices (and money) change. It would be fixed in any event because of, let us say, political pressures that are easy to rationalise in contemporary societies. The rule, then, is to set $m + b = \alpha$, where α is a fixed positive constant. In this situation we can easily show that the result of an increased deficit is the generation of a higher rate of inflation; there is, though, no crowding-out effect on k in this instance. To see this, note that in Equation 5.58, with $m + b = \alpha$ substituted in, we would have the result that $\partial k / \partial \Delta = 0$ directly. Since there is no effect of a growing deficit on capital intensity, there is also no effect on output (or on the product market in general). In addition, real per capita wealth remains at its initial steady-state level in this case.

We may also derive the effect on the inflation rate and on nominal interest rates by means of very straightforward calculations. For the *inflation rate*, from the government budget constraint, we have that $\pi^e = \Delta / \alpha - \delta$ and so $\partial \pi^e / \partial \Delta = 1 / \alpha$. That is, the increase in the rate of inflation induced by a growing deficit is actually proportional to the deficit. For the interest rate, we note that to keep $m + b$ constant, the interest rate must rise, and it must rise in proportion to the higher rate of inflation. To see this, combine Equations 5.59 and 5.60 to get

$$\frac{\partial i_b}{\partial \Delta} = \frac{(n_3 + n_4)}{\alpha n_3 (1 - u_p)} > 0 \tag{5.70}$$

This expression will be positive for $n_3 + n_4 < 0$. This condition is a reasonable one that assumes that equities are a closer substitute for bonds than they are for money.

Before going on to our last case we should summarise the results obtained in the last three sections. For one thing we have shown that under real interest-rate controls – in Subsection 5.4.3 – changes in the level of the government's deficit provoke much greater market interdependence than in the cases when there are quantity controls – as in Subsection 5.4.4. As such, the result (of the interest-rate control policy) is to spread the effect of a larger deficit on to both the rate of inflation and capital intensity. Under quantity controls (in 5.4.4 and 5.4.5) there is a greater degree of market independence since product market effects can be separated from the financial market effects. Even so, there is still a considerable difference between the results of the two quantity-control policies. By fixing the rate of growth of nominal money balances, we find that the rate of inflation becomes exogenous and that the burden of adjustment falls on the product market. On the other hand, when government debt is fixed in real per capita terms, the product market is independent of the government's deficit, and the burden of a growing deficit falls on the financial markets – and produces (only) a higher rate of inflation. It is easy to imagine a government following such a policy, under present-day conditions.

5.4.6 Fixing the Rate of Real Per Capita Monetary Expansion

For our last case let us consider the situation that arises when the government fixes the rate of real per capita monetary expansion so that $M/PL = \Phi$, where Φ is a fixed positive constant. This, of course, is equivalent to the rule that $m(\pi^e + \delta) = \Phi$, given the definition of m and assuming a steady state with $m = \pi^e = 0$. Substituting $\Phi/(\pi^e + \delta)$ for m in Equations 5.58 to 5.61 and differentiating with respect to Δ, we obtain

$$
\begin{bmatrix}
\delta - sf'(1-\tau) & \delta(1-s) & \dfrac{-\delta(1-s)\Phi}{(\pi^e + \delta)^2} & 0 \\[2ex]
L_1 f' + L_2 f''(1-u_c)(1-u_p) + L_5 & L_5 & -L_3 - L_4 + \dfrac{\Phi(1-L_5)}{(\pi^e + \delta)^2} & L_3(1-u_p) \\[2ex]
g_1 f' + g_2 f''(1-u_c)(1-u_p) + g_5 & g_5 - 1 & -g_3 - g_4 - \dfrac{\Phi g_5}{(\pi^e + \delta)^2} & g_3(1-u_p) \\[2ex]
0 & -(\pi^e + \delta) & -b & 0
\end{bmatrix}
$$

$$
\begin{bmatrix}
\dfrac{\partial k}{\partial \Delta} \\[2ex]
\dfrac{\partial b}{\partial \Delta} \\[2ex]
\dfrac{\partial \pi^e}{\partial \Delta} \\[2ex]
\dfrac{\partial i_b}{\partial \Delta}
\end{bmatrix}
=
\begin{bmatrix}
0 \\[2ex]
0 \\[2ex]
0 \\[2ex]
-1
\end{bmatrix}
\tag{5.71}
$$

In order for the steady state to be stable in this case, a necessary condition for local stability is that the determinant in Equation 5.71 be negative. For this determinant (H) to be negative a set of sufficient conditions is that

$$
sf'(1-\tau) - \delta \quad \text{and} \quad g_3 L_5 - L_3 g_5 + L_3 < 0, \quad L_3 g_4 - g_3 L_4 > 0
$$

The last two of these conditions imply that the demand for money cannot be too interest inelastic with respect to the after-tax real rate of interest on government bonds. Indeed, the last two inequalities imply that $L_3 < \min\left[(g_3 L_4/g_4, g_3 L_5/(g_5 - 1))\right]$. Hence if L_3 is small there is a distinct possibility that in this case the steady state may be unstable; L_3 describes the effect of the real interest rate (on bonds) on the demand for money.

Solving Equation 5.71, we find that

$$\frac{\partial k}{\partial \Delta} = \frac{-\delta(1-s)(1-u_p)\left[mn_3/(\pi^e+\delta)+(g_3 L_4 - L_3 g_4)\right]}{H} < 0$$

(5.72)

so that an increase in the deficit lowers capital intensity. Furthermore, an increase in Δ will increase bond holdings, the rate of inflation and the interest rate – in the event that $f'(1-\tau)-\delta \geqslant 0$. In view of these results there is a possibility that an *increase* in the government deficit could be consistent with both a smaller capital intensity and a *lower* rate of inflation.[12] This result would occur because there is too much capital relative to the golden-rule level such that the increase in the deficit has the effect of crowding-out excessive capital by significantly raising the after-tax real interest rate through a decline of π^e. Whether or not this is a likely scenario depends, of course, on the empirical magnitudes of the behavioural relations within the model. However, it is still of interest to note that in a *stable* steady-state larger government deficits can be consistent with lower rates of inflation. This is a result that would be desirable in theoretical work in view of the difficulty there has been in contemporary empirical work establishing any connection between deficits and inflation.

Perhaps, in view of the complexity of the model discussed in Section 5.4, it would be just as well to provide a brief summary of our results. We have pointed out that in a three-asset model there is sufficient capacity to analyse independent monetary and fiscal policies. Then, in all cases starting with a stimulatory fiscal policy – in the form of an increased deficit – considered in the steady state, we examined several monetary policies and compared them with regard to their effect on capital intensity (in order to see the extent of crowding-out), on the rate of inflation and on the nominal interest rate. In the first policy we looked at, we assumed that the government also fixed the real rate of interest. In this case capital intensity decreased and the inflation rate increased (as the deficit increased). When, in the second policy, the inflation rate is fixed (via a monetary rule of holding constant the rate of growth of the nominal money stock), we will have crowding-out and a rise in the nominal interest rate. In the third policy we discovered that we can prevent crowding-out by fixing the rate of growth of the sum of real-money balances and real bonds (still under an increased deficit), but at the cost of a higher inflation rate again (and with a rise in the nominal interest rate). Finally, in the last policy exercise, when the rate of growth of real per capita money balances is fixed, an increased deficit is generally but not always associated with a rise in the nominal interest rate and with a rise in the rate of inflation. Thinking across all of these examples, we can see that in the final analysis an increased deficit generally must come at the expense of either capital intensity or the inflation rate, at least in a three-asset, three-sector dynamic model of the sort we have looked at here. There was, though, one case – where the growth rate of real cash balances was fixed – when an increased deficit could actually produce a lower inflation rate.

5.5 FISCAL AND MONETARY POLICY IN THE SHORT RUN

We may use the long-run model developed in Section 5.4 to generate short-run results if we fix the capital stock. We have, of course, considered short-run results elsewhere in this study, but nowhere have we done this in a really general way, and so this section, while an addendum to a chapter on the long run, actually contains standard and important policy material. Indeed, by doing it in this way we can 'back' the short-run out of the general long-run model so that we can readily compare the two sets of results. Of course the short run is, in any case, the context in which most economists prefer to think of policy. Several recent papers by Pyle and Turnovsky (1976) and Turnovsky (1977b, 1980) work toward the short-run solution; it is of interest here, though, to consider a more extensive – and explicit – short-run framework for policy analysis. The purpose of this section, then, is to offer a general short-run, continuous-time model in which there are three assets and three economic agents. This structure provides a framework sufficiently rich to provide differential effects for monetary and fiscal policies.

The model in Subsection 5.5.1 contains sectoral descriptions of the behaviour of households, firms and the government, in the short run. All sectors are constrained in both their flow and stock decisions, following Foley and Sidrauski (1971) and, more recently, Buiter (1980). The *household* receives labour income and interest from its bond holdings and 'pays' an inflationary tax on its money and bond holdings; this provides its flow constraint. The stock constraint for the household contains three assets – money, government bonds and corporate securities. The last two are assumed to be perfect substitutes in the eyes of final wealth-holders. *Business firms*, in this framework, have a flow constraint in which all of the revenues generated by production are paid out either to workers or to shareholders; their stock constraint is again a trivial one. Finally, the *government*'s (flow) budget constraint assumes that new revenue generated by money creation and bond issues fills up the gap between tax revenues and expenditures (plus the net costs of servicing the accumulated debt of the government). Putting this structure together with a description of the labour market in terms of an expectations augmented Phillips curve, we then consider the characterisation of short-run equilibrium. To close the model we need to specify the size of the government's deficit and its method of finance (bonds or money). This part of the exercise makes explicit the interconnection between fiscal and monetary policy as potential influences on short-run equilibrium.

When we do the policy exercises we will consider several important alternative policy scenarios in order to demonstrate the properties of the model and, of course, to provide explicit results for the policy ineffectiveness debate. The cases that we will consider include a money-financed and a debt-financed deficit and we will look at the possibilities of running a distinct monetary policy (say, a change in the rate of expansion of the money stock) when a fiscal policy is already established. While many of our results are similar to those of the standard policy conclusions of, for example, short run *IS–LM* analysis, we will be able to show that there are some anomalies which suggest that a broader range may be desirable on certain topics. First, though, we need to set up our model.

5.5.1 The Model

We will begin by restating the *flow constraint* for households from our previous versions. In this section we will actually follow the presentation of Section 5.2, where a short-run solution was discussed, but here we have a three-asset structure to consider.

$$C + S = \left(y + i_b \frac{B}{P} \right)(1 - u_p) - \pi^e \left(\frac{M + B}{P} \right) \tag{5.73}$$

Here the flows of consumption and savings are equal to after-tax income from labour and equities (denoted as y) and bonds (u_p is the proportional income-tax rate) less the expected capital loss from bond and money holdings because of inflation (π^e is the expected rate of inflation). P, in Equation 5.73, is the product price, and we are assuming that the expected rate of change of equity prices (P_f) is equal to the expected rate of change of product prices. We are, that is to say, following Turnovsky (1974) in that we are assuming that product and equity prices are different but that their expected rates of growth are equal. Equities, under these circumstances, are a perfect inflation hedge.

As before, we will require a *stock constraint* for the household. This is basically a portfolio constraint and appears as Equation 5.74.

$$M^d + B^d + P_f K_f^d = M + B + P_f K_f \tag{5.74}$$

Here K_f is a financial claim on the capital stock and P_f is its price, as already defined. Equation 5.74, clearly, describes the nominal wealth of the household.

For their disposal income, households, in this structure, now have $Z = (y + i_b B/P)(1 - u_p)$, and their consumption function is, accordingly,

$$C = H(Z) \qquad 0 < H' < 1 \tag{5.75}$$

with the clear implication that the capital gains and losses defined in Equation 5.73 – relating to 'real-money balance' and 'real-bond' effects – affect saving but do not affect consumption. With respect to those two effects we have, accordingly, advanced what is akin to a 'permanent income' or smoothing rationale, as is the fashion in this literature.

With respect to households' portfolio decisions, we adopt another simplification that is customary in this literature; this is that government bonds and corporate shares are perfect substitutes. This assumption carries with it the implication that the after-tax real rate of return on government bonds is equal to the after-tax real return on corporate shares as in $i_b(1 - u_p) - \pi^e = r(1 - u_p)$. By merging shares and bonds in this way, we can now take advantage of Walras's Law for stocks – as described by Turnovsky (1977a) – to eliminate the bonds-cum-shares market. Thus, to complete our picture of the financial markets we need only specify the money-demand function. This, in real terms, is

$$M^d/P = L(y, r(1 - u_p), -\pi^e, A)$$
$$L_1, L_3 > 0; \ L_2 < 0; \ 0 \leqslant L_4 < 1 \tag{5.76}$$

Note that $A = (M + B + P_f K_f)/P$ in this model.

Our interest in the short run is in an unemployment 'equilibrium', and so we will adopt the expectations-augmented Phillips relationship described below in Equation 5.77; in this sense this result, too, is attached to Chapter 2 of this survey. This equation shows that the rate of growth of the nominal supply price of labour (the rate of change of the nominal wage) is related to the difference between real income and full-employment real income and to the expected rate of inflation. Note that we are assuming that there is a fixed quantity of labour (N) which can be fully employed.

$$\pi_w = a(y - y^f) + \pi^e \qquad a > 0 \tag{5.77}$$

Labour income at full employment and the income from holding corporate shares defines y^f. Finally, we will treat π^e as an exogenous variable in our short-run analysis although it would not change the general meaning of our results in what follows to adopt the adaptive expectations formula of previous sections of this chapter (as we did in Equation 5.8). Of course, actual magnitudes will be altered if we do this, but that will not be a matter of concern in this purely theoretical discussion.

The second sector in the problem is that for the firm. We will assume that *firms* employ two inputs in the production process. This process is described by the production function

$$y = F(K, N^d) \tag{5.78}$$

with F assumed to be homogeneous of degree 1 with positive and diminishing marginal products. Here we will assume that all revenue is paid out to workers and shareholders and that there are no corporate income taxes, so that

$$F(K, N^d) = \frac{W}{P} N^d + r \frac{P_f K_f}{P} \tag{5.79}$$

In addition, if $N^d = N^s$, that is, if there is full employment, then we have that $y^f = F(K, N^f) = (W/P)N^f + r(P_f/P)K_f$. It will, further, be asserted that labour, in this model, will be paid its marginal product, so that

$$F_N(K, N^d) = \frac{W}{P} \tag{5.80}$$

In this event, assuming that F is homogeneous of degree 1 so that factor payments 'exhaust' the output and employing Equations 5.79 and 5.80, we obtain the result that

$$r P_f K_f = F_K(K, N^d) P K \tag{5.81}$$

Reorganising this expression we have

$$P_f K_f \left(\frac{r}{F_K(K, N^d)} - 1 \right) = PK - P_f K_f \tag{5.82}$$

This result states that the difference between the value of the firm's assets and the value of its equity is reflected by the difference between the rate of return on shares and the marginal product of capital.

The conception just described is, of course, akin to Tobin's 'q' (1969). Following this thought, we might expect it to provide some leverage on the investment behaviour of the firm, and so it does. That is, following Infante and J. Stein (1980), the difference between the rate of return and the marginal product of capital reflects a difference between the demand and supply prices of investment. In our context the supply price of investment is P, since the product is used for both consumption and investment purposes, while the demand price is P_f. Indeed, the difference between these prices guarantees the existence of a finite level of investment which we now specify as

$$I = I[F_K(K, N^d) - r] \qquad I(0) = 0; \quad I' > 0 \qquad (5.83)$$

With this expression we come to the end of our discussion of the business firm, in the short-run model.

The final agent in our short-run model is, of course, the *government*. The subject of this section really concerns the policy implications of the government's budget constraint in the short run, and so we now need to specify that relation as it exists in our present structure. Let us define $\Theta = \dot{M}/M$ and $\Phi = \dot{B}/B$ as the endogenous rates of growth for money and bonds respectively. The government budget constraint, then, can be written as

$$\Theta(M/P) + \Phi(B/P) = (\tau - u_p)y + [r(1 - u_p) + \pi^e](B/P)] \qquad (5.84)$$

The left-hand side of this expression reflects the flow of new funds from the issue of new money and government bonds while the right-hand side represents the difference between government expenditures and tax receipts – τ being the expenditure rate – plus interest payments on bonds. With regard to this last, recall that $i_b(1 - u_p) = r(1 - u_p) + \pi^e$ from the assumption of perfect substitutes that we described above.

5.5.2   Policy Specifications and Short-run Equilibrium

In this subsection we will characterise the nature of short-run equilibrium in the model that we have just described and spell out the nature of the policy options open to the government. Let us begin with the labour market. Returning to Equation 5.80, after defining $v = F_N(K, N^d)$ as the marginal product of labour, we can write that relation dynamically as

$$\dot{v}/v = \pi_w - \pi \qquad (5.85)$$

π_w, here, is the rate of growth of the demand price of labour, and the subtraction of π (the actual rate of inflation) provides us with an expression that is equal to the rate of growth of the marginal product of labour. By combining Equations 5.77 and 5.85 we can immediately establish the result that

$$\dot{v}/v = a(y - y^f) + \pi^e - \pi$$

Following Infante and Stein (1980) and Turnovsky (1977c), we assume that the rate of growth of the marginal product of labour is always zero ($\dot{v} = 0$); this implies that the *labour-market equilibrium* condition is

$$\pi = a(y - y^f) + \pi^e \qquad (5.86)$$

This is the product-price version of the expectations-augmented Phillips relation, approximately as described in Chapter 2.

For *product-market equilibrium*, using the definition of Z established in Equation 5.75, we have the direct result that

$$H\left(\left(y + r\frac{B}{P}\right)(1 - u_p) - \pi^e\frac{B}{P}\right) + I\left(f(K, y) - r\right) + \tau y = y \qquad (5.87)$$

We are, of course, asserting that $C + I + g = y$. In this expression it again should be noticed, with respect to the investment function, that we have used the fact that $N^d = j(K, y)$ from the production function so that $f(K, y) = F_K(K, j(K, y))$, where $f_K < 0$ (since $F_{KK} < 0$ and $F_{KN} > 0$) and $f_y > 0$ (since $F_{NN} < 0$). These results occur because F is homogeneous of degree one with diminishing marginal products.

Finally, by substituting $f(K, y)K/r$ for $P_f K_f/P$ (from Equation 5.81) we can directly write out the *money-market equilibrium* condition as

$$L\left(y, r(1 - u_p), -\pi^e, \frac{M + B}{P} + f(K, y)\frac{K}{r}\right) = \frac{M}{P} \qquad (5.88)$$

In this event the complete description of short-run equilibrium consists of Equations 5.84, 5.86, 5.87 and 5.88.[13]

For short-run equilibrium the problem is to determine the seven unknowns y, r, π, Θ, $m = M/P$, Φ, and $b = B/P$, given K and π^e. There are, though, only four equations. What we have to do, to close the model, is to specify government macroeconomic policy. Traditionally, in short-run analysis the government budget constraint is taken as an 'accumulation' equation that does not affect the temporary equilibrium. In this event the variables $\Theta m = \dot{M}/P$ and $\Phi b = \dot{B}/P$ and the government budget constraint (Equation 5.84) do not form part of the short-run equilibrium. In addition, the stocks of nominal money and bonds are generally assumed to be fixed so that the model boils down to three equations (5.86, 5.87 and 5.88) and three unknowns (y, r and π). With M and B fixed, indeed, the method by which the government finances its expenditures or changes in tax rates is actually irrelevant in the short run. That is, in response to changes in the rates τ or u_p, the government will alter the rate of expansion of money or bonds (i.e. $\dot{M}$ or $\dot{B}$) relative to the price level which, in turn, will change the nominal stock of money or bonds in the next temporary equilibrium. But in our model we want to investigate how manipulation of the government budget constraint affects short-run equilibrium; this requires an explicit accounting for 'deficit policy' just as it did in the long-run case. In the short run, though, our variables will not all be growing at the same rate, and therefore the policy specification is necessarily somewhat more detailed than is typical for short-run macromodels. There are, though, sufficient differences in the results to justify this effort.

First consider a *money-financed deficit*; this we will define as the case in which the government adjusts nominal money balances to the nominal value of the deficit while bonds are tied to changes in the price level. What this means is that m is changed, by policy, to fill up the gap between the right-hand side of Equation 5.84, while b is held fixed. With b fixed, then $\dot{B}/B = \dot{P}/P$ so that $\Phi = \pi$; the rate of growth of bonds must equal the rate of inflation. To close the model we need to lay on one more restriction from the budget constraint; this is a setting for Θ. That is, in the money-financed situation m is endogenous, b and Θ are fixed, and $\Phi = \pi$, which is also endogenous. This leaves us with four equations and with four unknowns (y, r, π and m). Conversely, for a *bond-financed deficit*, m and Φ are fixed, $\Theta = \pi$, and the endogenous variables are y, r, π and b. It should be emphasised that, in the long run, Θ must equal Φ, but that in the short run – our context – this equality need not hold. Indeed, when Θ is fixed in the money-financed case, the variable Φ adjusts to Θ over time. The converse holds for the bond-financed case. Finally, we note that for the government budget constraint to affect short-run equilibrium we must specify macroeconomic policy, not in terms of the stocks (so that the adjustment is in the flows) as is traditionally done, but rather in terms of the flows (represented by Θ and Φ) so that the adjustment is in terms of the stocks.

Models explicitly considering the government budget constraint share a difficulty with respect to the stability of the equilibrium for the bond-financed case. This problem is well known (since Blinder and Solow (1973) and Infante and Stein (1976)) for long-run equilibrium as discussed by Christ (1978). The reason for the potential instability is the presence of interest payments in both the government budget constraint and in real disposable income. The fact that, on the one hand, interest can be compounded and, on the other, that the government must also finance its interest payments requires a further constraint in order to avoid an explosive result. Christ's solution to the problem is to treat the sum of government expenditures and before-tax interest payments as exogenous; this solves the stability problem directly but seems a somewhat artificial solution because it implies an asymmetry. That is, it is not clear why we want to assume that the government treats its expenditures as exogenous and its income as endogenous. There is an alternative, and this is to treat the government deficit as exogenous. In this way the deficit itself becomes a policy variable. This is done by Foley and Sidrauski (1971), Turnovsky (1980) and Feldstein (1980a), who do not, though, deal with the instability problem but with the role of the deficit. That is, we can define Δ as the fixed real value of the deficit, and thus Equation 5.84 becomes

$$\Theta(M/P) + \Phi(B/P) = \Delta \tag{5.89}$$

We will proceed to carry out the various policy experiments with this relation in place of 5.84.

5.5.3 Policy Experiments in the Short-run Model

(A) A Money-financed deficit

For a money-financed deficit, as pointed out above, we will assume that $b = b^0$ and that Θ is fixed (and thus $\Phi = \pi$). These conditions imply the following relations in place of our earlier equilibrium conditions. Note that we now will employ the notation $m = M/P$, $b = B/P$, for convenience.

$$H(y(1-\tau) + \Delta) + I(f(K, y) - r) + \tau y = y \tag{5.90}$$

$$L[y, r(1 - u_p), -\pi^e, m + b^0 + f(K, y)(K/r)] = m \tag{5.91}$$

$$\Theta m + (a(y - y^f) + \pi^e)b^0 = \Delta \tag{5.92}$$

Note that Equation 5.92 is a combination of the government budget constraint and the labour-market equilibrium condition. In this system y, r and m are the variables that are to be determined.

As shown in Figure 5.2, we can obtain a traditional *IS* curve from Equation 5.90. This relationship is defined as $r = \alpha(y)$, where $\alpha' < 0$ when $(H' - 1)(1 - \tau) + I'f_y < 0$. From Equation 5.91, *given m*, which is now

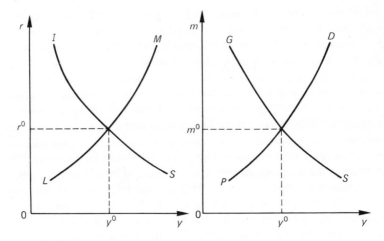

Figure 5.2   Short-run equilibrium – money-financed case

endogenous, we obtain the *LM* curve, defined as $r = M(y)$, with $M' > 0$. We may collapse the system further by substituting $r = \alpha(y)$, the *IS* curve, into the *LM* curve and eliminate the interest rate between the two functions. The result is defined in terms of the two remaining endogenous variables, *m* and *y*. The slope of this function, which we will call the *PD* curve, is then calculated as

$$\frac{dm}{dy} = \left(L_1 + L_4 f_y \frac{K}{r} + \left(L_2 - L_4 f \frac{K}{r^2} \right)\alpha' \right) \Big/ (1 - L_4) > 0$$

In more compact notation we can describe this *PD* curve as $m = \mu(y)$ with $\mu' > 0$; it appears in Figure 5.2 also. This is a kind of aggregate-demand curve, of course, but with *m* rather than the price level on the vertical axis. *m*, it should be recalled, is real-money balances.

The supply-side representation for the (m, y) plane comes originally from a combination of the labour-market equilibrium condition and the government budget constraint (as represented by Equation 5.92). We will call this the *GS* curve and can calculate its slope as

$$dm/dy = -ab/\Theta < 0$$

It also appears in the right-hand panel of Figure 5.2. More compactly, this relationship can be written as $m = \Sigma(y)$, with $\Sigma' < 0$. This curve, of course, differs from the usual aggregate-supply curve by being defined in terms of real-money balances (rather than the price level) and by including the government budget constraint. At any rate Figure 5.2·

captures the essence of the short-run policy model that we have developed to this point.

Suppose, then, that there is an increase in the real value of the deficit. The effect of this on real income is readily calculated as being

$$\frac{\partial y}{\partial \Delta} = -\frac{H'}{\Omega}\Theta\left(L_2(1-u_p)-L_4f\frac{K}{r^2}\right)+\frac{I'}{\Omega}(1-L_4)>0 \tag{5.93}$$

and shows a positive effect from an expansion of the deficit on real income. Here Ω is the determinant of the matrix of coefficients derived from Equations 5.90 to 5.92 and $\Omega' > 0$ from the condition for a negatively sloped IS curve that we described above. We will not list these solutions here, in the interest of economy.

The intuition for this result is as follows. First, the increase in Δ increases real disposable income, and so the IS curve shifts to the right; this, in turn, shifts the PD curve to the right. The increased deficit also shifts the LM curve to the right and the GS curve to the right. The net effect is upward on income in the short run and ambiguous on the nominal interest rate (as it turns out). The interest-rate result is comforting in view of empirical results that we have referred to elsewhere (on the effect of the U. S. deficit). We note that the effect on real-interest rates is similarly ambiguous while those on real-money balances and, of course, on the inflation rate are unambiguously positive. On net, these results differ from those standard in the typical IS–LM style literature in that in the usual situation the increase in real income is smaller than that shown here and the interest-rate effect is generally found to be positive. This is, essentially, the result of including the government budget constraint in the description of the short-run equilibrium. These seem to be important qualifications to the standard short-run paradigm.

A question which might arise about the operation of this model concerns the role of an independent *monetary policy* in the event that the deficit is money-financed. We will consider two types of monetary policy – a simple monetary expansion and an open-market operation. For the monetary expansion let Θ, the rate of growth of the nominal stock of money, increase. Equations 5.94, 5.95 and 5.96 show these effects on real income, the real-interest rate, and real-money balances.

$$\partial y/\partial \Theta = \frac{m}{\Omega}I'(L_4-1)<0 \tag{5.94}$$

$$\partial r/\partial \Theta = \frac{m}{\Omega}[(H'-1)(1-\tau)+I'f_y](L_4-1)>0 \tag{5.95}$$

$$\partial m/\partial\Theta = \frac{-m}{\Omega}\left[((H'-1)(1-\tau)+I'f_y)\left(L_2(1-u_p)\right.\right.$$
$$\left.\left.-L_4f\frac{K}{r^2}\right)+I'\left(L_1+L_4f_y\frac{K}{r}\right)\right]<0 \tag{5.96}$$

We are able to obtain signs for each of these effects, as noted. Thus, given a deficit that is money-financed, an increase in the rate of monetary expansion actually decreases real income and real balances and increases the real rate of interest. Furthermore, and paradoxically, it *decreases* the rate of inflation since

$$\partial\pi/\partial\Theta = a(\partial y/\partial\Theta)<0$$

Of course the price level is rising. This result occurs in this literature from time to time, usually because of imposing some restriction such as – in our model – that of an established deficit that is itself money-financed.

The rationale for this result is as follows. A rise in the rate of growth of the money stock – given the real value of the deficit – is consistent with a lower *level* of real-money balances. In order for real-money balances to fall, the real-interest rate must rise and real income must fall. Since Θ is rising and m is falling, we must have a higher product price level. The higher-product price level (with the higher Θ) means that the inflation *rate* is lower (i.e. it means that the rate of growth of the price level decreases although the level is higher). Indeed, by fixing Θ, in effect, the monetary authorities force portfolio holders to adjust to Θ when, at the same time, the fiscal authorities are holding Δ constant.

The second type of monetary policy that we mentioned is an open-market operation. To carry this out, let us assume that the government increases the nominal value of outstanding bonds so that b increases. We find, in this case, that

$$\partial y/\partial b = \frac{I'}{\Omega}\left[-\pi+L_4(\pi-\Theta)\right] \tag{5.97}$$

$$\partial r/\partial b = \frac{1}{\Omega}\left[(H'-1)(1-\tau)+I'f_y\right](-\pi+L_4(\pi-\Theta)) \tag{5.98}$$

$$\partial m/\partial b = \frac{-\pi}{\Omega}\left[(H'-1)(1-\tau)+I'f_y\right]\left(L_2(1-u_p)-L_4f\frac{K}{r^2}\right)$$
$$-\frac{I'}{\Omega}\left[\pi\left(L_1+L_4f_y\frac{K}{r}\right)-abL_4\right] \tag{5.99}$$

To help establish signs here we note the appearance of the term $\pi-\Theta$ in

5.97 and 5.98; this measures the difference between the rate of growth of nominal money balances and the rate of inflation. Thus, if $\Theta - \pi \geqslant 0$, then the open-market operation (that is, the increase in b) will reduce real income and raise the real-interest rate. Recall, in thinking about this result, that $\Phi = \pi$ and Θ is exogenous so that we have the inflation rate adjusting to the monetary rule. The money-market effect in 5.99 is not so readily determined and is, in any case, peripheral to the drift of this study.

Let us attempt a summary of Subsection A. With regard to a money-financed deficit – when the fiscal deficit is already growing – real income grows, as do real-money balances and the inflation-rate and real-money balances, but the effect of a growing deficit on the interest rate (however measured) is ambiguous. Monetary policy, in this context, when represented as an increase in the rate of growth of money given the real value of the government deficit, decreases real income and real-money balances (and increases the real-interest rate). Paradoxically, it actually decreases the rate of inflation. A policy of open-market operations, when the rate of growth of money is not less than the rate of inflation, leads to a decline in real income and a rise in the real-interest rate.

(B) *A Bond-financed deficit*

The alternative to the policy just considered is, of course, that of a bond-financed deficit. For this case, as we have already discussed, we set $m = m^o$ and fix Φ with $\Theta = \pi$. These conditions imply equilibrium relations similar to Equations 5.90 and 5.91, but we must replace Equation 5.92 with the following expression.

$$\Phi b + [a(y - y^f) + \pi^e]m^o = \Delta \tag{5.100}$$

This alternative is simply the result of assuming that the deficit is bond-financed. We will consider, in the remainder of this section, the analytics of macropolicy when there is a bond-financed deficit and offer some comparisons with the money-financed case. The endogenous variables are now y, r, π and b.

When expansionary fiscal policy is represented by an increase in Δ (and we have bond-financing) the results are generally less precise than in the money-financed case. The effect on real income is now

$$\frac{\partial y}{\partial \Delta} = -\frac{H'\Phi}{\Omega_1}\left[L_2(1 - u_p) - L_4 f\frac{K}{r^2}\right] - \frac{I'L_4}{\Omega_1} \tag{5.101}$$

Here Ω_1 is the counterpart to Ω in the money-financed case. In order for $\Omega_1 > 0$, we must have $(H' - 1)(1 - \tau) + I'f_y < 0$ and $\Phi(L_1 + L_4 f_y K/r)$

$-amL_4 > 0$; we also assume that $(H'' - 1)(1 - \tau) + H'am + I'f_y < 0$. The second condition just stated is required to preserve the direct relationship between real income and the interest rate in the money market. Even so, with $\Omega_1 > 0$, the effect on y is ambiguous because of the wealth effect in the money-demand function. We would require $L_4 = 0$ to get a sign for $\partial y / \partial \Delta$ (> 0). Hence, in the event that a growing deficit is financed by bonds, real income may *fall* even in the short run.

With regard to the other variables, then, an increase in the deficit increases the interest rate and the real value of government bonds, as described in Equations 5.102 and 5.103.

$$\frac{\partial r}{\partial \Delta} = -\frac{L_4}{\Omega_1} \left[(H' - 1)(1 - \tau) + I'f_y \right]$$

$$+ \frac{H'}{\Omega_1} \left[\Phi \left(L_1 + L_4 f_y \frac{K}{r} \right) - amL_4 \right] > 0 \qquad (5.102)$$

$$\frac{\partial b}{\partial \Delta} = \frac{1}{\Omega_1} \left(L_2 (1 - u_p) - L_4 f \frac{K}{r^2} \right) [(H' - 1)(1 - \tau)$$

$$+ H'am + I'f_y] + \frac{I'}{\Omega_1} \left(L_1 + L_4 f_y \frac{K}{r} \right) > 0 \qquad (5.103)$$

Both of these effects offset each other in equilibrating the product and money markets since the increase in b leads to an increase in consumption and money demand, while the increase in r decreases investment and money demand. The effect that dominates will determine the movement in y that is needed to restore equilibrium.

As mentioned above, it is possible to compare the effects of fiscal policy on real income under the two financing regimes discussed in the Subsections A and B. In order to do this, we set $m^o = b^o$ and $\Theta = \Phi$. The result is that, with the right-hand side of Equation 5.101 positive, we have

$$\left. \frac{\partial y}{\partial \Delta} \right|_{b = b^o} \qquad - \left. \frac{\partial y}{\partial \Delta} \right|_{m = m^o} > 0$$

Thus the money-financed deficit is more expansionary.[14] This results because the demand for bonds must increase in the bond-financing case while the demand for money must increase in the money-financed case. In order to bring about these changes, y must increase relatively more under money-financing since money and bonds are transactions substitutes given the stock constraint of the households in Equation 5.74, while the interest rate must increase relatively more under bond-financing in order for individuals to alter their portfolios in favour of bonds. Indeed, when the right-hand side of Equation 5.101 is positive, we also have that

$$\frac{\partial r}{\partial \Delta}\bigg|_{m=m^o} \qquad -\frac{\partial r}{\partial \Delta}\bigg|_{b=b^o} > 0$$

Thus, consistently, the interest rate rises more in the bond-financed case.

While these results are not, on the whole, surprising in the short-run literature, the reader should note (a) that we have backed this short-run model out of a long-run one and (b) that the long-run results with respect to real income of Blinder and Solow (1973) are precisely the opposite of those just described. Their bond-financing case is *a priori* unstable. Christ (1978), then, deals with this problem by treating all government payments as exogenous so that bond-financing is stable and money-financing is unambiguously more expansionary. The result here is therefore consistent with that of Christ, but it now refers to the short run, with the government deficit being given. Here, in addition, there is a clear comparison of interest-rate effects that does not appear in the literature just mentioned.

The next (and last) topic in this chapter concerns the potential role of monetary policy when the given deficit is bond-financed. When we discussed money-financing in Subsection A, we compared an explanation of the rate of growth of money and an open-market operation; now the correct comparison is between open-market operations and an expansion of the rate of growth of real bonds. For various reasons – one of which is space – we will limit our discussion here to the case of the open-market operation.

When we have an open-market operation (under bond-financing of a given deficit), we represent this by an expansion in m. The effects are

$$\frac{\partial y}{\partial m} = \frac{I'}{\Omega_1}[\Phi(1-L_4)+\pi L_4] > 0 \tag{5.104}$$

$$\frac{\partial r}{\partial m} = \frac{1}{\Omega_1}[(H'-1)(1-\tau)+I'f_y](\Phi(1-L_4)+\pi L_4) < 0 \tag{5.105}$$

$$\frac{\partial b}{\partial m} = -\frac{\pi}{\Omega_1}[(H'-1)(1-\tau)+I'f_y]\left(L_2(1-u_p)-L_4 f_y \frac{K}{r^2}\right)$$
$$-\frac{I'}{\Omega_1}\left[\pi\left(L_1+L_4 f_y \frac{K}{r}\right)-am(1-L_4)\right] < 0 \tag{5.106}$$

and they are all determinate with income expanding and with the real-interest rate and real-bond-holdings declining as a result of the monetary expansion. These results are certainly not unusual in the short-run literature.

Again we can set up a comparison between the two financing regimes in Subsections A and B and compare the effects of open-market operations. We do this by setting $m^o = b^o$ and $\Phi = \Theta \geqslant \pi$. The effects are

$$\frac{\partial y}{\partial m}\bigg|_{m=m^o} + \frac{\partial y}{\partial b}\bigg|_{b=b^o} = (\pi - \Theta)(L_4 - 1) + L_4(\pi - \Theta)$$

Here, if the rate of growth of nominal money-balances equals the rate of inflation ($\pi = \Theta$), then open-market operations have identical effects on real income irrespective of the method of financing the deficit; that is, an increase in m is equivalent to a decrease in b. In addition, if the wealth effect on money demand is sufficiently small, for example if $L_4 = 0$, then the relative effectiveness of open-market operations depends entirely on the differential $\Theta - \pi$. If this difference is positive, then open-market operations are stronger in influencing real income under money-financing. The converse is true for $\Theta - \pi < 0$. We finally note that for interest-rate effects, if $\Theta = \pi$, open-market operations are equivalent in the two cases. If $L_4 = 0$ (or if it is sufficiently small) and with $\Theta - \pi > 0$, then open-market operations have a stronger impact on the interest rate under bond-financing, while when $\Theta - \pi < 0$, the converse is true. Thus, the results depend on the rate of growth of the real stock of government debt compared to the rate of inflation.

Again, let us offer a brief summary of a very technical discussion. For a bond-financed deficit, when the deficit increases, the effect on real income is ambiguous while the real-interest rate and real-bond-holdings actually increase. A comparison of this case with the money-financed deficit produces the conclusion that the real-income adjustment is greater in the money-financed case while the interest-rate adjustment is greater under bond-financing. Open-market operations (still assuming that the deficit is bond-financed) raise real income and lower the real-interest rate. In addition, we are able to compare the effects on real income and the real-interest rate for an open-market operation under the two financing regimes. The determining element is whether the rate of growth of the real stock of government debt exceeds, equals or is less than the rate of inflation. Indeed, when these two rates are equal, the effects of an open-market operation are identical in the two financing regimes.

6 Keynesian and Monetarist Perspectives on the Policy Debate

> If the Treasury were to fill old bottles with bank-notes, bury them at suitable depths in disused coal mines which are then filled up to the surface with town rubbish, and leave it to private enterprise ... there would be no more unemployment.   KEYNES, 1936, p. 129

6.1   INTRODUCTION

Since the 1930s there has been a running debate between a group who might loosely be called 'Keynesian-activists' and a rival group of 'monetarist-classicists' which has involved most of the theoretical and empirical issues raised so far in this survey. Being overly-specific for the moment, monetarists are often associated with the idea that changes in the quantity of money are linked to changes in the price level and that the link is a causal one – from money to prices; as classicists they may view macropolicy as either unnecessary or, even, positively harmful in an uncertain world where adjustment takes a significant amount of time. In the same terms, Keynesians can be associated with notions of market imperfection and price sluggishness and, assuming it is feasible, with the need to undertake systematic policies to counteract the cyclical consequences of these (and any other) imperfections. At this level the issues are clear enough, but there is still no sense of the dynamics of this debate – in particular no sense of what has been resolved and of where the debate may go in the future. It will be the task of this chapter, then, to attempt to extract from this literature those results that are of particular value in clarifying the roles of monetary and fiscal policies in our times. This will be done in a way that deliberately plays down the many disputes that dot this landscape.

The major issue that still divides, let us say, neo-Keynesians from neo-monetarists concerns the way markets work. We have considered this topic in some depth in Chapters 3 and 4 and do not need to go over that ground again. By implication, we will argue that many issues actually have been resolved in this long debate, in the special sense in which one can claim resolution in the study of economics. By this we mean that there is a set of topics for which 'theoretical opinion' is pretty much agreed as to what the empirical issues are and for which empirical work has pretty much reached the point where those who could be persuaded by the evidence have in fact been persuaded. This material, at least until there are fresh eruptions, represents a finished body of work that is the common heritage of macroeconomists. What is surprising, though, is that one can still find a substantial literature, not all of it in a popular mode, that is written as if there actually has been very little progress on these policy issues. This unfortunate state of affairs suggests that macroeconomics is at best a chaotic and undisciplined topic area; indeed, it has also spawned a multiplicity of labels – e.g. neo-Keynesian, Marxo-Keynesian, and even bastard-Keynesian – which are used to identify the branches of the two schools of thought as they appear to emerge from the fray.

What is regrettable about the fragmentation, if such exists, is that the fundamental consistency of thought within each of the two approaches is obscured by what often seem to be doctrinal disputes. The confusion thus created is exacerbated by the tendency for the representative Keynesian to be an advocate of policy actions of all sorts – and for what are often liberal political opinions – and for the representative monetarist to tend to support policy inaction at the macroeconomic level – and to hold what are often conservative political opinions.[1] In the confusion, and, one suspects, often in deliberation, the clean lines of the debate have been rubbed over so much that if one is not careful he is apt to be seriously misled as to what evidence would improve the resolution of a particular issue. Thus a major part of the effort of this chapter will be to state a consensus view, when it exists, both across and within the two opposing perspectives. The remaining empirical and theoretical differences will be described, too, with the reminder that earlier chapters contain much of the more vital of this material.

The remainder of this chapter will attempt to reorient the debate, first, by eliminating the subcategories of each school and, then, by treating the whole debate as essentially a progression toward a clearer understanding of the macroeconomic policy choices that a nation could reasonably expect to have. We will begin with Keynes, following a historical line that begins with the initial Keynesian revolution and then discuss its progression as it solidifies into something that H. G. Johnson (1971) calls the 'Keynesian orthodoxy'. This material will run from Keynes up to the neo-Keynesians whose work we have already considered in earlier chapters. The discussion is conducted along the lines of the 'history of

Keynesian thought', but we will continue to focus primarily on macropolicy issues in order to give the discussion a structure consistent with the themes of this study. Our broad topics will consider the economics of Keynes, the nature of the Keynesian revolution and a still active debate (in Subsection 6.3.4) over 'fiscalism' as it exists in certain Keynesian writings and as it is contrasted with certain notions of monetarism in this literature.

With respect to monetarism, we will get under way in Section 6.4 with an attempt to define our way out of the problem by listing the main 'working propositions' of the dominant mainstream monetarists (Friedman, Meltzer, Laidler, Poole, for example). This framework is then illustrated in Subsection 6.4.1 with reference to the often-tested Friedman–Meiselman (1963) model and in Subsection 6.4.3 with reference to the still-used St Louis model. These standard monetarist paradigms have been thoroughly vetted, of course, with the main points of weakness involving the possibilities (a) that these models fail to specify causality correctly, (b) that the reduced-forms estimated contain endogenous variables as regressors, a variation of (a), and (c) that certain relevant variables have been omitted to the disadvantage of non-monetary (particularly fiscal) factors, primarily.

6.2 MONETARY AND FISCAL POLICY IN THE WORKS OF KEYNES

It is not really surprising that the Keynesians (e.g. Hicks, Samuelson, Tobin, etc.) altered the models of Keynes to achieve a new set of insights into how monetary and fiscal policies affect the economy. It is also not surprising that Keynesian theorists have adopted some of the material of the monetarists, if only because some of the monetarists' proposals have been demonstrated empirically. What is surprising is that Keynes himself has enjoyed somewhat of a revival not only in terms of his formulation of the roles of monetary and fiscal policy, but also because of his interest in the possibility of disequilibrium in a capitalist economy. This is not to say that disequilibrium is a new idea, for it has been an important topic throughout the debate, but instead to say that Keynes's ideas, *per se*, have been reintroduced into the recent discussion. Thus, the following is not entirely an essay in the history of ideas but, instead, is intended to be a refresher course in the relevance of the writings of Keynes (and, in Section 6.3, the Keynesians) to current topics. It is hoped that, after the discussion of these two sections, a reasonably clear picture of the characteristics of a 'representative Keynesian' will emerge.

We have used the word 'revolution' in connection with Keynes and his descendants, and it is appropriate, before narrowing the topic to policy issues, to consider the aptness of this designation. Following Johnson (1971), we can certainly accept the view that Keynesianism was an explicit attack on an established (classical) orthodoxy which was itself ineffective in explaining and prescribing the appropriate policy for persistent unemployment. The Keynesian alternative, then, was based on contemporaneous developments in general equilibrium theory, on econometric and statistical innovations and on the potential of real demand-side shocks both for explaining real-business cycles and for providing a justification for counteracting demand-side (policy) shocks. It became a revolution partly because of the apparent relevance of its prescriptions in what was thought to be a chronically depressed capitalist economy and because of the 'professional' zeal of some of its adherents. But it grew to develop its own orthodoxy and for that and other more pertinent reasons was attacked on certain fronts by the monetarist 'counter-revolution' which we will describe in similar terms in Section 6.4.

For Keynes, monetary policy works primarily by altering the long-term rate of interest and with it the rate of real-capital formation. That is, because of the existence of a well-defined speculative (asset) demand for money, a change in the supply of money (via an open-market operation) will tend to affect the long-term rate of interest and thereby to affect business investment. There are two major links in this chain on which Keynes (and the Keynesians) have focused attention. These concern the interest-elasticity of the investment-demand function and, to a lesser degree, the interest-elasticity of the demand for money.

With regard to the investment-demand function, Keynes, basically, offers us casual empiricism. That is, after dividing the influences on investment into 'short-period changes in the state of long-term expectations' and 'changes in the rate of interest', he finds the latter a 'great, though not a decisive, influence on the rate of investment' so that (1936, p. 164), 'For my own part I am now somewhat sceptical of the success of a merely monetary policy directed towards influencing the rate of interest.' This, actually, is partly due to the (long-term) rate of interest not being 'decisive' in the investment decision and partly because of his doubts concerning the ability of the authorities to alter the long-term interest rate. With regard to the latter, the problem arises, in the first instance, because 'the rate of interest is a highly psychological phenomenon'.[2] That is, while the authorities can readily control the short-term interest rate through open-market operations (in short-term securities), in order to reach the long-term rate, they must buck the forces of 'convention' since (p. 203), '*Any* level of interest which is accepted with sufficient conviction as *likely* to be durable *will* be durable. . . .' This is all the more apparent when the interest rate has fallen to a level that is generally considered to be unsafe. Such rigidity cannot be overcome by 'a monetary policy which strikes public opinion as being experimental in character or easily liable to change' (p. 203). On net (p. 204), 'The difficulties in the way of maintaining effective demand at a level high enough to provide full employment, which ensue from the association of a conventional and fairly stable long-term rate of interest with a fickle and highly unstable marginal efficiency of capital, should be, by now, obvious to the reader.' These observations have served as the backbone of the Keynesian position since the publication of the *General Theory* and were undoubtedly derived from British experiences in the early 1930s.[3]

In the foregoing the interest-elasticity of the demand for money has not had a strong role to play and that is in accord with recent views of this effect (see Lieberman, 1979). The policy problem is that of trying to induce spending responses via monetary or fiscal policy, and for that almost any interest-rate response at all will do. With regard to the mechanics of this, especially when the authorities are trying to push the interest rate lower, Keynes suggests two things that they could do to improve their grip. These are (a) to eschew dealing only in short-term securities and (b) to deal in securities which are riskier than those they usually deal in. For (b), they could even deal in securities issued by private firms if necessary. While these efforts would impart a direct and potentially quicker and more decisive influence on the credit markets, they still would not deal with the liquidity trap in which (p. 207), 'the monetary authority would have lost effective control over the rate of interest.' 'But whilst this limiting case might become practically import-ant in future, I know of no example of it hitherto. Indeed, . . . there has not been much opportunity for a test.' (p. 207) It is interesting that Keynes actually readily dismisses an idea that was for several generations an important element in the 'money doesn't matter' position of the Keynesians, and it is also interesting that his observation is made during the mid-1930s after the worst of the Great Depression was past. Indeed, his comments on the events in the early 1930s in the United States suggest that he felt that a liquidity crisis (a shortage) was at hand, not a liquidity trap.

As pointed out, Keynes's name is frequently mentioned as a founder of 'fiscalism', and so it is also useful to document his position on the usefulness of fiscal policy. As it turns out, he has little to say on the subject, but what he does say is quite forceful. With respect to fiscal policy in the *General Theory* it is clear that Keynes sees it as operating in a parallel way to a shift in investment except that (p. 119), 'we have to assume that there is no offset through decreased investment in other directions, – and also, of course, no associated change in the propensity of the community to consume'. The factors which would reduce the effect are any rise in the interest rate on account of the method of financing the policy, any rise in the price of capital goods, any increase in the demand for money (if confidence were increased, so might the holding of 'liquidity'), and any leakage abroad. This is largely a discussion of what later becomes known as 'crowding-out'. Of course, the degree of this effect clearly depends on the state of excess capacity in the system, and so (p. 127), 'public works even of doubtful utility may pay for themselves over and over again at a time of severe unemployment, if only from the diminished cost of relief expenditure'. This line of reasoning he pursues, producing a passage in which there almost appears to be a combined monetary–fiscal policy (p. 129): 'If the Treasury were to fill old bottles with banknotes, bury them at suitable depths in disused coal mines which are then filled up to the surface with town rubbish, and leave it to private enterprise . . . there would be no more unemployment.' In sum, it is 'more sensible to build homes . . . but if there are political and practical difficulties . . . the above would be better than nothing'.

6.3   THE KEYNESIAN REFORMULATION

From, roughly, 1940 until the mid-1960s a well-defined body of thought grew up around the foregoing, which was pretty much dominant (although occasionally challenged) on questions of macro-modelling and macropolicy. To go almost right to the end, in 1965 it was Solow's judgement that (1965, p. 146), 'I think that most economists feel that short-run macroeconomic theory is pretty well in hand. . . . The basic outlines of the dominant theory have not changed in years. All that is left is the trivial job of filling the empty boxes, and that will not take more than 50 years of concentrated effort at a maximum.' Similarly, W. W. Heller (1966, p. 116) asserts that 'we have harnessed . . . the economics that has been taught in the nation's classrooms for some twenty years . . . to the purposes of prosperity, stability, and growth', and also that (p. 72) 'the [1964] tax cut itself . . . described as a 'triumph' of high-test

Keynesian economic therapy . . . will richly repay its debts to the textbooks by supplying the classic example of modern fiscal policy and multiplier economics at work'.

As we have seen in earlier chapters, the years immediately after 1965 have not been particularly kind to the Keynesians. We do not need to go over that story again here; rather, in this section we wish to summarise these unified Keynesian positions on monetary and fiscal policies and distinguish them from the work of Keynes.

6.3.1 The Aggregative Structure of Keynesianism

As Leijonhufvud (1968) has pointed out, there are a number of basic theoretical differences between Keynes and the representative Keynesian. To begin with, Keynes arranges the sectors of his model differently from the Keynesians, by dividing his economy into consumer goods, non-money assets, labour services and money. In this structure the entity 'non-money assets' includes capital goods and bonds while 'money' includes all short term securities.[4] The consequence, then, is that the short-term interest rate is irrelevant for policy, and it is the long-term rate which must be controlled by policy (directly, if necessary) in order to influence investment. In contrast, the Keynesians, on the whole, add together consumption and investment and treat bonds and money as separate aggregates; labour services are then the fourth aggregate.[5] The representative interest rate in their model, thus, becomes a short-term interest rate.[6] In this case it becomes rather easy to see why, in the Keynesian system, the interest rate is thought to exert little effect on investment spending – it is a short-term interest rate, after all.[7] This, of course, shuts off an important potential avenue of influence for monetary policy – an avenue that, on the whole, Keynes apparently has more faith in than the Keynesians do.

The point just made about the Keynesian aggregative structure is suggestive, of course, but the main line of attack on this problem is, and should be, empirical. Especially influential in establishing the irrelevance of interest rates to investment decisions are the Oxford studies (e.g. of Meade and Andrews, 1938) and work by Klein (1954), J. R. Meyer and Kuh (1957), and Meyer and Glauber (1964). Klein, for example, argues that a large 'subjective risk premium' attached to investment decisions is sufficiently large to swamp changes in interest rates. In any case, he feels, businessmen are very conservative (preferring short to long payoffs) and have a psychological preference for using retained earnings (for which, quite possibly, they neglect to calculate an opportunity cost). Meyer and Kuh think that a considerable part of investment is 'autonomously' determined – leaving little for an endogenous variable such as the interest rate to do – while Meyer and Glauber favour a role for the interest rate in reining-in an expansion, although not for a recession, when the financial constraints are loosened. It should be emphasised that these views are essentially empirical and so must be taken as appropriate in this debate. Indeed, to this day, studies of investment regularly turn up low interest elasticities although it is arguable that the elasticities are large enough for monetary policy to gain some leverage.

The second major theoretical proposition of the Keynesian years reflecting on the effectiveness of monetary policy concerns the effects of price and wage inflexibility in a system subject to shocks. What is apparently a theoretical device in Keynes to concentrate attention on disequilibrium states, by allowing that there is short-run sluggishness in prices and wages, becomes, at least in some hands, the basis of a serious condemnation of the market system. In short, monopolistic practices, conservative pricing strategies, and unions (and even governments) become important elements in explaining why classical mechanisms (relative and absolute price changes) cannot be counted on to restore equilibrium quickly enough, at least when monetary policy is the instrument of that influence. In Keynes 'involuntary' unemployment is the result of the resistance by labourers to a money wage cut; this occurs because (Leijonhufvud, 1968, p. 95), 'In equilibrium, the system is "confused" and transactors act on the basis of faulty information.' Thus unemployment is partly due to speculation (on the future course of wages) and partly due to the result of actions taken on the basis of faulty or misused information (perhaps concerning what a worker's colleagues are earning).

Keynes, then, can be associated with the idea that unemployment is consistent with a classical system, but one in which a change in demand imposes an information constraint on traders who are thereby forced to engage in 'false' or disequilibrium trades. The amount of income thereby generated is less than that which would ensure full employment (a further constraint on demand) and one can readily imagine a cumulative cycle generated in this way. This is, of course, simply a theory of the real business cycle and it follows a process that, presumably, can be started off by shocks of some kind. The Keynesians, in their turn, formally developed a shock/cumulative-effect mechanism but, at least early on, motivated the appearance of unemployment in terms of monopoly power, cost-plus pricing rules, and the like. These two systems, accordingly, have different policy implications with firmness (and monetary and fiscal policy) playing a role in Keynes, while for the Keynesians, price controls, anti-monopoly policy, as well as fiscal and monetary policy, themselves setting up direct and contradictory shocks, are central to the policy.

Suppose, for example, that the system is shocked by an oil embargo which drives up the price of oil internationally. If business firms use short-run cost-plus pricing, they will mark up their prices. Assuming, first, that the money supply does not increase, then there will be, in effect, monetary tightness (as judged by the inadequacy of the existing quantity of money to support the new price structure). The higher price level will also induce higher excise and sales taxes which, after all, generally are not indexed, and so fiscal policy will tighten, too. This demand-side contraction would be accompanied by the supply-side shock, but the effect on demand is separate and removable. In particular, a policy to *accommodate* the demand-side part of the shock would be one of increasing the money supply. In effect (Blinder as quoted in Klamer, 1983, p. 164), 'the monetary accommodation is aimed at not letting the supply side shock contaminate the demand side. . . . If it were just a supply side shock . . . it may turn out that the optimal policy is not to accommodate it at all. After all, you can't fight the reduction in potential output.' But whether you undertake the policy also depends on how 'permanent' the supply-side shock is since, after all, there is no point entering the fray if the Arab cartel is likely to break down in the near future.

At this point we should consider some recent discussions – and some empirical speculations – bearing on this shock/rigidity rationale for fiscal and monetary policy. Our authors, for the remainder of this section, probably should be called neo-Keynesians – if any labels are appropriate. In the United States, the early 1970s brought crop failure and oil-supply restrictions; these are real shocks that would normally be expected to produce real-impact effects and, if prices are sluggish, cumulative real effects (cycles). The initial (impact) effect is unavoidable – since lost oil and lost crops cannot be re-created – but the authorities can offset the multiplier-accelerator effects induced by price sluggishness by, in effect, providing sufficient extra nominal income (R. J. Gordon, 1975). This is the policy of 'accommodating nominal income', and it produces inflation as a by-product (via the monetary expansion). If the accommodation is not forthcoming, then a recession occurs (in this story). Indeed, it is widely thought that a failure to accommodate was responsible for the 1974–5 recession in the United States (and elsewhere, possibly). Note that if the inflation is actually resisted by monetary means, a 'demand-side shock' could itself occur which would intensify (or create?) a recession (Fischer, 1985).

To analyse the possibilities, Phelps (1978) develops some exact results, following Gordon's lead (Gordon uses a two-sector model). Phelps employs an *IS–LM* framework, in both static and dynamic versions, to predict the exact amount of monetary accommodation necessary to restore full employment (assuming that the money wage does not itself decline sufficiently to bring this about automatically). With regard to the lack of accommodation in 1974–5 in the United States, Phelps argues that the policy was the result of the acceptance by the Federal Reserve of 'monetarism'. In particular, the authorities may have accepted the (classical) notions that

(a) the system would right itself quickly in any case and that
(b) the accommodation would have been ineffective anyway.

This last would follow from rational expectations, if nothing else.[8]

As rational expectations has invaded the discussion, the debate over monetary accommodation has broadened and has produced some unusual results. Blinder (1981), by this time having a second (1979) oil-related shock to consider, compares the Lucas (1973) model with the Fischer (1977) contract model in order to pin down the potential for monetary accommodation under rational expectations. As Blinder points out (p. 428), rational expectations can help the economy in that 'Part of the problem of adjusting to an energy shock is getting real wages down to the level dictated by the reduced marginal productivity of labor. To the extent that labor and management do this voluntarily . . . employment and output will not have to fall as much as if they do not.' Blinder then goes on to assume that OPEC has an informational advantage in comparison wih private agents in the prediction of the growth of the money stock; the authorities also have this informational edge, and so the potential effect of stabilisation policy is established.

In the Lucas model if OPEC real-price hikes are perceived to be *permanent*, then the authorities may well want to *reduce* the money supply so as to eliminate any unanticipated inflation, provided, of course, that this does not reduce aggregate demand and itself generate a recession (as in Fischer, 1985). (This would be the major factor producing any policy-correctible real effect.) There is no scope for accommodation in this case unless, of course, private agents only gradually learn that the real shock is permanent (as in Brunner,

Cukierman and Meltzer, 1980), while the government knows better, sooner. If, on the other hand, OPEC real-price hikes are seen as *transitory*, then there would likely be a role for accommodation, although in this case the authorities (as usual) would have to balance the social costs and benefits from the tradeoff between price stability and output stability. The Fischer model that Blinder employs raises an additional possibility since here long-term contracts will produce effects even from anticipated shocks. But the bottom line of this work is the result that under rational expectations we cannot be certain which way to push the money supply following a supply shock, and thus we cannot be sure whether to accommodate or disaccommodate.

6.3.3 The Term Structure of Interest Rates

A third area in which Keynes and the Keynesians differ markedly is, loosely, on the term structure of interest rates. An empirical term structure of interest rates relates the yields of different bonds to their maturities and is typically, but certainly not inevitably, upward-sloping. In theoretical work a representative short-term rate and a representative long-term rate generally measure the term structure and that is one way to read much of the following discussion. In Leijonhufvud's words (1968, p. 153) Keynes may be interpreted as having a two-asset model consisting of 'a means of payment and a title to a permanent income stream'. For the Keynesians, Leijonhufvud says: 'Reading the income-expenditure literature chronologically gives one an impression of a gradual "unfunding" of the representative financial asset over time, ending in the "bills only" model of recent and current money-demand theory.'

As we have seen, Keynes discusses policy in terms of (a) using the central bank's influence over short-term rates to alter (sticky) expectations and thereby to reach out to the more important long-term interest rate or, (b) preferably, interfering directly in the long-term market. His pessimism is not necessarily elasticity-based (as already noted), but also concerns the authorities' ability to stick to a policy long enough to impress those who would make investment-spending decisions.

The Keynesian version of policy in a term-structure context begins with Hicks's (1946) reformulation of I. Fisher's basic *expectations hypothesis*. To Hicks, long-term rates are determined by investors in the course of their speculations about the future course of the short-term interest rate. Although there is a constitutional weakness in the market in that there is a scarcity of long-term funds to be lent (so that there is a liquidity premium), this would not be important in the conduct of monetary policy and long-term rates would not move unless expectations of future action are affected in some way. Presumably these expectations would be independent of any but the most firmly conducted open-market operations (as in Keynes) and, as a deduction, it does not matter at which end of the term structure the policy is conducted. This last seems to be a difference between Hicks and Keynes since Keynes advocates dealing directly in the long-term market, but Keynes actually is only suggesting that there can be long lags in the reformulation of expectations. (This leads directly to the question, why not speed up the process and lend money directly to business investors?)

The obvious alternative to the expectations hypothesis is one in which lenders (borrowers) specialise in particular maturities, carving out a 'preferred habitat' for their funds (debts) that they are normally reluctant to leave. Financial markets differentiated by term-to-maturity, in this case, would be segmented, and monetary policy effects would be largely confined to the market (e.g. the T-bill market) in which the operation is carried out. An early and lucid exposition of the *segmentation hypothesis* is that of Culbertson (1957), while Modigliani and Sutch (1967) state the basic 'preferred habitat' version of the theory. To see how this general notion reinforces Keynesian ideas of the appropriate role of monetary policy, we can consider two not-entirely-dead policies of the early 1950s and 60s – 'operation twist' and 'bills only'.

Suppose, to begin with, that the segmentation view is correct and that term-differentiated bond markets are relatively insulated from each other. Suppose, as well, that one accepts Keynes's view and feels that only by changing a long-term rate – and hence affecting business investment – would a policy have any sizeable effect on the economy. Under these conditions one might well try to aim at long-term rates directly by conducting monetary policy in long-term securities and be relatively certain, since those involved in the long-term market (e.g. insurance companies and other institutional investors) would not move away from their preferred maturities, that the desired interest-rate change would occur.[9] Indeed, the possibility exists that one might deal out a tight-money policy at the short end of the market – working in the Treasury bill market – in order (for example) to increase the attractiveness of one's currency in foreign-exchange markets – while at the same time inducing lower rates at the long end to stimulate growth (or to prevent the temporary short-term policy from adversely affecting fixed-capital formation). This policy, which, if it actually works, might twist the usual upsloping yield-maturity curve into something flatter or even down-sloping, was part of the policy discussion (and maybe even part of the actual policy framework) in the early 1960s. It resurfaces from time to time, especially in the Press.

A policy somewhat related to Operation Twist, with, at least in one case, a similar historical pedigree, is that of 'bills only'. The central bank, it is argued, would be better off conducting open-market operations only in Treasury bills because the T-bill market is the only one broad enough to absorb the effects of a decisive policy without changing interest rates significantly and thus without upsetting capital markets. This policy is also based on there being strong segmentation effects in the market with respect to term to maturity, for broadness and narrowness of the market is not an issue if all rates move together because of speculative forces (as in the pure expectations theory). This policy has not been referred to by name in recent years (at least by the policy-makers), but it is abundantly clear that modern central banks actually deal primarily in short-term securities although at rare times they do deviate from this strategy.

The alternative scenario to segmentation is one in which the *expectations hypothesis* is appropriate. Basically, the argument is twofold, first, that in this case long-term rates are averages of expected short-term rates and, second, that only by altering expectations of interest rates would the authorities be able to influence long-term rates.[10] Putting it another way, investors will not care where they are along the structure, and if, for example, the authorities attempt to drive down the long rate by buying long-term securities, investors themselves will simply switch from long to short securities (which now have a relatively more attractive yield), and will thus drive down short-term rates as well. In this view, then, long and short securities are basically such close substitutes that long and short rates tend to move together. Quite clearly, under this view, neither of the two policy approaches just discussed is possible, since (a) the authorities cannot readily force relative interest rates away from what speculators expect (Operation Twist) nor (b) can they derive any special benefits from dealing at any particular point on the yield structure (Bills Only). It would be nice to report that these important theoretical issues have been resolved, but they have not been, although a truly enormous literature exists. No doubt, the truth about the term structure is somewhere in between, but quite possibly it is closer to the expectations end than to the hedging end, at least if recent surveys, incorporating the results of rational expectations tests, stand up.

6.3.4 Fiscalism

The Keynesian revolution has stimulated a keen interest in fiscal policy and a lively debate over the relative merits of fiscal policy versus monetary policy. To be sure, much of this discussion is a debate among policy activists, for advocates of policy rules often have no real enthusiasm for this topic. Even so, as we shall see, there are many who think that this is a mainstream monetarism versus Keynesianism topic. At any rate, active fiscalism – the strategy of using fiscal policy to control aggregate demand – is the subject of this section, while monetarism (either active or passive) will come on in Section 6.4.

By fiscal policy, to rephrase the definition used in Chapter 5, we mean all tax and spending activities of a national government that affect the size but not the composition (money versus bonds) of the national debt. By monetary policy, on the other hand, we mean, in effect, a policy that is concerned with the composition of the debt but not with its size (Hansen, 1958). This distinction is best illustrated with respect to the government's budget constraint. That is, in Equation 6.1, we show that the government's deficit δ, which arises because of a difference between receipts and expenditures, generally can be financed in three ways – via bond issues, money creation and tax revenues.

$$\delta = G - T = dB/dt + dM/dt \qquad (6.1)$$

Thus, an increase in G or a decrease in T – a fiscal policy, that is to say – could require borrowing or money creation and therefore an increase in the deficit. An open-market operation, on the other hand, would merely determine the ownership of existing stocks of bonds and money and not affect δ directly. Indeed, if we consolidate national government agencies so that both fiscal and monetary policy can be dealt with by whoever operates Equation 6.1, then monetary policy would be described by exactly offsetting movements in B and M with, as stated, no effect on δ (at least directly). As we will point out in Chapter 7, such a consolidation of the 'policy authority' is a common feature in countries that conduct 'demand-management' policies (but not, of course, in all countries).

After Keynes popularised and extended the case for using fiscal means in economic stabilisation, a rising tide of economic opinion promoted 'fiscalism' as a major supplement to the prevailing monetary methods of control. In the United States the peak came in 1964, with the Kennedy–Johnson tax cut, and in this case the debate made it abundantly clear that many economists felt they were winding up the Keynesian revolution at this point (see H. Stein, 1969). The principal stumbling-block to that time had been concern over the size of the deficit (H. Stein, 1969, p. 455).

For years economists had regarded the budget-balancing dogma as the main obstacle to rational decisions about fiscal policy. They had looked forward to the day when, the budget-balancing doctrine having been laid to rest, compensatory policy would take its place and decisions would be based on a calculation – presumably made by economists – of the tax and expenditure policies that would yield 'economic stability', meaning high employment and stable prices or the best compromise between these goals. When the day came in 1964 the ambition was achieved only partially and loosely. But still a significant step was made.

The observation then was that high deficits (and debt) had not previously been associated with any very serious effects – except possibly some repressed or actual inflation – as a casual glance at the Second World War experience would suggest, and so both active and passive fiscal policy, to counteract the employment effects of the general business cycle, provided a set of effective tools that were at hand (H. Stein, 1969, p. 460):

> Although it was in practical effect a large part of the fiscal revolution, this willingness to accept automatic variations in the budget position was not all of the revolution. The revolution also included the belief that fiscal decisions, not merely passive acceptance of what would happen anyway but active decisions, should be governed by the attempt to stabilize the economy and that these fiscal decisions should be the primary reliance for keeping the economy at a high but non-inflationary rate of operation.

And yet, as H. Stein points out (1969, p. 463), there simply was no strong empirical evidence for this position. That is:

> The general acceptance of compensatory finance as the basic principle of fiscal policy did not rest on any conclusive scientific demonstration that a policy of compensatory finance had worked or would work. The scientific issues were still unsettled in the mid-1960s when the history related here ends.

We shall concern ourselves here with the 'fiscal revolution', if such there was, reminding the reader that in Chapters 3 to 5 we have gone over much of the evidence that has been accumulated on the policy effects of various fiscal policies.

Among the many who spoke up forcefully for fiscal policy in the early days, Alvin Hansen stands out. Hansen, writing in 1949, argues that a combination of the liquidity trap and the low-interest elasticity of investment renders monetary policy useless in practice. The trap takes care of monetary policy during depressions and (p. 161)

> the monetary weapon to curtail an over-all excess of effective demand has the peculiar characteristic that it is scarcely at all effective unless the brakes are applied so vigorously as to precipitate a collapse. It would be interesting to know how high the interest rate would have to be pushed, in a period of inflationary pressure, before it could have a substantial effect on investment and consumption outlays.

Or (p. 163). 'It would be an easy matter to stop a man from becoming excessively corpulent by strangling him to death'. Thus it is that (p. 142) 'modern countries place primary emphasis on fiscal policy in whose service monetary policy is relegated to the subsidiary role of a useful but necessary handmaiden'. With regard to fiscal policy, Hansen argues that

> Urgently necessary, if we are going to implement a really effective anticyclical policy, is a flexible tax system. Nothing is more immediately important than a wider public understanding of this important issue. ... The modern fast-moving economy, with its tendency toward violent fluctuations, cannot be managed effectively, on the basis of an unchanging tax structure. ...

This, Hansen feels, requires an effort on the part of Congress to share its taxing powers with the Executive in order to promote the required flexibility.

The material described in Subsection 6.3.2 and the discussion so far in this section presents the Keynesians as almost monolithic in their insistence on the view that money does not matter and that fiscal policy can and will provide a stabilised macrosystem. That description has created what is essentially a straw man, and so, in the remainder of this section, at least on the issues of fiscalism versus monetarism, we will attempt to document the position of some representative neo-Keynesians, stopping short, however, of a full description since neo-Keynesians have written so much of the basic material on rational expectations and other topics (as described in earlier chapters).

The most obvious adjustment to the stereotype just described is the neo-Keynesian position that, after all, money does matter. This may surprise those who have been brought up on the textbook versions of the theory, but it is readily documented. For one thing, Keynesians recently seem happy to accept the essential long-run neutrality proposition of the monetarists; consider the following statement by J. Stein (1981, p. 139): 'Keynesians, monetarists, and new classical economists agree that the steady-state rate of inflation is closely related to the growth of the money supply, and that monetary policy cannot affect the equilibrium rate of unemployment.' The differences arise in the transition to the steady state. As an example of a Keynesian position on the short run, we have this by Blinder and Solow (1974, p. 9):

> The monetarist critique is sometimes described by its proponents as a defense of the proposition that monetary policy matters against the 'Keynesian' belief that it does not. But since most contemporary Keynesians do in fact believe in the effectiveness of monetary policy, the monetarist argument usually turns out to be a defense of the proposition that fiscal policy does not matter against the belief that it does.

This, of course, turns the tables neatly although, to be sure, the business about fiscal policy not mattering is essentially an empirical finding (from the St Louis model or from work on the 'Ricardian equivalence theorem') and not necessarily a matter of monetarist principle.[11] Indeed, returning to J. Stein (1976, p. 2), we can also read that 'A neo-Keynesian could accept Brunner's propositions that monetary impulses are a major factor accounting for variations in output and employment. . . '. Stein then goes on to argue that neo-Keynesians still do not accept the idea that fiscal policy (too) cannot be used in controlling inflation (see also Modigliani, 1977). There is, then, not much space between Keynesians and (as we shall see) monetarists on these important points, but significant empirical questions remain concerning the actual magnitudes, duration, and stability of fiscal and monetary policies in the short run.

6.3.5 Some Brief Notes on an Emerging post-Keynesianism

At this point we would be remiss if we did not address one further twist of the Keynes–Keynesian plot involving a 'new' generation of Keynesians who are generally referred to as 'post-Keynesians'. The general idea uniting this group is that what is essential to the policy debate are Keynes's notions that alternative policies have to be considered in a real world that is dominated by *uncertainty* (i.e. chaos) and by *disequilibrium*. It seems to be a matter of principle to the post-Keynesians that Keynes actually took this position; in this event he could be explained as denying that the existing framework could be patched up by counteracting the cumulative process (the cycle) with monetary and fiscal policy. Indeed – so goes the post-Keynesian literature – it is actually the Keynesians, when they translate Keynes (inaccurately) into contemporary non-stochastic general equilibrium models, who bring about this misdirection to the policy debate. In fact, by choosing an equilibrium structure, they have played into the hands of the similarly equipped neoclassical monetarists. The resulting synthesis, then, as described here and in earlier chapters, has little to do with Keynes and, more importantly, little to do with reality (with, for example, the relative effectiveness of fiscal and monetary policy).

Keynes, to be sure, can be read as having an interest in disequilibrium and uncertainty. *Disequilibrium* in this context means that the system has no tendency to settle into a stationary state but, instead, diverges, perhaps explosively, from any position it might take after it is shocked. Disequilibrium in this sense occurs if the parameters take on certain values (as the Keynesians thought they did (see Hicks, 1950) or if the system just is not an equilibrium structure (as Karl Marx and his successors maintain). In this respect the post-Keynesians are often not clear, in my judgement, and may well have adopted a Marxist position in which class-conflict and disorder is driven by an overly-efficient production structure. *Uncertainty*, in this literature, means a lack of ability to predict the future which is so 'deep' that we cannot even assign a probability distribution to our beliefs. Faced with such uncertainty, economic agents who are necessarily forced by the private-enterprise system to construct dynamic plans for consumption and production will do so only with the greatest difficulty and with such inconsistency (between *ex-ante* savings and investment) that equilibrium (of I and S) is only a chance and empirically uninteresting event.

Keynes certainly referred to disequilibrium and uncertainty, and he spoke to the inadequacy of both monetary and fiscal policy for the fine-tuning exercises that are associated with the Keynesians. Keynes also argues that it might be necessary to Socialise investment to some extent, but whether this is a needed – but desperate – strategy or merely a reference to the crowding-out phenomenon is not easy to say. It is known, however, that he put his blessings on both the Samuelson (1939) and Harrod (1939) dynamic models and on the Hicks (1937) *IS–LM* apparatus. These are, in the terminology of earlier chapters, equilibrium paradigms although for certain values of the parameters the equilibrium would be an unstable one (especially in the Harrod model). We have worked this out for the Samuelson model (in Chapter 1) and it has been demonstrated elsewhere for the Hicks general equilibrium model although, curiously, it does not hold for Keynes's case of the liquidity trap (Patinkin, 1965). But, Keynes's views aside, equilibrium may not exist and uncertainty may be a serious concern, and so the post-Keynesian position deserves consideration although strictly speaking not in a macropolicy book since such policy is unlikely to help in a world that fits their description.

Speaking of such matters, Hicks (1974) reconstructs Keynesian economics so that it also looks back to Keynes in a fashion that seems to have borrowed a bit from the post-Keynesian literature. Hicks, first, offers a distinction between 'fixprice' and 'flexprice' models – Keynesianism featuring the first and neo-monetarism the second – and he does so in the context of the behaviour of business inventories. In a flexprice model it can be argued that traders hold inventories of commodities that are sufficient to absorb shocks to the system under normal conditions; here, on the one hand, prices would react to shocks while, on the other, the cumulative process (the multiplier) is not set into motion since actual stocks are always equal to desired stocks (by the action of the flexprice). In a fixprice model, desired stocks generally are not equal to actual, since re- or de-stocking must occur when prices do not adjust, so that the multiplier process (and fiscal policy) has broader scope. Indeed, disequilibrium, defined as a situation in which actual stocks are unable to catch up with desired stocks, is a distinct possibility. This seems to be a point of agreement with the post-Keynesians. In the flexprice model, such a pattern would be expected to occur only outside the normal range of experiences of economic agents (i.e. for large shocks, as described in Leijonhufvud, 1973). This inventory-adjustment framework (which we discussed briefly in Chapter 3), then, offers a reconstruction of Keynesianism (based on the idea of stock adjustment in Keynes's monetary theory) which is a little more satisfying than simply relying on imperfections such as 'money illusion' in the labour supply function as Keynes himself did.

The preceding, by reconstructing the debate around a potential empirical issue – the relative dominance of fixprice and flexprice markets – revives fiscal policy (via the multiplier); Hicks also attempts a reconstruction of the Keynesian view on monetary policy by going back to the original text. Keynes, it will be recalled, suggests that monetary policy works but does so mainly by affecting the long-term interest rate; the Keynesians, in turn, restructure Keynes's model so that the effect (if any) is through short-term rates. What Hicks (1974) suggests is that money should be considered largely as a 'running asset' (as working capital) that (a) is hard to measure because it exists in an amorphous bundle of running assets, many of which are physical in nature and (b) is easy to supplement by means of credit lines and overdrafts and is, in any case, subject to rapid technical change (which is more rapid if the authorities squeeze on it). This part of the reconstruction is essentially an attack on monetarism in that (some) monetarists have opted for M1 targets and a stable demand for money as an essential prop in the use of monetary policy. Hicks's fungible running assets would not serve well in this context.

With respect to actual situations, Hicks sets up a distinction between *autoeconomies*, which do not have an elastic private-sector lending mechanism and in which firms must hold stocks of liquid assets and *overdraft economies* that do have a lending mechanism so that firms need not rely on their stocks of liquid assets in a pinch. In an autoeconomy (such as the United States), he says, monetary policy directly alters private sector stocks of liquidity so that restocking is necessary; in a word, it has a real effect by, for example, affecting spending plans. Monetary policy also has an effect in so far as flexprices (interest rates or money prices) produce wealth effects on private-sector spending decisions. In an overdraft economy (such as the United Kingdom), in contrast, firms do not suffer any apparent liquidity constraint when money is tightened (they, themselves, have no stocks of liquidity, and their suppliers (the banks) will tend to pass on directly to them the cost of the tight-money policy, for example. The banks, themselves, inhabit an overdraft economy, and they will draw on the readily available, but more expensive, sources of liquidity from their suppliers (e.g. the 'lender of last resort' or the Euro-dollar market). It is even conceivable that the private-sector response to higher interest rates would be the creation of new forms of liquidity – by a sort of 'institutional elasticity' – and banks themselves could take the lead in this activity perhaps, again, with the help of the government. The upshot is that in an overdraft economy – especially one which is fixprice so that wealth effects are shut off – a monetary restraint which is designed to attack the stock of liquidity, and thereby to create a constraint on private-sector spending plans, will actually be reduced to having little effect, since liquidity is widely available in secondary markets (at a price). In this comparison, then, we see monetary policy would tend to work in an autoeconomy such as the United States, and 'monetarism' is appropriate there, but does not work in the overdraft, fixprice UK economy, where monetarism is inappropriate. That this is not a universally accepted definition of monetarism will be demonstrated in Section 6.4. Whether it is good economics awaits effective empirical testing (and, certainly, further theoretical elucidation).

6.4 MONETARISM

Above we mentioned H. G. Johnson's (1971) recommendation that we treat the Keynesian movement as a revolution and the monetarist as a counter-revolution. An economic counter-revolution presumably arises for the same reasons as a revolution – as an attack on an orthodoxy that has failed to deal with important real-world problems – but it could easily stand on a narrower base to the extent that it exists primarily to correct certain specific (alleged) deficiencies in the existing orthodoxy. Thus the monetarist model also employs a general equilibrium technology (see M. Friedman, 1970, 1971) and also uses basically the same monetary theory as Keynes (see M. Friedman, 1956), but it differs both in its attempt to isolate and estimate simple 'reduced'-form relationships and in its insistence on distinguishing between nominal and real interest rates. Where it is at its strongest, though, is in its convincing explanation of the determinants of inflation and in its apparent consistency with the earlier classical tradition that tends to treat inflation as a monetary phenomenon. It gained popularity, says Johnson, primarily because inflation became a pressing problem in Western economies, and it petered out as a movement (as Johnson predicted it would) after large-scale unemployment returned (in the early 1980s) and concern about inflation waned. In addition, its central proposition that 'money matters' has been grafted on to a new rational expectations orthodoxy which has elements drawn from both sides in the Keynesian/monetarist controversy, and this, too, has made the monetarist position less distinct.

Monetarists have often been characterised in terms of a list of basic principles, and while such a list conveys some of the flavour of the monetarist approach, it also tends to create the impression that monetarists can be split into numerous factions. This impression, indeed, occurs because in most of these lists there is at least some material to which any particular monetarist would not subscribe; this is all the more obvious in that many of the propositions are empirical in nature, in any case, and estimates, quite frankly, differ a lot. Part of the problem of identifying a *representative monetarist* stems from the dominance of Milton Friedman in the debate; indeed, his views (or, really, those of a small set of original monetarists), have often been identified as representing the consensus position even when substantial disagreement could be found among the monetarists. This, for example, appears to be the view of Morgan (1978), who identifies the following as the major monetarist propositions. Note that there is a footnote attached which refers either to Friedman's works or to those of other early monetarists in order to illustrate the point that this list may be drawn up over too narrow a set of economists to be fairly representative of the monetarist position.

(a) The demand for money is a stable function of a limited number of observable variables of which permanent income is the most important. Interest rates are not regarded as important determinants of the demand for money.

(b) The money supply is exogenously determined by the monetary authorities.

(c) The big insight of the quantity-theory approach (because the substitution effects between money and assets are weak) is that a discrepancy between money demand and money supply will be eliminated by a rise in (spending and thus in) nominal income.

(d) It takes large changes in income to restore equilibrium in the money market in view of the dependence of money demand on the level of nominal permanent income rather than on the level of nominal income.

(e) Empirical work supports these propositions, and other work establishes that money leads nominal national income by (on average) sixteen months.

(f) The transmission mechanism of monetary policy is basically through private portfolios in terms of asset substitution effects and interest-induced wealth effects.

(g) The money stock is the appropriate indicator of monetary policy, and it is important to distinguish between real and nominal interest rates.

(h) There is a long and variable lag between money and money income which precludes the use of monetary policy as a short-run stabilising device. In the long run the government should maintain a steady growth of the money stock.

(i) Fiscal policy should be avoided because of its crowding-out effect on private spending.[12]

To get a sense of the dynamics, the range and the differences of monetarist propositions, consider two more recent collection of principles put forward by monetarists whose views seem to represent at least some of the evolution of the position, particularly as the empirical evidence has come in. One of these is Laidler's (1981); a monetarist, then, holds

(a) a quantity theory of money approach either in terms of Friedman's 'restatement' (1956) or in terms of the naïve theory that doubling money somehow doubles prices,
(b) an expectations-augmented Phillips curve,
(c) a monetary approach to the balance of payments[13] and
(d) an antipathy toward monetary or fiscal policy and a preference for rules – especially a monetary growth rule – over discretion in macropolicy.

To this list we can add the following (ignoring any repetitions) from Poole (1978).

(e) In the short run a change in the rate of growth of the money stock – especially if anticipated – will affect real national income. Indeed, the business cycle is primarily caused by monetary instability.
(f) The correlation between money and other variables reflects a causation running from money to these other variables and not the converse.
(g) It is technically possible to control the money stock, and thus the government should be held responsible for the consequences of monetary instability.

and even

(h) Households and firms should be assumed to be rational utility and profit maximisers.

This last arises in part from a rejection of micro-oriented cost-push or market-failure theories of inflation and partly in recognition of some monetarists' recent interest in rational expectations. Notice that point (e) here is a point that is decisively rejected by the 'strong' rational expectations approach; indeed strong rational expectations would decisively reject (e) and (f), as well as many of the points on the earlier lists in this section. This might suggest, then, the sense in which we are dealing with the 'history of monetarist thought' in this discussion.

As a second example of the non-monetarist's view of monetarism, by far the most ambitious is that of Mayer (1978), who deals with the macro issues that have dominated our discussion to this point and brings up a number of micro points, as well as some material that seems normative. Mayer adds to the above lists the

(a) belief in the inherent stability of the private sector,
(b) reliance on small rather than large econometric models,
(c) use of the reserve base or a similar measure as the indicator of monetary policy,
(d) use of the money stock as the proper target of monetary policy,
(e) a relatively greater concern about inflation than about unemployment compared to other economists, and
(f) a dislike of government intervention.

Thus (c) and (d) bring up yet another distinction – between targets and indicators – that clearly does exist in monetarist writings as we will see in Chapter 7; (a) would be rejected by Keynesians and (possibly) by rational expectations economists (in favour of neutrality); (b) refers mainly to the well-known Friedman–Meiselman, St Louis and Brunner–Meltzer models (the first two are discussed below) and to little else; and (f) is clearly normative and political, and probably best describes the views of certain individuals (e.g. Milton Friedman) rather than those of the representative monetarist whom we are trying to pin down.[14] Indeed, it is worth pointing out in this context that if one thinks the authorities are powerless to control unemployment in any systematic way, then he ought to be able to argue for less policy, without losing his liberal credentials. Point (e), finally, is flatly untrue and is the result of the monetarist insistence that inflation is a serious problem (not that unemployment is not also a serious problem). As H. G. Johnson (1971) explains, this insistence is somewhat self-serving in view of the special advantages monetarist models have in explaining the inflation/money linkage, but in any case, most short-run monetarist models contain unemployment/inflation tradeoffs and no firm view as to the proper shape of the social welfare structure between them.

6.4.1 The Friedman–Meiselman Model

This and the next major section will return to a distinction made in Chapter 1 on structural versus reduced-form models and address some questions concerning widely used monetarist-style models.[15] The model we will discuss here is the Friedman–Meiselman (1963) 'monetary multiplier' model which attributes changes in nominal income to prior changes in the nominal money supply. The study was met with considerable debate in the 1960s and the dispute still lingers on, in a somewhat different context (as discussed in Chapters 3 and 4). In the next section we will present the monetarist-inspired St Louis model of Andersen and Jordan (1968) and Andersen and K. M. Carlson (1970); this model has also continued to attract empirical support to the present and has had its share of controversies. What these two models have in common is that they are explicitly monetarist, that they are small and that they can be described as reduced-form, for the most part. In this event, while it is not exactly a fact, we can here record Mayer's judgement (1978, p. 24) that 'while Keynesians prefer large-scale structural models, monetarists prefer small reduced-form models'. This preference, Mayer says, arises because monetarists regard the transmission process between money and its final effects as too complicated to capture with a detailed structural model so that a reduced form that abstracts from these complexities may give one reliable (and broad) results which may be the best one can do under the circumstances. Put this way we immediately see a potential empirical confrontation – between certain detailed structural models and the 'monetarist' reduced-form models – that can be resolved by comparing their estimating and forecasting abilities. But first things first, and so we will now consider these two models (a) as typical monetarist models and (b) as of some potential value in tracking and predicting the economy.

The Friedman–Meiselman (FM) model is the first and certainly the simplest of the well-known reduced-form models of the monetarists. In the original paper two alternative 'theories' of what determines nominal income are proposed, one Keynesian and one representing the 'money hypothesis'. These are

$$Y = a_1 + b_1 M + e_1 \quad \text{or} \quad C = a + vM \tag{6.2}$$

$$Y = a_2 + b_2 A + e_2 \quad \text{or} \quad C = a_2 + (b_2 - 1)A \tag{6.3}$$

Here A is autonomous expenditures (net investment, net exports, and the government deficit), and M is the exogenously determined money stock. Since in equilibrium, $Y = C + A$, it is necessary as well to adjust Equation 6.3 to avoid the simultaneous equations inconsistency that would arise because of the induced correlation between A and the error term (e_2) in the second equation. Equation 6.2 has no such problem since M is directly exogenous (by assumption). To deal with the problem in 6.3, we can subtract A from both sides of this equation; this explains the right-hand side of 6.3. Equation 6.2 is then rewritten in terms of consumption for comparability. In the FM study Equation 6.1 'predicts' money national income for the United States somewhat better than does 6.3;

this is for annual data over the 1897 to 1958 period. This result is obtained for both nominal and real versions and for several transformations (and subsets) of the data as well as for results when both monetary and fiscal variables appear in the same equation (as they do in the St Louis equation described below). Friedman and Meiselman conclude (p. 166):

> The results are strikingly one sided. Except for the early years of the Great Depression, money . . . is more closely related to consumption than is autonomous expenditures. . . . Such correlation as there is between autonomous expenditures and consumption is in the main a disguised reflection of the common effect of money on both.

This clearly creates the impression that money (and possibly *only* money) matters.

The FM model was immediately controversial and the dispute is a continuing one, although the topics have changed somewhat over the years. Concerning the income/expenditure theory in Equation 6.3, Ando and Modigliani (1965) complain that the consumption function is misspecified directly,[16] as well as in the sense of having an independent variable that is correlated with the error term because of mutual endogeneity. In their terminology some of A (and M in the money-multiplier equation) is itself 'induced' and so neither equation is a proper reduced form. Ordinary least-squares estimates, in this circumstance, would tend to be inconsistent. In their contribution to this debate DePrano and Mayer (1965) point out that FM imply that fiscal policy is likely to be ineffective (they cite Friedman's *Capitalism and Freedom* (1962) in this connection); they produce the argument that these stripped-down versions of the theory actually do injustice to the (more structural) Keynesian theory. Taken as a whole, these three studies, along with another by Hester (1964), succeed in comparing upwards of twenty measures of A with M. This kind of empirical 'grid search' is not very satisfying, although it certainly is invited by the agnostic approach of FM. In the years after the debate, studies of the basic model have proliferated, often, but not always, to the advantage of the monetary hypothesis.[17] In particular, in these later studies money matters, although the role of money compared to autonomous expenditures is certainly not always of the comparative strength that FM found it to be.

The simultaneous equations' problem which was not faced directly in any of these early studies is basically the subject of the 'reverse causation' literature that we shall discuss in Subsection 6.4.2. Before that, however, it is worth mentioning some other statistical (etc.) problems that have been brought up in this debate. In one paper, Christ (1973) explains the determination of money income by means of the policy variables that actually appear in the US government's budget constraint. For monetary policy he recommends using not M but H, where the latter is high-powered money (basically the reserves of the banking system plus currency in the hands of the public) which is more likely to be exogenous. Christ finds both expenditure and monetary variables influential in general, but both with a weakened influence in recent years (1948–70). In a second paper, Poole and Kornblith (1973) use the FM model (and the St Louis equation to be discussed shortly) as well as the models of their critics to attempt forecasts of the post-1963 data. The results are proclaimed 'disappointing' in that a policy based on any of these simple models does not predict very well. The models are equally inefficient, however, in their predictions. Indeed, in a similar sort of study, but one using a small econometric model, Kmenta and P. E. Smith (1973), using US data for 1954–63, find that neither fiscal nor monetary policy matter much and, when their effects could be identified, might have contributed to instability (although the overall model, a fifth-order-difference equation, shows damped oscillations (i.e. was stable)). This last is not actually inconsistent with monetarism, at least as Milton Friedman has laid down the rules.

The monetary-multiplier dispute has also turned out to be somewhat of a proving ground for statistical techniques, and this is one of its more enduring characteristics. For example, Savin (1978), noting that the FM model generally produces unsatisfactory Durbin–Watson statistics (at least when it is not tested with distributed lags or in first-difference form), re-estimates the model on US data using a maximum-likelihood autoregression technique. Savin, indeed, argues that the correct Keynesian position is that fiscal policy should be used when the economy is far from equilibrium and monetary policy otherwise. In this case the 1930s would be the only part of the FM sample in which one might reasonably expect fiscal policy to show up since that is (wartime aside) the only time when major anti-cyclical fiscal policies were undertaken in the FM data period. Of course, the debate is really over the influence of a concept broader than just a fiscal influence (A is *all* exogenous expenditures), but, be that as it may, Savin's tentative results with a second-order autoregressive structure reduce the influence of M, generally, and elevate that of A for the 1930s, as compared to the FM result.

In a different sort of test, and returning to the basic problem that has bothered many of the critics of FM, Burns (1975) questions whether the protagonists have ever established exactly what it is they are trying to demonstrate (p. 32):

> Thus, while it is agreed in general terms that the debate concerns the *relative stability* of the response of economic activity to monetary and expenditure policy, there has been no consistent definition of this concept nor has there been any statement concerning the underlying statistical properties necessary to make such a concept meaningful.

Burns suggests that, under these conditions, the standard fixed-coefficients models should be abandoned in favour of a 'random coefficients' technique. In this he follows the advice of Zellner (1966), who argues that this approach is generally useful for macroeconomics because of aggregation problems.[18] Burns works his tests on US data for 1929–58; over a period where FM find monetary influences more stable, he finds no support for their position and, indeed, weak support for autonomous expenditures. These results are reversed, however, in a later paper that uses the same basic approach (but with some technical improvements) so that Burn's revised position comes out in favour of FM's argument that the monetary multiplier is the more stable one (see Burns, Thomson and R. J. Smith, 1977). The same random-coefficients approach is repeated over the ten-model data space of Poole and Kornblith (1973), who earlier argued that all of these simple models predict poorly. In this last test, Burns and Thomson (1975) find expenditure policy to be very much more unstable than monetary policy for a large variety of expenditure-policy models.

Using yet another recently popular approach, Cho (1979) proposes a spectral analysis of the relations between consumption (C) and, alternatively, money (M), FM autonomous expenditures (A), and Ando–Modigliani (AM) autonomous expenditures (A^*). An examination of the 'auto-spectral densities' of the four series shows that long-run components dominate the frequency compositions of M and short-run components dominate for A and A^*, while C has important elements of both. A 'coherence-square' calculation (roughly an R^2) further suggests an appropriate duration of the connection between A^* and C of 8–20 quarters while the high-coherence squares between M and C are for components having a duration greater than fifteen quarters. Looking at the 'phase' (to try to determine whether a series leads or lags another) Cho finds an 'out-of-phase' relation between A and C which he suggests shows that the FM measure of autonomous expenditures is not truly exogenous; this point has been made repeatedly in the literature. Money matters in these tests, so FM are right on this point, but so too does $A*$, particularly in the short-term cyclical frequencies where money was not so effective, so AM, too, are right, at least with regard to this particular statistical procedure.

6.4.2 Reverse Causation in the Friedman–Meiselman Model

To define 'reverse causation' we must begin by laying down some rules for causality itself. This is primarily a statistical topic, at least if we put aside philosophical matters as we certainly shall. There is no universally accepted definition of causality, as it turns out, but the one most used in economics is known as *Granger causality* (see Granger, 1969). A useful statement of this in a time-series context is by Sims (1972, p. 544): 'The time series Y is said to 'cause' X relative to the universe U (U is a vector time-series including X and Y as components) if, and only if, predictions of $X(t)$ based on $U(s)$ for all $s < t$ are better than predictions based on all components of $U(s)$ except $Y(s)$ for all $s < t$.' A more prosaic, and somewhat different, version of this is provided by Feige and Pearce (1979, p. 521): 'Heuristically, Granger's notion of causality states that X "causes" Y if the past history of X can be used to predict Y more accurately than simply using the past history of Y.' A variant of this, along with a thorough review of the theory, is provided by Pierce and Haugh (1977).

An appropriate test of causality is suggested by the following which is also due to Sims (1972, p. 541). 'If and only if causality runs one way from current and past values of some list of exogenous variables to a given endogenous variable, then in a regression of the endogenous variables on past, current, and future values of the exogenous variables, the future values of the exogenous variables should have zero coefficients.' This last provides one with an exact procedure, now known as the *Sims test*, in which a distributed-lag equation with 'whitened' (or 'prefiltered') residuals is employed.[19] Indeed, as Sims points out, many relationships involving distributed lags in popular use in macroeconomics (e.g. tests of the permanent-income hypothesis) contain implicit statements on causality which probably should be tested. We note, though, that this Sims procedure does not deal explicitly with contemporaneous causation, only lagged (i.e. only 'proper' causation).

Sims employs his test on U.S. quarterly data for 1947–69 and finds – for either the monetary base (MB) or M1 as determinants of GNP – that tests of GNP on M1 and on MB were significant (by an F-test), and so were the reversed tests of M1 and MB on GNP. For future values, those of GNP are highly significant in explaining M1 (so, by his test, GNP is ruled out as a cause of M1), while future values of M1 are not significant in explaining GNP. This, broadly, supports the monetarist position on causation. Sims concludes that (p. 542),

> the most conservative way to state the results for money and income is that they show it to be unreasonable to interpret a least squares lag distribution for money on GNP as a causal relation, and that they provide no grounds for asserting that distributed lag regressions of GNP on money do not yield estimates of a causal relation. It is natural, and I believe appropriate, to phrase the result more positively: the data verify the null hypothesis that distributed lag regressions of GNP on money have a causal interpretation.

In Sim's study the general F-test is not passed when the causation of P (the GNP deflator) is assumed to be MB. Further testing for inflation is carried out in a study by Berman (1978) on US quarterly data (1956–77); Berman finds that (p. 6) the 'Sims test of Granger causality supports the hypothesis of unidirectional causality running from changes in M1 growth to changes in inflation. The correct specification for the M1 model is a stable 10-quarter distributed lag with uniformly sized weights.' He also finds MB a less effective predictor of the rate of inflation. In a study already referred to, Feige and Pearce (1979) work over the same data space (1947–69, quarterly US data) with three tests. A test for the independence between Y and M1 or MB found these aggregates to be independent of each other. Similarly, a direct test of Granger causality of their own devising does not establish that money causes income or the reverse. With a Sims test, however, Sims's conclusions are broadly upheld. The difference, they feel, lies in Sims's test procedure. In particular, his future 'lags' are arbitrarily shorter than his past lags and his prefiltering technique (he uses $1 - 1.5\,L + 0.5625\,L^2$ where L is the lag operator) is basically arbitrary (Sims says, p. 545, 'This filter approximately flattens the spectral density of most economic time series'.) Feige and Pearce present alternatives and then establish that the choice of prefiltering technique alters the results even when they all 'successfully' whiten the residuals.[20] They conclude that Sims's finding that money causes nominal income, but not the converse, cannot be claimed on the basis of their results, although in truth it really seems as if the Sims test, at least as applied here, is extremely sensitive to alternative specifications.

There are other tests on the US data. Mehra (1978) uses the Sims test with the monetary base (*MB*) for quarterly US data from 1952 to 1972. He concludes that *MB* affects both nominal and real income in the short run, but only nominal income (i.e. the price level) in the long run. He is challenged by Stephens (1980) on the grounds that, in essence, fiscal policy may not have been effective in the period in question (rather than ineffective in principle). This conjecture is supported empirically, to some extent.[21] McMillan and Fackler (1984), tackling the question of how to specify the unknown lag structure of the money/income relationship find bi-directional causality between narrow money and income, while broad money (M2) causes money income. Further investigations of the lag structure by Thornton and Batten (1985), however, do not confirm the $M_2 \rightarrow Y$ result (in favour of M1 and M2 $\leftrightarrow Y$). They argue that the Granger test is sensitive to the lag specification (which suggests that contrary results are likely to appear in future tests); they also argue that if there actually is a unidirectional relation in this area, it is probably between the monetary base and nominal income. It should be recalled that earlier studies (mentioned above) often rejected this possibility.

On the UK data the FM comparison has not produced as strong a case for monetarism partly, no doubt, because fiscal policy (and other exogenous effects) are more evident. Williams, Goodhart and Gowland (1976) perform the first British calculations using the Sims test on measures of narrow and broad money (and GDP) and find evidence that causation might run both ways. Putnam and Wilford (1978) argue, in a theoretical paper, that the results of Williams *et al.* are influenced by the nature of the international payments system (fixed rates) in the period 1958–71 in which the United Kingdom was not a reserve-creating country (while the United States was). The United Kingdom, consequently, finds its monetary base has a large endogenous 'international reserve assets' component and its price level is determined exogenously (its components actually determined in world markets). The reserve assets are endogenous because (p. 245) 'the balance of payments reflects attempts by individuals to maintain equilibrium money balances as they adjust their expenditures and receipts'. A similar argument is advanced by Mills and Wood (1978), and in a separate paper Mills (1980a) performs a test using a 'direct' causality test,[22] on data spanning the period from 1963 to 1977. He finds that conventional filtering techniques in the Sims test do not reduce the residuals to white noise while their performance is somewhat better in the direct test. The reverse causation (*Y* on *M*) is, in any case, even more strongly evident than in the Williams *et al.* study.

Mills (1980b) also uses the more agnostic 'vector autoregression' procedure. His reasoning, following Sims (1980), is that in this case all variables (he has four) are treated as endogenous; in his words (p. 2): 'Since such macromodels may be regarded as unrestricted reduced forms, restrictions based on a priori theorizing are able to be ignored. Of course, some restrictions, notably lag lengths, are required. . . '. A good reason for wishing to ignore the restrictions is that they are often rather strong; they are there, of course, to ensure proper identification. In the event, on the UK data from 1880 to 1978 the model fits well, although some instability shows up after 1972. Broadly, monetarist conclusions are upheld, but there are also sufficient feedback effects so that reverse causation is *also* upheld; that is, there is evidence of what we are calling 'bi-directional' causality. Mills suggests that the results are certainly in favour of policy effectiveness although at the same time the interactions are sufficiently complicated so as to make it difficult to implement a monetary policy.

On the *Canadian* data, Barth and Bennett (1974) employ the Sims test to the effect that they find reverse causation between M1 and nominal GNP. A second test by Hsiao (1979) confirms this and also finds causation running from nominal GNP to M2. The data in the second case are quarterly from 1955 to 1977. There have been a number of challenges to the Barth and Bennett results (Sarlo, 1981, Auerbach and Rutner, 1978, and Sharpe and M. B. Miller, 1975) which involve the data, seasonality, the arbitrary whitening of the residuals and the fixed/flexible-rate topic already mentioned for UK tests. With the exception of the Sharpe–Miller result, reverse causation seems to stand up pretty well in the Canadian case, especially over recent years. On quarterly *Irish* data (1960–75) Geary (1977) finds that M1 leads nominal GNP while Komura (1982) on three segments of *Japanese* data (in the 1955 to 1980 period) finds 'bi-directional' influence between M2 and nominal and real income (but money does lead prices). Both of these studies use the Sims test. Dyreyes, Starleaf and Wang (1980) use two test procedures in addition to the Sims test on the data for six countries. They find bi-directional causality in Japan and the United States, money causing income in Australia and Canada, income causing money in the United Kingdom, and no relation at all in Germany. A separate Australian study by Fiebig (1980) supports the monetarist claim of a link between money and income, while finding some contemporaneous feedback from income to money; this last required a modification of the Sims test, of course. Taking all of these tests together, we can hardly claim that this is a settled issue since econometric problems (and data problems) abound; indeed, to say the least, no clear cross-country generalisations can be made at this stage.

6.4.3 The St Louis Model

The Friedman–Meiselman monetarist model is not, in general, utilised by economists in any practical exercises, but a closely related model – the St Louis model – is. This model was developed at the Federal Reserve Bank of St Louis (see Andersen and Jordan, 1968, and Andersen and K. M. Carlson, 1970) in order to provide an empirically viable small-scale monetarist model. In fact, it has since been used mostly as a forecasting tool or as a prop in the continuing monetary versus fiscal policy debate.

The St Louis model consists of five basic equations and three identities as described, for example, in Andersen and K. M. Carlson (1974). The best-known equation is the 'St Louis equation' and explains total spending in terms of the distributed lags of two exogenous variables, one representing monetary policy and one representing fiscal policy.

$$\Delta Y_t = f_1(\Delta M_t, \ldots, \Delta M_{t-n}, \Delta E_t, \ldots, \Delta E_{t-n}) \tag{6.4}$$

It is this reduced-form equation that has been the subject of most of the controversy; its similarity to the 'multiplier' equations (6.2 and 6.3), taken together, is apparent. The second equation in the model is a price equation in which D represents demand pressure and ΔP^e represents the expected change in prices.

$$\Delta P_t = f_2(D_t, \ldots, D_{t-n}, \Delta P_t^e) \tag{6.5}$$

Anticipated price changes are derived from another reduced form (of past price changes) of

$$\Delta P_t^e = f_3(\Delta P_{t-1}, \ldots, \Delta P_{t-n}) \tag{6.6}$$

while demand pressure is defined by the identity

$$D_t = \Delta Y_t - (X_t^F - X_{t-1}) \tag{6.7}$$

where X_t^F is full-employment output. The fourth behavioural equation in the model is an interest-rate equation (that is, a 'liquidity preference' equation) representing the demand for money; the supply of money is assumed to be determined exogenously.

$$i_t = f_4(\Delta M_t, \Delta X_t, \ldots, \Delta X_{t-n}, \Delta P_t, \Delta P_t^e) \tag{6.8}$$

The fifth and last behavioural relation then explains the unemployment rate in terms of G – the GNP 'gap'.

$$U_t = f_5(G_t, G_{t-1})$$ (6.9)

The gap, in turn, is explained by a second identity:

$$G_t = (X_t^F - X_t)/X_t^F$$ (6.10)

Here X_t is the actual real GNP. The third and last identity in the model, then, defines real-spending changes.

$$\Delta X_t = \Delta Y_t - \Delta P_t$$ (6.10)

The St Louis model has eight contemporaneous endogenous variables (ΔY_t, ΔP_t, ΔP_t^e, ΔX_t, D_t, i_t, G_t, and U_t) and two exogenous policy variables (ΔE_t and ΔM_t) as well as the benchmark variable X_t^F. Equations 6.4 and 6.6 are *ad hoc* reduced-form equations while the remaining equations have at least some endogenous variables as right-hand variables.[23] The model is actually separable into blocks in that the five equations 6.4 to 6.7 and 6.11 can be solved for the five variables ΔY_t, ΔP_t, D_t, ΔX_t, and ΔP_t^e and, given these values, the remaining equations can be solved for i_t, U_t and G_t recursively. In the original papers, when simulations with the model are undertaken, monetary policy generally only affects nominal variables, fiscal policy has no significant effect on nominal GNP, and the model shows damped oscillations after shocks (in X_t^F, E_t and M_t).

Most of the empirical controversy over the St Louis model involves Equation 6.4. That equation is not inherently biased against fiscal policy – measurement problems, issues of exogeneity and omitted variables aside – and in at least some tests it has turned up a positive role for fiscal policy, although monetary policy still generally dominates (compare B. M. Friedman (1977) and Gramlich (1971) with Batten and Hafer (1983)). The problems just mentioned have produced a literature, to be discussed in a moment, but one further problem we will not discuss at length concerns the method used to estimate the distributed lag in the St Louis equation. The technique generally employed is the Almon lag procedure, but this has come in for some heavy criticism (see Schmidt and Waud (1973)) because of the likelihood of generating specification errors whenever the parameters (degree and lag length) are not known *a priori*. This difficulty can be overcome by using 'specification error tests', and when this is done by Harper and Fry (1978), the result is an improved fiscal response (compared to the uncorrected form) although the monetary policy response is still larger and faster. On the other hand, Batten and Thornton (1983), using the Pagano and Hartley (1981) technique for fitting distributed lags efficiently, argue that the policy conclusions of the St Louis model do not depend on the choice of parameters of the Almon lag (i.e. on the degree and length of lag choices).

There are, then, two general questions that have been raised about the St Louis model. The first of these is the concern that M (or F) is itself partly endogenous – in view of the oft-stated policy of the Federal Reserve of stabilising interest rates – so that the estimators of the equation are inconsistent. The second is that there are omitted variables so that, again, inconsistency exists in the estimators. We will discuss the first issue as another example of reverse causation later in this section; with regard to the second point there is actually a specific issue raised in support of the fiscalist position. This is that, as constructed, the model is directly biased against fiscal policy and in favour of monetary policy. Suppose, then, that the St Louis equation is estimated as

$$\Delta Y = \alpha_1 \Delta M + \alpha_2 \Delta G + v \tag{6.12}$$

when the correct model is really

$$\Delta Y = \beta_1 \Delta M + \beta_2 \Delta G + \beta_3 \Delta E + u \tag{6.13}$$

If, as may generally be supposed, the omitted variable ΔE is directly related to ΔG and ΔM, then another equation in the structure is given by

$$\Delta E = \tau_1 \Delta M + \tau_2 \Delta G + w \tag{6.14}$$

Combining Equations 6.13 and 6.14, representing the correct structure, we then produce the correct reduced-form St Louis equation of

$$\Delta Y = (\beta_1 + \beta_3 \tau_1)\Delta M + (\beta_2 + \beta_3 \tau_2)\Delta G + z \tag{6.15}$$

where the coefficients of ΔM and ΔG provide the correct interpretation of the coefficients α_1 and α_2 in Equation 6.12. Indeed, $\beta_3 \tau_1$ and $\beta_3 \tau_2$ measure the bias, and they could clearly indicate the direction of the bias, at least for certain obvious omitted variables. To consider an example, suppose that E is investment and that it is dependent on the interest rate. In this event, increased government spending could increase the interest rate and crowd out investment (so $\tau_2 < 0$) while an increase in the money supply could directly lower the interest rate and thus increase investment spending (so that $\tau_1 > 0$). For this situation, Equation 6.15 would show a stronger effect (a higher coefficient) for ΔM – interpreted as α_1 when it is really $\beta_1 + \beta_3 \tau_1$ – and a lower value for fiscal policy (as represented by the coefficient on ΔG). Modigliani and Ando (1976) and Van Order (1978) have variations on this theme. For a recent summary of these and other econometric issues see Stockton and Glassman (1985).

The debate over 'causation' in the St Louis model has covered many of the topics already considered in our discussion of monetarism (and in earlier chapters). An obvious way to demonstrate causality is to attempt direct forecasts on out-of-sample data in comparison (say) with the *MPS* or some other comparable model. In an early study Poole and Kornblith (1973) find the St Louis model comparably incompetent in its forecasting, as noted above. More recently, Hafer (1982) conducts causality tests (on U.S. data) which imply that *M* affects nominal GNP while two measures of fiscal influence do not (establishing no 'reverse causation'), and he exhibits some results for some out-of-sample forecasts which suggest that given *M*, fiscal influences do not add significantly to the prediction of nominal GNP (with the variables written in rate-of-growth form). More explicit forecasting of the money multiplier is attempted by Hafer, Hein and Kool (1983), who argue that (p. 22) 'For such a control procedure to function properly, the monetary authorities must be able to predict movements in the multiplier with some accuracy.' They claim, indeed, on U.S. data, that using a Box–Jenkins and a multi-state Kalman-filter forecasting procedure and a 'St Louis-type' equation would be useful in stabilising GNP growth rates. In a similar vein, but using the price equation 6.5 from the St Louis model in addition to the St Louis equation, L. H. Meyer and Varvares (1981) argue that the U.S. inflation predictions of the St Louis model are not as good as those from a model that employs either a Phillips relation or a monetarist-style reduced form for inflation. The latter two versions are, however, equally effective in predicting inflation. Some of this work, though, is subject to the Lucas critique, at least when 'fixed coefficient' models are used to convey the results of policy simulations; the problem is potentially very serious in the St Louis model (P. A. Anderson, 1978). For an example of a paper which ignores this advice see Arestis, Frowen and Karakitsos (1978). Here a small-model approach to the data of four open economies yields fiscal dominance over monetary in Germany, Canada and the United Kingdom, but the reverse for the United States (although fiscal does matter in that last case).

The possibility of 'feedback' and hence a breakdown of exogeneity is also involved in the choice of policy targets by the authorities. If, for example, the authorities follow the policy of stabilising the interest rate (or the level of free reserves), they will introduce a correlation between *M* and the errors of Equation 6.12; this would, of course, produce bias in the OLS studies of this equation. That is, when the authorities stabilise nominal interest rates, they will actually destabilise nominal income. Thus, whenever there are shocks to the system (e.g. in the error in 6.12), the authorities would pump in money (for example) in order to hold i_t constant. In this case nominal income would rise (and so would M) and so would the error in Equation 6.12. A second problem of this same sort lies in the unidentified influence of other objective variables on the policy variables (i.e. M or E) themselves (Goldfeld and Blinder, 1972, Crotty, 1973, and S. H. Stein, 1980). These alternative objectives are not identified in this framework, but responses to them could show up as correlation between M and the errors of Equation 6.12 as long as either M is the policy instrument or there is an interrelationship between M and any other policy instrument. Indeed, the problem is potentially severe enough to reverse completely the thrust of the generally anti-fiscalist results in this literature.

To all of this the monetarists have responses. For one thing, monetarists can certainly claim, until it is decisively proved otherwise, that Equation 6.12 is the correct reduced form and that all omitted exogenous variables are irrelevant. For another, it is certainly arguable that government spending and tax changes are, in fact, rarely used policy tools and that the widely used tools (at least in the United States) involving the stimulation of investment (e.g. the investment tax credit or accelerated depreciation) have not been very effective in practice. In short, fiscal policy does not matter because it really has not been used in ways that would give it a chance to have a major impact. Monetarists also could take the position that any increase in government spending will, in any case, induce offsetting changes in other expenditures (crowding-out) in which case Equation 6.12 is still correct, at least in the long run. Finally, monetarists could point to the probability that the so-called structural models are really reduced form in part and that they certainly could suffer either from the omission of relevant variables and/or from other sorts of misspecification. This last is all the more obvious in the event that these structural models have problems of aggregation (and hence of interpretation). The evidence for this comes, paradoxically, from the assertions of Keynesians themselves, who maintain that there are significant union or monopoly effects or that prices are set by 'mark-up' rather than by marginal principles. Some of this discussion will be resumed in Chapter 7 with reference to the aggregation of money.

7 Objectives, Instruments, Targets and Indicators

> Undeniably, the Federal Open Market Committee (FOMC), which decides and executes open market policy for the Federal Reserve System, is much of the time in the dark about what has been going on in the economy. In saying this, we do not mean to be at all derisive. It is simply that the Committee decides policy each day.
>
> KAREKEN, MUENCH and WALLACE, 1973, p. 156

7.1 INTRODUCTION

To those most closely associated with macropolicy, many of the basic issues in the design of policy are represented by the topics discussed in this chapter. To begin with, the policy authorities have to define and measure the concepts with which they are working; they also have to interact with the various established political entities in order to determine the specific values of the objective variables and, on occasion, the permissible values of the instruments. 'Price stability' is an example of an objective variable here, and 'an inflation rate between two and four per cent' is a specific value; in turn, the open-market operations, the central bank's discount rate and the table of income-tax rates are examples of instruments. In between the *objectives* and *instruments*, in the usual design of policy, lie the intermediate variables – the money supply, the fiscal deficit and interest rates. It is through these variables that policy can be conceived of as flowing and from these variables the authorities might select both *targets* at which to aim their instruments and *indicators* of the general effectiveness of their policy (and of the need for new policies). This chapter, then, considers recent contributions to the literature on the potential practice of macroeconomic policy structured around these four broad concepts.

Chapter 7 actually begins with a discussion of the objective variables themselves and with some documentation of the empirical work on 'reaction functions', as these were first described in Chapter 1. Both conceptual and measurement problems have to be dealt with here, for a capable policy design requires clarity about its objectives, but the discussion in this first section generally will stick to the conceptual problems – some of which involve even political considerations – and leave the measurement problems to Section 7.4 on targets and indicators. When we come to targets and indicators we will discuss them in the traditional way – as stops along the roadway between instruments and objectives – as well as in a fashion suggested by the requirements of rational expectations models. In particular, we will consider the information-content of the intermediate variables – of the interest rate and especially of the money stock – and we will also attach our discussion of both aggregation and the signal-extraction problem (in Section 7.5) to this discussion. The latter topic will bring up questions of the value of leading, coincident and lagging indicators, although this particular problem is an incidental topic in this study.

The authorities generally can be assumed to have direct control over the instruments of their policy; in fact, these variables are usually precisely calibrated (and therefore easily measured). Section 7.3 takes up this discussion in terms of the actual practices of Western governments. It would be inaccurate to say that the instruments are not influenced by developments in the economy, of course; in fact, by setting their instruments on the basis of feedback from the economy, the authorities actually render their instruments endogenous in an important sense. What is exogenous, actually, is the selection of the value of the objective variables (and, of course, other variables that are exogenous to the economic system (e.g. the weather)).

The variables mentioned above as instruments (e.g. tax rates) are not the ones usually referred to as playing that role in theoretical and, certainly, in practical discussions of macroeconomic policy. Indeed, the money supply, the interest rate and even the size of the budgetary deficit often assume this role in the basic policy models in this literature. What distinguishes these 'instruments' from the others is that they are potentially subject to direct feedback from the economy; this, of course, raises the issue of reverse causation discussed in Chapter 6. In that material we found evidence in favour of reverse causation in a number of instances involving these concepts, and thus at this point claims for their exogeneity as a general matter simply cannot be sustained.

The variables just described do have a place in a coherent policy design, however, as *targets* or as *indicators*. The need for such variables arises because the authorities cannot hit their objectives precisely and because the transmission of their policy is somewhat unpredictable in its timing; in this event the authorities need to gather information (and respond to it) as their policy unfolds. This is where these 'quasi-instruments' come in – as intermediate variables that can serve either as targets or as indicators of monetary policy. That is, after setting a policy instrument, the authorities watch their intermediate targets (perhaps the interest rate) to see if the policy is going through; they judge the final impact, on, for example, the price level, in terms of how an indicator (such as a measure of the money stock) reacts. This important distinction will be discussed in Section 7.4 in various ways, but for now we just need to point out that, as a first approximation, a target variable itself should be precisely calibrated and easily hit and an indicator should have an unambiguous theoretical connection with the objective variables being influenced (and measured).

7.2 THE OBJECTIVES OF MACROECONOMIC POLICY

A macropolicy discussion actually should begin with an analysis of the objectives of macroeconomic policy. For a policy to be at all coherent the practitioners of policy must systematically enumerate and quantify their objectives – if possible – and distinguish intermediate from final object- ives. Specific references can be found in the literature to the following general objectives, although the qualifying words attached change with the circumstances. These are price-level stability, full employment, a satisfactory balance of payments (or a stable exchange rate) and a sufficiently rapid rate of growth. To this we could add, in certain circumstances, a stable capital market as a kind of intermediate objective that some observers seem to rate pretty highly.

Consider, first, the price level (that is, the inflation rate). If prices grow steadily at, say, 2 per cent per year, then an economy can accommodate itself to the situation by (for example) applying automatic indexation clauses or by constructing pay scales that reflect the expected inflation rate. Further, since market interest rates will tend to reflect the expected rate of inflation and since, with a steady 2 per cent inflation, expected inflation will tend to be equal to actual inflation, nominal interest rates will simply tend to be marked up by 2 per cent so that capital markets will not be unduly disturbed by such an inflation. Thus, the frustration of expectations and many of the undesirable distributional effects of a variable inflation rate probably would not occur to any great extent. Thus, a potential objective variable is the rate of change of a representa- tive price index at some desired value (or range of values). In fact, most, if not all, societies clearly have a well-defined desired range for the rate of change of prices, quite possibly but certainly not inevitably, centred around a zero rate, at least where this is at all feasible.[1]

With regard to full employment, the first question which arises concerns whether or not the usual measure, unemployment as a percentage of the labour force, is the appropriate objective variable. For one thing, the monetary authorities may be instructed to watch the level of employment rather than the rate of unemployment, leaving the latter to social rather than macroeconomic policy. Second, the rate of unemployment will not reflect (a) the underemployment that results from workers taking jobs that do not fully utilise their skills or (b) the fact that the size of the labour force itself will tend to vary with the condition of the economy. In hard times, for example, disappointed workers may quit the labour force, never again to compete for jobs (although they may for some time be assumed to be job-hunting (by the government)). Furthermore, there are other problems of labour-force participation to worry about. In recent years in a number of Western economies, for example, women have increased their participation rate partly (in effect) filling up the spaces created by a rising male unemployment rate. Thus, while total employment has risen overall, 'visible male unemployment' has also been rising to relatively high levels (historically). Perhaps, indeed, there is a variable 'natural' rate of unemployment, not likely to settle at a zero per cent of the labour force, which the authorities should keep in mind when they select a target (that is, a desired) rate; see Chapter 2, above, for considerably more on this topic.

With regard to international objectives, any discussion must reflect the rapid changes in this area in recent years. In the days when the International Monetary Fund (IMF) supervised an active fixed-rate system many countries attempted to follow the rules and keep their fixed exchange rates within narrow bands. In this period we often see a very real conflict between a country's apparent internal objectives and those defined by the group of nations in the IMF. A country, in this period, used its stocks of gold, IMF balances, Special Drawing Rights (after 1968) and convertible currencies for the front-line battle to defend the 'parity' of its currency and often fought behind the lines either to control the domestic economy or to influence the parity by means of fiscal and (especially) monetary policy. But the IMF system has been swept away and now the world stock of 'reserves' consists mainly of convertible currencies – dominated by the US dollar – and attempts to control exchange rates are now at most half-hearted. Thus, while it is not easy to be precise over what is being done in particular cases (the United States, for example, rarely conducts any firm policy toward its exchange rate), it is still important to realise that exchange-rate changes figure in policy discussions and on occasion even provoke monetary reactions when things seem to be going particularly 'badly' – whatever that might mean (it sometimes means increased variability).

Since the Second World War there has been a vigorous discussion, much of it carried on in the political arena, over the possibility of defining a growth objective. In all likelihood, the authorities of most countries have not used monetary policy energetically to boost the rate of growth of the economy and have used fiscal policy only sparingly in this role, but, even so, there is a wide-ranging debate over this objective. The discussion of growth is often a complicated one, partly because of the issues of pollution, depletion of resources, and the like, but as things stand there is basically no precise work on the tradeoffs among growth and these other areas. Even so, it seems likely that the fiscal and monetary literature will eventually get around to these issues. (See Kaldor (1971) for a discussion and Snower (1981) for a rare analysis of this more general problem.)

Above we referred to an intermediate objective that is sometimes important; this is the question of the degree of stability of the domestic capital markets. In practice this stability is usually defined in terms of the behaviour of one or more key interest rates (most notably the Treasury-bill rate or mortgage-interest rates). While we have already discussed the role of interest-rate stability at several points in this study (particularly in Chapters 1 and 2), here we wish to emphasise its position as an explicit objective by itself. In particular, a stable-interest rate suggests to some observers that capital markets are also orderly. This stability, then, is valued because it may well provide a good background for a successful growth policy, especially in so far as it leads to a stable climate for long-term capital formation. Indeed, somewhat loosely, we could go as far as to say economic orderliness in general may well be helpful to growth and even to the achievement of the other objectives (see Pissarides, 1972). For example, frequent and/or large changes in policy variables can cause expensive portfolio adjustments, extended legislative sessions, changes in payslips and other forms, not to mention all the real adjustments in the allocation of resources brought about by the shock to the system (and to its stock of relevant information). What this broader perspective amounts to is considering as an objective that of 'no policy changes' as compared to the other more activist concerns enumerated above.

This leaves us with two important questions remaining with regard to objectives: the extent of interactions among objectives and an enumeration of what the objectives have actually been in a number of important cases. The first point is rather simply stated. The objective variables we have defined – $\dot{P}/P$, U, $\dot{y}/y$ and B (for the balance of payments or the exchange rate) – can all be visualised as final endogenous variables in a general macroeconomic model of an open economy. As such, they will be mutually endogenous in general, so that achievement in one area may be either at the expense of or complementary to achievement in another area. Thus, if there were such a thing as a stable Phillips curve, then U and $\dot{P}/P$ would be contradictory in the sense that to produce less unemployment (via a macropolicy) the authorities would have to accept more inflation, as measured by the slope of the Phillips curve. In contrast, as noted, two objectives may go together to some extent. An example of such a complementarity occurs when a policy of more rapid growth – when carried out – actually reduces unemployment at the same time. Since it cannot always be said whether or to what extent the objective variables are contradictory or complementary in actual cases (and, indeed, there may well be differences associated with different instruments or at different times), we should probably leave it that the variables are mutually endogenous and construct our models with sufficient flexibility to comprehend this. In this connection, although it has provided an example, the Phillips curve (or Okun's Law or any of the other empirical 'truths' of this sort) does not really provide a firm enough basis for choice among policies that are substitutes (as we saw in Chapter 2). Nevertheless, the interaction of objectives is a reality that must be dealt with.

All Western governments do make such choices in practice, and there have been numerous studies of their objectives, building essentially on something like the reaction function model of Chapter 1. What is done, in these cases, is essentially to regress the objectives on the policy variables – using, in effect the 'revealed preferences' of the authorities to decode their actual policy tradeoffs. That is, if α represents the coefficient on unemployment and β that on inflation, then, assuming the model fits well (so that the instrument settings are actually 'explained' by the data), then α/β represents the revealed tradeoff between the two objectives. What emerges from a comparison over many countries (see the survey in Parkin and Bade, 1977) is that most countries show some interaction between two or even three objectives (which are not the same across countries) when monetary policy 'instruments' are employed as the dependent variables. (Fiscal measures have generally not shown up (statistically) in these tests.) Indeed, the actual numbers produced often seem to make sense (see Reuber, 1964, Dewald and H. G. Johnson, 1963, D. Fisher, 1970, and Pissarides, 1972) although these studies rarely consider the endogeneity issue (the money stock is often employed as the instrument) and generally set up a single-equation format, even though the problem is patently simultaneous-equation in nature. We shall continue on the subject of instruments in the next section.

7.3 THE INSTRUMENTS OF FISCAL AND MONETARY POLICY

In our discussion of policy to this point we have said very little of a specific nature about who the macropolicy authorities really are and about what instruments they employ in trying to advance their objectives. For the authorities two types of arrangement presently seem to be in vogue in the developed countries which actually employ fiscal and monetary policy to any extent. These are arrangements in which:

(a) fiscal and monetary policy are placed under the control of the central government or in which
(b) fiscal policy is placed under the control of the central government and monetary policy is placed under the control of a separate (centralised) monetary authority.

It is impossible to generalise further than this, though, because practice varies so much across countries (Parkin and Bade, 1977).

In the United States, for example, the Federal Reserve carries out monetary policy while the Congress enacts the legislation that either enables or sets up the machinery to carry out fiscal policy. In reality, in the United States, much of the decision power for fiscal policy rests with the President and a few leaders in Congress and for monetary policy with the Chairman of the Board of Governors of the Federal Reserve (himself confirmed in his position by Congress although as an appointee of the President). If the newspapers are any guide to the situation, these separate entities often have conflicting views of the magnitude and timing of monetary and fiscal actions appropriate at particular times. Germany, Switzerland and Canada have this style of decision-making with several agencies (or their heads) responsible for the policies.

But more often one finds a centralised authority responsible for both monetary and fiscal policy; thus the Bank of England Act of 1946 says 'The Treasury may from time to time give such direction to the Bank as after consultation with the Governor of the Bank they think necessary in the public interest . . . ' and the structures of Australian, Belgian, Italian, French, Japanese, Dutch and Swedish policies all exhibit a similar fiscal and monetary policy integration. However, while this removes an element of conflict in policy formulation, this arrangement need not produce a harmonious final product, especially if all of the interaction between fiscal and monetary policy is not appreciated. As well, it is worth pointing out that a divided authority could operate as a constraint on (for example) careless or premature actions that might have been better not to have been taken.

Turning to the actual instruments employed, let us consider a broad list of fiscal and monetary policy tools, pretty much without comment. For *fiscal policy*, the main discretionary policy tools are changes in government spending, changes in tax rates – considering all sorts of tax rates as proper game – and changes in withholding exemptions, depreciation guidelines and the like. Much of the tax literature is in terms of investment tax credits, depreciation guidelines, and, of course, personal and corporate income-tax rates, but there are other suggestions that surface from time to time. Among these, in a stabilisation context, are the sales tax (Branson, 1973), a tax-based incomes policy (Seidman, 1978), the employment tax credit (Fethke, Policano and Williamson, 1979), and even 'labour taxes' (Benavie, 1981). We should also note the existence of a huge literature on non-discretionary 'automatic' stabilisers which are not part of our subject material, but are certainly part of any overall fiscal design. (See Blinder and Solow (1974), Smyth (1974), McCallum and Whitaker (1979) and Sheffrin (1981) for a cross-section.)

For *monetary policy* the main instruments are open-market operations, changes in reserve requirements or in the liquidity constraints imposed on commercial banks and/or other financial intermediaries and changes in the central bank's lending rate (to commercial banks or to an intermediary such as the British discount houses). The authorities may also consider general and specific – that is, 'selective' – credit control as part of their domain; this would bring in direct controls on interest rates (e.g. ceiling rates), controls on minimum payments for instalment (hire-purchase) contracts, maximum lending periods for certain types of loans and even direct controls on the quantity of lending (Silber, 1975). Partly under this heading we might also find controls on capital spending or on stock and bond market activity (as in the form of the American margin requirements that impose minimum down-payments on securities transactions). There is also the possibility of direct control in the form of (for example) firm warnings directed to the commercial banks about the quantity of their lending. One also comes across direct wage and price controls or, more usually, wage and price guidelines. Finally, both lists of policy instruments include an element of direct persuasion (sometimes called 'moral suasion' in the literature); this is a device which is almost always part of any actual policy although the final effect is almost certainly small (and, whether small or not, is certainly unquantifiable). This is a considerable list, clearly, and, as noted, it is usually in the hands of a reasonably unified and central authority. There is, then, at least the possibility that the multiplicity of instruments will make it possible to reach a multiplicity of objectives, but, as we shall see, there are a lot of problems that intervene.

7.4   THE TARGETS AND INDICATORS OF MACROECONOMIC POLICY: A THEORETICAL DISCUSSION

In the discussion of objectives and instruments to this point we have worked with the provisional assumption that whatever concept we are dealing with has an unambiguous definition in an empirical sense. For the instruments defined in Section 7.3 this does not seem a serious problem, but for the objectives, since the concepts discussed are generally aggregates – e. g. of consumer prices, unemployment rates and the rate of growth of real GNP – we need to consider further the basic index-number problem that arises when 'constructed' aggregates are used for policy purposes. To take up the objectives of policy in this context would be redundant, however, since we have covered that topic elsewhere (D. Fisher, 1983); as a consequence, we will work with the intermediate variables and, in particular, in Subsection 7.4.1, with the monetary quantities. In any case this is probably the most important literature we could look at in view of the recent interest in, and practice of, direct money stock or reserve control.

In a fundamental sense the monetary quantities discussed in Subsection 7.4.1 are indicators of what we might loosely call the stock of 'moneyness' in the economy. We are, actually, led to adopt an empirical approach to this problem because of the heterogeneous nature of monetary products. Indeed, transactions accounts and savings accounts have different blends of the underlying characteristics of money – as mediators in exchange or as stores of value – and so we will suggest that a viable approach would be to utilise received consumer theory in the search for a useful 'indicator' of monetary services. We could then propose to control this entity as if it were a direct-policy instrument.

There is, though, a more general targets–indicators problem which we have to deal with; this arises because of all the potential uncertainties and lags that can (and probably do) arise in the conduct of policy. This topic considers the operating rules and provisional techniques that the authorities actually employ in order to achieve the best possible results in an uncertain and possibly unstable world. The gist of the problem is that the authorities have to feel their way along in order to know the effect of past changes in their instruments, as well as in order to identify all other influences on the situation at hand. In this task they use a set of targets that can be hit by the policy instruments and a set of indicators that measure their progress in achieving some desirable combination of values of their objective variables. In this part of the chapter – in 7.4.2 – we will look at the formal literature on the targets–indicators problem, leaving to Section 7.6 the discussion of the actual practices of modern policy authorities. Such empirical notes as we have will also appear in Section 7.6.

There is one other major area of interest in this literature, and that involves rational expectations. We suggested back in Chapter 2 that rational expectations brings information-processing into the mainstream of dynamic policy models, but we actually have presented only sparse examples of this particular advantage. To pick up on questions of information-gathering, we first look at an early paper on hyperinflations (Cagan, 1956) in which there exists a conflict between rational and adaptive expectations as predictors of inflation. In particular, it seems that the adaptive expectations approach (of Cagan) throws away useful information about the determination of inflation rates which, assuming it is readily obtainable information, economic agents would not want to do. Pursuing the question of information-gathering we next refer to a more general treatment of the issues that arise under the broad heading of a consideration of the 'signal extraction' problem; some of this material is drawn from Sargent (1979). Finally, to complete the story on rational expectations we look at a paper by Feige and Pearce (1976) in which an explicit cost-of-information approach is attempted. This sort of work is surprisingly rare in this literature. The discussion appears in Section 7.5.

7.4.1 On the Monetary Aggregates

In this subsection we wish to extend an earlier survey (D. Fisher, 1983) on the definition of money in order to consider the circumstances under which certain monetary aggregates might serve effectively as measures of 'moneyness' for policy purposes. The present practice in most countries is to classify certain bank and public sector financial liabilities arbitrarily as either 'narrow' money (M1) – that is, balances that can be used for transactions purposes – or 'broad' money (M2, M3), where the latter usually include M1 plus savings (and time) deposits and other accounts on which drafts usually cannot be written directly. On occasion very large denomination deposits are included in monetary measures even though it is admitted that the users are generally not individuals but business firms looking for a decent return on funds that are accumulating for (often) some financial purpose. All of these measures (M1, M2, etc.) are frequently redefined by the authorities, usually because the monetary measure shows – or is expected to show – 'erratic' behaviour in the face of institutional or technological changes (such as the introduction of automatic transfers among accounts). Indeed, the dominant reasons for this recently have been financial innovations that have, it seems, changed the basic characteristics of various financial commodities and, it is usually alleged, increased substitutability among many of these entities.

The brute-force way to approach this problem, and the way generally employed, is to try various combinations of selected financial variables using statistical procedures to identify the best candidate among the various alternative definitions. A suggested procedure is to identify the purpose at hand and then to compare the various aggregates in this particular role. Thus (Friedman and Schwartz, 1970, p. 90) 'there is a subtotal, labeled "money" for convenience, which is useful to distinguish because it is related to other magnitudes in a fairly regular and stable way, though its particular content may be different from place to place or time to time'. The 'other economic magnitudes' may be the value of nominal GNP or, even, concepts as difficult to grasp empirically as the demand for money (see G. S. Laumas, 1968). The latter enters the problem because (Laidler, 1969, p. 515) 'as far as the definition of money is concerned the most important issue has been the identification and measurement of a stable aggregate demand for money function'. This connects with our policy problem in this section because (Laidler, 1969, p. 515) 'A "more stable demand function" is precisely one that permits the consequences of shifting the supply of money to be more easily and accurately predicted.' That is, if we find a more stable demand for money, then the money concerned – M1, M2 or whatever – will be a good indicator of (and possibly a target for) the pressure of monetary policy on the economy.

In two important senses the foregoing really begs the fundamental question we are posing in favour of some empirical gymnastics. For one thing, it supposes that there is some concept called 'the supply of money' which can be manipulated directly without raising any comparable problem of measurement. This is not so, though, for all of the definitions proposed so far include the liabilities of privately-owned financial institutions; these liabilities are generally not controlled directly, but are merely influenced by, for example, open-market operations. The financial institutions are also, and at the same time, influenced by market forces – even just on the liability side – so in principle an indicator of the money supply itself is needed before we can claim the identification of money demand. For another thing, it is an act of almost boundless faith to construct our aggregates merely by adding together the various components, without employing index-number theory in their construction. It might be hoped, of course, that for a certain time and place we might find a close relation (historically, of course), but, for the United States at least (Barnett, 1984, pp. 165–6) 'the simple sum M1 aggregate is the only official monetary aggregate whose behavior even remotely approximates that of a well-designed index number'. Even M1 is not particularly good from this point of view (and the authorities often put weight on M2 and M3 if M1 looks particularly shaky) and so policy mistakes will occur that can materially reduce the effectiveness of policy.

The issue at hand is substitutability among the potential assets since (Barnett, 1984, p. 165), 'It is well known in aggregation theory that aggregation by simple summation is valid only when aggregating over goods that are perfect substitutes.' We can approach this topic either by means of a system of demand equations for the various assets – measuring the relevant elasticities of substitution and plotting the behaviour over time – or by means of the construction of the 'ideal' indices of monetary quantities (the Divisia or Fisher Ideal indices), where ideal indices are those that are based on (i.e. approximate) the true indices suggested by formal aggregation theory. We will pursue both of these topics in the remainder of this section.

The utility approach to the substitution problem can work either with money operating through the utility function – as a result of substituting money into that function through the constraints – or with money entering directly into the function as if it provides direct services (e.g. liquidity, convenience) to the representative economic agent.[2] While not everyone appreciates the beauty of the direct-utility approach, it does have the considerable advantage of employing a standard and well-known paradigm, so, without further apology, because of a desire to be clear about the theoretical issues involved, we will proceed.

The representative consumer can be assumed to maximise

$$u_i = U_i(c_t, \ldots, c_{t+T}; x_t, \ldots, x_{t+T}; B_{t+T})$$
$$i = t, \ldots, t + T \tag{7.1}$$

where c and x are vectors of consumer goods and financial commodities (the former flows, the latter stocks) and B is a long-term bond that has no moneyness to it. T defines the agent's horizon. The suitable constraint, of course, is a dynamic one, but rather than complicate things, we can invoke Hadar's collapsibility theorem (1971): that is, if a multiperiod utility function is maximised subject to some appropriate set of wealth constraints, assuming that optimal plans are revised every period, there exists a one-period utility function that if maximised subject to a single wealth constraint yields a set of demand functions that trace out the time path. This produces the following problem for the current period

$$u_t = U_t(c_1, \ldots, c_n; x_1, \ldots, y_m) \tag{7.2}$$

with

$$\sum_{j=1}^{n} p_j c_j + \sum_{i=1}^{m} \pi_i x_i = M'_t \tag{7.3}$$

where M'_t defines current resources and π_i is the 'user cost' associated with the ith financial commodity.[3] This last is based on the representative non-money asset that appears in $7.1 - B_{t+\tau} -$ and, for the ith asset is

$$\pi_{it} = (r_t^* - r_{it})/(1 + r_t^*) \tag{7.4}$$

where r_t^* identifies the yield on the bond (B). This is one way of getting at the implicit yield on monetary assets, by comparing it with an alternative asset (B) that provides no 'pecuniary' services. If the individual uses money and forgoes interest then the forgone interest is the user cost (which is equal, at the margin, to the value of the pecuniary services).

If we do not wish to estimate the larger demand system implied by Equations 7.2 to 7.4, we can further assume weak separability between the financial assets and consumption goods; this, at least, is what the literature generally does. We can, then, estimate (simultaneously) a set of monetary demand equations for the components of M1, M2, etc., where the structure of the problem is to maximise

$$u_t = U_t(x_{1t}, \ldots, x_{mt}) \tag{7.5}$$

subject to

$$\sum_{i=1}^{m} \pi_{it} x_{it} - M_t = 0 \tag{7.6}$$

where M_t represents the resources devoted to this class of commodities. The simultaneity will be recognised by imposing the standard restrictions of consumer theory,[4] and the aggregation across consumers can be checked by testing the significance of the aggregation on various proposed collections of financial commodities (e.g. currency, demand deposits and NOW accounts); the separability is also testable. If all goes well – that is, if the coefficients are well-determined, etc., and if the aggregation across consumers goes through – then the derived elasticities of substitution among the financial commodities can be examined to determine those that might reasonably be aggregated. In this literature – whether or not the aggregation across consumers has been checked – the results generally suggest that the elasticities are too low (and too unstable) for simple-sum aggregations of even M1 to be safe indicators of what final users think money is.[5] This implies that we must construct our index using a weighted average, where, we will argue, the weights are those suggested by superlative index-number theory.

The superlative index approach to defining a monetary indicator is based on economic theory; its purpose is to achieve as valid a measure of moneyness as possible, given that we can never expect to construct a perfect measure. The basic problem confronting us is studied under the equivalent headings of the 'composite-goods theorem' or 'the index-number problem'. In order to construct an aggregate that obeys the laws of economic theory (negative substitution elasticities, symmetrical preferences, etc.) the following is a necessary and sufficient condition (Hicks, 1946, p. 33). 'A collection of physical things can always be treated as if they were divisible into units of a single commodity so long as their relative prices can be assumed to be unchanged, in the particular problem at hand'. In short, when prices change (the only interesting case), those changes must be equi-proportionate among the elements of the aggregate.[6] Failing this at some level (statistically), the constructed entity will have no meaning in economic theory and will be a treacherous element in any policy design, as a target, as an indicator, or (of course) as the dependent variable in a demand for money function. The problem is that of an 'unstable' definition (Barnett, 1980) that can translate into an unstable policy (or demand-for-money function) quite apart from any actions of economic agents.

The current procedure used by the authorities of all countries with these sorts of policies is to construct simple sum aggregates of the monetary quantities. We have argued that this is most likely to produce unsatisfactory numbers and have suggested that empirical studies generally confirm this position. The next best thing to do would be to construct arbitrary weights based on budget shares at some base period (a Laspeyres index); the problem here is that after a price change, because of the substitution effect, the old budget shares will not reflect the actual economic decisions taken at the set of new prices. The theoretical answer to this is to employ aggregation theory in which aggregator functions are constructed; in the case of consumers this aggregator function is a representative utility function, in effect. What we do is estimate the parameters of the utility function – assuming, arbitrarily, some specific functional form – in order to be able to construct weights for the price index at relative prices that differ from the original ones; the quantity index is the 'dual' of this price index. The problem is that the true utility/aggregator function is unknown, as are the details of its parameterisation so that the appearance of instability of the index can re-enter the problem. The Laspeyres index, in this case, can be interpreted as a linear approximation of the true but unknown aggregator function, but it is not a very good approximation although it is likely to be better than the weightless index generally employed by the monetary authorities.

It is here that we might consider a formulation in terms of 'ideal' statistical index-number theory; this approach is designed to provide higher-order approximations to the underlying aggregator functions. The statistical approach, to put the cart before the horse, has the properties that

(a) the index numbers do not depend upon any unknown parameters,
(b) there is no need to specialise the underlying utility function, and
(c) the statistical index is a function of both prices and quantities.[7]

Among the potentially large class of superlative indices the Fisher Ideal and the Divisia stand out. Of these two, the Divisia has a particularly straightforward interpretation; for one thing (Barnett, 1981, p. 221) 'Hulten ... has proved that in continuous time the Divisia is always exact for *any* consistent (... weakly separable) aggregator function. Hence, no index number can be better than the Divisia in continuous time'.

The Divisia is constructed as follows. For M_{it} being the quantity of financial asset i at time period t, then the share of M_{it} of total 'expenditures' in the class of financial assets is (in discrete time):

$$S_{it} = (\pi_{it} M_{it}) \bigg/ \left(\sum_{j=1}^{n} \pi_{jt} M_{jt} \right) \tag{7.7}$$

Here π is the user cost defined in Equation 7.4. In continuous time the Divisia index would be the line integral of the differential

$$d \log M = \sum_{i=1}^{n} S_i d \log M_i \tag{7.8}$$

In discrete time we could approximate 7.7 with

$$S_{it}^* = \tfrac{1}{2}(S_{it} + S_{it-1})$$

and then the Divisia would be constructed from

$$\log M_t - \log M_{t-1} = \sum_{i=1}^{n} S_{it}^* (\log M_{it} - \log M_{it-1}) \tag{7.9}$$

It is this formulation that has the theoretical and statistical backing to measure 'moneyness', once we have settled on a class of representative assets. It should be noted again that the weights here (in Equation 7.7) depend on both prices and quantities and that the prices are user costs, reflecting, in effect, the opportunity costs of holding monetary financial assets relative to some benchmark non-monetary asset.

Does using a Divisia index make a difference for money as a target, as an indicator or as an input into, for example, the demand for money? For economic models – and by implication for both targets and indicators – it does. Barnett (1980) shows that some apparent shifts in the demand for money in the United States are removed if a Divisia rather than a simple-sum index is employed. This finding is repeated for a test of money as a potential target in another paper (Barnett and Spindt, 1979), where the information content of the Divisia is shown to dominate the simple-sum. As an indicator (as, in the sense defined below, a target-indicator), Barnett (1984) shows that the differences between Divisia and simple-sum estimates of M1 and, especially, M2 and M3, are considerable on recent US data. This should alarm anyone who relies on any of these money-stock indicators for almost any conceivable purpose.

7.4.2 Targets and Indicators: A Formal Distinction

The literature on which this subsection is based has seen sparse in recent years, but the reason is not that anything is really settled. The context we consider is that of trying to conduct a coherent policy when adequate information is unavailable and when the effects of economic shocks are spread out (generally unevenly) over time. This is, of course, the problem of conducting policy anywhere but on the blackboard. In fact, in order to conduct a policy of the sort described in earlier chapters the authorities need to know the general shape of the structure of the economy; this includes being able to discern the impact of exogenous forces and identifying the size, significance and stability of the parameters of a correct model of the system. Putting aside rational expectations for the moment, this is clearly a task that is beyond the technology of economics, and so a literature that searches for policies with 'low-information' requirements has evolved.

In fact, the macropolicy authorities will generally try to make do with the best model they possess; what they possess, really, is a series of partly verified hypotheses (for example that the demand for money may be a stable function of a few key variables or that a Cobb–Douglas production function might provide a satisfactory basis for the aggregate-supply function), some often inconsistent (and often seriously inaccurate) forecasts from econometric models and from other less formal sources, and a great deal of largely unverifiable intuition on how certain markets – mainly financial – actually function. Since they are likely to feel better about their grip on the behaviour of the financial markets, it is small wonder that the authorities will try to implement a less ambitious policy than one based on a full macroeconometric model (with or without rational expectations). This alternative generally takes the form of selecting certain variables to be *targets* (Brunner and Meltzer, 1969, p. 2), 'The target problem is the problem of choosing an optimal strategy or strategies to guide monetary policy operations in the money markets under the conditions of uncertainty and lags in the receipt of information about the more remote goals of policy' and certain other variables to be *indicators* (p. 16): 'The problem of selecting an indicator of monetary policy is equivalent to the problem of finding a scale that allows us to make reliable statements comparing the thrust of various policy combinations.' It is, however, possible that a single variable could perform both functions as we shall see when we look at more precise definitions (and at the results of empirical tests).

One might at first glance think, in view of the fact that the authorities possess reasonably full information about their own instrument settings, that they possess sufficient information to measure the impact of policy adjustments on the final variables in the system, but, for a number of reasons this is not so. One major difficulty is that all sorts of lags exist in the response of the system to various impulses; and not only do the lags vary from cause to cause, but they also vary from period to period (apparently), making it most difficult to disentangle the effects of policy and non-policy influences. Even more serious, perhaps, are the results of trying to conduct a policy when the structure of the economy is not well-defined or, for that matter, when it cannot be 'defined' in this sense because of the influence of changing rational expectations. Finally, the policy is also vulnerable to the quality of the data employed in the models and at some points the data are very weak, indeed. The frequent and sizeable revisions of GNP, consumer spending and the like bear witness to the potential of this problem.

In this context, then, formal criteria for targets and indicators have been suggested in an attempt to cut through the high-information requirements of the 'full model' approach without laying on a lot of structure. Following Saving (1967), for example, we could set up formal criteria for targets as follows. Policy targets must be

(a) quickly and firmly influenced by the instruments at hand, and
(b) readily and accurately measurable.

The first condition is perfectly understandable, while the latter condition rules out such subjective notions as the 'tone and feel' of the market because such concepts would be unquantifiable, essentially, such that two different observers would be likely to provide two different estimates of their magnitude (see Guttentag, 1966, and Atkinson, 1969). Immediately, we can see why interest rates are such a popular monetary target variable; they are readily observable on a daily basis, and they seem to respond directly to monetary pressures. For fiscal policy the targets are much harder to specify, and we find, really, little reference to this particular concept in the fiscal policy literature.

Still following Saving (1967), then, the *indicators* of policy could be chosen on the basis of what they tell us about the influence of policy instruments on the final variables. The usually stated condition is that

(a) the indicator variables should have a direct, short, statistically firm, and theoretically unambiguous connection with the objective variables.

This is, as we shall see, approximately what we should want if the indicators 'Granger-cause' the objective variables. As it stands, though, all we get from this first condition is a measure of *all* of the influences on the final variables; what we really need to know to complete the policy design is what the policy influence alone has been. Thus, Saving proposes a second condition, rather difficult to model in practice, which is that

(b) the indicators efficiently separate the determinants of the target variables into exogenous and policy-determined components.

In sum, we must choose our indicator for both its closeness to the final variables and its ability to divide the influences of (other) exogenous factors from the policy factors as determinants of the targets. In any case, we would not need this second condition if the targets could be uniquely hit by the monetary authorities or if the target and the indicator variables were the same thing.

7.5 MONETARY POLICY TARGETS AND INDICATORS AND RATIONAL EXPECTATIONS

The foregoing is designed to explain formally what the policy authorities do in the event that they must grope along because of insufficient information. This is the same environment that has spawned rational expectations, and so it is interesting to take a look at several results which refer to the use of information-providing variables (also called 'indicators') as part of individual or official strategy. Here it will be obvious, if it has not been to this point, that the indicators literature should be thought of as an integral part of the rational-expectations approach to macroeconomic policy, even though we have not produced any results under rational expectations so far in this chapter.

In earlier chapters we have argued that information costs provide the major new element in the rational-expectations approach; at the same time we have said nothing very specific about this in our discussion to this point. In this respect we are only following the literature, but we should now at least introduce some work that attempts to deal with this important element of the theory. As we will see, this material will tie into our discussion of indicators nicely. To begin with, if individuals have all of the information relevant to their decision-making and if we then (implicitly) assume that information is costless, then we are led to argue that they should not make any mistakes at all – or, at any rate, that we can judge the power of the theory in terms of the strength of its predictions. That is, if it predicts poorly, the theory is rejected either because random events have swamped systematic events or because economic agents have made systematic errors. This rigid interpretation is really not in the spirit of the definition of rational expectations given in Chapter 3, although it does have the advantage of providing a direct test. Of course, the rational-expectations theory could never survive so strict a test, either.

Much of the rational-expectations literature actually concerns itself with predictions of the inflation rate – using a monetary-quantity indicator and/or the past history of inflation rates – and so this is the obvious place to begin our discussion. The classic paper on this topic – but one that is not in a rational-expectations format – is actually Cagan's (1956) study of seven twentieth-century hyperinflations. A hyperinflation can be defined as a condition in which rises in the price level 'are considered sufficiently large to be analysed independently of output changes' (J. L. Evans and Yarrow, 1981, p. 61). In Cagan's cases, over periods of time up to two years, the price level rose as many as 3.81 $\times 10^{27}$ times (and, in that case, the stock of currency expanded 1.19 $\times 10^{25}$ times). Cagan's model follows immediately (following Sargent and Wallace, 1973).

Assume, first, that the equilibrium in the money market is given by

$$\log (M/P)_t = \alpha \pi_t^e + \tau y + \delta + u_t \qquad \alpha < 0, \tau > 0 \tag{7.10}$$

where π_t^e is the expected inflation rate (r, the real rate of interest, is assumed to be constant) and y is the log of real income. We can, as noted, assume that y is constant (at least for the hyperinflation case), and we can further assume that money demand is always equal to money supply (as we did, in effect, in 7.10). With respect to expected inflation (π_t^e) Cagan assumes that economic agents form their expectations adaptively as in

$$\pi_t^e = (1 - \lambda) \sum_{i=0}^{\infty} \lambda^i \pi_{t-i} \qquad 0 \leqslant \lambda < 1 \tag{7.11}$$

with actual (historical) inflation rates on the right. In this literature this expression is often referred to as 'permanent prices'.

We can rewrite Equation 7.11, using the lag operator (L) as

$$\pi_t^e = ((1 - \lambda)/(1 - \lambda L)) \pi_t \tag{7.12}$$

Then, by lagging Equation 7.10 one period and subtracting the result from 7.10 we obtain a first-differenced form for the money-market equilibrium of

$$\log (M_t/M_{t-1}) \equiv \mu_t = \pi_t + \alpha(\pi_t^e - \pi_{t-1}^e) + u_t - u_{t-1} \tag{7.13}$$

We can then substitute Equation 7.12 into 7.13 and solve for the actual rate of inflation; this yields the rather cumbersome expression given as Equation 7.14:

$$\pi_t = \frac{\dfrac{1 - \lambda L}{1 + \alpha(1 - \lambda)}}{1 - \left[\dfrac{\lambda + \alpha(1 - \lambda)}{1 + \alpha(1 - \lambda)}\right]L} \mu_t - \frac{\dfrac{1 - \lambda L}{1 + \alpha(1 - \lambda)}(1 - L)}{1 - \left[\dfrac{\lambda + \alpha(1 - \lambda)}{1 + \alpha(1 - \lambda)}\right]L} u_t \tag{7.14}$$

This is a first-order difference equation for π (in μ and u and their lags).

In Equation 7.14 the actual rate of inflation depends on its own history (because of L in the denominator) and on the history of the rate of growth of the money stock. This is, to emphasise the point, the actual way the price level evolves under an adaptive expectations rule such as

Equation 7.12 when the quantity of money is determined exogenously, as we are assuming. We are, that is to say, assuming adaptive expectations, as Cagan does, and setting up (but not solving) the resulting difference equation for the inflation rate.

Cagan, actually, substitutes Equation 7.11 directly into 7.10 by the use of the proxy for permanent prices; his solution is

$$\log (M/P)_t = \alpha(1 - \lambda) \sum_{i=0}^{\infty} \lambda^i \pi_{t-i} + \tau y + \delta + u_t \tag{7.15}$$

There are two objections to this procedure. For one thing if we assume prices actually evolve according to 7.14, then equation (7.15) shows that the terms π_{t-i} and u_t will be correlated. That is, Equation 7.14 shows that the shocks in the money-demand curve will influence the actual inflation rate so that if both enter Equation 7.15 the application of ordinary least squares will produce inconsistency. For a second thing, and this involves rational expectations directly, the public is being assumed (by Cagan) to use Equation 7.12 to predict prices when prices actually evolve according to Equation 7.14, which is, of course, a different path. This would be irrational and a systematic error results; the public, if it also included in its information set the behaviour of the money stock and the interactions of Equation 7.14 could actually improve its forecasts over what Cagan proposes. With better forecasts, then, the public could also improve its expected utility, which is what all this activity is about in the first place. Of course we are mixing rational and adaptive expectations here as if it were logical to have rational expectations in an adaptive-expectations world. Some further work on this model, in the rational-expectations context is by Bisignano (1975) and by J. L. Evans and Yarrow (1981); the latter show that in certain cases the rational-expectations equilibrium is unstable while the adaptive is not, depending on the policy rule adopted by the authorities. But, one fervently hopes, this particular literature is not germane to current policy problems and so we will turn to other matters.

As a second topic consider the situation when the authorities know the model of the economy, in a particular sense to be defined below, and are themselves faced with an information problem because certain stochastic variables are known only with a lag. The treatment is that of Kareken *et al.* (1973), with some help from Sargent (1979). Here we are basically returning to our rules-versus-authorities discussion of Chapter 1, but with material that ties in with our current discussion of monetary targets and indicators. The expectations of the government will here be 'rational' – more or less – although this is a context in which the lags in information-gathering would justify adaptive expectations. We will say something about how the private sector reacts to all this at the end.

The authorities, in this problem, will try to control nominal GNP (Y) and will do so with three intermediate variables; these are

central bank assets (A),
the stock of bank deposits (M), and
a nominal interest rate (R).

The data on assets and nominal interest rates are available each day (with a one-day lag) while deposits are available with a one-week lag and GNP is available only at the beginning of each quarter. This is approximately correct except for (in the United States) 'flash' estimates of GNP (and its components) which were available before the end of the quarter. Then, for a linear model, assuming there is only one target variable and assuming that the structure is known with certainty (i.e. the constants and slopes of the linear model are known), we find (Kareken *et al.*, 1973, p. 157), 'It is optimal for the central bank, in guessing initial conditions for the current day, to use all such observations as have become available since it last decided open market policy.' This, indeed, is what we saw in Chapter 1 with a very basic structure. In face, in such a simplified set-up, the authorities will find it optimal to re-solve the model for optimal values of their instruments each day, to the extent that new information implies that either initial conditions or the parameters have changed (and to the extent that the costs of running the model permit it).

In the foregoing, policy settings are changed each day – even with a known structure – because, of course, estimated initial conditions change each day. Furthermore, the central bank does not use an 'intermediate-target variable' at all (i.e. an R^* or an M^*), but sets up its problem with *expected values* for all variables, revising its guesses as to the initial conditions and adjusting its instruments when (and as) expected values deviate from actual values. This is an important distinction, for it implies that in a policy set-up with these assumptions there is no target variable at all, but only information-providing intermediate variables (indicators, really) that enable the authorities to fix up a new set of initial conditions, resimulate the policy and redeploy its instruments.

Assume, then, the following model. Let the *IS* curve be

$$Y_t = \alpha_0 + \alpha_1 R_t + a_t \quad (1)$$

with $\alpha_1 < 0$. For the money market, where the intermediate variables we are interested in are determined, assume that the demand for money (deposits) is given by

$$M_{dt} = \alpha_2 + \alpha_3 Y + \alpha_4 R_t + a_t(2) \qquad (7.16)$$

with $\alpha_3 > 0$, $\alpha_4 < 0$, and the supply by

$$M_t = \alpha_5 + \alpha_6 R_t + \alpha_7 B_{dt} + a_t(3) \qquad (7.17)$$

with $\alpha_6, \alpha_7 > 0$. Here B_{dt} defines the demand for desired reserves on day t; the $a_t(i)$ are shocks, to be discussed in a moment. Assuming $B_t = B_{dt}$ and $M_{d_t} = M_t$ in equilibrium, we would have an *LM* curve of

$$R_t = \beta_0 + \beta_1 Y_t + \beta_2 A_t + \beta_3[a_t(2) - a_t(3)]. \qquad (7.18)$$

The authorities, then, will try to minimise a quadratic loss function (unweighted because there is only one objective) as in

$$L = \sum_{t=1}^{Q} (Y_t - Y^*)^2 \qquad (7.19)$$

This function runs over all future periods. The authorities do so knowing (by assumption) all of the particular αs and βs – since they know the structure of the model – but only knowing the general form of the stochastic process that determines the $a_t(i)$, as in

$$a_t(i) = \rho_i a_{t-1}(i) + u_t(i) \qquad |\rho_i| < 1 \qquad (7.20)$$

and not the values of the $a_t(i)$ themselves. It is through this condition – describing the business cycle in effect (both real and nominal) – that the past has an influence on the present, in this model.

Kareken *et al.* (1973) show that the decision rule in Equation 7.19 boils down to a rule in terms of the current day only on account of the assumptions of the model (a single objective and linearity). To see this, let us employ a different terminology and a slightly simpler model (due to Sargent, 1979). A reduced form for GNP that is similar to that which we would get from the above system can be written as

$$y_t = \lambda y_{t-1} + b(L)M_t + c(L)R_{t-1} + \varepsilon_t \qquad (7.21)$$

where $b(L)$ and $c(L)$ are lag operators describing the following processes

$$b(L) = \sum_{i=0}^{\infty} b_i L^i \qquad c(L) = \sum_{i=0}^{\infty} c_i L^i$$

These describe the influence of past values of M and R on GNP. The error term in 7.21 is assumed to be interpreted in such a way that 7.21 is a regression equation. The authorities are then assumed to try to minimise

$$E_{t-1}((y_t - y^*)^2)$$

with, as noted, poor information on y (measured quarterly). The information on lagged M and lagged R is assumed to be contained in the information set Ω_{t-1} whence we can describe the authorities' problem as setting the money stock (its 'target') such that

$$P[y_t : \Omega_{t-1}, M_t] = y^* \tag{7.22}$$

This describes the projection (regression) of y_t on Ω_{t-1} and M_t and shows how the setting for the policy 'target' variable (M_t) is determined by the expected value for y_t, conditional on M_t and on the information available in Ω_{t-1}.

To find the optimal feedback rule for M_t in terms of the information available on past R and M, we can proceed as follows (still following Sargent, 1979). Recognising the Koyck lag in 7.21 we can rewrite that expression as

$$(1 - \lambda L)y_t = b(L)M_t + c(L)R_{t-1} + \varepsilon_t$$

Then, dividing through by $(1 - \lambda L)$ we have

$$y_t = [b(L)/(1 - \lambda L)]M_t + [c(L)/(1 - \lambda L)R_{t-1} + [1/(1 - \lambda L)]\varepsilon_t$$

This eliminates y_{t-1}, in effect. Since ε_t is independent of all values of R and M, this last expression is also a regression equation of the form

$$P[y_t : \Omega_{t-1}, M_t] = [b(L)/(1 - \lambda L)] M_t + [c(L)/(1 - \lambda L)]R_{t-1}$$

This, then, provides the left-hand side of Equation 7.22. Substituting for $b(L)$ and $c(L)$ we find that the optimal value for M_t is

$$M_t = [(1 - \lambda)/b_0]y^* - [c(L)/b_0]R_{t-1} - \sum_{i=1}^{\infty} b_i L^i M_t / b_0 \tag{7.23}$$

Clearly, then, the optimal setting of the 'target' or control variable M_t depends on the fixed objective (y^*) and on the information in Ω_{t-1}. This consists of all of the data on R and M as these variables affect y_t. These are essentially indicator relationships as defined above.

From an inspection of this result it is clear that

(a) the 'target' M_t will be changed each period as new data come in, so that the use of a fixed target strategy is clearly suboptimal.

Kareken *et al.* point out that the American FOMC follows such a suboptimal rule, setting targets for R and M and then sticking to these targets as time passes and as new data roll in; this is with reference to 1972 (and earlier), but since then there has been no obvious change in their strategy, with the switch to monetary targets in 1979 (to the extent this was done) still not meeting the Kareken *et al.* objection (p. 170) that 'the use of an intermediate target variable necessarily involves some waste of information which, if initial conditions matter, is valuable.' It is valuable, that is to say, if the intermediate variables are indicators, for

(b) all information that affects y_t – whatever its source – is in principle useful in setting the feedback rule. This is the indicator function, but this concept is conceivably much wider than merely intermediate financial variables.

(c) Finally, we note that y still shows cycles in this scenario.

This last follows from the fact that if the rule 7.23 is followed, then

$$y_t = \lambda y_{t-1} + (1 - \lambda)y^* + \varepsilon_t \tag{7.24}$$

which still has serial correlation in it since it is not possible to remove the effects of the lagged values of y_{t-1} (which are not known soon enough) by picking a value of M_t.

The result just described also provides a contribution to the debate over whether to follow a simple monetarist rule (as discussed in Chapter 1) or to use a broader set of variables. But there is another problem and this is that the information itself may be sufficiently incorrect that a feedback policy – which requires accurate information *including* forecasts – may be worse than a rule on these grounds alone. One study that concludes just that, with reference to the 1973–5 period in the United States, is by Craine, Havenner and J. Berry (1978). They find that the misinformation provided by erroneous price forecasts is severe enough so that there are greater losses associated with the information-sensitive feedback policy than with the monetary rule (in the Friedman sense). The losses are measured with an arbitrary loss function for the authorities (several of these are tried without upsetting the conclusions). The authors argue (p. 781) that the period in question is so traumatic that it is 'roughly equivalent to a wing falling off' an airplane and that 'more normal times . . . would certainly give the advantage to feedback strategies'. This seems an unwarranted empirical assertion (what, for example, is 'normal'?), but the point – that much of this work ignores the quality of information in an information-sensitive environment – is both valid and important in the policy context. The point also applies to the quality of the monetary data, of course, and there is no reason to be complacent about that either (Pierce, *et al.*, 1980, and Pierce, 1980).

Returning to our main theme, then, we see that the result just given is also sympathetic to a Keynesian view of the world, and, says Sargent (1979) in this it depends on the existence of

(a) simultaneity in the economic structure,
(b) lags in the system that impart some predictability to economic variables, and
(c) a relatively constant structure of the lags.

Thus (p. 356), 'the monetary authority should in general revise its planned setting to its policy instruments each time it receives some new and surprising reading on a variable that is determined simultaneously with a variable like GNP or unemployment that it is interested in controlling'. Under rational expectations, though, if economic agents have the same model and data, they will counteract the systematic policy settings even though they are day-to-day, leaving no role for policy (but leaving the cycle in y_t). The authorities, that is to say, could not close the gap between y_t and y^* by the use of any feedback rule based on generally available information (and a common model). This result is hinted at in Chapter 1, proved in Chapter 3 and continues to hold here, under the assumed conditions, of course.

For our final result in this section let us consider some work on the problem of information costs that is provided in an interesting paper by Feige and Pearce (1976). In the basic rational-expectations model, economic forecasts arise from the use of a 'correct' model of the economy which itself includes the variables being forecasted. This model has some definite costs attached to it – the cost of obtaining the data, the cost of setting it up on the computer, etc. – so economic agents, if rational, will trade off the expected benefit with the costs and decide what procedure to adopt. The costs could be so high that economic agents would not build models of any sort and would, instead, get 'close enough' to the truth merely by monitoring the past values of the variables being predicted. In this event we would run into the 'observational equivalence' problem of Chapter 3 again since adaptive expectations would also suggest the same procedure, although not necessarily on 'cost-of-information' reasoning.[8]

To set up a structure that is reasonably sympathetic to these issues, Feige and Pearce construct a simple model in which information costs appear explicitly. In this model total costs are divided into those of obtaining information ($\Sigma c_i I_i$) and those associated with forecasting errors; here I_i represents the quantity of the ith type of information. While we are thinking of indicators, broadly, an example might be the following. Suppose that we are forecasting the inflation rate but that economic agents make forecasting errors in predicting the inflation rate, of $\pi_t - \pi^e$. Assume also that the direct costs of this error are measured by a quadratic-loss function as in

$$c = k(\pi_t - \pi_t^e)^2 \tag{7.25}$$

In turn, this forecasting error can be assumed to be a function of the quantity and type of information used, as in

$$(\pi_t - \pi_t^e)^2 = f(I_1, \ldots, I_n) \qquad f_i' > 0 \tag{7.26}$$

Here we treat k as positive (in 7.25) and argue that an 'increase' of information of type i (an increase of I_i) directly reduces the squared forecasting error in 7.26.[9] The outcome is the standard cost minimisation result that $c_i = -kf'$ for $i = 1, \ldots, n$.

Feige and Pearce do not really use the model just postulated, but it stands as a useful first attempt to set down formally an information cost paradigm. Instead, they set up a Box–Jenkins ARIMA (autoregressive integrated-moving-average) model to measure the information content in past inflation rates and then look to see if other information might improve their first approximations. This is a straight indicators approach. The general ARIMA model is

$$\Phi(L)(1-L)^d \pi_t = \Theta(L)a_t \tag{7.27}$$

where a represents a random shock and L is the lag operator, as before. In this formulation the function $\Phi(L)$ is a polynomial of order p describing the autoregressive structure, and the function $\Theta(L)$ is a polynomial of order q describing the moving average process.[10] We can argue that $\pi_t = \alpha_t \pi_{t-1} + \alpha_2 \pi_{t-2} + \ldots + a_t$ describes the evolution of prices. Call this $\alpha(L)\pi_t = a_t$. Since, from Equation 7.27 we have the result that

$$[\Phi(L)(1-L)^d / \Theta(L)] \pi_t = a_t$$

we can equate these two expressions so that

$$\Phi(L)(1-L)^d / \Theta(L) = \alpha(L) = 1 - \alpha_1 L - \alpha_2 L^2 - \ldots \tag{7.28}$$

Then, since we can estimate the parameters of $\Phi(L)$ and $\Theta(L)$ we can obtain estimates of the weights α_i by equating the coefficients of like powers of L in the two equations in 7.28.

Feige and Pearce's preliminary empirical results establish that for the United States data the ARIMA model efficiently utilises all of the information inherent in past inflation rates; the lags are not, however, of the simple distributed lag type commonly employed in this literature. They then consider what additional value a *leading* indicator might be in forecasting; to be useful, a leading indicator must (p. 509) 'reduce the expected mean square forecast error below that of the models based solely on past inflation rates. For an economically rational agent, this criterion is not sufficient, since he will use the leading indicator only if the predictive benefits outweigh the costs.'

A leading indicator, they argue, must first meet the condition of Granger causality (the leading indicator, to some extent, must cause the inflation rate) before it would be included in a cost calculation (look, again, at the discussion of causality in Chapter 6). The procedure Feige and Pearce employ is from Haugh (1972), and the potential leading indicators they look at are monetary quantities and the high-employment budget surplus (see below). They can identify no causality, and hence (at any cost) the leading indicators would not be used. Of course, the 'cost of information' is not really part of this empirical work (because it is not needed) so that what remains are a hypothesis, some useful results and a clear exposition of how to handle such models, if such information is to be further considered for its 'cost effectiveness'.

7.6   FISCAL INDICATORS IN PRACTICE

Let us, first, consider the fiscal-policy literature on (targets and) indicators. We have already noted that there really is no fiscal-target literature to look at – in the sense defined above – and we should further note that when the word 'target' appears in fiscal discussions, it most often refers to the desired value of the objective variables; indeed, we find scant reference to the intermediate targets that are so much discussed when monetary policy is the subject (see below). By default, then, our fiscal discussion will be concerned mainly with the identification of effective indicators – as if there were no useful distinction between targets and indicators – in so far as they identify the strength of fiscal policy. Note that we will not anywhere discuss the details of how deficits, etc., might be measured in practice; a useful summary of these problems is in Boskin (1982).

The first measure of fiscal influence proposed and the one most often appearing in the textbooks is the actual (or realised) budgetary deficit (or surplus). This has long been in disfavour, though (Colwell and Lash, 1973, p. 321):

To separate cause from effect, the fiscal index should be free of the influence of changes in GNP so that changes in the index can give an unambiguous measure of the change in fiscal policy. The actual surplus, the difference between actual Federal tax receipts and expenditures, cannot serve as an accurate indicator because it is influenced by movements in economic activity.

Even so, in these days of two-stage least-squares and other econometric devices this is not a compelling argument, and a deficit that is itself the predicted value from a regression in which instruments and exogenous variables are the independent variables certainly may be successful as a fiscal indicator. That is, we need not reject the budget deficit as an indicator, but we must arrange for its 'purification' before its role as an indicator is assessed empirically. Even so, a chorus of writers agrees with Colwell that we should just drop it.[11]

As an alternative indicator a concept known as the 'full-employment surplus' (*FES*) has been devised (see Blinder and Solow, 1973). This is,

$$FES = T(y^*, t) - g \tag{7.29}$$

where the function T depends on tax rates (t) and on 'full-employment' GNP (y^*); g, here, is real government expenditures. In a static economy y^* is a datum, and as long as g and t are exogenous, we have a potentially useful measure of fiscal influence. But, even in a static context, certain problems emerge. First,

(a) The balanced budget theorem proves that government purchases are stronger than tax receipts as a policy tool. The *FES* in this form treats them as alike.

One answer, since it is certainly true that some taxes are paid out of savings, is to calculate a *weighted FES* of

$$FES_w = cT(y^*, t) - g \tag{7.30}$$

where c is the propensity to consume. This still leaves a second problem which applies to both 7.29 and 7.30.

(b) At less than full employment the effect of a change in the vector of tax rates may be different in magnitude and even sign from the effect at full employment.

That is, tax revenues, and hence the effect of (say) a set policy with both corporate and income taxes changed, may depend on who is working and able to pay the tax as well as the extent to which corporate profits are depressed. Indeed, it is conceivable that tax revenues would fall when a tax rise is instituted if corporate profits are reduced and workers idled.

These are results from a static version of the problem; in a growing (or inflationary) economy the *FES* has another problem. This is the appearance, assuming fixed tax rates (fixed tax brackets), of a built-in fiscal 'drag'. That is, a growing economy will generate steadily increasing tax revenues (we must grow in a per spending unit form) 'siphoning too much of the economic substance out of the private economy and thereby choking expansion' (W. W. Heller, 1966, p. 65). The problem for the indicators *FES* and FES_w is that in Equations 7.29 and 7.30 an endogenous influence, as variable as the influence of growth on tax revenues, will be confused with the discretionary policy changes. We note, as well, that inflation causes a similar effect, more pronounced in so far as inflation is also associated with an increase in government revenues (and hence government expenditures, at least in some circumstances). Finally, we might as well point out that the full-employment level of GNP is not necessarily exogenous but could be taken to be partly endogenous. In this case it would have to be determined in the model, of course.

There are several other fiscal indicators in the literature, mostly designed to deal with the less than full-employment situation in which we typically find ourselves. One of these is the weighted initial surplus (IS_w) of Oakland (1969) which uses the initial level of income as the fixed basis for comparison, as in Equation 7.31.

$$IS_w = w_1 c + w_2 t y^* - g_e \tag{7.31}$$

Here c is the constant in the tax function, g_e is exogenous government expenditures, and y^* is the initial level of income. IS_w provides a kind of impact measurement which is not readily used for a time series (since y^* varies) but which can certainly be used for the sort of period-to-period changes that actual policy sometimes contemplates. A similar concept appears in the Blinder and Solow paper. This is the weighted standardised surplus (SS_w) as in

$$SS_w = \frac{dG - cT_t dt}{1 - c(1 - T_y)} \tag{7.32}$$

Here T_t and T_y are derivatives of the tax function, dG and dt are the policy changes, and c – the weight – is the propensity to consume.[12] This concept is essentially an impact multiplier equation for the change in government spending, adjusted (standardised) for the effect of the change in tax revenues ($-cT_t dt$) on the level of tax revenues. This equation can readily be generalised for a more complicated structure; as well, it can be used to measure the impact of automatic stabilisers (by deducting these from total autonomous effects on income). If t and G are instruments of policy and if we rule out feedback, then we can predict our policy impact if the relation with SS_w (or any other measure that meets these conditions) is stable. This stability is not guaranteed by the procedure we have adopted here since we are still subject to having a correct model of the economy. Indeed, worries over the measurement of the data, the level of disaggregation, the endogeneity of G, the consistency of fiscal and monetary policy objectives and the interactions between fiscal and monetary policy effects all surface here to leave important empirical and theoretical questions.

The model used to support this equation is the Blinder and Solow 'rock-bottom' model. Infante and J. Stein argue that this model has some peculiar properties (1976, p. 488), 'either bond financed deficit spending is unstable or the cumulative fiscal policy multiplier . . . is negative' and smaller than the one for money-financed deficit spending. These are non-Keynesian conclusions derived by imposing stability on the rock-bottom model. They are direct contradictions to the Blinder and Solow conclusions (they, in turn, do not impose stability). Another Infante and Stein result is a non-monetarist one; in their model, in the stable form (p. 492), 'the impact effects of a rise in the money supply, with government spending held constant, are to raise income and prices; however the cumulative effects will be to lower income and prices'. These comments essentially should return us to the literature discussed in Chapter 5.

Currently the most discussed measure of the fiscal influence is something called the 'cyclically adjusted federal debt' (or 'budget'). Some years ago, Hendershott (1968) suggested that a useful monetary indicator would be the 'neutralized money stock' and, while this did not exactly catch on, it resurfaces from time to time. The fiscal version of this, as noted, is the cyclically adjusted federal debt (see de Leeuw and Holloway, 1985). The general idea is to identify a reference trend for GNP (a y^* in our earlier terminology); to calculate a set of cyclical tax elasticities (as GNP changes) for the various types of receipts and expenditures in the budget; and then to take gaps between trend GNP and actual GNP, apply the tax elasticities and use the result to compute a cyclically adjusted budget. The first part of this, the establishment of the reference GNP, is usually arbitrary (using 'high-employment' or 'potential' GNP), and for this de Leeuw and Holloway propose a new measure in which the reference trend is computed by filtering out the cycle. The filter is not done using time series methods – as we might want to see on this problem – but employs NBER methodology. At any rate as their empirical results suggest, such an adjustment does alter the results. In particular, the cyclically adjusted debt does have an influence on nominal GNP and a positive effect on interest rates. When tests for the effect of a growing debt on capital formation are included, there is even a suggestion of a crowding-*in* effect. But this is a new measure, and the results are not all in.

7.7 MONETARY TARGETS AND INDICATORS IN PRACTICE

In this section we will generally look at distinct material on, alternatively, targets and indicators. We begin, however, with a monetarist literature that makes no distinction. That is, the monetarists generally seem to argue that the target problem and the indicator problem can be resolved in favour of a single variable that does both jobs. For example, Schwartz (1969) defines the best choice for a monetary target to be one which

(a) is measurable,
(b) is subject to control by the central bank, and
(c) is a reliable *indicator* of monetary conditions.

At the time of her work, for Canada, she says, this target-indicator was 'credit market conditions', for Japan it was the 'balance of borrowed reserves' and for the United Kingdom, there were as many as four targets in use: short-term interest rates, the level of bank advances, the cost and availability of credit and deposits or the quantity of money. In the case of the United Kingdom, Schwartz owns that the first target may be used as an indicator of the others (in particular, the second or fourth target). Schwartz argues that (a) credit conditions do not meet her first conditions, (b) interest rates, the volume of borrowed reserves, or credit conditions do not meet her second, and (c) bank assets, credit, loans, interest rates and credit conditions do not meet her third. On the other hand, deposits and the money supply meet all three. She offers some evidence.

Turning to the work of Keran (1970) – again written in the monetarist tradition – we have the following list of indicator characteristics.

(a) They should be responsive to the instruments.
(b) They should have an unambiguous relation with total demand.
(c) They should have a close and consistent relation with the final variables.

Thus, Keran's first condition is really Schwartz's second and his second and third are essentially her third and thus encompass the target. Within this framework Keran performs regressions (ignoring his first (target) condition) for six countries and concludes that generally the monetary measures perform better than the interest-rate measures. Finally, Tanner (1972) considers five criteria (modelled on all of the above) and compares five potential targets-indicators. After removing (other) exogenous influences from the final variables (see the discussion of the weighted standardised surplus described above) Tanner concludes that the five target-indicators can be rated as follows: the money stock or the monetary base are good, the neutralised money stock or the monetary full-employment interest rate are acceptable and the interest rate is unacceptable.[13] These rankings, though, are purely on statistical fit and thereby ignore Schwartz's first condition and, of course, the second one with which we began this discussion.

As another piece of this empirical collage, consider the offering of Saving (1967); it was his set-up which we used to frame the distinction in Subsection 7.4.2. In that paper Saving considers four monetary indicators – the rate of interest, the level of free reserves, the money stock and the monetary base. The problem with the rate of interest is that it also moves pro-cyclically in the absence of policy. That is, since stabilisation policy also calls for a procyclical movement in the interest rate, it would be hard to pick out the policy effect from the general effect. Clearly, we need a separate indicator. Assuming that free reserves (excess reserves less borrowed reserves in the Federal Reserve System) move contra-cyclically, we still have the same problem. During an upswing, as the endogenous interest rate rises, free reserves held by banks will tend to decline; the decline in free reserves as a result of the endogenous influence will be applauded since policy would also call for a reduction in free reserves (see Meigs, 1962). The money stock, by itself, tends to move pro-cyclically as well; in this case, since policy is to make it move contra-cyclically, policy may become too perverse, producing unnecessary cycles (we can, of course, neutralise it). Finally, the monetary base may not move cyclically at all and so would be a good indicator of monetary policy. Saving notes that nothing said about the weakness of the interest rate as an indicator precludes its use as a target. Indeed, we suspect that monetary policy has generally tended toward the use of a measure of the money stock as an indicator and the nominal interest rate (or credit-market conditions) as a target, despite frequent pronouncements to the contrary. As pointed out in Chapter 2, the *nominal* interest rate does not make a good target because effectiveness here is bought at the cost of price-level instability. The effectiveness appears to be there in certain cases (Pindyck and Roberts, 1976) meaning that it may well be easier to control the interest rate than the money stock (whatever the instruments selected to do the job). The *real* interest rate is not subject to the same instability problem as the nominal rate, but it is so difficult to measure that its use in any policy could produce results that are inferior to, even, no policy at all. For a recent discussion of this last issue see Santoni and Stone (1982) and Walsh (1983).

Above, we pointed out that an effective way to define an indicator variable is in terms of whether it Granger-causes the objective variable in question. From this point of view, in a recent paper Davidson and Hafer (1983) tested seven potential indicators on US data for nominal and real income (including three non-monetary (debt) measures). While this sort of testing often provokes a rash of competing studies, this particular effort is properly structured around Granger causality. Davidson and Hafer report that M1 Granger-causes both nominal and real GNP while GNP (generally) does not cause M1. M2 passes in relation to nominal GNP but not real. All other variables fail the test. In addition, Davidson and Hafer test the target condition (they call it a question of 'controlability') using the 'adjusted monetary base' and the seven candidates for indicators. Once again M1 is Granger-caused by the monetary base, and much of its variation is explained by the base while the non-monetary indicators fail to respond to the base and the broad money-stock measures are largely unpredicted by the base. The upshot is that among the financial variables studied, M1 (up to 1980) not only is the only one that fits *both* target and indicator criteria, but also fits convincingly. So, as pointed out several times in this chapter, a single variable can pack all this informational clout, although this is for a particular time and place and in comparison with a particular set of alternatives. (Another example may well be Australia, although there some troublesome feedback occurs between the monetary targets and the instruments (Sharpe and Volker, 1980).)

Notes and References

1 An Overview: Basic Policy Models without Rational Expectations

1. We should note from the outset that while it may seem to be a matter of principle as to what is included in the sets 'endogenous' and 'exogenous' this is actually not the case. Obviously some variables influence the economy without there being a converse relationship – the weather is one such – and hence are truly exogenous. But modelling limitations have a lot to do with this dichotomisation as well and variables are often simply assumed to be exogenous for convenience. Foreign influences are often treated in this way (or simply ignored) and variables that have often been hard to measure (or determine) – such as spending on plant and equipment – also end up as exogenous variables in empirical studies.

2. In what follows, the tradeoffs among the objectives will be derived by comparing weights. An alternative would be to estimate the tradeoffs directly; a functional form that would do the job would be the translog disutility function as in

$$\log d = \alpha_0 + \sum_i \alpha_i \log (y_i^* - y_i) + \tfrac{1}{2} \sum_i \sum_j \alpha_{ij} \log (y_i^* - y_i) \log (y_j^* - y_j)$$

This function could then be applied, with its constraints, to the problem studied above. No tests of this function appear in the literature in this context, and there do not appear to be any direct estimates of the tradeoffs either.

   Note that the quadratic function itself has some problems. Most notably it treats upward and downward deviations symmetrically (this seems unlikely) and it dramatically increases the importance of large deviations.

3. We see, as a technical matter, that $(B_1 F)^{-1}$ must exist; furthermore, since this matrix has dimension $p \times p$, where p is the number of objectives, we see that the number of objectives must equal the number of intermediate variables and hence, by our argument above, the number of instruments. This is a standard result in this literature.

4. In a paper of Friedlaender (1973) the model is estimated with values of the objectives ($\tilde{y}^*$) and with the lagged values of the endogenous variables (the $\tilde{y}$). But this use of actual objectives is the exception in this literature, which generally estimates Equation 1.16 with $\tilde{y}$ (and $\tilde{I}_{t-1}$); the reason, of course, is that the authorities do not generally publish their exact objectives.

5. If $\rho_{uv} \neq 0$ the same results can easily hold, but only for particular values of the parameters (see Poole (1970) for a discussion).

6. This can also be seen directly from the calculation of

$$\frac{\partial L_m}{\partial b_2} = 2a_1(a_1 b_1 + b_2)^{-3} \sigma_u \sigma_v \left[b_2 \left(b_1 \frac{\sigma_u}{\sigma_v} + \rho_{uv} \right) - a_1 \left(\frac{\sigma_v}{\sigma_u} + b_1 \rho_{uv} \right) \right]$$

which is positive for $b_1(\sigma_u/\sigma_v + \rho_{uv}) < 0$. This is approximately the condition favouring monetary control, for $\rho_{uv} = 0$.

7. The polynomial $A(L)$ is rational if it can be expressed as the ratio of two finite-order polynomials in L. See Jorgenson (1966) for a discussion.

8. To see that 1.36 can solve 1.33, carry out the lag operation; the operation of the denominator on

$$c_1\lambda_1^t \quad \text{and} \quad c_2\lambda_2^t$$

reduces those expressions to zero. Note that it is quite likely that such models will show explosive roots, a case which is basically economic nonsense.

9. Blanchard (1981b) argues that for US data (1947–78) equation 1.28 would be

$$y_t = \quad 1.34\,y_{t-2} - 0.42\,y_{t-2} + e_t$$
$$(16.4) \qquad (5.21)$$

This shows damped oscillations ('humps') as the typical US pattern. Blanchard argues that this humped pattern comes mainly from the behaviour of investment. The data here are detrended logarithms of real income.

10. Sargent and Wallace (1976) note that this result also holds for systems that have multiple goals and instruments and more equations and more lags in the system.

11. We will provide a different, and more detailed, version of this system in Chapter 2, when we consider the natural-rate hypothesis.

2 The Natural-rate Hypothesis and Other Matters

1. M. Friedman (1970) is one who essentially takes this approach to explaining the different positions. Friedman's explanation is in terms of a 'missing equation' in the standard IS/LM framework that is supplied in different ways by Keynesians ($P = P_0$) or monetarists ($y = y_f$).

2. The new term in Equation 2.2 can also be rationalised by a 'dispersion' or 'aggregation' hypothesis. Phillips suggested that labour markets were 'tight' during upturns and 'loose' during downturns, but an alternative, suggested by Lipsey, argues that because of the convexity of the Phillips curve, individual micro curves will tend to lie below the (observed) average of all micro curves. This is a technical point, of course, but Lipsey has gone further and suggested that it has a real-world rationale. In particular, during upturns individual industries have different experiences, with the pressure on wages and prices coming from the aggressive and expanding industries which exert a pressure on resources that is greater than their relative shares of the input markets. In downturns, conversely, no firms are putting pressure on wages and prices, and the curve resumes its normal shape. But the few empirical tests of this aggregation hypothesis are not very encouraging (see Archibald, 1969, and Archibald, Kemmis and Perkins, 1971).

3. Another early theoretical derivation is due to Laidler and Corry (1967).

4. Representative early papers of this sort are by Samuelson and Solow (1960), Klein and Bodkin (1964), Kaliski (1964) and Bowen and R. A. Berry (1963).
5. For the production function $y = \Phi(K, L)$, the total derivative, with K fixed, is $dy = \Phi_L \, dL$. Since, around equilibrium, dL is a measure of unemployment, we may substitute directly (where dy is approximated by $y - y_f$ and dL is approximated by $L - L_f$). Since $u = L - L_f$ we have the expression in the text, after linearising (see Turnovsky (1977c)).
6. For productivity see Hines (1968), Black and Kelejian (1970), Perry (1970) and R. J. Gordon (1971). The profit rate appears in Perry (1970), while trade-unions figure in Hines (1964, 1968) and Ashenfelter *et al.* (1972). A study with taxes and wage-and-price controls is by R. J. Gordon (1972).
7. This equation is an approximation. $£C$ received one period in the future would be discounted as in $C/((1 + r^e)(1 + \pi^e))$ where π^e is the expected inflation rate. Thus the correct form for Equation 2.11 is actually $i = r^e + \pi^e + r^e\pi^e$.
8. If the bonds were price-indexed bonds, then no such corrections would be needed. Very few of these actually exist, however.
9. This is known as the Gibson Paradox. It is called a paradox because high-interest rates are supposed to be associated with low-investment and consumption. One often reads of a cost-push link between i and p (or π), but the dynamics of most of these kinds of theory are usually not fully specified.
10. They might do this because they reject Equation 2.11 or, more realistically, because they have no idea where r^e is and, given other objectives (such as to hold unemployment below its natural rate), their policy has this effect, unintentionally.
11. See Turnovsky (1977c) for a simple Phillips curve version of this. Phelps (1968) has produced a variant of the above that is based on the idea that firms try to maintain a desired 'wage differential' and pass on any wage increases in the form of higher prices. Turnovsky also summarises the Phelps paper.
12. This was a British test. The incomes policies were judged to be 'on' in 1947–50, 1956 and 1961–4.
13. For example,

$$\partial F / \partial(P^*/P(1 + i)) = K[N, P^*/(1 + i)] - C^* \partial F/\partial A$$

where $K[\cdot]$ is a substitution effect (< 0) and $C^*(\partial F/\partial A)$ is, as assumed, small. C^* is optimal consumption (the agent is maximising an intertemporal utility function).
14. β_4 comes out to zero in their empirical work and is subsequently dropped.
15. The equation for the natural rate is

$$U^* = \frac{\tau + S_2(1 - \Phi(C, \sigma^2))}{\tau + S_0\Phi(C, \sigma^2) + S_2(1 - \Phi(C, \sigma^2))}$$

where τ represents Point (a), C represents Point (b), S_2 represents Point (c), S_0 is the frequency of new job offers and σ^2 is the coefficient of variation of the distribution of job offers.
16. The Phillips curve, as above, comes from the assumption of adaptive expectations. Reference' here should also be made to Lucas and Prescott (1974), McCall (1970) and Gronau (1971).

17. Tobin (1972) argues that a congestion effect may lower the ability of workers to locate a suitable job (i.e. in cases when the pool of unemployed is too large) while R. E. Hall (1975) suggests that the equilibrium pool is too small because business firms overutilise it (they do not account for the effect on the pool of other firms fishing in the same waters). Prescott (1975) poses the question and Mortensen (1984) surveys this literature on the 'efficiency' of the natural rate.

18. Santomero and Seater (1978) classify the search models as microfoundations although in truth much of the foregoing seems to be just microeconomics with *ad hoc* aggregations, if any. They also briefly discuss other microfoundations. Among these are papers introducing market failure arising from Keynesian notions of involuntary unemployment (e.g. Clower (1965), Barro and H. Grossman (1971, 1976) and Tobin (1972)) and papers involving asymmetry in the way markets clear (e.g. Ross and Wachter, 1973) or between employers' and workers' price expectations (e.g., Brunner and Meltzer, 1976).

19. More convincing evidence of the same sort is provided by Topel (1983), who shows that officially-unemployed workers (in the United States) are generally laid off, and by Mattila (1974), who shows that 'job switchers' generally do not have a period of unemployment. This is not totally discouraging because (a) unemployment would still tend to have the pattern suggested in the theoretical work just discussed and (b) the search model itself can be revised to capture the idea of job search while the worker is employed. Burdett (1978) provides one such model, in which the worker accepts the first job that matches the value of his leisure and continues to search (while employed) until his reservation wage is reached. The two 'wages' are not equal because of information costs.

20. The distinction between a 'subjective' and 'objective' distribution that is implicit here has been questioned by Swamy and Tinsley (1982). In a sense, especially under rational expectations as we shall see, the (sum of the) subjective distributions equals the objective distribution if economic agents act on their guesses as the rational-expectations theory assumes they do.

21. An explanation of this appears in Sargent (1979, p. 209); there the Lucas model is explained as a 'signal-extraction' problem.

22. Barro's model has both real and nominal sectors and accordingly, has the same variance property only under certain conditions (involving restrictions on the values of the price and wealth elasticities of aggregate demand and aggregate supply). In Barro's version the variance of relative prices (the variance of $p_t(z) - \bar{p}_t$) increases with increases in the variance of aggregate demand.

23. We should note that the result for the effect on the Barro (1976) test (i.e. the effect of unanticipated money) was similar.

24. Azariadis (1981) disagrees, arguing that, in effect, since markets are incomplete and producers sell implicit labour contracts to their workers which contain insurance against employment mistakes, there is a permanent tradeoff that may even be positive as in M. Friedman's case.

25. Firms might hoard workers, workers might shorten their period of search, etc.

26. The work cited in these last few paragraphs involves mostly microeconomic modelling and thus is somewhat beyond the scope of this chapter. A representative paper, offering a 'risk-averse worker' hypothesis for the inflation-variance of inflation correlation is by Cosimano (1983). Papers by H. I. Grossman (1981), Azariadis (1975, 1981) and Brunner, Cukierman and Meltzer (1980) involving risk in product and labour markets are also relevant here.

3 Rational Expectations I: Basic Theories

1. As Maddock and Carter (1982, p. 41) say, 'rational expectations is the application of the principle of rational behaviour to the acquisition and processing of information and to the formation of expectations'.
2. This rule applies to $t + 1$ and t only. Because of actual random shocks in $t + 1$, $t + 2$, etc., the forecasting errors ε_2 and ε_3 (conditional on I_t) will generally be serially correlated.
3. The government may, of course, forecast using a rational-expectations operator instead of the distributed lag, but (a) it does not (yet) and (b) it still could make errors (see below and in Chapter 4). In any event the distributed lag is, as Lucas says, a 'minimum variance estimator' and likely to be the one used.
4. Of course this is just an example and the whole section just a theoretical argument, so care needs to be taken not to claim that this proves policy will not work in actual cases.
5. For (a) $M_t = \tau_1 M_{t-1} + \mu_t$ then (b) $EM_t = \tau_1 M_{t-1}$, clearly. In this case subtracting (b) from (a) we have that the error in the prediction of the money stock, under rational expectations, is

    $$M_t - EM_t = \mu_t$$

    i.e. is random. Substituting this expression into Equation 3.24 we have

    $$y_t = y_n + (\alpha/(\alpha + \beta_1))(\beta_2\mu_t - \varepsilon_t) - \varepsilon_t$$

    which is, of course, in the same form as 3.18, as claimed.
6. If adaptive expectations rule, then there is a long-run effectiveness to policy. That is, if price expectations are described by

    $$p_t^e = \rho p_{t-1} + (1 - \rho)p_{t-2} + \ldots$$

    then it will always be possible to drive a wedge between p_t^e and p_t, until economic agents catch on to a given systematic change in τ_1, and so y_t can be affected, in the obvious direction.
7. Recall R. E. Hall's argument (1975), discussed in Chapter 2, that u_t is in fact highly serially correlated so that an expression such as $u_t = u_{nt} + \mu_t$ is unlikely to hold. Hall favours theories that explain the cyclical pattern of u_n (see below, under the 'real-business cycle').
8. We should note here another extension to the Sargent–Wallace and McCallum papers by Fethke and Jackman (1982). They show that Poole's original results – that under certain conditions money control is preferable to interest-rate control and vice versa – hold up when there is costly wage indexation.

9. As Lucas (1980) points out, one can build a cyclical theory of the cycle in terms of the structural parameters alone, but with the assumption of explicit disequilibrium new 'free' parameters describing the adjustments to disequilibrium must be introduced. Thus Lipsey's explanation of the Phillips curve, in effect, has a full structure of the labour and an adjustment parameter in $\alpha(N_d - N_s)$. This parameter can be estimated, or absorbed into the others, but it – and the disequilibrium method – is not necessarily better at explaining cycles than the Hicks–Samuelson model of Chapter 1. There we generated cycles in real variables – and could have gone on to include unemployment easily enough – merely with reference to the two structural parameters α and β. It seems that if we are to have 'parsimony of parameters' the difference equation approach, particularly in so far as it is based on careful thought about the structure (does not spending today depend on past decisions?), has some advantages.

10. R. J. Gordon (1981) has an effective verbalisation of Lucas's theory.

11. Is it 'rational' for firms to do this? Published and stable prices might be good business and changes in these listings are certainly costly (Okun, 1975).

12. We should mention here a literature that motivates real cycles in terms of the risk-aversion of workers. In a discussion of this effect by Sheffrin (1983) it is pointed out that evidence collected by J. Grossman (1979) in a test of the 'ineffectiveness' proposition actually shows that most of the fluctuations in unemployment are apparently due to fluctuations in the *natural* rate of unemployment. An explanation which is consistent with this literature is that risk-averse workers respond to procyclical variations in their risks by tacking a risk premium on to their wage demands. This produces a procyclical pattern to the natural rate of unemployment. See Cosimano (1983) for some further theoretical work on this topic.

13. There are, in a word, real effects, but they are quantitatively insignificant. This is not a particularly clear insight, at least to this reader.

14. The debate over this is extensive; see Barro (1974), and the discussion in Chapter 4.

15. R. E. Hall and Jorgenson also look at accelerated depreciation, the shortening of capital lifetimes, and a first-year write-off, all of these on post-war US policy experience.

4 Rational Expectations II: Extensions and Empirical Tests

1. Among the recent surveys of this literature, one finds R. J. Gordon (1981), Begg (1982), Minford and Peel (1983), Sheffrin (1983) and Attfield, Demery and Duck (1985).

2. The diversification can occur because of transactions costs in trading assets other than money or because of risk-aversion. It also arises in models in which money is directly inserted into the utility function (along with other stocks).

3. Among the specific surprises that Barro discusses are those around the Korean War, the sudden drop in the rate of change of M in 1960 (followed by a rise in U, of course). Barro makes some predictions for the 1974–7 period using coefficients estimated over 1941–73.

4. A Canadian study by Wogin (1980) using Barro's approach obtained similar results (only unanticipated money matters) as does another, on British data, by Bellante, Morrell and Zardkoohi (1982).

5. There are still problems having to do, for example, with the possibility that past and present anticipated *future* monetary growth is not ruled out as an avenue for monetary influence (see Buiter, 1983). This point is similar to one frequently raised by Tobin (e.g. 1972) concerning the possibility that the direction of causation could be from P to M even though M leads P if M increases in anticipation of its need later (when price pressures, for other reasons, occur). Buiter mentions several other concerns about the Barro–Rush–Attfield (*et al.*) procedures.

6. There are, of course, exceptions to this, among which Patinkin (1965) and Brunner and Meltzer (1972) stand out in the macro-theoretic literature.

7. A few references are in order here, for those wishing to search this literature. For pre-rational material one could try the Commission on Money and Credit (1961), Federal Reserve Bank of Boston (1971), Hansen (1973), Jaffee (1971), Radcliffe Report (1959), W. L. Smith (1959), Tobin and Brainard (1963), or the summary of these and other studies in D. Fisher (1976). More recent surveys have been included in the present study.

8. This is done with reference to a debate over the 'rationality' of certain popular price and interest rate (survey) expectations data. See Pesando (1975) and, especially, Pearce (1979) for some of the problems with these data.

9. O'Brien (1981) looked at the policy directives of the Federal Open Market Committee to the manager of the Open Market Account (at the New York Federal Reserve Bank) to see if the directives would have been useful to the public if they had been issued at the time of the FOMC meeting rather than after a long (up to six weeks') delay. His answer is that they do not have any information value and this was confirmed in a second test (1982). O'Brien employed the assumption of rational expectations in his tests.

10. Walsh, in another paper of the same vintage (1982b), goes into a great deal more detail about this application of the Lucas critique; in this he is following Lucas and Sargent (1981).

11. In a recent paper Belongia and Sheehan (1985) raise the possibility that econometric problems may have caused the expected announcement to fail to perform. Accordingly, they re-evaluate much of the literature described in the last few paragraphs and find 'contrary evidence' to the efficient-markets hypothesis.

12. Another paper that takes up the causality issue is by Caves and Feige (1978), who argue that on the US data 'reverse' causation from stock prices to money can be established, utilising a Granger-type test. See Chapter 6 for more on Granger causality in the money-income context.

13. This is similar to the well-known 'snapback' effect discussed by Tucker (1966), Laidler (1968) and Howrey (1969).

14. This last is called the 'Mundell effect' (1971).

15. The model does not permit private agents to learn anything else nor does it permit the government to build a stock of credibility by announcing a policy and then producing it (so that a later 'surprise' could affect expectations). We will consider this last in Subsection 4.4.2.

16. Above we noted the 'inflationary finance' motive for inflation. This is another reason (other than the cost/unemployment tradeoff) for ending up with more inflation than is optimal in a sequential policy model.

17. We should note the existence here of a literature on how social security is perceived by consumers. It is a related topic because, of course, the system is financed by taxes and because it may be included as a potential future benefit by consumers. Recent typical empirical papers taking contrasting views of this are by Feldstein (1974) and Barro (1979c). We will not go further with this topic, however, since this literature is not germane to fiscal policy in the (cyclical) sense.

18. One readily finds sizeable effects of fiscal policy on interest rates (etc.) if he uses adaptive or static expectations; for an example see Cohen and Clark (1983).

19. Perhaps, of this list, the worst of the lot are the data problems. Sheehan is well aware of this, but uses as his measures of fiscal influence the net Federal debt and the high-employment deficit. The former does not account for real-income changes and the latter misses off-budget items (see, also, the discussion in Eisner and Pieper (1984)). In addition (Seater, 1985) one should be concerned with the effect of inflation on the actual outstanding debt and with the real value of state and local deficits. The studies in this literature, as described by Seater and by Sheehan, differ so widely with respect to their measurement of the fiscal influence as to make any firm conclusions impossible at this stage. See the discussion of fiscal indicators in Chapter 7.

20. There are a few other direct studies. In one such, McMillan and Beard (1980) find a mild fiscal accommodation on US data; a survey of a mountain of material appears in the *Economic Review*, Federal Reserve Bank of Atlanta (Aug 1982).

5 Monetary and Fiscal Policy in the Long Run

1. The development of the models of this chapter is due to Jeffrey I. Bernstein, who has kindly let me have them for inclusion in this study. All errors are, of course, chargeable to my account.

2. Because our concern is the long run or the steady state, we shall not present results from the disequilibrium literature here. This caveat refers in particular to the Keynes–Wicksell models (see J. Stein, 1969, 1971). In any event Fischer (1972) has shown that a consistent Keynes–Wicksell model – that is, a product-market disequilibrium model – becomes identical to the neoclassical vintage model in the steady state.

3. For what follows we also assume that J and n are twice continuously differentiable and are homogeneous of degree one in Py and PA. Note that the following results hold for the partial derivatives of Equations 5.5 and 5.6 because of the definition of wealth:

$$J_1 + n_1 = 0, \quad J_2 + n_2 = 1, \quad \text{and} \quad J_3 + n_3 = 0.$$

4. We will assume that F is twice continuously differentiable and is homogeneous of degree one in capital and labour.

5. Notice that if we had written the demand for money as $m = kL(f' + \pi^e)$ then $\varepsilon > 1$ would hold. We are, in effect, generalising the demand for money over such a formulation while retaining a useful property of the capital intensity of the demand for money.

6. I. Fisher (1898) proposed that the nominal rate of return on an asset changes in proportion to the rate of inflation, thereby causing the real rate of return to be constant. However, because capital intensity increases with the rate of inflation, then the real rate of return (r) falls as in

$$\partial r / \partial \theta = f'' (\partial k / \partial \theta) < 0$$

Feldstein (1976), in turn, has pointed out that we should not expect the right-hand side of this equation to exceed 0.01.

7. We are ignoring capital gains taxes here. Note, also, that r is now the before-tax rate of return to shareholders.

8. For a discussion of endogenous corporate finance see Feldstein, J. Green and Sheshinski (1978, 1979).

9. The assumption that $H_2 < 0$ may seem a little strong to some readers. An alternative would be to assume that

(a) $sf' - \delta < 0$

(b) $L_3(\pi^e + (\delta/s)) + (L_4 - 1)m < 0$

(c) $f''k/f' > -1$

In which case we could deduce that $H_2 < 0$. The first of these conditions is just the stability condition for the barter economy and the third is the empirical judgement that the capital-intensity elasticity of output is itself inelastic. The second condition can be shown to depend on the inflation-rate elasticity of money balances. This is negative and if it is sufficiently inelastic the sign on (b) would be negative. These comments provide some economic background to the assumption in the text.

10. We can get this result if we assume

$$-L_3 \frac{\pi^e}{m} > \frac{(L_4 - 1)\pi^e s}{\pi^e s + \delta}$$

The term on the left is the 'inflation-rate elasticity of the demand for money' referred to in note 9, above. It is, therefore, part of the overall stability condition for this model.

11. The effect on wealth is actually ambiguous and depends on $f'(1 - \tau) - \delta$.

12. When the rate of inflation does increase, the demand for money falls and, because the demand for bonds rises, there are ambiguous effects on the level of government debt and on real wealth.

13. Although we are not interested in long-run equilibrium in this section, it should be noticed that the characterisation of the stationary state (since we are only concerned with the short run, we did not bother specifying a labour growth rate) with $\dot{K} = 0$ leads to $I(F(K, y) - r) = 0$. The marginal product of capital equals the rate of return on corporate shares and therefore (from Equation 5.82) the value of equity equals the value of the firm's assets. In addition, with $\dot{\pi}^e = 0$, then $\pi = \pi^e$ and so $y = y^f$. The long-run equilibrium is one with full employment.

14. To see this result set $a = 0$ (which defines a vertical Phillips relationship) and then

$$\left.\frac{\partial y}{\partial \Delta}\right|_{b = b^o} - \left.\frac{\partial y}{\partial \Delta}\right|_{m = m^o} = \frac{I'}{\Omega_1} > 0$$

as claimed.

6 Keynesian and Monetarist Perspectives on the Policy Debate

1. It needs to be emphasised that many monetarists are not in favour of employing monetary policy instead of fiscal policy and are, in fact, opposed to activist macropolicy of any sort, even though they think money matters. This point is frequently misunderstood in the literature.
2. Keynes (1936, p. 202). One page later he adjusts his wording in favour of it being 'a highly conventional, rather than a highly psychological, phenomenon'.
3. We should note here the argument in Patinkin (1976) that Keynes of the *Treatise* (1930) is much more optimistic about the usefulness of monetary policy and introduced public expenditures as an alternative policy tool in case it was necessary to use interest rates for exchange-rate objectives. In 1936 Britain's exchange rate was floating so the views expressed here represent a sharp revision (1930–6) of views on the relative usefulness of monetary and (as we shall see) fiscal policy.
4. Leijonhufvud (1968) argues that Keynes's model is a two-commodity model (consumer goods and capital goods) in effect. Froyen (1976) takes issue with this, with reference to more recently available Keynesian memorabilia, arguing that the *Treatise* provides a two-sector model while the *General Theory* is actually a one-sector model (as it is portrayed in (for example) the *IS–LM* framework).
5. The device for combining consumption and investment is an aggregate production function in which a single good is produced at a constant relative price between the two. There is no aggregate production function in Keynes.
6. The four aggregates require three relative prices (w, p and i_s or i_L). On term-to-maturity grounds the margin might reasonably be supposed to be between money and its closest substitute, Treasury bills. All securities of longer term to maturity would then be dominated and basically irrelevant to money holding.
7. We are here neglecting the liquidity trap, which was widely employed in textbooks, although it has generally not been more than the 'extreme' Keynesian case, even to the Keynesians.
8. For example, see Barro (1976) who argues that the policy could make the adjustment to the real shock more painful. There is some empirical support for the notion that the 1974 shock had minimal real-output effects (we will argue below that it was not 'accommodated') and the 1979 oil shock had no discernible real effects (compare Burbridge and Harrison (1981) with Frye and Gordon (1980)). This, basically, supports (a) in what is bound to be a continuing literature.

9. We are here referring to a variation of the segmentation theory known as the 'preferred habitat' of the representative investor. See Modigliani and Sutch (1967).

10. A forward rate can be calculated from a yield structure by comparing adjacent yields, one for an n period bond and one for an $n-1$ period bond, both calculated at the same time (t). A formula to do this is due to Hicks (1946) and is

$$1 + r_{nt} = \frac{(1 + R_{nt})^n}{(1 + R_{n-1t})^{n-1}}$$

Here R_{n-1t} is a yield (lifted from the newspaper, for example, and r_{it} is the forward rate. The expectations hypothesis, then, argues that this forward rate is also an expected rate determined, in effect, by the actions of those who participate in this market.

11. One can find support for the notion that some monetarists believe that fiscal policy does not have any effect, but this does not include Friedman. As M. Friedman says, in his well-known debate with W. W. Heller (1969, p. 48): 'The basic difficulties and limitations of monetary policy apply with equal force to fiscal policy.' So his position is anti-activist, not anti-effect. This seems an important distinction. On the other hand, M. Friedman has also said that (1962, p. 83) after an increase in government expenditure not even money income goes up, let alone real income. This judgement is delivered in the context of an example. He also has suggested that fiscal policy has a role to play in influencing long-run changes in real income (M. Friedman, 1970), as have many others in this long debate.

12. For (a) a reference is M. Friedman (1959b); perhaps the strongest claims for stability appear in Laidler (1971), who says (p. 91) that 'The evidence in favour of the existence of a stable relationship between the aggregate demand for real balances and a few variables is overwhelming'. (b) is more a matter of assumption in monetarist models than a matter of principle; for examples of models see Andersen and Jordan (1968) or M. Friedman (1970, 1971); for some evidence see Cagan (1965). For (e), Friedman's early studies seem a little incomplete, by modern standards; a more recent effort to the same effect is by Berman (1978). For (f) see Pesek and Saving (1967). For the first part of (g) see Schwartz (1969); for the second see I. Fisher (1898) or M. Friedman (1968). For (h) see M. Friedman (1959a).

13. In this list, aside from numerous omissions, the main departure from the list above is point (c). This is explained in Laidler's paper, but see also H. G. Johnson (1977).

14. Mayer would agree with this point. For a discussion of these issues, and numerous references, see Aschheim and Tavlos (1979).

15. It should be emphasised, in line with the discussion to this point, that we mean only that these are the models of several economists as monetarists, quite possibly, and not that they should ever be taken as representative of monetarism except, perhaps, in an historical sense.

16. The consumption function in the income-expenditure theory is $C = f(Y_d)$ where Y_d is disposable income. In general, $Y_d \neq A$.

17. A 'short list' of these studies is as follows. On UK data Barrett and Walters (1966) finds the autonomous investment equation outperforming the money multiplier. Walters (1966) also finds that the money equation itself does not work well in the post-Second World War period (he refers to this as a chaotic money market). In general, though, money matters in these two studies. More ambitiously, Argy (1970) searches for a strong monetary multiplier (and did some comparisons of M versus A) on data for seventeen different countries. He finds generally poor results for the monetary multiplier (except in Belgium, Finland and Italy). His data are over the 1951–67 period.

    A Canadian study by Macesich (1964) obtains the same result as FM, broadly. With a revised measure of autonomous expenditures, however, P. S. Laumas and Zerbe (1971) find A and M roughly equal in their effects.

18. Below, under 'reverse causation' we will discuss a vector autoregression procedure used by Mills (1980b) on UK data. Mills's concern is with identification in the model but has in common with Burns the idea that an agnostic approach may be best in cases in which no strong *a priori* line emerges.

19. If the variables are not prefiltered then the results of this test will obscure the relation between X and Y to the effect that the F-test would be invalid. Of course the whitening is arbitrary, but it is necessary to remove the serial correlation in the residuals of the OLS equation. The weakness is that information is filtered out so that what remains is a kind of 'as if' test with an indeterminately lower range of applicability than one might wish. The prefiltering is also arbitrary and that, too, has caused some empirical problems in some of the basic studies in this literature.

20. Whether or not the data are seasonally adjusted is also an issue. Feige and Pearce (and Sims) agree that they should be unadjusted, but when they are unadjusted the Sims prefilter apparently leaves the residuals serially correlated.

21. Curiously, Mehra (with Spencer, 1979) had already argued that the St Louis equation (an equation with both monetary and fiscal variables in it) shows evidence of reverse causation for fiscal but not for monetary policy. See below for more on the St Louis equation.

22. The Sims test, as described above, is shown to be equivalent to the following direct test (p. 4); 'Y does not cause M ... if M is no better predicted by including present and past values of Y along with its own past values than it can be by just including these own past values'. This test is also referred to as the 'Granger test' by Sargent (1976a) and by Mehra (1977). The latter provides a useful explanation.

23. We refer to 6.4 and 6.6 in this way since they are not, in general, the reduced-form equations from a complete model, as discussed in Chapter 1.

7 Objectives, Instruments, Targets and Indicators

1. In some underdeveloped countries, where the desired inflation rate is set well above zero, inflation is directly part of the fiscal (i.e. revenue-creating)

machinery. In that event it is a great help to have a stable demand for money (see Nichols, 1974).

2. A standard example of the first is to assume that money saves time in transactions; that time is divided among transactions, productive, and leisure activities; and that leisure activities, as proxied by the time spent on them, directly provide utilities. See Saving (1971).

3. The user cost is here defined in the sense of Jorgenson (1963); the explanation of the theory used in this section is based on Barnett (1976, 1981).

4. This involves the usual Cournot and Engel aggregations and restrictions on the diagonal and off-diagonal terms of the substitution matrix. The set of restrictions that usually fails to hold (empirically) is that involving the symmetry of the substitution effects.

5. Two examples of this methodology, on this problem, and arriving at these conclusions are provided by Ewis and D. Fisher (1984, 1985); the consumer technology in these studies is Translog and Fourier, respectively. Other studies offering similar conclusions are by Barnett (1980, 1981) and Offenbacher (1979), while an early paper arriving at a different conclusion is by Chetty (1969). For an extension of the substitution framework to the topic of currency substitution – to the open economy, that is to say – see Ewis and Fisher (1984) and, especially, G. Sims and Takayama (1980). The latter has a nicely worded explanation of the theoretical argument (which involves duality theory).

6. The standard proof of this is in H. Green (1964). Another way to put this condition is that the utility function of the representative consumer (Barnett, 1980, pp. 14–15) 'requires the goods over which it is defined to be perfect substitutes in identical ratios. In other words, the components of the quantity index must be indistinguishable to the consumer'.

7. A pure price index exhibits only price effects while a quantity index contains only quantity effects; thus the non-parametric approach suggested here has the disadvantage that no such simple interpretation can be given to it. Properties (1) and (2) are advantages, of course.

8. Nelson (1975) points out that if we only use the lagged values of the particular variable being predicted (in a multivariate model) our forecasts will be inefficient in general (in the sense of generally providing higher mean-squared forecasting errors). It is still, though, a matter of expected cost versus expected benefit, as to what procedure will be adopted. An empirical study of inflation expectations in the context of the UK wage equation (by Ormerod, 1982) concludes that while rational expectations gives results with greater explanatory power than 'mechanistic' forecasts, the advantage is probably not sufficient to justify the considerable additional expense involved in generating the rational-expectations equation (in a large-scale model).

9. Note, though, that this formulation begs any question concerning the distinction between the quantity and the quality of information. Of course it could be an index of the quality of information, the quantity of information, or both, if suitably measured.

10. The Cagan model, as just described, had weights of $(1 - \lambda L)\lambda^i$ and a lag structure of $(1 - \lambda)\pi_t = (1 - \lambda L)a_t$ and so can be described in terms of Equation 7.27 readily: the order of the lag process in Cagan's case is unity and λ is the moving-average parameter.

11. The most influential recent work on fiscal policy is that of Blinder and Solow (1974); they agree completely. Indeed, at this stage there appear to be no dissenters.

12. If $y = c[y - T(y, t) + A + G]$ then we can totally differentiate and solve for dy to obtain

$$dy = \frac{dA}{1 - (\partial c/\partial y)(1 - \partial T/\partial y)} + \frac{dG - [(\partial c/\partial y)/(\partial T/\partial t)]dt}{1 - (\partial c/\partial y)(1 - \partial T/\partial y)}$$

This is Equation 7.32, in the term on the far right. Of course, this is a standard multiplier framework. Note, particularly, that if all exogenous and fiscal influences are removed from dy, then the residual could be attributed to monetary policy. See also Blinder and Goldfeld (1976) and Artis and C. Green (1981) for a British application.

13. We have already discussed the money stock versus the interest rate in this sense in Chapter 1 and elsewhere in this study. The idea of the neutralised money stock belongs to Hendershott (1968) and comes from a consideration of the endogeneity issue. In particular, economic activity itself imparts a strongly pro-cyclical movement to the money stock which is not really policy-induced. By analogy with the full-employment surplus, Hendershott calculates a 'trend utilization of resources' neutralised money stock. He finds a contracyclical pattern for this indicator in the 1952 to 1964 US data. This index shares with the *FES* the property that away from full-employment (or trend-adjusted full employment) anomalies develop. These would occur for a non-linear trend or, of course, a cyclically unstable demand for money. As well, some procyclical monetary mistakes are neutralised. See above for a discussion of the neutralised fiscal indicator.

Bibliography

ALBERRO, J. (1980) 'The Lucas Hypothesis on the Phillips Curve: Further International Evidence', *Journal of Monetary Economics* (Oct).

ALOGOSKOUFIS, G. (1983) 'The Labour Market in an Equilibrium Business Cycle Model', *Journal of Monetary Economics* (Jan).

—— and C. A. PISSARIDES (1982) 'A Test of Price Sluggishness in the Simple Rational Expectations Model: U.K. 1950–1979', mimeo, London School of Economics (Jan).

ANDERSEN, L. C., and K. M. CARLSON (1970) 'A Monetarist Model for Economic Stabilization', *Review*, Federal Reserve Bank of St Louis (Apr).

—— and K. M. CARLSON (1974) 'St Louis Model Revisited', *International Economic Review* (June).

—— and J. JORDAN (1968) 'Monetary and Fiscal Actions: A Test of Their Relative Importance in Economic Stabilization', *Review*, Federal Reserve Bank of St Louis (Nov).

ANDERSON, P. A. (1978) 'Rational Expectations Forecasts from Nonrational Models', mimeo, Federal Reserve Bank of Minneapolis (Apr).

ANDO, A., and F. MODIGLIANI (1965) 'The Relative Stability of Monetary Velocity and the Investment Multiplier', *American Economic Review* (Sep).

ARAK, M. (1977) 'Some International Evidence on Output–Inflation Tradeoffs: Comment', *American Economic Review* (Sep).

ARCHIBALD, G. C. (1969) 'The Phillips Curve and the Distribution of Unemployment', *American Economic Review* (May).

—— R. KEMMIS and J. W. PERKINS (1971) 'Excess Demand for Labour, Unemployment and the Phillips Curve: A Theoretical and Empirical Study', mimeo, University of Essex (Dec).

ARESTIS, P., S. F. FROWEN and E. KARAKITSOS (1978) 'The Dynamic Impacts of Government Expenditure and the Monetary Base on Aggregate Income: The Case of Four OECD Countries, 1965–1975', *Public Finance* (no. 1–2).

ARGY, V. (1970) 'The Role of Money in Economic Activity: Some Results for 17 Developed Countries', International Monetary Fund *Staff Papers* (Nov).

ARTIS, M. J., and C. GREEN (1981) 'Using the Treasury Model to Measure the Impact of Fiscal Policy, 1974–79', mimeo, University of Manchester (June).

ASCHAUER, D. A. (1985) 'Fiscal Policy and Aggregate Demand', *American Economic Review* (Mar).

ASCHHEIM, J., and G. S. TAVLOS (1979) 'On Monetarism and Ideology', *Quarterly Review*, Banca Nazionale del Lavoro (June).

ASHENFELTER, O. C., G. E. JOHNSON and J. H. PENCAVEL (1972) 'Trade Unions and the Rate of Change of Money Wages in the U.S. Manufacturing Industry', *Review of Economic Studies* (Jan).

ATKINSON, T. R. (1969) 'Tone and Feel of the Market as a Guide for Federal Open Market Operations', in K. BRUNNER (ed.) *Targets and Indicators of Monetary Policy* (San Francisco: Chandler).

ATTFIELD, C. L. F., D. DEMERY and N. W. DUCK (1981a) 'Unanticipated Monetary Growth, Output and the Price Level: UK 1946–1977', *European Economic Review* (June/July).
—— —— —— (1981b) 'A Quarterly Model of Unanticipated Monetary Growth, Output and the Price Level in the UK, 1963–1978', *Journal of Monetary Economics* (Nov).
—— —— —— (1985) *Rational Expectations in Macroeconomics* (Oxford: Blackwell).
—— and N. W. DUCK (1983) 'The Influence of Unanticipated Money Growth on Real Output: Some Cross-Country Estimates', *Journal of Money, Credit and Banking* (Nov).
AUERBACH, R. D., and J. L. RUTNER (1978) 'A Causality Test of Canadian Money and Income: a Comment on Barth and Bennett', *Canadian Journal of Economics* (Aug).
AZARIADIS, C. (1975) 'Implicit Contracts and Underemployment Equilibrium', *Journal of Political Economy* (Dec).
—— (1981) 'A Re-examination of Natural Rate Theory', *American Economic Review* (Dec).
BAILEY, M. J. (1962 [1971]) *National Income and the Price Level* (New York: McGraw-Hill).
BARNETT, W. A. (1976) 'The User Cost of Money', *Economic Letters* (vol. 1, no. 2).
—— (1980) 'Economic Monetary Aggregates: An Application of Index Number and Aggregation Theory', *Journal of Econometrics* (Sep).
—— (1981) *Consumer Demand and Labor Supply: Goods, Monetary Assets and Time* (Amsterdam: North-Holland).
—— (1984) 'Recent Monetary Policy and the Divisia Monetary Aggregates', *The American Statistician* (Aug).
—— and P. A. SPINDT (1979) 'The Velocity Behavior and Information Content of Divisia Monetary Aggregates', *Economic Letters* (vol. 4, no. 1).
BARRETT, C. R., and A. A. WALTERS (1966) 'The Relative Stability of Monetary and Autonomous Expenditure Multipliers in the U.K.', *Review of Economics and Statistics* (Nov).
BARRO, R. J. (1974) 'Are Government Bonds Net Wealth?', *Journal of Political Economy* (Nov/Dec).
—— (1976) 'Rational Expectations and the Role of Monetary Policy', *Journal of Monetary Economics* (Jan).
—— (1977a) 'Unanticipated Money Growth and Unemployment in the United States', *American Economic Review* (Mar).
—— (1977b) 'Long-term Contracting, Sticky Prices, and Monetary Policy', *Journal of Monetary Economics* (July).
—— (1978) 'Unanticipated Money, Output, and the Price Level in the United States', *Journal of Political Economy* (Aug).
—— (1979a) 'The Effect of Social Security on Private Saving: The Time Series Evidence', NBER Working Paper (Feb).
—— (1979b) 'Second Thoughts on Keynesian Economics', *American Economic Review* (May).
—— (1979c) 'On the Determination of the Public Debt', *Journal of Political Economy* (Oct).

—— (1979d) 'Unanticipated Money Growth and Unemployment in the United States: Reply', *American Economic Review* (Dec).

—— (1980) 'Federal Deficit Policy and the Effects of Public Debt Shocks', *Journal of Money, Credit and Banking* (Nov).

—— (1981a) 'Unanticipated Money Growth and Economic Activity in the United States', in *Money, Expectations and Business Cycles* (New York: Academic Press).

—— (1981b) 'The Equilibrium Approach to Business Cycles', in *Money, Expectations and Business Cycles* (New York: Academic Press).

—— and D. B. GORDON (1983a) 'Rules, Discretion and Reputation in a Model of Monetary Policy', *Journal of Monetary Economics* (July).

—— —— (1983b) 'A Positive Theory of Monetary Policy in a Natural Rate Model', *Journal of Political Economy* (Aug).

—— and H. I. GROSSMAN (1971) 'A General Disequilibrium Model of Income and Employment', *American Economic Review* (Mar).

—— —— (1976) *Money, Employment and Inflation* (Cambridge: Cambridge U.P.).

—— and Z. HERCOWITZ (1980) 'Money Stock Revisions and Unanticipated Money Growth', *Journal.of Monetary Economics* (Apr).

—— and M. RUSH (1980) 'Unanticipated Money and Economic Activity', in S. FISCHER (ed.) *Rational Expectations and Economic Policy* (Chicago: University of Chicago Press).

BARRON, J. M. (1975) 'Search in the Labor Market and the Duration of Unemployment', *American Economic Review* (Dec).

BARTH, J. R., and J. T. BENNETT (1974) 'The Role of Money in the Canadian Economy: An Empirical Test', *Canadian Journal of Economics* (May).

BATTEN, D. S., and R. W. HAFER (1983) 'The Relative Impact of Monetary and Fiscal Actions on Economic Activity: A Cross-Country Comparison', *Review*, Federal Reserve Bank of St Louis (Jan).

—— and D. L. THORNTON (1983) 'Polynominal Distributed Lags and the Estimation of the St Louis Equation', *Review*, Federal Reserve Bank of St Louis (Apr).

BAUMOL, W. J. (1961) 'Pitfalls in Contracyclical Policies: Some Tools and Results', *Review of Economics and Statistics* (Feb).

BEGG, D. K. H. (1982) *The Rational Expectations Revolution in Macroeconomics* (Baltimore, Md: Johns Hopkins U.P.).

BELLANTE, D., S. O. MORRELL and A. ZARDKOOHI (1982) 'Unanticipated Money Growth, Unemployment, Output and the Price Level in the United Kingdom: 1946–1977', *Southern Economic Journal* (July).

BELONGIA, M. T., and R. G. SHEEHAN (1985) 'The Efficient Markets Hypothesis and Weekly Money: Some Contrary Evidence', mimeo, Federal Reserve Bank of St Louis.

BENAVIE, A. (1981) 'Stabilization Policies Which Reverse Stagflation in a Short Run Macromodel', *Southern Economic Journal* (July).

BERKMAN, N. A. (1978) 'On the Significance of Weekly Changes in M1', *New England Economic Review* (May/June).

BERMAN, P. I. (1978) *Inflation and the Money Supply in the United States, 1956–1977* (Lexington, Mass.: Lexington Books).

BISIGNANO, J. (1975) 'Cagan's Real Money Demand Model with Alternative Error Structures', *International Economic Review* (June).

BLACK, S. W., and H. H. KELEJIAN (1970) 'A Macro Model of the U.S. Labor Market', *Econometrica* (Sep).

BLANCHARD, O. J. (1981a) 'Output, the Stock Market, and Interest Rates', *American Economic Review* (Mar).

—— (1981b) 'What is Left of the Multiplier Accelerator?', *American Economic Review* (May).

—— and L. H. SUMMERS (1984) 'Perspectives on High World Interest Rates', mimeo, NBER (Nov).

—— and M. W. WATSON (1984) 'Are Business Cycles All Alike?', mimeo, NBER (June).

BLEJER, M. I., and L. LEIDERMAN (1980) 'On the Real Effects of Inflation and Relative-price Variability: Some Empirical Evidence', *Review of Economics and Statistics* (Nov).

BLINDER, A. S. (1981) 'Monetary Accommodation of Supply Shocks under Rational Expectations', *Journal of Money, Credit, and Banking* (Nov).

—— and S. FISCHER (1980) 'Inventories, Rational Expectations, and the Business Cycle', *Journal of Monetary Economics* (Nov).

—— and S. M. GOLDFELD (1976) 'New Measures of Fiscal and Monetary Policy, 1958–73', *American Economic Review* (Dec).

—— and R. M. SOLOW (1973) 'Does Fiscal Policy Matter?' *Journal of Public Economics* (Nov).

—— —— (1974) 'Analytical Foundations of Fiscal Policy', in A. S. BLINDER *et al.*, *The Economics of Public Finance* (Washington, D.C.: Brookings Institution).

BLOCK, M. K., and J. M. HEINEKE (1973) 'The Allocation of Effort under Uncertainty: The Case of Risk-averse Behavior', *Journal of Political Economy* (Mar/Apr).

BODIE, Z. (1976) 'Common Stocks as Hedges Against Inflation', *Journal of Finance* (May).

BOMBERGER, W. A., and G. E. MAKINEN (1976) 'Inflation, Unemployment, and Expectations in Latin America: Some Simple Tests', *Southern Economic Journal* (Oct).

BONOMO, V., and J. E. TANNER (1983) 'Expected Monetary Changes and Relative Prices: A Look at Evidence from the Stock Market', *Southern Economic Journal* (Oct).

BOSCHEN, J. F. (1985) 'Employment and Output Effects of Observed and Unobserved Monetary Growth', *Journal of Money, Credit and Banking* (May).

—— and H. I. GROSSMAN (1980) 'Tests of Equilibrium Macroeconomics Using Contemporaneous Monetary Data', NBER Working Paper.

BOSKIN, M. (1982) 'Federal Government Deficits: Some Myths and Realities', *American Economic Review* (May).

BOWEN, W. G., and R. A. BERRY (1963) 'Unemployment Conditions and Movements of the Money Wage Level', *Review of Economics and Statistics* (May).

BRANSON, W. H. (1973) 'The Use of a Variable Tax Rate for Stabilization Purposes', in R. A. MUSGRAVE (ed.) *Broad-based Taxes: New Options and Sources* (Baltimore, Md: Johns Hopkins U.P.).

BRAY, M., and D. M. KREPS (1981) 'Rational Learning and Rational Expectations', mimeo, Stanford University.

BRUNNER, K., A. CUKIERMAN and A. H. MELTZER (1980) 'Stagflation, Persistent Unemployment and the Permanence of Economic Shocks', *Journal of Monetary Economics* (Oct).

—— and A. H. MELTZER (1969) 'The Nature of the Policy Problem', in K. BRUNNER (ed.) *Targets and Indicators of Monetary Policy* (San Francisco: Chandler).

—— —— (1972) 'Money, Debt and Economic Activity', *Journal of Political Economy* (Sep/Oct).

—— —— (1976) 'The Phillips Curve', in K. BRUNNER and A. H. MELTZER (eds) *The Phillips Curve and Labor Markets* (Amsterdam: North-Holland).

BRYANT, J., and N. WALLACE (1984) 'A Price Discrimination Analysis of Monetary Policy', *Review of Economic Studies* (Apr).

BUCHANAN, J. M. (1976) 'Barro on the Ricardian Equivalence Theorem', *Journal of Political Economy* (Apr).

BUITER, W. (1980) 'Walras' Law and All That – Budget Constraints and Balance Sheet Constraints in Derived Models and Continuous Time Models', *International Economic Review* (Feb).

—— (1983) 'Real Effects of Anticipated and Unanticipated Money: Some Problems of Estimation and Hypothesis Testing', *Journal of Monetary Economics* (Mar).

BULL, C., and R. FRYDMAN (1983) 'The Derivation and Interpretation of the Lucas Supply Function', *Journal of Money Credit and Banking* (Feb).

BURBIDGE, J., and A. HARRISON (1981) 'Testing for the Effects of Oil-price Rises Using Vector Autoregressions', mimeo, McMaster University (Sep).

BURDETT, K. (1978) 'Employee Search and Quits', *American Economic Review* (Mar).

BURMEISTER, E., and A. R. DOBELL (1970) *Mathematical Theories of Economic Growth* (London: Macmillan).

BURNS, M. E. (1975) 'The Relative Stability of Aggregate Economic Relations; Friedman and Meiselman Revisited', *Manchester School* (Mar).

—— and P. J. THOMSON (1975) 'The Relative Stability of Responses to Monetary and Expenditure Policy in the United States: A Random-coefficients Approach', mimeo, University of Manchester.

—— —— and R. J. SMITH (1977) 'The Relative Stability of Responses to Monetary and Expenditure Policies: Some Results of Investigations Using a Random-coefficients Framework', mimeo, Monash University.

CAGAN, P. (1956) 'The Monetary Dynamics of Hyperinflation', in M. FRIEDMAN (ed.) *Studies in the Quantity Theory of Money* (Chicago: University of Chicago Press).

—— (1965) *Determinants and Effects of Changes in the Money Stock, 1875–1960* (New York: Columbia U.P.).

CANTO, V. A., M. C. FINDLAY and M. R. REINGANUM (1983) 'The Monetary Approach to Stock Returns and Inflation', *Southern Economic Journal* (Oct).

CARGILL, T. F., and R. A. MEYER (1974) 'Wages, Prices and Unemployment: Distributed Lag Estimates', *Journal of the American Statistical Association* (Mar).

CARLINO, G. (1982) 'Interest Rate Effects and Inter-temporal Consumption', *Journal of Monetary Economics* (Mar).

CARLSON, J. (1977) 'A Study of Price Forecasts', *Annals of Economic and Social Measurement* (Winter).

CARLSON, K. M. (1978) 'Does the St Louis Equation Now Believe in Fiscal Policy?', *Review*, Federal Reserve Bank of St Louis (Feb).

CAVES, E. W., and E. L. FEIGE (1978) 'Efficient Markets, Stock Returns and the Money Supply', mimeo, University of Wisconsin-Madison (July).

CHETTY, V. K. (1969) 'On Measuring the Nearness of Near-Moneys', *American Economic Review* (June).

CHO, D. W. (1979) 'The Relative Stability of Monetary Velocity and the Investment Multiplier in the United States: Some Additional Evidence', *Southern Economic Journal* (Apr).

CHRIST, C. F. (1973) 'Monetary and Fiscal Influence on U.S. Money Income, 1891–1970', *Journal of Money, Credit and Banking* (Feb).

—— (1978) 'Some Dynamic Theory of Macroeconomic Policy Effects on Income and Prices under the Government Budget Constraint', *Journal of Monetary Economics* (Jan).

—— (1979) 'On Fiscal and Monetary Policies and the Government Budget Constraint', *American Economic Review* (Sep).

CICCOLO, J. (1978) 'Money, Equity Values and Income', *Journal of Money, Credit, and Banking* (Feb).

CLOWER, R. W. (1965) 'The Keynesian Counter-Revolution: A Theoretical Appraisal', in F. H. HAHN and F. P. R. BRECHLING (eds) *The Theory of Interest Rates* (London: Macmillan).

COHEN, D., and P. B. CLARK (1983) 'The Effects of U.S. Fiscal Policy on the U.S. Economy', mimeo, Board of Governors of the Federal Reserve System.

COLWELL, P. F., and N. A. LASH (1973) 'Comparing Fiscal Indicators', *Review of Economics and Statistics* (Aug).

Commission on Money and Credit (1961) *Money and Credit* (Englewood Cliffs, N.J.: Prentice-Hall).

COOPER, R. V. L. (1974) 'Efficient Capital Markets and the Quantity Theory of Money', *Journal of Finance* (June).

CORNELL, B. (1983) 'Money Supply Announcements and Interest Rates: Another View', *Journal of Business* (Jan).

COSIMANO, T. (1983) 'Risk Averse Behavior and Normal Employment', mimeo, Texas A & M University (Sep).

COX, W. M. (1985) 'Inflation and Permanent Government Debt', *Economic Review*, Federal Reserve Bank of Dallas (May).

CRAINE, R., A. HAVENNER and J. BERRY (1978) 'Fixed Rules vs. Activism in the Conduct of Monetary Policy', *American Economic Review* (Dec).

CROTTY, J. R. (1973) 'Specification Error in Macro-econometric Models: The Influence of Policy Goals', *American Economic Review* (Dec).

CUDDINGTON, J. T. (1980) 'Simultaneous-equations Tests of the Natural Rate and Other Classical Hypotheses', *Journal of Political Economy* (June).

CUKIERMAN, A. (1979) 'The Relationship between Relative Prices and the General Price Level: A Suggested Interpretation', *American Economic Review* (June).

—— and P. WACHTEL (1979) 'Differential Inflationary Expectations and the Variability of the Rate of Inflation', *American Economic Review* (Sep).

—— —— (1982) 'Relative Price Variability and Nonuniform Inflationary Expectations', *Journal of Political Economy* (Feb).

CULBERTSON, J. M. (1957) 'The Term Structure of Interest Rates', *Quarterly Journal of Economics* (Nov).

DANFORTH, J. P. (1979) 'On the Role of Consumption and Decreasing Absolute Risk Aversion in the Theory of Job Search', in S. A. LIPPMAN and J. J. McCALL (eds) *Studies in the Economics of Search* (New York: North-Holland).

DAVIDSON, L. S., and R. W. HAFER (1983) 'Some Evidence on Selecting an Intermediate Target for Monetary Policy', *Southern Economic Journal* (Oct).

DEATON, A. (1977) 'Involuntary Savings Through Unanticipated Inflation', *American Economic Review* (Dec).

DECANIO, S. J. (1979) 'Rational Expectations and Learning by Experience', *Quarterly Journal of Economics* (Feb).

DE LEEUW, F., and T. M. HOLLOWAY (1985) 'The Measurement and Significance of the Cyclically Adjusted Federal Budget and Debt', *Journal of Money, Credit and Banking* (May).

DEPRANO, M., and T. MAYER (1965) 'Tests of the Relative Importance of Autonomous Expenditure and Money', *American Economic Review* (Sep).

DEWALD, W. G., and H. G. JOHNSON (1963) 'An Objective Analysis of the Objectives of American Monetary Policy, 1952–61', in D. CARSON (ed.) *Banking and Monetary Studies* (Homewood, Ill.: Irwin).

DICKS-MIREAUX, L. A., and J. C. R. DOW (1959) 'The Determinants of Wage Inflation: United Kingdom, 1946–1956', *Journal of the Royal Statistical Society* (series A, pt 2).

DRISCOLL, M. J., J. L. FORD, A. M. MULLINEUX and S. SEN (1983) 'Money, Output, Rational Expectations and Neutrality: Some Econometric Results for the UK', *Economica* (Aug).

DWYER, G. P. (1982a) 'Money, Income, and Prices in the United Kingdom, 1870–1913', mimeo, Emory University (Jan).

—— (1982b) 'Inflation and Government Deficits', *Economic Inquiry* (July).

DYREYES, F. R., D. R. STARLEAF and G. H. WANG (1980) 'Tests of the Direction of Causation between Money and Income in Six Countries', *Southern Economic Journal* (Oct).

ECKSTEIN, O. (1964) 'A Theory of Wage–Price Process in Modern Industry', *Review of Economic Studies* (Oct).

—— and G. FROMM (1968) 'The Price Equation', *American Economic Review* (Dec).

EISNER, R., and P. J. PIEPER (1984) 'A New View of the Federal Debt and Budget Deficits', *American Economic Review* (Mar).

EVANS, J. L., and G. K. YARROW (1981) 'Some Implications of Alternative Expectations Hypotheses in the Monetary Analysis of Hyperinflations', *Oxford Economic Papers* (Mar).

EVANS, P. (c. 1982) 'Monetary Policy and the Determination of Interest Rates', mimeo.

—— (1983) 'Price-Level Instability and Output in the United States', *Economic Inquiry* (Apr).

—— (1985) 'Do Large Deficits Produce High Interest Rates?', *American Economic Review* (Mar).

EWIS, N. A., and D. FISHER (1984) 'The Translog Utility Function and the Demand for Money in the United States', *Journal of Money, Credit and Banking* (Feb).

—— —— (1985) 'Toward a Consistent Estimate of the Demand for Monies: An Application of the Fourier Flexible Form', *Journal of Macroeconomics* (Spring).

FAIR, R. C. (1979) 'An Analysis of the Accuracy of Four Macro Econometric Models', *Journal of Political Economy* (Aug).

FAMA, E. F. (1975) 'Short-Term Interest Rates as Predictors of Inflation', *American Economic Review* (June).

—— (1981) 'Stock Returns, Real Activity, Inflation and Money', *American Economic Review* (Sep).

—— and M. R. GIBBONS (1980) 'Inflation, Real Returns, and Capital Investment', mimeo, University of Chicago, Graduate School of Business (Aug).

—— and G. W. SCHWERT (1977) 'Asset Returns and Inflation', *Journal of Financial Economics* (Nov).

FEDERAL RESERVE BANK OF BOSTON (1971) *Consumer Spending and Monetary Policy: The Linkages.*

FEIGE, E. L. and D. K. PEARCE (1976) 'Economically Rational Expectations: Are Innovations in the Rate of Inflation Independent of Innovations in Measures of Monetary and Fiscal Policy?', *Journal of Political Economy* (June).

—— —— (1979) 'The Casual Causal Relationship between Money and Income: Some Caveats for Time Series Analysis', *Review of Economics and Statistics* (Nov).

FELDMAN, M. (1982) 'Learning and Convergence to Rational Expectations', mimeo, University of California at Santa Barbara.

FELDSTEIN, M. S. (1974) 'Social Security, Induced Retirement, and Capital Accumulation', *Journal of Political Economy* (Sep).

—— (1976) 'Inflation, Income Taxes and the Rate of Interest: A Theoretical Analysis', *American Economic Review* (Dec).

—— (1980a) 'Fiscal Policies, Inflation, and Capital Formation', *American Economic Review* (Sep).

—— (1980b) 'Inflation and the Stock Market', *American Economic Review* (Dec).

—— (1982) 'Government Deficits and Aggregate Demand', *Journal of Monetary Economics* (Jan).

—— J. GREEN and E. SHESHINSKI (1978) 'Inflation and Taxes in a Growing Economy with Debt and Equity Finance', *Journal of Political Economy* (Apr).

—— —— —— (1979) 'Corporate Financial Policy and Taxation in a Growing Economy', *Quarterly Journal of Economics* (Aug).

—— and L. H. SUMMERS (1977) 'Is the Rate of Profit Falling?', *Brookings Papers* (no. 1).

—— —— (1978) 'Inflation, Tax Rates and the Long Term Interest Rate', *Brookings Papers* (no. 1).

FETHKE, G. C., and R. JACKMAN (1982) 'Optimal Monetary Policy, Endogenous Supply and Rational Expectations', mimeo, London School of Economics (Mar).

—— and A. J. POLICANO (1981) 'Long-term Contracts and the Effectiveness of Demand and Supply Policies', *Journal of Money, Credit and Banking* (Nov).

—— —— (1984) 'Wage Contingencies, the Pattern of Negotiation and Aggregate Implications of Alternative Contract Structures', *Journal of Monetary Economics* (Sep).

—— —— (1985) 'Monetary Policy and the Timing of Wage Contract Negotiations', mimeo, University of Iowa (May).

—— and S. H. WILLIAMSON (1979) 'Macroeconomic Implications of Employment Tax Credit Policy', *Southern Economic Journal* (Oct).

FIEBIG, D. G. (1980) 'The Causal Relationship between Money and Income in Australia', *Australian Economic Papers* (June).

FISCHER, S. (1972) 'Keynes–Wicksell and Neoclassical Models of Money and Growth', *American Economic Review* (Dec).

—— (1977) 'Long-term Contracts, Rational Expectations and the Optimal Money Supply Rule', *Journal of Political Economy* (Jan).

—— (1980) 'On Activist Monetary Policy with Rational Expectations', in S. FISCHER (ed.) *Rational Expectations and Economic Policy* (Chicago: University of Chicago Press).

—— (1985) 'Supply Shocks, Wage Stickiness and Accommodation', *Journal of Money, Credit and Banking* (Feb).

FISHER, D. (1970) 'The Instruments of Monetary Policy and the Generalized Trade-off Function for Britain, 1955–1968', *Manchester School* (Sep).

—— (1976) *Monetary Policy* (London: Macmillan).

—— (1978) *Monetary Theory and the Demand for Money* (London: Martin-Robertson).

—— (1983) *Macroeconomic Theory: A Survey* (London: Macmillan).

FISHER, I. (1898) 'Appreciation and Interest', *American Economic Review*.

FOLEY, D. K., and M. SIDRAUSKI (1971) *Monetary and Fiscal Policy in a Growing Economy* (London: Macmillan).

FOSTER, E. (1978) 'The Variability of Inflation', *Review of Economics and Statistics* (Aug).

FRENKEL, J. A. (1975) 'Inflation and the Formation of Expectations', *Journal of Monetary Economics* (Oct).

FRIEDLAENDER, A. F. (1973) 'Macro Policy Goals in the Post-war Period: A Study in Revealed Preference', *Quarterly Journal of Economics* (Feb).

FRIEDMAN, B. M. (1977) 'Even the St Louis Model Now Believes in Fiscal Policy', *Journal of Money, Credit and Banking* (May).

—— (1979) 'Optimal Expectations and the Extreme Information Assumptions of "Rational Expectations" Macromodels', *Journal of Monetary Economics* (Jan).

—— (1982) 'Lessons from the 1979–82 Monetary Policy Experiment', *American Economic Review* (May).

FRIEDMAN, M. (1956) 'The Quantity Theory of Money – A Restatement', in M. FRIEDMAN (ed.) *Studies in the Quantity Theory of Money* (Chicago: University of Chicago Press).

—— (1959a) *A Program for Monetary Stability* (New York: Fordham U.P.).
—— (1959b) 'The Demand for Money: Some Theoretical and Empirical Results', *Journal of Political Economy* (Aug).
—— (1962) *Capitalism and Freedom* (Chicago: University of Chicago Press).
—— (1968) 'The Role of Monetary Policy', *American Economic Review* (Mar).
—— (1970) 'A Theoretical Framework for Monetary Analysis', *Journal of Political Economy* (Mar/Apr).
—— (1971) 'A Monetary Theory of Nominal Income', *Journal of Political Economy* (Mar/Apr).
—— (1977), 'Inflation and Unemployment', *Journal of Political Economy* (June).
—— and W. W. HELLER (1969) *Monetary and Fiscal Policy* (New York: Norton).
—— and D. MEISELMAN (1963) 'The Relative Stability of Monetary Velocity and the Investment Multiplier in the United States, 1897–1958', in E. C. BROWN *et al., Stabilization Policies* (Englewood Cliffs, N.J.: Prentice-Hall).
—— and A. J. SCHWARTZ (1963) *A Monetary History of the United States* (Princeton: Princeton U.P.).
—— —— (1970) *Monetary Statistics of the United States* (New York: Columbia U.P.).
FRIEND, I., and J. HASBROUCK (1982) 'Effect of Inflation on the Profitability and Valuation of U.S. Corporations', mimeo, University of Pennsylvania, Wharton School.
FROYEN, R. T. (1976) 'The Aggregative Structure of Keynes's *General Theory*', *Quarterly Journal of Economics* (Aug).
—— and R. N. WAUD (1980) 'Further International Evidence on Output–Inflation Tradeoffs', *American Economic Review* (June).
—— —— (1984) 'The Changing Relationship between Aggregate Price and Output: The British Experience', *Economica* (Feb).
—— —— (1985) 'Demand Variability, Supply Shocks and the Output–Inflation Tradeoff', *Review of Economics and Statistics* (Feb).
FRYE, J., and R. J. GORDON (1980) 'The Variance and Acceleration of Inflation in the 1970s: Alternative Explanatory Models and Methods', mimeo, Northwestern University (Aug).
GARBADE, P. J., and P. WACHTEL (1978) 'Time Variation in the Relationship between Inflation and Interest Rates', *Journal of Monetary Economics* (Nov).
GEARY, R. C. (1977) 'Money and Inflation in Ireland, 1960–1975, with Some Observations on Relationships between Time Series', *Review*, Bank of Ireland (Feb).
GERMANY, J. D. (1978) 'Can the Effects of Unanticipated Policy be Estimated?', mimeo.
GOLDFELD, S. M., and A. S. BLINDER (1972) 'Some Implications of Endogenous Stabilization Policy', *Brookings Papers* (no. 3).
GOODHART, C. A. E. (1975) *Money, Information and Uncertainty* (London: Macmillan).
GORDON, D. F. (1974) 'A Neo-Classical Theory of Keynesian Unemployment', *Economic Inquiry* (June).

GORDON, R. J. (1971) 'Inflation in Recession and Recovery', *Brookings Papers* (no. 1).

—— (1972) 'Wage-Price Controls and the Shifting Phillips Curve', *Brookings Papers* (no. 2).

—— (1975) 'Alternative Responses of Policy to External Supply Shocks', *Brookings Papers* (no. 1).

—— (1977) 'World Inflation and the Sources of Monetary Accommodation: A Study of Eight Countries', *Brookings Papers* (no. 2).

—— (1981) 'Output Fluctuations and Gradual Price Adjustment', *Journal of Economic Literature* (June).

—— (1984) 'Supply Shocks and Monetary Policy Revisited', *American Economic Review* (May).

—— and S. R. KING (1982) 'The Output Cost of Disinflation in Traditional and Vector Autoregression Models', *Brookings Papers* (no. 2).

GRAMLICH, E. (1971) 'The Usefulness of Monetary and Fiscal Policy as Discretionary Stabilization Tools', *Journal of Money, Credit and Banking* (May).

GRANGER, C. W. J. (1969) 'Investigating Causal Relations by Econometric Models and Cross-spectral Methods', *Econometrica* (July).

GREEN, H. A. J. (1964) *Aggregation in Economic Analysis* (Princeton: Princeton U.P.).

GRICE, J. W. (1981) 'Wealth Effects and Expenditure Functions: A Survey of the Evidence', in M. J. ARTIS and M. H. MILLER (eds) *Essays in Fiscal and Monetary Policy* (Oxford: Oxford U.P.).

GRONAU, R. (1971) 'Information and Frictional Unemployment', *American Economic Review* (June).

GROSSMAN, H. I. (1974) 'The Cyclical Pattern of Unemployment and Wage Inflation', *Economica* (Nov).

—— (1977) 'Risk Shifting and Liability in Labor Markets', *Scandinavian Journal of Economics* (no. 2).

—— (1981) 'Incomplete Information, Risk Shifting and Employment Functions', *Review of Economic Studies* (Apr).

GROSSMAN, J. (1979) 'Nominal Demand Policy and Short-run Fluctuations in Unemployment and Prices in the United States', *Journal of Political Economy* (Oct).

—— (1981) 'The "Rationality" of Money Supply Expectations and the Short-run Response of Interest Rates to Monetary Surprises', *Journal of Money, Credit and Banking* (Nov).

GUTTENTAG, J. (1966) 'The Strategy of Open Market Operations', *Quarterly Journal of Economics* (Feb).

HADAR, J. (1971) *Mathematical Theory of Economic Behavior* (Reading, Mass.: Addison-Wesley).

HAFER, R. W. (1982) 'The Role of Fiscal Policy in the St Louis Equation', *Review*, Federal Reserve Bank of St Louis (Jan).

—— and S. E. HEIN (1982) 'Monetary Policy and Short-term Real Rates of Interest', *Review* Federal Reserve Bank of St Louis (Mar).

—— —— and C. J. M. KOOL (1983) 'Forecasting the Money Multiplier: Implications for Money Stock Control and Economic Activity', *Review*, Federal Reserve Bank of St Louis (Oct).

HAHN, F. H. (1969) 'On Money and Growth' *Journal of Money, Credit and Banking* (May).

HALL, R. E. (1975) 'The Rigidity of Wages and the Persistence of Unemployment', *Brookings Papers* (no. 2).

—— (1978) 'The Macroeconomic Impact of Changes in Income Taxes in the Short and Medium Runs', *Journal of Political Economy* (Apr).

—— and D. W. JORGENSON (1967) 'Tax Policy and Investment Behavior', *American Economic Review* (June).

—— —— (1969) 'Tax Policy and Investment Behavior: Reply and Further Results', *American Economic Review* (June).

HAMBURGER, M. J., and L. A. KOCHIN (1972) 'Money and Stock Prices: The Channels of Influence', *Journal of Finance* (May).

—— and B. ZWICK (1981) 'Deficits, Money and Inflation', *Journal of Monetary Economics* (Jan).

HANSEN, A. H. (1949) *Monetary Theory and Fiscal Policy* (New York: McGraw-Hill).

HANSEN, B. (1958) *The Economic Theory of Fiscal Policy* (Cambridge, Mass.: Harvard U.P.).

—— (1973) 'On the Effects of Fiscal and Monetary Policy: A Taxonomic Discussion', *American Economic Review* (Sep).

HANSON, J. A. (1980) 'The Short-run Relation Between Growth and Inflation in Latin America: A Quasi-rational or Consistent Expectation Approach', *American Economic Review* (Dec).

HARPER, C. P., and C. L. FRY (1978) 'Consistent Empirical Results with Almon's Method: Implications for the Monetary versus Fiscal Policy Debate', *Journal of Finance* (Mar).

HARROD, R. (1939) 'An Essay in Dynamic Theory', *Economic Journal* (Mar).

HAUGH, L. D. (1972) 'The Identification of Time Series Interrelationships with Special Reference to Dynamic Regression Models', Ph.D. dissertation, University of Wisconsin-Madison.

HELLER, W. P., and R. M. STARR (1979) 'Capital Market Imperfection, the Consumption Function, and the Effectiveness of Fiscal Policy', *Quarterly Journal of Economics* (Aug).

HELLER, W. W. (1966) *New Dimensions of Political Economy* (Cambridge, Mass.: Harvard U.P.).

HENDERSHOTT, P. H. (1968) *The Neutralized Money Stock* (Homewood, Ill.: Irwin).

HERCOWITZ, Z. (1981) 'Anticipated Inflation, the Frequency of Transactions and the Slope of the Phillips Curve', mimeo, Foerder Institute, Tel Aviv University (Dec).

HESTER, D. (1964) 'Keynes and the Quantity Theory: Comment on Friedman and Meiselman CMC Paper', *Review of Economics and Statistics* (Nov).

HICKS, J. R. (1937) 'Mr. Keynes and the Classics: A Suggested Interpretation', *Econometrica* (Apr).

—— (1946) *Value and Capital* (Oxford: Clarendon Press).

—— (1950) *A Contribution to the Theory of the Trade Cycle* (Oxford: Clarendon Press).

—— (1974) *The Crisis in Keynesian Economics* (Oxford: Blackwell).

HINES, A. G. (1964) 'Trade Unions and Wage Inflation in the United

Kingdom, 1893–1961', *Review of Economic Studies* (Oct).

—— (1968) 'Unemployment and the Rate of Change of Money Wage Rates in the United Kingdom, 1962–1963: A Reappraisal', *Review of Economics and Statistics* (Feb).

HOLLAND, A. S. (1984) 'Does Higher Inflation Lead to More Uncertain Inflation?', *Review*, Federal Reserve Bank of St Louis (Feb).

HOMA, K. E., and D. M. JAFFEE (1971) 'The Supply of Money and Common Stock Prices', *Journal of Finance* (Dec).

HOWARD, D. H. (1978) 'Personal Saving Behavior and the Rate of Inflation', *Review of Economics and Statistics* (Nov).

HOWREY, E. P. (1967) 'Stabilization Policy in Linear Stochastic Systems', *Review of Economics and Statistics* (Aug).

—— (1969) 'Distributed Lags and the Effectiveness of Monetary Policy', *American Economic Review* (Dec).

HSIAO, C. (1979) 'Autoregressive Modelling of Canadian Money and Income Data', *Journal of the American Statistical Association* (Sep).

HUBERMAN, G., and G. W. SCHWERT (1985) 'Information Aggregation, Inflation and the Pricing of Indexed Bonds', *Journal of Political Economy* (Feb).

INFANTE, E. F., and J. L. STEIN (1976) 'Does Fiscal Policy Matter?', *Journal of Monetary Economics* (Nov).

—— —— (1980) 'Money-financed Fiscal Policy in a Growing Economy', *Journal of Political Economy* (Apr).

JAFFEE, D. (1971) *Credit Rationing and the Commercial Loan Market* (New York: Wiley).

JOHNSON, H. G. (1971) 'The Keynesian Revolution and the Monetarist Counter-revolution', *American Economic Review* (May).

—— (1977) 'The Monetary Approach to Balance of Payments Theory and Policy: Explanations and Policy Implications', *Economica* (Aug).

JORGENSON, D. W. (1963) 'Capital Theory and Investment Behavior'. *American Economic Review* (May).

—— (1966) 'Rational Distributed Lag Functions', *Econometrica* (Jan).

JOVANOVIC, B. (1979) 'Job-matching and the Theory of Turn-over', *Journal of Political Economy* (Oct).

JUSTER, F. and L. D. TAYLOR (1975) 'Towards a Theory of Saving Behavior', *American Economic Review* (May).

KALDOR, N. (ed.) (1971) *Conflicts in Policy Objectives* (Oxford: Blackwell).

KAREKEN, J. H., T. MUENCH and N. WALLACE (1973) 'Optimal Open Market Strategy: The Use of Information Variables', *American Economic Review* (Mar).

KALISKI, S. F. (1964) 'The Relation Between Unemployment and the Rate of Change of Money Wages in Canada', *International Economic Review* (Jan).

KATSIMBRIS, G. M. (1985) 'The Relationship between the Inflation Rate, Its Variability and Output Growth Variability', *Journal of Money, Credit and Banking* (May).

—— and S. M. MILLER (1982) 'The Relation between the Rate and Variability of Inflation: Further Comment', *Kyklos* (no. 3).

KERAN, M. W. (1970) 'Selecting a Monetary Indicator–Evidence from the United States and Other Developed Countries', *Review*, Federal Reserve Bank of St Louis (Sep).

—— (1971) 'Expectations, Money and the Stock Market', *Review*, Federal Reserve Bank of St Louis (Jan).

KEYNES, J. M. (1930) *A Treatise on Money* (London: Macmillan, 1958 ed.).

—— (1936) *The General Theory of Employment, Interest and Money* (New York: Harcourt, Brace).

KIHLSTROM, R. E., and J.-J. LAFFONT (1979) 'A General Equilibrium Entrepreneurial Theory of Firm Formation Based on Risk Aversion', *Journal of Political Economy* (Aug).

KING, R. G., and C. I. PLOSSER (1984) 'Money, Credit, and Prices in a Real Business Cycle', *American Economic Review* (June).

KLAMER, A. (1983) *Conversations with Economists* (Totowa, N. J.: Rowman & Allenheld).

KLEIN, L. R. (1954) *The Keynesian Revolution* (New York: Macmillan).

—— and R. G. BODKIN (1964) 'Empirical Aspects of the Trade-offs Among Three Goals: High Level Employment, Price Stability and Economic Growth', in *Inflation, Growth and Employment* (Englewood Cliffs, N.J.: Prentice-Hall).

KMENTA, J., and P. E. SMITH (1973) 'Autonomous Expenditures versus Money Supply: An Application of Dynamic Multipliers', *Review of Economics and Statistics* (Aug).

KOCHIN, L. A. (1974) 'Are Future Taxes Anticipated by Consumers?', *Journal of Money, Credit and Banking* (Aug).

KOMURA, C. (1982) 'Money, Income and Causality: The Japanese Case', *Southern Economic Journal* (July).

KORMENDI, R. (1983) 'Government Debt, Government Spending and Private Sector Behavior', *American Economic Review* (Dec).

KOSKELA, E., and M. VIREN (1980) 'The Variance Hypothesis on the Output–Inflation Tradeoff: Evidence from Scandinavia', *Scandinavian Journal of Economics* (no. 4).

KYDLAND, F. E., and E. C. PRESCOTT (1977) 'Rules Rather than Discretion: The Inconsistency of Optimal Plans', *Journal of Political Economy* (June).

—— —— (1980) 'A Comparative Theory of Fluctuations and the Feasibility and Desirability of Stabilization Policy', in S. FISCHER (ed.) *Rational Expectations and Economic Policy* (Chicago: University of Chicago Press).

—— —— (1982) 'Time to Build and Aggregate Fluctuations', *Econometrica* (Nov).

LAHIRI, K. (1977) 'A Joint Study of Expectations Formation and the Shifting Phillips Curve', *Journal of Monetary Economics* (Apr).

LAIDLER, D. (1968) 'The Permanent Income Concept in a Macro-economic Model', *Oxford Economic Papers* (Mar).

—— (1969) 'The Definition of Money: Theoretical and Empirical Problems', *Journal of Money, Credit and Banking* (Aug).

—— (1971) 'The Influence of Money on Economic Activity – A Survey of Some Current Problems', in G. CLAYTON *et al.* (eds) *Monetary Theory and Policy in the 1970s* (Oxford: Oxford University Press).

—— (1981) 'Monetarism: An Interpretation and an Assessment', *Economic Journal* (Mar).

—— and B. CORRY (1967) 'The Phillips Relation: A Theoretical Explanation', *Economica* (May).

LAUMAS, G. S. (1968) 'The Degree of Moneyness of Savings Deposits', *American Economic Review* (June).

LAUMAS, P. S., and R. O. ZERBE (1971) 'The Relative Stability of Monetary Velocity and Investment Multiplier in Canada', *Journal of Money, Credit and Banking* (Nov).

LEIDERMAN, L. (1979) 'Expectations and Output-Inflation Tradeoffs in a Fixed-exchange Rate Economy, *Journal of Political Economy* (Dec).

—— (1980) 'Macroeconomic Testing of the Rational Expectations and Structural Neutrality Hypotheses for the United States', *Journal of Monetary Economics* (Jan).

LEIJONHUFVUD, A. (1968) *Keynesian Economics and the Economics of Keynes* (Oxford: Oxford U.P.).

—— (1973) 'Effective Demand Failure', *Swedish Economic Journal* (Mar).

LEVHARI, D., and D. PATINKIN (1966) 'The Role of Money in a Simple Growth Model', *American Economic Review* (Oct).

LEVI, M. D., and J. H. MAKIN (1980) 'Inflation Uncertainty and the Phillips Curve: Some Empirical Evidence', *American Economic Review* (Dec).

—— (1981) 'Factors Affecting Monetary Policy in an Era of Inflation', *Journal of Monetary Economics* (Nov).

LIEBERMAN, C. (1979) 'The Interest Elasticity of Money Demand, Liquidity, and Reverse Causation', *Economic Inquiry* (Oct).

LIPSEY, R. G. (1960) 'The Relation Between Unemployment and the Rate of Change of Money Wage Rates in the United Kingdom, 1862–1957: A Further Analysis', *Economica* (Feb).

—— (1974) 'The Micro Theory of the Phillips Curve Reconsidered: A Reply to Holmes and Smyth', *Economica* (Feb).

—— (1976) 'The Place of the Phillips Curve in Macro Economic Models', mimeo, Queen's University, Ontario (Mar).

—— and M. PARKIN (1970) 'Incomes Policy: A Reappraisal', *Economica* (May).

LOGUE, D. E., and R. J. SWEENEY (1981) 'Inflation and Real Growth: Some Empirical Results', *Journal of Money, Credit and Banking* (Nov).

—— and T. D. WILLETT (1976) 'A Note on the Relation between the Rate and Variability of Inflation', *Economica* (May).

LONG, J. B., and C. I. PLOSSER (1983) 'Real Business Cycles', *Journal of Political Economy* (Feb).

LUCAS, R. E. (1972a) 'Econometric Testing of the Natural Rate Hypothesis', in O. ECKSTEIN (ed.) *The Econometrics of Price Determination* (Washington, D.C.: Board of Governors of the Federal Reserve System).

—— (1972b) 'Expectations and the Neutrality of Money', *Journal of Economic Theory* (Apr).

—— (1973) 'Some International Evidence on Output–Inflation Trade-offs', *American Economic Review* (June).

—— (1975) 'An Equilibrium Model of the Business Cycle', *Journal of Political Economy* (Dec).

—— (1976) 'Econometric Policy Evaluation: A Critique', in K. BRUNNER and A. H. MELTZER (eds), *The Phillips Curve and Labor Markets* (New York: North-Holland).

—— (1980) 'Methods and Problems in Business Cycle Theory', *Journal of Money, Credit, and Banking* (Nov).

—— and E. C. PRESCOTT (1974) 'Equilibrium Search and Unemployment', *Journal of Economic Theory* (Feb).

—— and L. A. RAPPING (1969a) 'Price Expectations and the Phillips Curve', *American Economic Review* (June).

—— —— (1969b) 'Real Wages, Employment, and Inflation', *Journal of Political Economy* (Sep/Oct).

—— and T. J. SARGENT (1981) 'Introduction', in R. E. LUCAS and T. J. SARGENT (eds) *Rational Expectations and Econometric Practice* (Minneapolis: University of Minnesota Press).

McCALL, J. J. (1970) 'Economics of Information and Job Search', *Quarterly Journal of Economics* (Feb).

McCALLUM, B. T. (1977) 'Price-Level Stickiness and the Feasibility of Monetary Stabilization Policy with Rational Expectations', *Journal of Political Economy* (June).

—— (1980) 'Rational Expectations and Macro-Economic Stabilization Policy', *Journal of Money, Credit, and Banking* (Nov).

—— (1981) 'Price Level Determinacy with an Interest Rate Policy Rule and Rational Expectations', *Journal of Monetary Economics* (Nov).

—— and J. K. WHITAKER (1979) 'The Effectiveness of Fiscal Feedback Rules and Automatic Stabilizers under Rational Expectations', *Journal of Monetary Economics* (Apr).

McDONALD, J. (1975) 'Wages and Prices in Australia: On the Short- and Long-run Trade-offs Between Inflation and Unemployment', *Australian Economic Papers* (Dec).

MACESICH, G. (1964) 'The Quantity Theory and the Income–Expenditure Theory in an Open Economy: Canada, 1926–1950', *Canadian Journal of Economics* (Aug).

MADDOCK, R. and M. CARTER (1982) 'A Child's Guide to Rational Expectations', *Journal of Economic Literature* (Mar).

McGEE, R. T., and R. T. STASIAK (1985) 'Does Anticipated Monetary Policy Matter?', *Journal of Money, Credit and Banking* (Feb).

McMILLAN, W. D., and T. R. BEARD (1980) 'The Short Run Impact of Fiscal Policy on the Money Supply', *Southern Economic Journal* (July).

—— and J. S. FACKLER (1984) 'Money vs. Credit Aggregates: An Evaluation of Monetary Policy Targets', *Southern Economic Journal* (Jan).

MARIANO, R. S., and J. J. SEATER (1985) 'New Tests of the Life Cycle and Tax Discounting Hypotheses', *Journal of Monetary Economics* (Mar).

MATTILA, J. P. (1974) 'Job Quitting and Frictional Unemployment', *American Economic Review* (Mar).

MAYER, T. (1978) *The Structure of Monetarism* (New York: Norton).

MEADE, J. E., and P. W. S. ANDREWS (1938) 'Summary of Replies to Questions on Effects of Interest Rates', *Oxford Economic Papers* (Oct).

MEHRA, Y. P. (1977) 'Money Wages, Prices, and Causality', *Journal of Political Economy* (Dec).

—— (1978) 'An Empirical Note on Some Monetarist Propositions', *Southern Economic Journal* (July).

—— and D. E. SPENCER (1979) 'The St Louis Equation and Reverse Causation: The Evidence Reexamined', *Southern Economic Journal* (Apr).

MEIGS, A. J. (1962) *Free Reserves and the Money Supply* (Chicago: University of Chicago Press).

MEYER, J. R., and R. R. GLAUBER (1964) *Investment Decisions, Economic Forecasting and Public Policy* (Cambridge, Mass.: Harvard U.P.).

—— and E. KUH (1957) *The Investment Decision: An Empirical Study* (Cambridge, Mass.: Harvard U.P.).

MEYER, L. H., and C. VARVARES (1981) 'A Comparison of the St. Louis Model and Two Variations: Predictive Performance and Policy Implications', mimeo, Washington University of St Louis (Nov).

—— and C. E. WEBSTER (1982) 'On the Real Effects of Imprecise Monetary Control', in L. H. MEYER (ed.) *Improving Money Stock Control: Problems, Solutions and Consequences* (Amsterdam: Kluwer–Nijhoff).

MILLS, T. C. (1980a) 'Money, Income and Causality in the U.K. — A Look at the Recent Evidence', *Bulletin of Economic Research* (May).

—— (1980b) 'Investigating the Long Run Interaction between U.K. Macroeconomic Aggregates: An Exercise in Vector Autoregressive Modelling', mimeo, University of Leeds.

—— and G. E. WOOD (1978) 'Money-Income Relationships and the Exchange Rate Regime, *Review*, Federal Reserve Bank of St Louis (Aug).

MINFORD, P. and D. PEEL (1980), 'The Natural Rate Hypothesis and Rational Expectations – A Critique of Some Recent Developments', *Oxford Economic Papers* (Mar).

—— —— (1981) 'The Role of Monetary Stabilization Policy under Rational Expectations', *Manchester School* (Mar).

—— —— (1983) *Rational Expectations and the New Macroeconomics* (Oxford: Martin-Robertson).

MIRON, J. A. (1985) 'Financial Panics, the Seasonality of the Nominal Interest Rate and the Founding of the Fed.', mimeo, University of Michigan (Mar).

MISHKIN, F. S. (1982a) 'Does Anticipated Monetary Policy Matter? An Econometric Investigation', *Journal of Political Economy* (Feb).

—— (1982b) 'Does Anticipated Aggregated Demand Policy Matter? Further Econometric Results', *American Economic Review* (Sep).

MITCHELL, D. W., and H. E. TAYLOR (1982) 'Inflationary Expectations: Comment', *American Economic Review* (June).

MODIGLIANI, F. (1977) 'The Monetarist Controversy, or Should We Foresake Stabilization Policies?', *American Economic Review* (Mar).

—— and A. ANDO (1976) 'Impact of Fiscal Actions on Aggregate Income and the Monetarist Controversy: Theory and Evidence', in J. STEIN (ed.) *Monetarism* (Amsterdam: North-Holland).

—— and R. SUTCH (1967) 'Debt Management and the Term Structure of Interest Rates: An Empirical Analysis of Recent Experience', *Journal of Political Economy* (Aug).

MORGAN, B. (1978) *Monetarists and Keynesians* (London: Macmillan).

MORTENSEN, D. T. (1970a) 'A Theory of Wage and Employment Dynamics', in E. S. PHELPS (ed.) *Microeconomic Foundations of Employment and Inflation Theory* (New York: Norton).

—— (1970b), 'Job Search, the Duration of Unemployment and the Phillips Curve', *American Economic Review* (Dec).

——(1984) 'Job Search and Labor Market Analysis', mimeo, Northwestern University.

MULLINEAUX, D. J. (1980) 'Unemployment, Industrial Production and Inflation Uncertainty in the U.S.', *Review of Economics and Statistics* (May).

MUNDELL, R. A. (1971) *Monetary Theory* (Pacific Palisades, Calif.: Goodyear).

MUTH, J. F. (1961) 'Rational Expectations and the Theory of Price Movements', *Econometrica* (July).

NEFTCI, S., and T. J. SARGENT (1978) 'A Little Bit of Evidence on the Natural Rate Hypothesis from the U.S.', *Journal of Monetary Economics* (Apr).

NELSON, C. R. (1975) 'Rational Expectations and the Predictive Efficiency of Economic Models', *Journal of Business* (July).

—— (1976) 'Inflation and Rates of Return on Common Stocks', *Journal of Finance* (May).

—— and C. I. PLOSSER (1982) 'Trends and Random Walks in Macroeconomic Time Series', *Journal of Monetary Economics* (Sep).

—— and G. W. SCHWERT (1977) 'Short Term Interest Rates as Predictors of Inflation: On Testing the Hypothesis that the Real Rate of Interest is Constant', *American Economic Review* (June).

NICHOLS, D. A. (1974) 'Some Principles of Inflationary Finance', *Journal of Political Economy* (Mar/Apr).

—— D. H. SMALL and C. E. WEBSTER (1983) 'Why Interest Rates Rise When an Unexpectedly Large Money Stock is Announced', *American Economic Review* (June).

OAKLAND, W. H. (1969) 'Budgetary Measures of Fiscal Performance', *Southern Economic Journal* (Apr).

O'BRIEN, J. M. (1981) 'Estimating the Information Value of Immediate Disclosure of the FOMC Policy Directive', *Journal of Finance* (Dec).

—— (1982) 'The Information Value of the FOMC Policy Directive under the New Operating Procedure', mimeo, Board of Governors, Federal Reserve System (Dec).

O'DRISCOLL, G. P. (1977) 'The Ricardian Nonequivalence Theorem', *Journal of Political Economy* (Jan).

OFFENBACHER, E. K. (1979) 'The Substitutability of Monetary Assets', Ph.D. thesis, University of Chicago.

OKUN, A. M. (1970) *The Political Economy of Prosperity* (New York: Norton).

—— (1975) 'Inflation: Its Mechanics and Welfare Cost', *Brookings Papers* (no. 2).

—— (1978) 'Efficient Deflationary Policies', *American Economic Review* (Mar).

ORMEROD, P. (1982) 'Rational and Non-rational Expectations of Inflation in Wage Equations for the United Kingdom', *Economica* (Nov).

PAGAN, A. R., A. D. HALL and P. K. TRIVEDI (1983) 'Assessing the Variability of Inflation', *Review of Economic Studies* (Oct).

PAGANO, M., and M. J. HARTLEY (1981) 'On Fitting Distributed Lag

Models Subject to Polynomial Restrictions', *Journal of Econometrics* (June).

PARKIN, M. (1973) 'The Short Run and Long Run Trade-offs Between Inflation and Unemployment in Australia', *Australian Economic Papers* (Dec).

—— and R. BADE (1977) 'Central Bank Laws and Monetary Policies: A Preliminary Investigation', in M. G. PORTER (ed.) *The Australian Monetary System in the 1970s* (Monash University).

PARKS, R. W. (1978) 'Inflation and Relative Price Variability', *Journal of Political Economy* (Feb).

PATINKIN, D. (1965) *Money, Interest and Prices* (2nd ed.) (New York: Harper & Row).

—— (1976), *Keynes' Monetary Thought* (Durham, N.C.: Duke U.P.).

PEARCE, D. K. (1979) 'Comparing Survey and Rational Measures of Expected Inflation: Forecast Performance and Interest Rate Effects', *Journal of Money, Credit and Banking* (Nov).

—— (1982) 'The Impact of Inflation on Stock Prices', *Economic Review*, Federal Reserve Bank of Kansas City (Mar).

—— and V. V. ROLEY (1982) 'The Reaction of Stock Prices to Unanticipated Changes in Money', mimeo, Federal Reserve Bank of Kansas City (Sep).

PEEL, D., and P. MINFORD (1980) 'The Natural Rate Hypothesis and Rational Expectations – A Critique of Some Recent Developments', *Oxford Economic Papers* (Mar).

PERRY, G. L. (1966) *Unemployment, Money Wage Rates and Inflation* (Cambridge, Mass.: MIT Press).

—— (1970) 'Changing Labor Markets and Inflation', *Brookings Papers* (no. 3).

—— (1972) 'Unemployment Flows in the U.S. Labor Market', *Brookings Papers* (no. 2).

PESANDO, J. (1974) 'The Supply of Money and Common Stock Prices: Further Observations on the Econometric Evidence', *Journal of Finance* (June).

—— (1975) 'A Note on the Rationality of the Livingston Price Expectations', *Journal of Political Economy* (Aug).

PESARAN, M. H. (1982) 'A Critique of the Proposed Tests of the Natural Rate – Rational Expectations Hypothesis', *Economic Journal* (Sep).

PESEK, B. P., and T. R. SAVING (1967) *Money, Wealth and Economic Theory* (New York: Macmillan).

PHELPS, E. S. (1966) *Golden Rules of Economic Growth* (New York: Norton).

—— (1967) 'Phillips Curves, Expectations of Inflation and Optimal Unemployment over Time', *Economica* (Aug).

—— (1970a) 'The New Microeconomics in Employment and Inflation Theory', in E. S. PHELPS *et al.*, *Microeconomic Foundations of Employment and Inflation Theory* (New York: Norton).

—— (1970b) 'Money Wage Dynamics and Labor Market Equilibrium', in E. S. PHELPS *et al.*, *Microeconomic Foundations of Employment and Inflation Theory* (New York: Norton).

—— (1978) 'Commodity-supply Shock and Full-Employment Monetary Policy', *Journal of Money, Credit and Banking* (May).

—— and J. B. TAYLOR (1977) 'Stabilizing Powers of Monetary Policy under Rational Expectations', *Journal of Political Economy* (Jan).

PHILLIPS, A. W. (1954) 'Stabilization Policy in a Closed Economy', *Economic Journal* (June).

—— (1958) 'The Relationship between Unemployment and the Rate of Change of Money Wage Rates in the United Kingdom, 1861–1957', *Economica* (Nov).

PIERCE, D. A. (1980) 'Sources of Error in Economic Time Series', mimeo, Special Studies Section, Board of Governors, Federal Reserve System.

—— and L. D. HAUGH (1977) 'Causality in Temporal Systems', *Journal of Econometrics* (May).

—— D. W. PARKE, W. P. CLEVELAND and A. MARAVALL (1980) 'Uncertainty in the Monetary Aggregates: Sources, Measurement and Policy Effects', mimeo, Board of Governors, Federal Reserve System.

PINDYCK, R. S., and S. M. ROBERTS (1976) 'Instruments, Intermediate Targets, and Monetary Controllability', *International Economic Review* (Oct).

PISSARIDES, C. A. (1972) 'A Model of British Macroeconomic Policy, 1955–1969', *Manchester School* (Sep).

POOLE, W. (1970) 'Optimal Choice of Monetary Policy Instruments in a Simple Stochastic Macro Model', *Quarterly Journal of Economics* (May).

—— (1978) *Money and the Economy: A Monetarist View* (Reading, Mass.: Addison-Wesley).

—— and E. B. F. KORNBLITH (1973), 'The Friedman–Meiselman CMC Paper: New Evidence on an Old Controversy', *American Economic Review* (Dec).

PRESCOTT, E. C. (1975) 'Efficiency of the Natural Rate', *Journal of Political Economy* (Dec).

PUTNAM, B. H., and D. S. WILFORD (1978) 'Money, Income and Causality in the United States and the United Kingdom: A Theoretical Explanation of Different Findings', *American Economic Review* (June).

PYLE, D. H., and S. J. TURNOVSKY (1976), "The Dynamics of Government Policy in an Inflationary Economy: An "Intermediate Run" Analysis', *Journal of Money, Credit and Banking* (Nov).

RADCLIFFE REPORT (1959) *Report* of the Committee on the Working on the Monetary System, Cmnd 827 (London: HMSO).

REICHENSTEIN, W., and F. BONELLO (1982) 'Aggregate Supply Considerations and the St Louis Equation', *Journal of Economics and Business* (July).

REUBER, G. L. (1964) 'The Objectives of Canadian Monetary Policy, 1949–61', *Journal of Political Economy* (Apr).

ROGALSKI, R. J., and J. D. VINSO (1977) 'Stock Returns, Money Supply and the Direction of Causality', *Journal of Finance* (Sep).

ROLEY, V. V. (1983) 'The Response of Short-term Interest Rates to Weekly Money Announcements', *Journal of Money, Credit, and Banking* (Aug).

—— and C. E. WALSH (1983) 'Monetary Policy Regimes, Expected Inflation and the Response of Interest Rates to Money Announcements', mimeo, NBER (Aug).

ROSS, S. A., and M. L. WACHTER (1973) 'Wage Determination, Inflation and the Industrial Structure', *American Economic Review* (Sep).

ROTHSCHILD, M. (1974) 'Searching for the Lowest Price When the Distribution of Prices is Unknown', *Journal of Political Economy* (July/Aug).

ROZEFF, M. S. (1974) 'Money and Stock Prices', *Journal of Financial Economics* (Sep).

RUTLEDGE, J. (1975) 'The Unemployment–Inflation Tradeoff: A Review Article', mimeo, Claremont Men's College.

SAMUELSON, P. A. (1939) 'Interaction between the Multiplier Analysis and the Principle of Acceleration', *Review of Economic Statistics* (May).

—— and R. M. Solow (1960) 'Analytical Aspects of Anti-Inflation Policy', *American Economic Review* (May).

SANTOMERO, A. M., and J. J. SEATER (1978) 'The Inflation–Unemployment Trade-off: A Critique of the Literature', *Journal of Economic Literature* (June).

SANTONI, G. J., and C. C. STONE (1982) 'The Fed and the Real Rate of Interest', *Review* Federal Reserve Bank of St Louis (Dec).

SARGENT, T. J. (1973) Rational Expectations, the Real Rate of Interest and the Natural Rate of Unemployment', *Brookings Papers* (no. 3).

—— (1976a) 'A Classical Macroeconomic Model for the United States', *Journal of Political Economy* (Apr).

—— (1976b) 'The Observational Equivalence of Natural and Unnatural Rate Theories of Macroeconomics', *Journal of Political Economy* (June).

—— (1979) *Macroeconomic Theory* (New York: Academic Press).

—— and D. M. HENDERSON (1973) 'Monetary and Fiscal Policy in a Two-sector Aggregative Model', *American Economic Review* (June).

—— and N. WALLACE (1972) 'Rational Expectations and the Dynamics of Hyperinflation', mimeo (University of Minnesota).

—— —— (1975) 'Rational Expectations, the Optimal Monetary Instrument and the Optimal Money Supply Rule', *Journal of Political Economy* (Apr).

—— and —— (1976) 'Rational Expectations and the Theory of Economic Policy', *Journal of Monetary Economics* (Apr).

—— and —— (1981) 'Some Unpleasant Monetarist Arithmetic', *Quarterly Review*, Federal Reserve Bank of Minneapolis (Fall).

SARLO, C. A. (1981) 'Money and Income in Canada: Comparative Causality Tests', mimeo, Wilfrid Laurier University (July).

SAVIN, N. E. (1978) 'Friedman–Meiselman Revisited; A Study in Autocorrelation', *Economic Inquiry* (Jan).

SAVING, T. R. (1967) 'Monetary-policy Targets and Indicators', *Journal of Political Economy* (Aug.).

—— (1971) 'Transactions Costs and the Demand for Money', *American Economic Review* (June).

SCHMIDT, P., and R. N. WAUD (1973) 'The Almon Lag Technique and the Monetary versus Fiscal Policy Debate', *Journal of the American Statistical Association* (Mar).

SCHWARTZ, A. J. (1969) 'Short-term Targets of Three Foreign Central Banks', in K. BRUNNER (ed.) *Targets and Indicators of Monetary Policy* (San Francisco: Chandler).

SEAKS, T. G., and S. D. ALLEN (1980) 'The St Louis Equation: A Decade Later', *Southern Economic Journal* (Jan).

SEATER, J. J. (1977) 'A Unified Model of Consumption, Labor Supply and Job Search', *Journal of Economic Theory* (Apr).

—— (1982) 'Are Future Taxes Discounted?', *Journal of Money, Credit, and Banking* (Aug).

—— (1985) 'Does Government Debt Matter? A Review Article', *Journal of Monetary Economics*.

SEIDMAN, L. S. (1978) 'Tax-based Income Policies', *Brookings Papers* (no. 2).

SHARPE, I. G., and M. B. MILLER (1975) 'The Role of Money in the Canadian Economy', *Canadian Journal of Economics* (May).

—— and P. A. VOLKER (1980) 'The Australian Monetary Base/Money Supply Relationship, 1964–1977', *Economic Record* (Dec).

SHEEHAN, R. G. (1985a) 'The Federal Reserve Reaction Function: Does Debt Growth Influence Monetary Policy?', *Review*, Federal Reserve Bank of St Louis (Mar).

—— (1985b) 'Money, Anticipated Changes, and Policy Effectiveness', *American Economic Review* (June).

SHEEHEY, E. J. (1979) 'Inflation, Unemployment, and Expectations in Latin America–Some Simple Tests: Comment', *Southern Economic Journal* (Apr).

SHEFFRIN, S. M. (1981) 'Taxation and Automatic Stabilizers', *Public Finance* (no. 1).

—— (1983) *Rational Expectations* (Cambridge: Cambridge U.P.).

SHILLER, R. J. (1980) 'Can the Fed Control Real Interest Rates?', in S. FISCHER (ed.) *Rational Expectations and Economic Policy* (Chicago: University of Chicago Press).

SIDRAUSKI, M. (1967a) 'Rational Choice and Patterns of Growth in a Monetary Economy', *American Economic Review* (May).

—— (1967b) 'Inflation and Economic Growth', *Journal of Political Economy* (Dec).

SIEGEL, J. J. (1985) 'Money Supply Announcements and Interest Rates: Does Monetary Policy Matter?', *Journal of Monetary Economics* (Mar).

SILBER, W. L. (1975) 'Selective Credit Policies: A Survey', in I. KAMINOW and J. M. O'BRIEN (eds) *Studies in Selective Credit Policies* (Federal Reserve Bank of Philadelphia).

SIMS, C. A. (1972) 'Money, Income and Causality', *American Economic Review* (Sep).

—— (1980) 'Macroeconomics and Reality', *Econometrica* (Jan).

SIMS, G., and A. TAKAYAMA (1980) 'Currency Substitution and the Translog Function', mimeo, Econometrics Society meetings.

SMALL, D. H. (1979) 'Unanticipated Money Growth and Unemployment in the United States: Comment', *American Economic Review* (Dec).

—— and D. A. NICHOLS (1984) 'The Effect of Money Stock Announcements on the Federal Funds Market', mimeo, University of Wisconsin–Madison (Apr).

SMITH, W. L. (1959) 'Financial Intermediaries and Monetary Control', *Journal of Finance* (May).

SMYTH, D. J. (1974) 'Built-in Flexibility of Taxation and Stability in a Simple Dynamic *IS–LM* Model', *Public Finance* (no. 1).

SNOWER, D. J. (1981) 'Stabilization Policies versus Intertemporal Policy Reversals', mimeo, Birkbeck College (June).

SOLOW, R. M. (1965) 'Economic Growth and Residential Housing', in M. D. KETCHUM and L. T. KENDALL (eds) *Readings in Financial Institutions* (Boston: Houghton–Mifflin).

STEIN, H. (1969) *The Fiscal Revolution in America* (Chicago: University of Chicago Press).

STEIN, J. L. (1969) 'Neoclassical and Keynes–Wicksell Monetary Growth Models', *Journal of Money, Credit and Banking* (May).
—— (1971) *Money and Capacity Growth* (New York: Columbia U.P.).
—— (1976), 'Introduction', in J. L. STEIN (ed.) *Monetarism* (New York: North-Holland).
—— (1981) 'Monetarist, Keynesian, and New Classical Economics', *American Economic Review* (May).
STEIN, S. H. (1980) 'Autonomous Expenditures, Interest Rate Stabilization and the St Louis Equation', *Review of Economics and Statistics* (Aug).
STEPHENS, J. K. (1980) 'An Empirical Note on Some Monetarist Propositions, *Southern Economic Journal* (Apr).
STOCKTON, D. J., and J. E. GLASSMAN (1985) 'The Theory and Econometrics of Reduced-form Nominal and Price Equations', *Southern Economic Journal* (June).
STROTZ, R. H. (1956) 'Myopia and Inconsistency in Dynamic Utility Maximization', *Review of Economic Studies* (no. 3).
SWAMY, P. A. V. B., and P. A. TINSLEY (1982) 'The Rational Expectations Approach to Economic Modelling', *Journal of Economic Dynamics and Control* (May).
TANNER, J. E. (1972) 'Indicators of Monetary Policy: An Evaluation of Five', *Quarterly Review*, Banca Nazionale del Lavoro (Dec).
—— (1979a) 'Fiscal Policy and Consumer Behavior', *Review of Economics and Statistics* (May).
—— (1979b) 'An Empirical Investigation of Tax Discounting: A Comment', *Journal of Money, Credit, and Banking* (May).
—— and J. M. TRAPANI (1977) 'Can the Quantity Theory be Used to Predict Stock Prices – or is the Stock Market Efficient?', *Journal of Finance* (Oct).
TATOM, J. A. (1981) 'Energy Prices and Short-run Economic Performance', *Review*, Federal Reserve Bank of St Louis (Jan).
TAYLOR, J. B. (1975) 'Monetary Policy During a Transition to Rational Expectations', *Journal of Political Economy* (Oct).
—— (1980) 'Aggregate Dynamics and Staggered Contracts', *Journal of Political Economy* (Feb).
—— (1982) 'Establishing Credibility: A Rational Expecatations Viewpoint', *American Economic Review* (May).
—— (1983) 'Comments', *Journal of Monetary Economics* (July).
THORNTON, D. L. (1984) 'Monetizing the Debt', *Review*, Federal Reserve Bank of St Louis (Dec).
—— and D. S. BATTEN (1985) 'Lag-length Selection and Tests of Granger Causality between Money and Income', *Journal of Money, Credit and Banking* (May).
TOBIN, J. (1955) 'A Dynamic Aggregative Model', *Journal of Political Economy* (Apr).
—— (1965) 'Money and Economic Growth', *Econometrica* (Oct).
—— (1969) 'A General Equilibrium Approach to Monetary Theory', *Journal of Money, Credit and Banking* (Feb).
—— (1970) 'Money and Income: Post Hoc Ergo Propter Hoc?', *Quarterly Journal of Economics* (May).
—— (1972) 'Inflation and Unemployment', *American Economic Review* (Mar).
—— and W. C. BRAINARD (1963) 'Financial Intermediaries and the

Effectiveness of Monetary Controls', *American Economic Review* (May).

TOPEL, R. (1983) 'On Layoffs and Unemployment Insurance', *American Economic Review* (Sep).

TOYODA, T. (1972) 'Price Expectations and the Short-Run and Long-run Phillips Curves in Japan, 1956–1968', *Review of Economics and Statistics* (Aug).

TUCKER, D. P. (1966) 'Dynamic Income Adjustments to Money Supply Changes', *American Economic Review* (June).

TURNOVSKY, S. J. (1972) 'The Expectations Hypothesis and the Aggregate Wage Equation: Some Empirical Evidence for Canada', *Economica* (Feb).

—— (1974) 'On the Role of Inflationary Expectations in a Short-run Macroeconomic Model', *Economic Journal* (June).

—— (1977a) 'On the Formation of Continuous Time Macroeconomic Models with Asset Accumulation', *International Economic Review* (Feb).

—— (1977b) 'Structural Expectations and the Effectiveness of Government Policy in a Short-run Macroeconomic Model', *American Economic Review* (Dec).

—— (1977c) *Macroeconomic Analysis and Stabilization Policy* (Cambridge: Cambridge U.P.).

—— (1980) 'Monetary and Fiscal Policy in a Long-run Macroeconomic Model', *Economic Record* (June).

—— and M. L. WACHTER (1972) 'A Test of the "Expectations Hypothesis" Using Directly Observed Wage and Price Expectations', *Review of Economics and Statistics* (Feb).

URICH, T. (1982) 'The Information Content of Weekly Money Supply Announcements', *Journal of Monetary Economics* (July).

—— and P. WACHTEL (1981) 'Market Response to the Weekly Money Supply Announcements in the 1970s', *Journal of Finance* (Dec).

VAN ORDER, R. (1978) 'On the Bias in Estimates of the Effects of Monetary and Fiscal Policy', *Review of Economics and Statistics* (May).

VINING, D. R., and T. C. ELWERTOWSKI (1976) 'The Relationship between Relative Prices and the General Price Level', *American Economic Review* (Sep).

VISCUSI, W. K. (1979) 'Job Hazards and Worker Quit Rates: An Analysis of Adaptive Worker Behavior', *International Economic Review* (Feb).

WALSH, C. E. (1982a) 'Interest Rate Volatility and Monetary Policy', mimeo, Federal Reserve Bank of Kansas City (Apr).

—— (1982b) 'The Effects of Alternative Operating Procedures on Economic and Financial Relationships', in *Monetary Policy Issues in the 1980s* (Federal Reserve Bank of Kansas City).

—— (1983) 'Should the Federal Reserve Establish a Real Interest Rate Target?', *Economic Review*, Federal Reserve Bank of Kansas City (June).

WALTERS, A. A. (1966) 'Monetary Multipliers in the U.K., 1880–1962', *Oxford Economic Papers* (Nov).

WEBSTER, C. E. (1982) 'The Effects of Monetary Policy when the Monetary Policy Rule is Unknown', mimeo, Washington University of St Louis (Mar).

WICKSELL, K. (1936) *Interest and Prices* (New York: Kelley, 1965 reprint).

WILDE, L. L. (1977) 'Labor Market Equilibrium under Nonsequential Search', *Journal of Economic Theory* (Aug).

WILLIAMS, D., C. A. E. GOODHART and D. H. GOWLAND (1976) 'Money, Income, and Causality: The U.K. Experience', *American Economic Review* (June).

WILLIAMSON, O. E., M. L. WACHTER and J. E. HARRIS (1975) 'Understanding the Employment Relation: The Analysis of Idiosyncratic Exchange', *Bell Journal of Economics* (Spring).

WOGIN, G. (1980) 'Unemployment and Monetary Policy under Rational Expectations', *Journal of Monetary Economics* (Jan).

YAWITZ, J. B., and L. H. MEYER (1976) 'An Empirical Investigation of the Extent of Tax Discounting', *Journal of Money, Credit and Banking* (May).

YOHE, W. and D. KARNOVSKY (1969) 'Interest Rates and Price Level Changes, 1952–1969', *Review*, Federal Reserve Bank of St Louis (Dec).

ZARNOWITZ, V. (1985) 'Recent Work on Business Cycles in Historical Perspective: A Review of Theories and Evidence', *Journal of Economic Literature* (June).

ZELLNER, A. (1966) 'On the Aggregation Problem, A New Approach to a Troublesome Problem', mimeo, University of Chicago.

Index